MW01194800

Making Our Neighborhoods,
Making Our Selves

Making Our Neighborhoods, Making Our Selves

GEORGE C. GALSTER

The University of Chicago Press
Chicago and London

The University of Chicago Press, Chicago 60637
The University of Chicago Press, Ltd., London
© 2019 by The University of Chicago
Published 2019
Printed in the United States of America

28 27 26 25 24 23 22 21 20 19   1 2 3 4 5

ISBN-13: 978-0-226-59985-4 (cloth)
ISBN-13: 978-0-226-59999-1 (e-book)
DOI: https://doi.org/10.7208/chicago/[9780226599991].001.0001

Library of Congress Cataloging-in-Publication Data

Names: Galster, George C., 1948– author.
Title: Making our neighborhoods, making our selves / George C. Galster.
Description: Chicago ; London : The University of Chicago Press, 2019. |
    Includes bibliographical references and index.
Identifiers: LCCN 2018030679 | ISBN 9780226599854 (cloth : alk. paper) |
    ISBN 9780226599991 (ebook)
Subjects: LCSH: Neighborhoods—United States. | United States—Social
    conditions. | Sociology, Urban—United States.
Classification: LCC HT123 .G258 2019 | DDC 307.3/3620973—dc23 LC
    record available at https://lccn.loc.gov/2018030679

♾ This paper meets the requirements of ANSI/NISO Z39.48-1992
(Permanence of Paper).

Portions of chapter 2 are reprinted from the article "What Is Neighbourhood?
An Externality-Space Approach" (*International Journal of Urban and Regional
Research* 10, no. 2, 1986), 243–323. Chapter 6, "Nonlinear and Threshold
Effects Related to Neighborhood," originally appeared in *Journal of Planning
Literature* (August 2018). Portions of chapter 8 are reprinted from the article
"Spatial Foundations of Inequality: An Empirical Overview and Conceptual
Model" by G. C. Galster and P. Sharkey (*RSF: The Russell Sage Journal of the
Social Sciences* 3, no. 2, 2017) and "The Mechanism(s) of Neighbourhood
Effects: Theory, Evidence, and Policy Implications" from *Neighbourhood
Effects Research: New Perspectives*, edited by M. van Ham, D. Manley, N. Bailey,
L. Simpson, and D. Maclennan. Portions of chapter 9 are reprinted from the
article "Neighbourhood Social Mix as a Goal of Housing Policy: A Theoretical
Analysis" (*European Journal of Housing Policy* 7 no. 1, 2007). Portions of chapter
10 are reprinted from "Neighborhoods and National Housing Policy: Toward
Circumscribed, Neighborhood-Sensitive Reforms" (*Housing Policy Debate*),
which is forthcoming.

CONTENTS

Neighborhoods occupy an exalted position of importance for decision makers in virtually every realm of life: households, dwelling owners, business owners, public officials, mortgage lenders, and home insurers. Households believe that the neighborhood affects their quality of life and the future opportunities for their children, and they move accordingly if they can. Residential property owners, mortgage lenders, property insurers, and retail businesspeople believe that the neighborhood affects their risk-adjusted rates of financial return. Local public officials believe that the neighborhood affects the quantity, type, and quality of public services that citizens will demand, and the tax base that constrains the degree to which officials can meet these demands. The well-known adage about what is crucial in real estate summarizes all of these beliefs: "Location, location, location."

Similarly, our public discourse is full of expressions that highlight the salience of neighborhoods in our everyday experience. Terms like "decaying inner city," "upscale quarter," "black ghetto," "slum area," "ethnic enclave," "gentrifying district," "immigrant barrio," "hipster village," and "transitional zone" are illustrative of how often we think about smaller-scale places within a broader metropolitan area.

An Epidemic of Myopia, and Hopefully a Cure

Because of its salience for so many, it is no wonder that the neighborhood has long been the focus of scholarly investigations. Indeed, during the last two score years dozens of significant books and hundreds of peer-reviewed journal articles have been published by economists, sociologists, political scientists, geographers, historians, and urban planners on issues related to the urban neighborhood.[1] Unfortunately, despite its breadth and depth, this body of work has been plagued by myopia in five dimensions: topic, discipline, paradigm, geographic level, and causation.

Topically, prior scholarly works fall into three broad categories, each of which is important but ultimately incomplete. Those in the first category try to explain the drivers and unfolding processes of neighborhood change—that is, *what affects neighborhoods*.[2] Those in the second category focus on the degree and means to which neighborhoods influence the behaviors and life chances of their residents—that is, *how neighborhoods affect us*.[3] Those in the last category consider how we as a society might successfully intervene to revitalize distressed neighborhoods—that is, *how we can affect neighborhoods so they will affect us better*.[4]

In rare instances, a major scholarly work will address two or more of these three domains. Two recent and deservedly influential works by sociologists fall into this notable category.[5] Patrick Sharkey discovers that the influences of disadvantaged urban neighborhoods are so pernicious that three-quarters of black children raised in them during the 1970s are likely to end up in similar environs when they are adults.[6] To break this intergenerational poverty trap, he argues for durable policies that will change the fundamental structures of poor places. In his monumental book on Chicago, Robert Sampson provides a deeply insightful investigation into the social processes that generate collective perceptions of neighborhoods, link neighborhoods via household mobility patterns, create variations in neighborhood-level conditions like social efficacy, and in aggregate produce stable spatial patterns of racial and economic stratification affecting residents' quality of life and opportunities in profound ways for extended periods.[7] Sampson argues for a structural urban neighborhood policy that should not only improve places of concentrated poverty, but also be cognizant of the broader interconnections among neighborhoods that might affect the efficacy of such initiatives. Despite their impressive scope, however, these two books pay little topical heed to market forces as influences on household mobility or housing investment behavior.[8] As I will demonstrate, the driver of neighborhood change is the housing market, which is metropolitan in scale yet establishes strong connections across local political jurisdictions and communities. A focus on the social processes within smaller geographies blinds us to larger external forces that impinge on what kind of people and what amount of money and other resources flow into any particular neighborhood, and what sorts of financial constraints limit the geographic alternatives for these crucial flows.

Unlike virtually all prior neighborhood scholarship, in this holistic analysis I attempt to be multidisciplinary in my approach, relying upon paradigms, concepts, and evidence from several social-scientific domains. In particular, from neoclassical economics I took as foundation the notion that in a capitalist society, markets generate price and profit signals that are the prime allocator of flows of self-interested people and rate-of-return-driven financial resources across metropolitan space. From geography, I relied upon the maxim that everything in space affects everything else in space, but more proximate things are more influential. From sociology, I drew upon the claims that stratification by race and class is a primary social fault line, that social context influences behavior, and that social and cultural distance matter as well as physical distance. From social psychology I learned that individuals construct their perceived reality in conjunction with interactions with others. From behavioral economics I drew the lesson that people do not always behave like fully informed, rational, maximizing *Homo economicus*, but instead often engage in informal intellectual heuristics based on wildly imperfect information. From developmental psychology, I distilled the essence not only of how proximal influences like family affect how children grow into adulthood, but of how distal influences like neighborhood and broader-scale contexts matter crucially as well.

As for paradigms, I am well aware that two competing schools of thought that fundamentally differ in their conception of archetypical humans have divided social science over at least the last half century. One school, associated with neoclassical economics and the rational choice school within political science, sees humans as fundamentally self-interested, atomistic decision makers who, on the basis of their predetermined preferences, make optimizing choices based on rational assessment of reasonably complete information. The other school, associated with sociology and social psychology, sees humans' preferences, perceptions, and behaviors as being profoundly shaped by the social community in which they are embedded; they are often other-regarding, ill-informed, and "irrational" in the neoclassical sense. Both paradigms are incomplete; neither provides a fully satisfactory foundation for understanding neighborhoods as effects of and influences upon individuals, let alone a broader account of human behaviors in an urban milieu. I attempt in this book to stake out a common-sense middle ground between these extreme views. Individuals typically are self-interested in pursuing their goals, but they often exhibit other-regarding behaviors. Their social and physical contexts influence people in profound cognitive, perceptual, and behavioral ways; yet so do the financial constraints imposed by their own budget, in combination with the prevailing pattern of housing prices and rents set by the marketplace.

There is a common myopia associated with the choice of a particular geographic scale of analysis. Many neighborhood-related studies focus only on the characteristics, internal processes, and dynamics of neighborhoods; rarely do they consider how individual behaviors drive aggregate neighborhood-level outcomes. Many studies examine two levels: how neighborhood characteristics affect individual residents. Rarely do they consider how individual behaviors—and, ultimately, neighborhoods—connect with local political jurisdiction or metropolitan-wide forces. My approach in this book is explicitly multilevel, considering individual, neighborhood, jurisdictional, and metropolitan scales. I focus on both economic and social forces connecting these micro-, meso-, and macro-levels in webs of mutually causal relationships.[9]

Finally, the presumed direction of causation is another source of myopia in the scholarship on neighborhood. Some studies start by taking the bundle of neighborhood characteristics as predetermined, and then probe what effects this bundle may have on individuals. Other studies start by taking individuals' preferences, income, and information as predetermined, and examine how those individuals move or invest in various circumstances. Still others try to understand how social interaction in the neighborhood shapes individuals' preferences and information. Finally, some studies posit shocks at the metropolitan area scale, causing an alteration of individual mobility and investment decisions that ultimately lead to neighborhood changes. In this book I consider all of these causal connections. Indeed, this book fundamentally is about understanding neighborhoods as embedded in complex, multilevel patterns of circular causation.

An Overview of This Book

In this book I develop analytical frameworks and marshal evidence, both of which permit a better understanding of the origins, nature, and consequences of neighborhood change. I offer strategies for making a more socially desirable palette of neighborhoods in American metropolitan areas. The proposition "We make our neighborhoods, and then these neighborhoods make us" serves as the foundation of this book. That is, our collective actions regarding where we live and invest financially and socially—done in the context of the laws, markets, and institutions we have established—will determine what characteristics our neighborhoods will manifest, and how these characteristics will evolve. Yet, these multidimensional characteristics of our neighborhoods—physical, demographic, economic, social, environmental, institutional—dramatically influence our information, attitudes, perceptions, expectations, behaviors, health, quality of life, and financial well-being; our children's development; and our families' opportunities for social advancement.

Unfortunately, private, market-oriented decision makers now governing human and financial resource flows among neighborhoods usually arrive at an inefficient allocation due to externalities, strategic gaming, and self-fulfilling prophecies. This failure systematically produces too little housing investment in many places and too much segregation by race and economic standing. Moreover, lower-socioeconomic-status black and Hispanic households and property owners typically bear a disproportionate share of the financial and social costs associated with underinvestment, segregation, and neighborhood transition processes, all while reaping comparatively little of their social benefits. Ultimately, our current neighborhoods create unequal opportunities. Because neighborhood context powerfully affects children, youths, and adults—while neighborhood contexts are extremely unequal across economic and racial groups—space becomes a way of perpetuating inequality of opportunity for social advancement.

To remedy these substantial market failures, I provide a comprehensive set of neighborhood-supportive policies and programs in the domains of housing investment, economic segregation, and racial and ethnic segregation. The principle of *strategic targeting* guides all the interventions I advocate. These programs emphasize voluntary but incentivized actions by households and property owners that will expand residential options and gradually alter the physical, socioeconomic, and racial landscape of American neighborhoods. I argue that these programs hold the prospect for commanding bipartisan support. It is my hope that this book provides a firm intellectual foundation and motivation for such enlightened intervention.

George C. Galster
May 2018

PART 1

Neighborhoods: Overarching Frames and Definitions

ONE

Introduction

Virtually everyone in the United States has grown up or lived in what they would consider a neighborhood. Despite this intimate familiarity, most people have little understanding of the forces that bring neighborhoods into being and make them change, the many ways in which neighborhoods influence our lives, whether these neighborhood-related processes are good or bad for society, and how we might intervene with public policies if we think neighborhood outcomes should be improved. In this book, I shed light on all these dimensions. To use a medical metaphor wherein the neighborhood is the "patient," this book develops principles for comprehending the etiology of disease, diagnosing the patient, assessing the disease's consequences for the patient, and providing an efficacious prescription.

More specifically, in this book I address in a holistic, multidisciplinary way the fundamental questions regarding neighborhoods by marshaling a half century worth of theory and evidence from many social sciences. What is the neighborhood? What drives changes in its residents' economic standing or racial/ethnic composition, physical conditions, and retail activities? How do households and property owners form expectations about neighborhood change and interact with each other? What are the idiosyncrasies of neighborhood change processes? What consequences for human and financial capital transpire when neighborhoods change, and who disproportionately bears the costs of such changes? Why do we have so many blighted neighborhoods and ones that evince little diversity on racial/ethnic or economic grounds? In what dimensions and through what mechanisms do neighborhoods affect their residents? Is the current constellation of American neighborhoods optimal from society-wide perspectives of efficiency and equity? In addressing these questions, I derive eight summary propositions. Based on this diagnostic analysis, I then advance public policy and planning prescriptions for dealing with three most significant problems associated with how we have made our neighborhoods: physical blight, economic segregation, and racial/ethnic segregation.

The Framing of This Book

I ground my analysis on two premises that jointly provide a holistic perspective on neighborhoods.[1] First, the nature and dynamics of the phenomenon we call the neighborhood result from the aggregation of individual behaviors driven primarily by two sets of actors—household occupants and owners/developers of residential property—operating within the framework of price signals and constraints provided by a predominantly capitalistic housing market operating at the metropolitan scale. Second, the character and dynamics of the neighborhood, in turn, affect a wide range of perceptions, behaviors, dimensions of well-being and socioeconomic opportunities of its resident adults and children. Put more succinctly, *we make our neighborhoods and then they make us.*[2]

In the next two sections, I provide overarching frameworks for these premises. I first focus on the determinants of individual household residential mobility, tenure choice, and residential property investment decisions, synthesizing the existing scholarship on these behaviors. Then I focus on how these two sets of decision makers are behaviorally linked, how their actions get aggregated to produce neighborhood-level outcomes, and how these aggregate outcomes in turn reflect back on the individual decision makers and their families, shaping their perceptions, behaviors, quality of life, and future opportunities. My frameworks are distinguished by their consideration of different spatial scales—individual, neighborhood, local political jurisdiction, and metropolitan area—and how the forces affecting neighborhoods are woven together in a complex web of mutually causal, self-reinforcing relationships.

Making Neighborhoods: Individual Decisions about Residential Mobility, Tenure Choice, and Property Investments

My unified framework for understanding the household's residential mobility and tenure choice behavior and the dwelling owner's investment behavior—the fundamental building blocks of neighborhood change—is represented diagrammatically in figure 1.1. In this and succeeding figures, rectangles denote sets of characteristics, attitudes, expectations, and behaviors, and presumed causal linkages between them are shown as arrows or

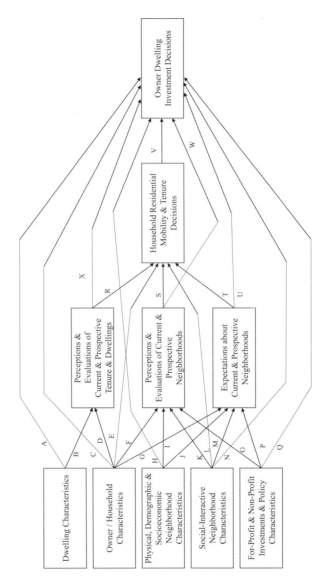

Figure 1.1. The objective and subjective determinants of individual household residential mobility, tenure, and property investment behaviors

"paths." In this part of the analysis, for simplicity I consider the stock of existing households, dwellings, and neighborhoods to be predetermined for the decision maker. Though expectations about future changes in existing and new neighborhoods are an essential part of the decision-making process, as I will amplify below, for the most part during the short period when households and property owners are actively deciding where to live, whether to own or rent, and how much to invest in properties, they take the current array of opportunities as essentially fixed. I will consider the longer-term decisions about adding to the housing stock via construction of new properties and rehabilitation of nonresidential properties later in this chapter, and especially in chapter 3.

During some short-term "snapshot" period of observation, the objective characteristics of the individual, the current dwelling occupied, the current neighborhood (including interactions with neighbors), prospective dwellings and neighborhoods, and any relevant private or public investments or policies supplying resources to the neighborhood can be considered predetermined—that is, taken as fixed values by the individual decision maker. Based on these currently experienced objective characteristics, the individual will form perceptions, mold beliefs, make subjective evaluations of the current dwelling and neighborhood (perhaps in relation to alternatives), and develop expectations about the future of the neighborhood.[3] Based on these objective characteristics and subjective perceptions, beliefs, evaluations, and expectations, the resident household will make a decision about remaining in the current location or moving, in combination with a closely related decision about whether to own or rent the occupied property. Based on analogous inputs, the owner of the dwelling under consideration (who might be the occupying household) will make a decision about whether to sell the property; hold it and either maintain, undermaintain, or improve its quality; or (in the extreme) abandon the property. In the case of owner-occupiers, these latter decisions must be made jointly.[4]

In sum, my framing posits that several distinct sets of objective characteristics of the individual and the context influence several subjective attributes of the individual. Together these objective, predetermined elements and subjective, "intervening" elements determine individual residential mobility, tenure choice and/or housing investment behavior. The causal impacts of objective individual and contextual characteristics upon these two decisions may be direct and/or indirect; that is, mediated to greater or lesser degree by the intervening subjective elements. Consider now in more detail in the next two subsections what comprises these various elements and how they may be interrelated in the context of received scholarship about residential mobility, tenure choice, and housing reinvestment behaviors.

Residential Mobility Behavior of Households

Five theories of voluntary[5] intraurban residential mobility have competed in the scholarly literature for decades, though they typically share many features and the lines among them are often blurred.[6] As I will demonstrate, the causal paths in figure 1.1 it views as predominant distinguish each theory.

The first, "life course" theory, posits that households move in a predictable pattern across their lifetimes.[7] Households evaluate their current residential situations in light of their current shelter needs associated with their particular stages in life: single, married without children, married with young children, married with older children, and so on. They typically deem the status quo no longer suitable when a new life stage emerges, whereupon mobility transpires. Features and size of the dwelling are often crucial in these situations, neighborhood context less so, from the perspective of life course theory. This theory sees paths E and B/D-R in figure 1.1 as salient.

The second, the "stress" theory, takes the view that households assess whether to move by comparing the satisfaction associated with current and potential residential environments.[8] Stress is defined as the difference between current and potential residential satisfaction, and is seen as being directly related to the probability of moving. Life-cycle transitions can generate stress, but so too can neighborhood conditions such as intolerable socioeconomic composition or racial transition. This theory expands the hypothesized salient paths in figure 1.1 to include not only those above in the "life course" theory, but also F/I/K-S.

The third perspective, the "dissatisfaction" theory, posits that mobility is a two-stage process that begins when a threshold of dissatisfaction is exceeded.[9] During the initial stage, households evaluate salient aspects of the current residential environment (potentially including those associated with both dwelling and neighborhood) in light of their needs and aspirations, yielding a certain high or low absolute degree of "residential dissatisfaction." If the household registers sufficient dissatisfaction, it will develop a desire to move and enters into the second stage of the process, which involves actively gathering information to assess alternative residential locations. The members of the household will make the decision to move if they can find a financially feasible alternative that prospectively offers some relief from their dissatisfaction. In this view, background characteristics of both the household and the residential context influence mobility desires and actions only through the intervening variable of the current absolute level of residential dissatisfaction; that is, only paths B/D-R and F/I/K-S in figure 1.1.

The fourth theory, "disequilibrium," posits that households attempt to maximize their well-being by consuming an "optimal" bundle of residential (dwelling and neighborhood) attributes.[10] At any moment, however, households may not reside in their optimal bundle (i.e., be in disequilibrium) because family or current residential circumstances may have changed since the original point of in-moving or because other, superior market opportunities may have arisen subsequently. The probability of moving out is directly related to the degree of such disequilibrium between the households' current and prospective feasible residential options, and inversely related to housing market search and moving costs. Market search will be undertaken whenever the expected benefits (marginal gain in well-being) of locating a more optimal, feasible alternative exceed the expected search costs. Although the marginal expected benefits of mobility are directly related to the current degree of disequilibrium residential consumption, there is no implicit threshold of absolute disequilibrium involved. Nevertheless, the salient paths in figure 1.1 would still be B/D-R and F/I/K-S.

In the fifth approach, "perceived net advantage," I synthesized aspects of the above theories and extended from them by drawing from behavioral psychology to include the role of future expectations.[11] At any particular moment, households may be seen as holding a multifaceted set of beliefs that inform a potential mobility decision, which concern both current and future (1) household needs and aspirations, (2) dwelling and neighborhood characteristics of occupied location and feasible alternative locations, and (3) financial and other adjustment costs associated with moving. Contemporary and futuristic beliefs are influenced not only by active market search but by passively acquired information gained through commuting, mass media, conversations, and so on.[12] Taking into account beliefs about its current and anticipated needs and aspirations, the household will comparatively evaluate which feasible alternative locations (both now and in the future) may best meet them over an extended time horizon. Mobility will be triggered when a feasible alternative evinces a prospective long-term advantage in fulfilling needs/aspirations (net of adjustment costs), as appropriately adjusted for uncertainty and time horizons. From the perspective of the perceived net advantage theory all direct and mediated causal paths to mobility shown in figure 1.1 are of potential salience.

One common implication of all these approaches to residential mobility, with the possible exception of the "life course," is that undesirable changes in the current neighborhood should increase the propensity to move out.[13] Many multivariate statistical studies have supported this implication by identifying several objective neighborhood indicators as robust predictors of greater mobility. These have included increasing crime and declining neighborhood physical quality,[14] lower homeownership rates,[15] higher (and growing) percentages of black neighbors[16] or lower-income neighbors,[17] and greater discrepancies between the household's income and that of the rest of the neighborhood.[18] Perceptions of disorder can also prove a powerful stimulant to moving out.[19]

Of equivalent importance for the analysis in this book, characteristics of the neighborhoods from which households may feasibly choose, not just those of the prospective individual dwelling, influence the choice of where a household moves once it decides to leave its current neighborhood. Opinion polls have found that most Americans prefer the option of an inferior dwelling located in a better neighborhood than an equally expensive option involving a superior house in an inferior neighborhood.[20] Researchers have found that when households are considering new potential neighborhoods, they most often are attracted to those having kin and friends,[21] predominantly residents of similar economic standing[22] and those of the same race or ethnicity.[23]

Housing Tenure Choice

There is much less theoretical dissention about the underlying factors that households weigh when considering whether to own or rent the dwellings they occupy.[24] The household first considers the financial resources available for the purchase of a home or the successful application for a mortgage: long-term ("permanent") income, assets, debt, credit rating (path E in figure 1.1). Then the prospective buyer must weigh the potential ongoing costs of holding the properties of the type, size, location, and features that are financially feasible. These costs include structural improvements, maintenance and repairs, local property taxes, federal income taxes (treatment of local tax and mortgage interest deductibility), hazard insurance, and expected equity appreciation (both for the home in question and for investments in alternative financial instruments); see path Q in figure 1.1. Finally, the household must assess the nonfinancial dimensions of homeowning: the value it places on independent control of the property and its terms of occupancy (path E in figure 1.1).

What should be clear from the foregoing summary of the tenure choice process is that it is inextricably bound up with mobility and neighborhood expectations.[25] The decision maker must project the length of stay in the dwelling being considered for purchase. It is usually sensible to incur the considerable out-of-pocket and time costs associated with home purchase only if the household plans to remain there for a number of years. Moreover, the expected duration of residency may influence the expected home equity appreciation. Due to this joint nature of the choice between residential mobility and tenure, I portray them in the same box in figure 1.1.

It also should be clear that neighborhood perceptions, evaluations, and expectations strongly influence the tenure choice process (paths R, S, and T in figure 1.1). If the only homes a household can afford are located in weak, declining neighborhoods, for example, households may forego homeowning because they perceive that it will tie them to an unsatisfactory quality of residential life, and will expect the appreciation of their property to be minimal. Alternatively, households in certain segments of the housing market may perceive that few rental options exist in desirable neighborhoods, whereupon their desires to buy a home will receive a boost. This shaping of whether we rent or buy property is one of a number of ways in which neighborhood affects us, a persistent theme that will be illustrated throughout this book.

Housing Investment Behavior by Owners

At any particular moment, the investment options faced by owners of existing dwellings are threefold: improve the quality of the structure, maintain quality at the current level, or allow quality to decline (either by passive undermaintaining or by active partitioning of the dwelling into one or more smaller units). Once an owner chooses the strategy, an amount of investment can be decided upon. The predominant theory of such decision making on the part of investors of residential properties presumes that they are motivated to choose in such a way that their expected financial rate of return is satisfactory (at least, if not maximized) compared to nonhousing investment alternatives, considering to some degree both immediate and future financial flows.[26]

The intertemporal nature of the housing investment decision and the durability of the investment once made focus attention on the central role played by the owner's expectations. Expectations about the future costs for housing improvements, the rate of structural depreciation, the interest rate for borrowed funds (i.e., the opportunity cost of savings), conditions in the surrounding neighborhood, and the rate of housing-price inflation jointly affect the perceived returns gained from expenditures on housing. All these expectations shape the owner's net operating income from the dwelling being occupied and its asset value when it is eventually sold. In the context of figure 1.1, direct paths A, C, H, Q and indirect paths F/I/O–W and G/J/P–U are relevant for the owner of residential property. Consider these causal influences in more detail.

Influences on owner's investment behaviors. Characteristics of the dwelling in question are independent, direct contributors to the observed housing investment behaviors (path A). Older structures usually deteriorate at a faster rate, thus presenting the owner with more frequently needed repairs to maintain constant quality. Dwellings with particular structural features render certain structural modifications extremely expensive; for example, those with sagging foundations are unlikely to support the addition of a second-story dormer, and those with obsolete wiring may not permit the installation of modern appliances or heating and cooling systems. A small lot may preclude the addition of a detached garage or a swimming pool. But beyond their physical features, dwellings may take on subjective and symbolic meanings for their owners that ultimate shape the sorts of investments that are made in them (path B-X).

Characteristics of the homeowner also directly influence the type of home investment strategy chosen and the expenditures allocated to its pursuit (path C). For example, owners with access to inexpensive yet skilled labor (perhaps their own) likely perceive home maintenance and repair costs as relatively low. The nature of the information one acquires shapes perceptions and expectations, of course; and the methods and extent of data acquisition vary by education, income, age, and family status of the owner (paths D-X, F-W, and G-U).[27]

The physical, demographic and socioeconomic character of the neighborhood in which a particular dwelling is located powerfully influences the type of investment strategies pursued. The value of the dwelling is not determined merely by its features and the lot on which it is located, but also by the surrounding environs' socioeconomic, racial, ethnic, age, and family-status composition, environmental amenities, local public-service and infrastructure quality, land-use patterns, and aggregate housing stock conditions (path H).[28] This means that the owner's perceived payoffs from incremental investments will depend on the current as well as future conditions of the surrounding neighborhood that are capitalized by the market (path I-W). These physical, demographic, and socioeconomic attributes of the neighborhood also provide clues to prospective changes in the milieu (path J-U).[29]

Finally, resources provided by the nonprofit and for-profit sectors may impinge on the owner's upkeep calculus. Governments, for instance, may directly subsidize housing repairs and improvements by providing grants or low-interest loans for this purpose (path Q). More indirectly, the actions of the public sector can greatly influence the perceptions and expectations held by owners, and thereby their subsequent investment activities (paths O-W and P-U). These actions may be substantive or symbolic. Examples of the former include improving neighborhood public parks, streets, lighting, or schools; encouraging the formation of local neighborhood organizations; or rezoning the area to permit or prohibit nonresidential land uses. Illustrations of the latter include the formation of a mayor's neighborhood advisory board with appointees from all neighborhoods, the designation of an official neighborhood X pride week, or the erection of signs proclaiming the boundaries, name, and history of each neighborhood. The for-profit sector, especially the local retail sector, can also have substantial influences on the attractiveness of a neighborhood, and thereby on the investment incentives of property owners.

Additional influences on owner-occupant's investment behaviors. Additional factors come into play for the property owner who also is the occupant. In such cases, the investment decision typically involves both "consumption" and "investment" dimensions.[30] First, maintaining or improving structural quality may be seen as increasing "utility" or well-being gained from consuming (i.e., living in) the dwelling, but it requires a sacrifice of income that could be spent otherwise. Reducing housing quality, on the other hand, sacrifices such housing-related utility but allows for greater consumption of other goods and services besides housing, especially if the generation of added income accompanies the quality decline. Such could be the case if an owner subdivided an erstwhile single-family dwelling to produce one or more rental properties. A second consideration likely for most homeowners is the wealth effect of such housing investment activity. If an owner placed importance on the value of the durable housing package as an asset beyond its current value as a consumer good, the calculus of the housing investment decision would be altered. In other words, spending money on one's home can be considered an investment, because it increases the eventual sales price of the home, and thus the wealth and future consumption possibilities of the homeowner.

The homeowner's decision is also related to time in a more complex way than is that of the absentee owner. The choice of housing versus non-housing expenditures cannot be fully understood in the context of a single moment. Because housing is a durable good, spending on it currently produces a useful flow of housing-related consumption services, as well as an augmented asset value for several subsequent periods. The degree to which any particular housing investment provides continuing consumption and asset benefits in the future depends on the rate of structural depreciation, the homeowner's rate of time preference, and changes in neighborhood conditions. The homeowner's decision thus involves not only choosing the desired mix of housing and nonhousing expenditures in the current period, but also this desired pattern of spending in the current period versus future ones.

Implicit in this discussion of the intertemporal nature of housing investment decisions by owner-occupants is the closely related decision about mobility. Obviously, a homeowner can adjust the amount of housing consumed by moving to a different dwelling, typically in conjunction with selling the previous home. The homeowner thus will sometimes contrast the well-being gained from pursuing a particular investment strategy for the current dwelling with that which can be gained from moving to another dwelling, possibly in a different neighborhood. Having formulated expectations and mobility plans, the homeowner makes a choice of housing versus nonhousing expenditures over the expected duration of tenure in the dwelling, within the set of constraints formed by both financial limitations of the owner and structural limitations of the dwelling. The former limitations consist of initial wealth, expected household income flows, and institutionally imposed borrowing constraints (path C in figure 1.1). The latter consist of the various architectural and mechanical idiosyncrasies of the physical structure that render alternative dwelling modification schemes more or less feasible in terms of incremental housing value gain versus modification cost (path A). Compared to those who plan to stay in their dwelling for a considerable period, homeowners who plan to move in the near future would be less concerned about the long-run consequences of current upkeep activities. That is, they would not be present to reap much of the stream of enhanced housing consumption provided by current upkeep, and hence would be less likely to undertake sizable amounts of such (path V).

The neighborhood is, of course, more than simply a place having particular physical features where particular types of autonomous individuals reside and into which financial resources flow. It is also an arena in which social interaction typically occurs among neighbors: they make friends, encourage conformity to collective norms, formulate solidarity sentiments, and pass along information. Another important distinguishing feature of owner-occupants as opposed to absentee owners is that the former are directly subject to this social dimension of the neighborhood in which they invest; the latter are not. This means that collectively those in the neighborhood have at least a potential for influencing the home investment behavior of homeowners residing there (path N).[31] This is the crucial distinction between owner-occupants and absentee owners that explains much of the observed differences in their housing investment actions.[32]

The social-interactive dimension of neighborhood may also have three indirect impacts on homeowners. First, social discourse among neighboring homeowners may provide a conduit for data sharing that tend to create common perceptions informing their investment decisions (path K-W). Second, it may reassure each individual owner that all the other homeowners in the neighborhood are likely responding to the same social pressures to maintain dwelling quality. Thus, homeowners in a neighborhood with a great deal of social cohesion may be more likely to be optimistic in their expectations (and in the market's evaluation) of the neighborhood's physical quality and property value projections (path M-U). Third, it may alter homeowners' expected longevity of tenure. Homeowners who are more attached to their neighborhood by strong social ties are less inclined to rupture these connections by moving out of the neighborhood, all else equal (paths L-V).

Making Our Neighborhoods: Aggregating Individual Decisions into Neighborhood Outcomes

The foregoing discussion summarized in figure 1.1 was based on the premise that those who wish to understand neighborhood dynamics must first understand the behavior of individual households and dwelling owners who ultimately determine the aggregate neighborhood outcomes. One must realize, of course, that in a broader, intertemporal framework, individual behaviors and aggregate neighborhood outcomes are related via mutually causal connections. In other words, individual actions in one period determine overall neighborhood characteristics in the next period through straightforward aggregation; these in turn affect subsequent individual perceptions, behaviors, evaluations, expectations and qualities of life.[33] Thus, not only do individual behaviors shape what neighborhoods are and how they change, but neighborhood conditions and stability affect individuals in turn, in a variety of powerful ways. Figure 1.2 illustrates this fundamental point about circular patterns of causation schematically.

At any particular moment summarized in figure 1.1, three factors will influence the decisions made by an individual (resident household and/or property owner) in the neighborhood under consideration. These include (1) the aggregate behaviors of other households and owners in the neighborhood (path B in figure 1.2); (2) the aggregate behaviors of other resource

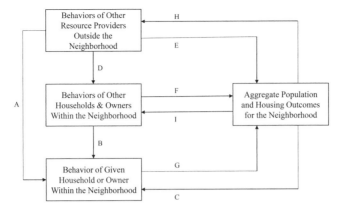

Figure 1.2. Individual behaviors and neighborhood outcomes: patterns of circular causation

providers in the public and for-profit sectors (path A); and (3) the current and expected future aggregate conditions in the neighborhood (path C). The individual undertakes a mobility, tenure, or housing investment behavior in ways described in the previous section, in conjunction with his or her personal and dwelling characteristics (path G). Concurrent with this individual's behavior, other households and property owners in the same neighborhood are also making mobility, tenure, and investment decisions (path F). Moreover, individual mortgage lenders, retail developers, and public policy makers are also making decisions that will affect the flow of resources into the particular neighborhood (path E). This welter of individual behavioral decisions will determine in aggregate what characteristics the neighborhood will exhibit in subsequent periods after the changes in residence and the real estate investments have come to fruition (paths E, F, and G). But if the aggregate characteristics that manifest themselves over time confound the original expectations held by the three sets of decision makers, further modifications of their behaviors likely will be generated (paths H, I, and C). Of course, such modifications of individual behaviors in turn may alter again the aggregate outcomes for the neighborhood, and the process of circular causation continues.

Neighborhoods Making Our Selves

Thus far, I have only considered how neighborhood conditions shape the mobility and tenure decisions of residents and the dwelling investment decisions of owners of property in the neighborhood, as summarized in paths I and C in figure 1.2. Though these influences are undoubtedly powerful, they by no means represent the full extent of how our neighborhoods shape us. There are three additional pathways through neighborhoods exert their effects on us.

First, neighborhoods directly shape how and where we collect data about our world, how we evaluate it and how we translate it into information useful for our decision-making. I discuss this pathway of neighborhood effect at length in chapter 5. Second, neighborhoods directly impinge on our mental and physical health by specifying the contextual influences to which we are exposed. The impacts of local schools, pollution, and violence are obvious illustrations. Finally, neighborhoods indirectly affect the human attributes that we acquire during the course of our lifetime by molding what options we perceive as most desirable and feasible. In this way, neighborhoods affect our decisions in the realms of fertility, education, employment and illegal activities, and thus influence the courses of our lives. These last two pathways are the subject of chapter 8.

A Holistic, Multilevel, Circular Causation Model of Neighborhoods

Prior sections have stepped through the components of a holistic view of how we make our neighborhoods and how they make our selves. It is helpful to visualize these connections in a unified fashion; see figure 1.3. It makes clear my position that to understand the causes and effects of neighborhoods one must embed them in a framework in which four spatial levels—metropolitan, local jurisdiction, neighborhood, and individual—are interconnected in mutually causal ways.

Previously, I explained the interconnections symbolized by paths A, B, and C in the context of figure 1.2. Aggregate population and physical characteristics of all neighborhoods in a local political jurisdiction will collectively affect what kinds of services and public institutions are demanded (parks, schools, safety forces, etc.), as well as the base of property, income, sales and other potential local taxes that can financially support such services and institutions (path D). Conversely, the combined tax/service package that the local jurisdiction provides to its citizens affects tautologically the quality of housing and the broader social characteristics of its constituent neighborhoods (path E). Finally, individual households and dwelling owners are interconnected with the metropolitan-wide housing market. As housing demanders and suppliers taken together, they "make the market" (path F); market signals in turn shape the mobility, tenure, and investment decisions

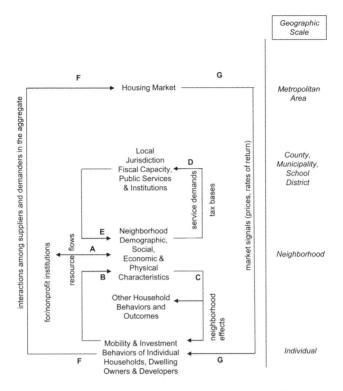

Figure 1.3. A holistic, multilevel, circular causation model of neighborhoods

of these individuals (path G). I amplify the analysis of these connections in chapters 3 and 4.

The Plan, Purposes and Propositions of This Book

I have organized this book to answer fundamental questions regarding neighborhoods in a coherent, cumulative manner. Chapter 2 addresses what a neighborhood is, whether it has definitive boundaries, and whether the "degree of neighborhood" can be measured. Chapters 3 and 4 address what drives changes in a neighborhood's housing and physical conditions, residents' economic standing or racial/ethnic ("racial" hereafter) composition, and retail activities. Chapter 5 addresses the question of how households and property owners acquire neighborhood-related information, form expectations about neighborhood change and interact with each other. Chapter 6 addresses the question of whether neighborhood change processes transpire in idiosyncratic, nonlinear ways. Chapter 7 addresses why we have so many blighted neighborhoods and ones that evince little diversity on racial or economic grounds. Chapter 8 addresses the mechanisms through which neighborhoods affect their residents. Chapter 9 addresses the consequences for human and financial capital that transpire when neighborhoods exhibit certain characteristics and change in particular ways, and addresses who disproportionately bears the costs associated with neighborhood processes. It also examines whether the current constellation of American neighborhoods is optimal from society-wide perspectives of efficiency and equity.

This book's first major purpose is to develop analytical frameworks and marshal evidence from across the social sciences that permit the reader to understand better the origins, nature, and consequences of neighborhood conditions and their dynamics. To this end, I advance eight core propositions related to how we make our neighborhoods and how they make us. These propositions also could be considered testable hypotheses.

- *Externally generated change:* Most forces causing neighborhoods to change originate outside the boundaries of that neighborhood, often elsewhere in the metropolitan area.
- *Asymmetric informational power:* Information about the absolute decline of the current neighborhood will prove more powerful in altering residents' and owners' mobility and investment behaviors than information about its relative decline or its absolute improvement.
- *Racially encoded signals:* Key types of information shaping perceptions and expectations about the neighborhood will influence the behaviors of residents and property owners, and a significant amount of such information lies encoded within the share of the black population in the neighborhood.
- *Linked threshold effects:* Individual mobility and housing investment decisions are triggered discontinuously once perceptions and expectations regarding the neighborhood have exceeded critical values. Aggregations of individual actions typically lead to large changes in neighborhood conditions only after these causal forces exceed a critical point. Once begun, aggregate changes in neighborhood conditions progress over time in a nonlinear fashion once they exceed another critical point. Many effects of neighborhood conditions on residents and property values only occur once critical values of conditions are exceeded, but eventually the marginal impacts of these conditions may wane at extreme values.
- *Inefficiency:* Decision makers in neighborhoods usually undertake an inefficient amount of activities of various sorts due to externalities, strategic gaming, and self-fulfilling prophecies. *Externalities:* Most decisions in neigh-

borhoods regarding mobility, property upkeep, and so on have impacts on neighbors that typically are not considered by the decision makers. *Gaming:* Expected payoffs perceived by some decision makers will be influenced by uncertain actions of other decision makers in the neighborhood. *Self-fulfilling prophecies:* If many individual decision makers share the same expectations about the neighborhood, they will behave collectively in a manner that brings about their expectation.

· *Inequity:* Lower-socioeconomic-status households and property owners typically bear a disproportionate share of the financial and social costs of neighborhood changes while reaping comparatively little of their benefits.

· *Multifaceted effect mechanisms:* Neighborhood context affects the attitudes, perceptions, behaviors, health, quality of life, and financial well-being of resident adults and children through a variety of causal processes.

· *Unequal opportunity:* Because neighborhood context powerfully affects children's development while neighborhood contexts are very unequal across economic and ethnic groups, space becomes a way of perpetuating unequal opportunities for social advancement.

This book's second major purpose is to show why and how we should make a more desirable palette of neighborhoods in American metropolitan areas. Based on diagnostic analyses culminating in the eight propositions above, the book builds a prima facie case that strategically targeted public policy interventions are required to make our neighborhoods more fair, humane, and productive environments for all Americans. Chapter 10 provides both overarching principles for strategic targeting interventions and specific prescriptions for public policy and planning initiatives dealing with the three most significant problems associated with how we have made our neighborhoods: physical blight, economic segregation, and racial segregation. It argues for programs that rely on voluntary but incentivized behaviors that gradually move toward a future of "opportunity neighborhoods": places of good physical quality, safety, diversity in economic and racial dimensions, and resources supplied by public, for-profit, and nonprofit institutions. Such neighborhoods could restore reality to the American promise of "equal opportunity," and serve as delivery systems for a new model of antipoverty policy and urban economic development.

TWO

The Meaning of Neighborhood

Since this book is about neighborhoods, it is only proper to define precisely the central concept at the outset. This seemingly straightforward task has proven wickedly difficult for scholars and no consensus has emerged. As Mark Aber and Martin Nieto put it, "Despite nearly 100 years of scholarly interest in neighborhoods, the question of what precisely constitutes a neighborhood remains unresolved and largely unexamined."[1]

The chapter is structured around three interrelated questions: How should neighborhood be defined? Does a neighborhood have unambiguous and consensual boundaries? Should neighborhood be thought of as a variable that differs in degree? I attempt to provide a definition that is acceptable yet inherently vague because of the heterogeneity of the multidimensional package of attributes that comprise it. Instead of talking about neighborhood as a place, I forward the idea that there are three distinct dimensions over which *the degree of neighborhood* varies across space: *congruence, generality and accordance.* In one extreme case, the values assumed by these three dimensions could signal an archetypical neighborhood commanding distinct, clear boundaries from the viewpoints of all decision makers of relevance for all important spatial attributes. In the opposite extreme case, the values assumed by these three dimensions signal that no meaningful neighborhood exists in this geographic space beyond that idiosyncratic one which an individual resident might perceive. Finally in this chapter, I suggest how these measures of neighborhood could be empirically tested, and reflect on how my concept of neighborhood as externality space overarches and advances the conventional views on neighborhood.

How Should Neighborhood Be Defined?

Urban social scientists have provided disparate answers to this question, stretching across many decades. Many have employed a purely geographic perspective. For example, Suzanne Keller defines neighborhood as a "place with physical and symbolic boundaries."[2] David Morris and Karl Hess label it "place and people, with the common sense limit as the area one can easily walk over."[3] "A geographically bound unit in which the residents share proximity and the circumstances within that proximity," is the definition employed by Robert Chaskin.[4] Michael Pagano says, "At minimum, most would agree that a neighborhood is a place in which people live, or at a more personal level, it is the area surrounding one's home. Neighborhoods are also assumed to have some sort of boundary to differentiate one from another."[5]

Others have attempted to integrate social and geographic perspectives, as in Howard Hallman's definition: "a limited territory within a larger urban area, where people inhabit dwellings and interact socially."[6] Donald Warren defines neighborhood as "a social organization of a population residing in a geographically proximate locale."[7] "Geographic units within which certain social relationships exist," is the term suggested by Anthony Downs.[8] Sandra Schoenberg specifies the neighborhood's defining characteristics as "common named boundaries, more than one institution identified with the area, and more than one tie of shared public space or social network."[9]

All these definitions offer some advantages but suffer from several shortcomings. They presume either a definitive (if unspecified) degree of spatial bounding or at least a minimal degree of social interrelationships within that space. Moreover, they underplay or overlook entirely numerous other features of the local residential environment that clearly affect its quality and desirability from the perspective of residents, property owners, public officials, and investors.

I believe that we can advance our understanding by defining neighborhood as follows:

> Neighborhood is the bundle of spatially based attributes associated with a proximate cluster of occupied residences, sometimes in conjunction with other land uses.

This definition owes its intellectual genesis to the work of Kelvin Lancaster, who originally formulated the notion of complex commodities as a multidimensional bundle comprised of simpler (albeit sometimes abstract) goods.[10] In this application, the spatially based attributes comprising the complex commodity called "neighborhood" consist of (in widely varying amounts across time and space):

· structural characteristics of the residential and nonresidential buildings: type, scale, materials, design, state of repair, density, landscaping, etc.
· infrastructural characteristics: roads, sidewalks, streetscape, utility services, etc.
· demographic characteristics of the resident population: age distribution; family composition; racial, ethnic, and religious group mix; etc.
· class status characteristics of the resident population: income, occupation and education composition
· tax and public service package characteristics: the quality of safety forces, public schools, public administration, parks and recreation, etc., in relation to the local taxes assessed
· environmental characteristics: degree of land, air, water, and noise pollution, topographical features, views, etc.
· proximity characteristics: access to major destinations of employment, entertainment, shopping, etc., as influenced by both distance and available transportation infrastructure
· political characteristics: the degree to which local political networks are mobilized, residents exert influence in local affairs through spatially rooted channels or elected representatives[11]
· social-interactive characteristics: intra- and extraneighborhood networks, degree of interhousehold familiarity, type and quality of interpersonal associations, residents' perceived commonality, participation in locally based voluntary associations, strength of socialization and social control forces, etc.[12]
· sentimental characteristics: residents' sense of identification with place, historical significance of buildings or district, etc.

The unifying feature of these attributes constituting the bundle called neighborhood is that they are *spatially based*. The characteristics of any attribute can be observed and measured only after one specifies a particular *location*. This is to say not that neighborhoods are homogeneous on any attribute, but merely that a distribution or profile can be ascertained once a space has been arbitrarily demarcated. Moreover, to say that attributes are spatially based does not mean that they are intrinsically coupled with the geography; some are (infrastructure, topography, buildings), whereas others are associated with individuals who lend their collective attribute to the space purely through aggregation once they occupy it. These more transient aspects of the space can be related to the residents tautologically (i.e., the class status and demographic characteristics above), their behaviors (i.e., the political and social-interactive characteristics above), or their emotional attachments (i.e., the sentimental characteristic above).

I emphasize that, while most of the attributes above usually are present to at least some extent in all neighborhoods, the quantity and composition of constituent attributes typically vary dramatically across neighborhoods within a single metropolitan area, let alone internationally. In my view, the only necessary and sufficient characteristic defining a neighborhood in all circumstances is "a proximate cluster of occupied residences"; all other attributes will vary by degree. This implies that, depending on the attribute package they embody, one can distinctly categorize neighborhoods by type or by quality. This is, of course, a tenet of social area analysis.[13] Unlike that classic school of thought, however, I extend the dimensions over which we can classify neighborhoods beyond the demographic- and status-related. The extension is necessary if one is to understand neighborhood change more fully, because key decision makers evaluate more than merely the demographic and status attributes of a space before investing in it or moving into it.

We consume commodities, of course, and in this sense neighborhood is no exception. Four distinct types of users potentially reap benefits from their consumption of neighborhood: households, property owners, businesses, and local government.[14] Households consume neighborhood through the act of occupying a residential unit and using the surrounding private and public spaces, thereby gaining some degree of satisfaction or quality of residential life. Residential property owners consume neighborhood by extracting rents or capital gains from the land and buildings owned in that location. Businesses consume neighborhood through the act of occupying a nonresidential structure (store, office, or factory), thereby gaining a certain flow of net revenues or profits associated with that venue. Local governments consume neighborhood by extracting tax revenues, typically from owners based on the assessed values of residential and nonresidential properties, and often by local income and sales taxes paid by residents.

Neighborhoods are also a venue for production, not simply consumption. In the most colloquial sense, neighborhoods often contain places of employment (often in the local retail or commercial sectors). Increasingly, "home offices" are becoming an important dimension of neighborhood-based production as well. Of course, scholars have long understood that the dwelling and the encompassing neighborhood are key environs for arguably the most important productive activity of all: the healthy, well-rounded development of children, youth, adolescents and young adults before they leave the paternal nest. I will delve into this vital aspect of how neighborhoods help make the next generation in chapter 9.

Does a Neighborhood Have Boundaries?

The fact that, once a space has been arbitrarily specified, we can measure spatially based attributes unambiguously does not necessarily imply, unfortunately, that *neighborhood* takes on an unambiguous spatial character. If all attributes were distributed uniformly within the same spatial scales *and* these scales could be demarcated by congruent boundaries, the place where one neighborhood stopped and another began (that is, where each attribute in the attribute bundle changed) could be designated in unambiguous geographic terms. However, the geographic scale across which an attribute varies often is highly dissimilar among attributes. For example, structural characteristics and those of the residents may vary dramatically over a few hundred feet, whereas public educational quality may only differ among enrollment zones for elementary schools, and air quality may be virtually constant across vast swaths of a metropolitan area.

Thus, my definition does not lead to the Holy Grail sought by much neighborhood analysis of the twentieth century: an unambiguous, meaningful, consensual bounding of urban neighborhoods. On the contrary, my definition suggests that any particular location is associated with characteristics that are *nested in space*, with a different level of the spatial hierarchy (and potential boundary) associated with each different component of its attribute bundle. It follows that households, investors, and scholars may well select different parsing of metropolitan space, depending on the particular neighborhood attributes (or, equivalently, the neighborhood typology) of interest or greatest importance for their decision.[15]

This implication is consonant with Gerald Suttles's conceptualization suggesting a multilevel spatial view of neighborhood.[16] Suttles argued that urban households could identify four scales of "neighborhood." At the smallest scale was the block face, the area over which parents permitted their children to play without supervision. The second level was the "defended neighborhood," the smallest area possessing a corporate identity as defined by mutual opposition or contrast to another area. The third level, the "community of limited liability," typically consisted of some local governmental body's district in which individuals' social participation was selective and voluntary. The highest geographic scale of neighborhood, the "expanded community of limited liability," was an entire sector of the city.[17] Subsequent household surveys have revealed that residents conceive of distinct spatial levels of neighborhood, which correspond closely to Suttles's theory.[18] In the context of my definition, I interpret the foregoing as suggesting that residents perceive several distinct clusters of neighborhood attributes, and that within each cluster the attributes vary at the same scale across roughly congruent spaces.

Moreover, it is precisely these *perceptions* of boundaries that are most critical in constructing theories or predictive models of neighborhood change, which is the purpose in this book. As I will explicate further in chapter 3, flows of human and financial resources produce the stock of attributes constituting neighborhood, and these flows will be governed by perceptions of key actors. The extent to which these actors will modify their resource flows will depend on whether they perceive that those attributes of particular relevance to them within *their* perceptual bounding of neighborhood have or are about to be changed.

My definition of neighborhood undergirds a complementary formulation of the behaviorally meaningful neighborhood in terms of *neighborhood externality space*. I define a person's externality space as the geographic area (containing the person's residence or property) over which changes initiated by others (people, institutions, governments, nature) in one or more of the aforementioned spatially based attributes are perceived as altering the well-being (use value and psychological or financial benefits) the individual derives from the particular location in which they live or own property.[19] These externality spaces possess three potentially quantifiable dimensions:

· "*congruence*:" the degree to which an individual's various externality spaces correspond to particular, predetermined geographic boundaries, such as those established by public officials
· "*generality*:" the degree to which an individual's externality spaces for different spatially based attributes correspond geographically
· "*accordance*:" the degree to which externality spaces for different individuals located in close proximity correspond geographically.

In the next section, I develop these three dimensions more rigorously and provide illustrative pictorial representations. I note at the outset that my formulation of neighborhood as externality space focuses on *others* who influence the well-being of the beholder by their proximate, spatially based actions. By doing so, I am not implying that the individual in question has no personal efficacy in shaping the neighborhood. Instead, I am arguing that for the purpose at hand of measuring neighborhood in multiple aspects, it is useful to focus on the externalities others are generating. Moreover, I recognize that the individual may in some cases influence the behavior of others nearby due to social interactions, collective norms, and other social processes. Nevertheless, as I amplify below, I believe that in observing how individuals respond to external stimuli not of their own making, the key dimensions of their neighborhood will be revealed.

Neighborhood as Externality Space

My purpose here is to present a new conceptualization of neighborhoods that is "realist"[20]— that is, grounded in the perceptions of people who are living and investing in them.[21] I develop algorithms whereby one can aggregate individual perceptions and quantify the differences in these perceptions. Finally, I suggest how one might make operational, geographic specifications of neighborhood based on empirical investigations that follow from these conceptualizations and algorithms. The operational specifications, in turn, open up a host of new possibilities for testing hypotheses of interest to theoreticians and policy makers alike. In other words, I attempt to link explicitly perceptual and spatial dimensions in order to derive a concept of neighborhood that is quantifiable and which holds the promise of improving our understanding of behavioral responses to proximate contextual changes that, in turn, produce aggregate alterations in neighborhood demographic and physical characteristics.

The fundamental way in which my approach to neighborhoods differs from previous attempts is that it is inductive rather than deductive. That is, prior attempts to specify neighborhood in a way that was perceptually meaningful have foundered on their inability to deduce precise geographic neighborhood boundaries from the theoretical constructs. I believe such a deductive approach is inherently fruitless. Rather, a meaningful theoretical conceptualization of neighborhood lays the groundwork for empirical tests in which the geographic boundaries of neighborhoods themselves become dependent variables. In this way, one does not beg the question of the existence of such boundaries, but rather they become the subject of hypotheses that one can test inductively. At this point, previous conceptual views about neighborhoods come into play; for it is precisely such characteristics as local social interaction, culture, sentiment, and symbolism that potentially can affect individuals' perceptions in an area to produce varying degrees of coincidence among their ecological views of neighborhood.

I do not view neighborhood as a unidimensional, dichotomous entity, something that either is or is not there. Rather, I view it as something that in aggregate is a quantifiable variable. One can measure its magnitude along interval scales in each of three dimensions: congruence, generality, and accordance. In other words, for any specific dimension of neighborhood, one does not consider here whether "it exists" or "does not exist," but rather the *degree to which* it exists over some particular geographic space.[22] I explain in the next subsections how the notion of an individual's externality space is foundational for the concept of neighborhood, and how the three dimensions of neighborhood can be measured.

Conceptualizing and Measuring Dimensions of Externality Spaces

One can specify a bespoke externality space (as defined above) from the perspective of a particular individual who is a resident or owner of property at the urban location under consideration. This specification considers the space over which particular changes are both perceived and adjudged nontrivial. In other words, it is the space over which stimuli indicative of changes in the quality of the individual's residential milieu provide the necessary (though not sufficient) conditions for behavioral responses of importance for neighborhood change: outmigration, alteration in home maintenance, dwelling sale, revisions in amount, type or locus of social interaction, and so on. Changes are herein specified as resulting from the actions of others which are *external* to the individual—that is, not the result of direct market or social transactions between the individual and the other person(s).[23] My focus is on changes that are exogenous to the individual, because the ultimate use of this formulation is as a tool for analyzing and predicting individual behavioral responses to such external stimuli that will lead to neighborhood change.[24] One could consider all sorts of externalities, in principle. Examples would be situations in which a public playground is built on a vacant lot on the block, a person of a different race moves into the house next door, a new city incinerator is built four blocks away, or several close friends move out of the neighborhood.

The geographic boundaries of this individual's externality space cannot be more precisely specified until one knows more about the externality under consideration, the individual's beliefs and attitudes, the local social networks between the individual and proximate others, and the spatial pattern of the individual's habitual travels. In other words, the externality space is a function of how individuals evaluate the particular externality, how their peers evaluate it, and whether they are aware of its existence, either firsthand through direct observation or secondhand through interpersonal communication.[25] I will delve in much greater depth into the ways that people acquire information about their neighborhoods in chapter 5.

Consider, initially, the externality of litter as an illustrative example. An individual may not readily perceive or be concerned about the presence of litter on an adjacent block, but would more likely do so if it were on the individual's own block. In such a case, the individual's externality space for litter would consist of the block face. Analogously, the externality space over which the individual is sensitive to the immigration of households of lower socioeconomic status is probably more expansive. Still larger may be the externality space for such externalities as new shopping centers or public facilities.[26]

Of course, exactly when some externality comes close enough for it to be perceived and assessed as influencing one's residential well-being or return on residential property investment depends on the characteristics of the observer. Elderly households, female-headed households, and households with children may be, for example, relatively more sensitive to the proximity of violent crime. Similarly, white bigots would have a larger externality space vis-à-vis new black residents than would more tolerant whites.

In the case of resident households (both renters and owner occupants), the externality space may also be influenced by the social character of the surrounding area. Although the social dimension of space may, itself, be the source of an externality, it also can influence the likelihood of individuals in that space perceiving a particular physical, demographic, or social interactive externality and the way in which they evaluate its consequences. For instance, if a person is embedded within a spatially dense social network (e.g., a traditional ethnic enclave), that person will be exposed to much secondhand information about and interpretation of spatial events that otherwise might not have been perceived through firsthand observation. The individual's evaluation of perceived information may also depend on the acculturation that has occurred in the local social milieu. As illustration, one who has resided for a long time amid professional-status residents might grow more favorably disposed toward valuing "everything in its place"—that is, rigid separation of land uses. This individual might therefore specify a more spatially extensive perceptual boundary for nonresidential land uses than would a person inculcated with the values of proximate working-class residents. These latter considerations may be included under the rubric "symbolic communities."[27] In chapter 5, I will provide an overarching model and more complete analysis of how neighborhood social-

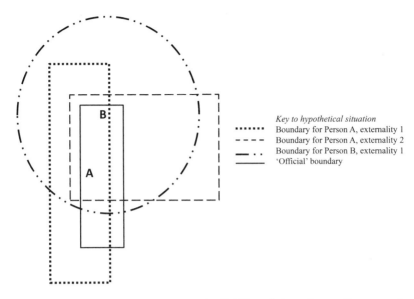

Figure 2.1. Hypothetical neighborhood with official boundaries and externality spaces of two residents

interactive contexts affect residents' acquisition and evaluation of information.

Figure 2.1 provides a simplified hypothetical portrait of spatial arrangements that will be useful in illustrating the issues at hand and in my proposed resolution. Figure 2.1 shows two people (A and B, who might be households or property owners) residing or owning at proximate locations shown inside an officially designated neighborhood (such as a census tract) defined by the solid-line border rectangle. Person A's externality space for a particular externality generator (#1) is delineated by the dotted-line rectangle; person B's corresponding space for the same externality is delineated by the dashed-dotted-line circle. Person A's externality space for a different externality (#2) is delineated by the dashed-line rectangle. Figure 2.1 illustrates all the challenges discussed above in defining boundaries of a neighborhood. The two people do not share the same perception of the area they consider their relevant "neighborhood" when externality #1 is occurring. Neither of these spaces corresponds perfectly with the official neighborhood boundary defined administratively. Finally, person B does not define the same neighborhood in the same way for all contexts.

I can now specify in more detail how to measure three dimensions of individuals' (that is, residents' or property owners') externality spaces:

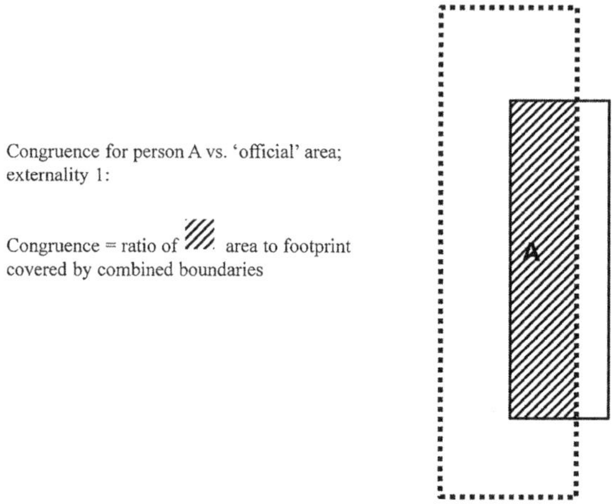

Congruence for person A vs. 'official' area;
externality 1:

Congruence = ratio of ⧄ area to footprint
covered by combined boundaries

Figure 2.2. Illustration of congruence

congruence, generality, and accordance.[28] Here I present these measures heuristically, using simplified graphic illustrations; I provide more formal, precise equations for each term in the appendix to this chapter. Individual *congruence* is the degree to which an owner's or resident's perceptual boundaries of the externality space for a particular externality corresponds to some predetermined geographic boundaries defined by streets, topographical features, or bureaucratic fiat that delineate an unambiguously bordered space containing the property to which the individual is attached.[29] One can quantify this degree of correspondence by the ratio of the area in which these spaces overlap and the total (nonduplicated) area covered by these two spaces. Alternatively formulated in set terminology, one can express individual congruence as the ratio of the intersection of these two sets and the union of these two sets. This measure ranges from a minimum of zero (when areas do not overlap) to a maximum of one (when areas overlap perfectly).

One can also demonstrate congruence graphically, using the hypothetical situation portrayed in figure 2.1. For this illustration, person A's congruence measure is visually portrayed in figure 2.2 as the ratio of the cross-hatched area in which the two spaces overlap to the area covered by the (nonduplicated) footprint of these two spaces.

The second individual dimension, *generality*, is the degree to which an individual's externality spaces correspond across a number of *different* externalities. The intuition of measuring this dimension is analogous to that for congruence: the average ratio of overlapping to footprint areas across pairs of

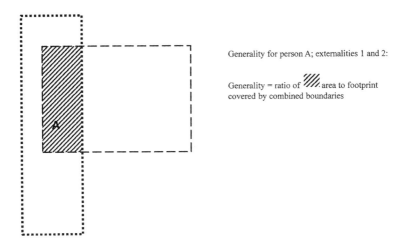

Figure 2.3. Illustration of generality

externality spaces specified for a variety of potential externalities, for all possible permutations of externality combinations (excluding duplications). Generality ranges from a minimum of zero (no overlap of spaces across externalities) to a maximum of one (the same perceptual spaces across all externalities for the individual). Figure 2.3 portrays this measure graphically. Generality for externalities 1 and 2 for individual A is the ratio of the cross-hatched area to the area of the footprint covered by the two spaces.

The third dimension is *accordance*: the degree to which all relevant individuals' externality spaces for a particular externality overlap. As in the above measures, one can define accordance as the ratio of the overlapping areas to the area of combined footprint of the two person's externality spaces; for more than two individuals, it is the average of these ratios across all individuals and all nonduplicated permutations of these pairwise comparisons. Accordance can also be illustrated visually with the aid of figure 2.4: the ratio of the cross-hatched area to the footprint area.

It is at the point where individual perceptions of neighborhood are aggregated over a spatial grouping of individuals that the operational geographic meaning of neighborhood has been typically rendered ambiguous in previous studies because there was no way to account for differences in people's mental maps of their neighborhood. One can avoid this by focusing on this question: *To what degree* does neighborhood exist in a particular place for a particular dimension? This alternative focus provides the basis for simultaneously *defining* and *measuring* neighborhood at the group level. Such an

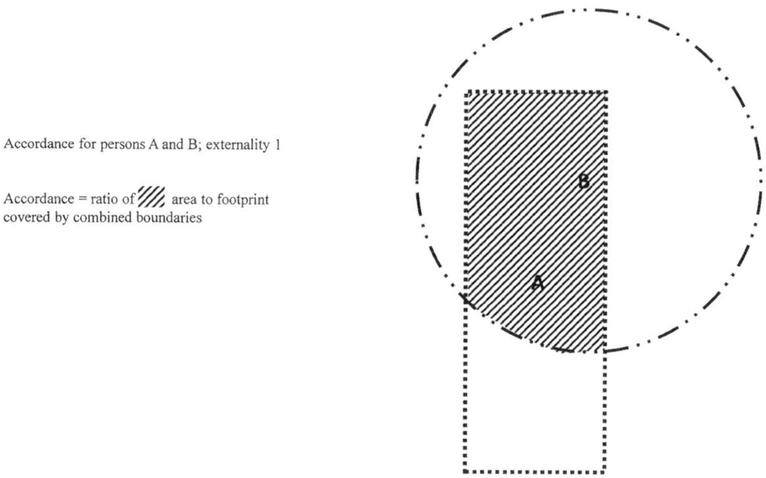

Accordance for persons A and B; externality 1

Accordance = ratio of ▨ area to footprint covered by combined boundaries

Figure 2.4. Illustration of accordance

analysis would revolve around the *aggregation* of individual measures of the three dimensions introduced above: congruence, generality, and accordance. It is a straightforward matter conceptually to take these notions and create more aggregate equivalent descriptors. One can simply compute averages of the pairwise comparisons of externality space overlaps across a number of individuals living and/or owning property in the locale under investigation and/or across several externality types, as is appropriate for the measure and aim of the investigation at hand. These aggregate measures could tell the researcher, in a strictly quantified way, the degree to which, in this area, (1) residents' perceived externality spaces corresponded to the official neighborhood boundaries, (2) residents perceived the same spaces for all externalities, and (3) residents' perceptions of the space over which a particular externality impinged were similar.

A Simplified Illustration of Measuring Dimensions of Neighborhood

Up to this point, I have presented congruence, generality, and accordance in heuristic and graphic terms. Here I supplement this with a simplified numerical example illustrating the point above about how a neighborhood's three dimensions could be measured in the aggregate, once information about residents' or owners' externality spaces was obtained. Consider the hypothetical situation portrayed in figure 2.5. Two residents living at locations A and B occupy this officially defined neighborhood (solid-line boundary),

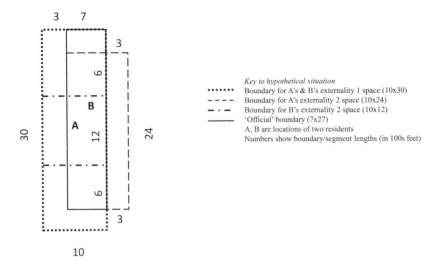

Figure 2.5. Illustration of measuring aggregate neighborhood congruence, generality, and accordance

which has an area of 189 (7 × 27, measured in hundreds of feet). To avoid an overly complex drawing, I show only three externality spaces. Residents A and B share an identical externality space when it comes to externality 1, a rectangle (dotted-line boundary) with area 300 (10 × 30). Residents A and B have different perceptions of the spaces over which externality 2 would impinge; the former specifies the rectangle (dashed-line boundary) with area 240 (10 × 24) and the latter the rectangle (dot-dashed-line boundary) with area 120 (10 × 12).

Beginning with congruence between persons A and B's (identical) externality 1 space and the official neighborhood, the overlap of spaces is exactly the rectangle of the officially defined neighborhood (area = 189). Thus, for both people the individual congruence for externality 1 is .63 (189/300). Congruence between person A's externality 2 space is .64, the ratio of the overlap area of the two spaces (168 = 7 × 24) to the footprint of the two spaces (261 = 189 + [3 × 24]). Congruence between person B's externality 2 space is .37, the ratio of the overlap area of the two spaces (84 = 7 × 12) to the footprint of the two spaces (225 = 189 + [3 × 12]). In this example, the aggregate congruence across all residents and externality types is the mean of these four individual-level measures: .57 ([.63 + .36 + .64 + .37] / 4). This measure has a straightforward interpretation: slightly more than half of the officially defined neighborhood area overlaps with the externality spaces perceived by residents in that place. This would imply that researchers,

planners, and policy makers who might be interested in predicting or influencing residents of this official neighborhood would do well to cast their
spatial focus on a different geography.

We proceed in an analogous fashion in computing generality for this illustration. For resident A, generality is .45: the ratio of overlap between the
two externality spaces ($168 = 7 \times 24$) to their combined footprint ($372 = 300$
$+ [3 \times 24]$). For resident B, generality is .40: the ratio of overlap between the
two externality spaces ($120 = 10 \times 12$) to their combined footprint (300).
The aggregate generality for this place is .425, the average of the residents'
figures. This aggregate measure tells us that the average resident of this place
has considerable variation in the perceived spaces over which different types
of externalities of relevance may impinge, since well less than half of the
cross-externality spaces share areas in common.

Finally, we can compute accordance for this illustration. Since residents
A and B share identical spaces regarding externality 1, accordance for that
externality equals one. For externality 2, the accordance value is .61: the
ratio of the externality 2 spaces in common for the residents ($168 = 7 \times 24$)
to their combined footprint ($276 = 240 + [3 \times 12]$). Averaging across the
two residents yields .80, the aggregate accordance for this place. This means
that, on average, residents here specify spaces for any particular externality that have 80 percent of their areas in common, suggesting considerable
homogeneity of perception and evaluation of externalities that may affect
their neighborhood.

Congruence, Generality, Accordance, and the Nature of Neighborhood

At this point we have the tools required to conceptualize what neighborhood means in a new way. In my externality space framework, neighborhood is *both defined and measured* by its aggregate congruence, generality, and
accordance. Each dimension may only be specified in terms of particular
perceptual group(s) and externality(ies) being perceived, depending on the
particular goals of the analyst. Once such a context has been specified, the
neighborhood associated with a predefined geographic place or group of individuals can be considered in terms of the degree to which it manifests congruence, generality, and accordance in the aggregate. For a predetermined
spatial set of *individuals*, should there be an area over which aggregate accordance and generality (for the particular externalities specified) were high,
it would imply not only that a meaningful neighborhood exists but that its
boundaries would be defined with little ambiguity or disagreement among
these individuals. If accordance and generality were low, however, we would

conclude that no collectively meaningful spatial neighborhood existed for this group. For a predetermined *geographic area* and the individuals contained therein, the degree to which neighborhood is manifested there would be primarily measured by aggregate congruence.[30] If aggregate congruence were low, we would conclude that the bureaucratically specified boundaries did not provide good proxies for the neighborhood as perceived by these individuals.

Making the Concept of Neighborhood as Externality Space Operational

Externality Spaces Exist

Due to its centrality to my formulation of neighborhood, it is important to recognize that externality space is not just a theoretical construct but an established fact. As I will discuss fully in chapter 9, a substantial body of sophisticated statistical modeling provides remarkably consistent, strong evidence that the housing market—and, by implication, current and prospective residents and property owners—behave as if externality spaces exist.[31] As illustration, this literature demonstrates that the value (that is, the capitalization of market actors' evaluations) of a dwelling is substantially affected if, within five hundred feet, a home suffers from a foreclosure, a property is abandoned, or a new infill construction project is completed. The spaces spreading from these externality generators may extend outward up to three thousand feet. Unfortunately, these studies can only take us so far in measuring the aspects of neighborhood I have delineated above, because they use market-wide averages and implicitly assume that the estimated externality spaces are circular in shape, as portrayed by person B's externality 1 space in figure 2.1. As such, they obscure the potential heterogeneity across space, individuals, and direction that are essential in ascertaining the degree to which neighborhood in its various dimensions exists in a particular locale.

An Empirical Strategy for Investigating Externality Spaces

My theoretical analysis implies that the way to convert the concept of neighborhood into an operational measure useful for empirical research and planning purposes is to measure boundaries of how individuals mentally map their externality spaces. Here is how one might undertake such an empirical investigation.

Depending on the ultimate analytical reason for the investigation, the researcher would first need to choose one particular externality (or manageable subset of them), as well as one or more particular group(s) of people upon whom to focus—that is to say, the particular dimension(s) over which neighborhood externality space will be assessed must be specified. For example, in a more narrowly focused study one might only want to explore behavioral responses of a certain type of household to the proximate in-migration of persons of lower socioeconomic status. At the other extreme, for broader urban planning purposes one might be interested in the parameters of a more general neighborhood for an expansive set of externalities that potentially might be regulated by land-use zoning as perceived by residents, owners, real estate brokers, and officers of financial institutions alike.

Second, and more dauntingly, the researcher would need to ascertain and map how the selected individuals perceived their externality space(s).[32] This would involve the administration of carefully designed surveys to reveal the distance at which respondents begin to perceive that certain generators of externalities affect them. In this vein, one could either query about *alternative hypothetical situations* and likely perceptions, or ascertain *actual perceptions of particular extant externalities* and, after noting the specific locations of respondent and externality(ies), infer a perception-distance relationship. Researchers have long used a technique analogous to the former to investigate, for example, how whites would evaluate alternative proximities of prospective black neighbors.[33] The potential weakness of this former approach is that the evaluations of hypothetical externalities may not correspond to evaluations of real ones if social acceptability bias influences the response to the hypothetical situation, or if respondents do not perceive the externalities in a particular instance.[34] The latter approach above is superior in this regard, since researchers are recoding the current perceptions and evaluations of existent externalities. The shortcoming of this latter approach is that the range of analysis is restricted to the set of externalities currently perceived, in varying degrees, by the sample of individuals in question, and this set may be extremely narrow, even potentially excluding the externality on particular interest to the researcher.

Whichever of the above techniques is used in the second step, the result would be a mapping of each particular externality space for each sampled individual. With these data about individuals' externality spaces, one could proceed to undertake several revealing investigations. If researchers took as given particular administratively specified boundaries of neighborhoods in the space over which data were collected, they could calculate for each neighborhood aggregate measures of generality using appendix equation 5, and accordance using equation 6 or 7, as appropriate. If one were attempting to designate the most meaningful neighborhood boundaries a priori, however, the goal would be to specify boundaries that exhaustively and mutually exclusively parsed the area under investigation such that one maximized the overall degree of congruence between the resulting neighborhoods and the relevant externality spaces of individuals located there. One could accomplish this with geographic information system (GIS) software, using an iterative procedure to identify boundaries that maximize aggregate congruence. This program also could calculate generality and accordance values for each of the spatially bounded neighborhoods resulting from the congruence-maximizing algorithm.

The preceding methodology would reveal to the researcher what the neighborhoods for the selected externalities and groups geographically looked like in the particular area. In addition, tests conducted with the congruence-maximizing algorithm could reveal how sensitive congruence was to slight alterations of boundaries, or in the number of neighborhoods specified. For instance, one might be particularly interested in how much congruence is lost when one adopts some previously established administrative or traditional boundaries, instead of the best ones achieving maximized congruence. The accordance and generality values calculated for the neighborhoods generated through GIS processing would also tell the investigator the degree to which these neighborhoods exist in similar ways across individuals in the sample and across various externalities.[35] In other words, the boundary yielding maximum congruence need not imply that congruence is high absolutely; accordance and generality may still be relatively low. Thus, one can assess from the methodology whether neighborhood is a meaningful construct for all or some of the locales under investigation.

Rory Kramer has recently applied my externality space concept in his empirical analysis of how people use attributes of geographic spaces to form clear boundaries that preserve racial segregation in Philadelphia.[36] Kramer puts forth an innovative method to define and measure spatial boundaries, using GIS tools to observe salient geographic break points in "racial externality" indicators that serve as markers separating communities. He focuses on one externality that he assumes white households (if not black households as well) negatively assess: a racial designation of potential neighbors that is different from their own. Instead of directly asking whites about the shape of their racial externality spaces, he draws inferences based on the observed population distribution: a neighborhood boundary (having substantial accordance) exists wherever there is a steep gradient (change) in the percentage of white residents as one takes alternative measurements across a short distance. He finds that several race-based neighborhood boundaries have proven remarkably resilient over time, and they typically correspond to political jurisdiction lines and/or features of the natural landscape and major transportation infrastructure. As pathbreaking as Kramer's empirical investigation is, the method he employs is inapplicable when considering externality spaces that are not delineated by easily visible characteristics of the residential population. It also does not consider potential variations in the degree of accordance, generality, and congruence across vast swaths of metropolitan space where the racial composition is similar.

As a final point, consider the contrasts between the methodology I suggested (or that Kramer employs) and the one conventionally used: asking residents to draw or name the boundaries of their neighborhood.[37] Certainly, the latter technique is operationally simpler. Once such maps are obtained, one might subject them to accordance and congruence calculations according to appendix equations 6 and 3, respectively, using GIS technology. This would be an interesting and informative exercise. There would remain residual ambiguity, however, concerning what types of externalities respondents were implicitly considering when making their maps. Thus, the implications drawn from these mental maps may not be transparent.

Rethinking Conventional Nostrums on Defining Neighborhood

Neighborhood as a Social Construct

How does the foregoing analysis comport with the conventional sociological notions of neighborhood as "arena for social interaction" and "symbolic community"?[38] Quite simply, the social dimension is herein viewed as a *variable* helping to delineate an individual's externality space, as I will elaborate upon in chapter 5. Borders specified by tradition and collective sentiment can indeed sometimes serve as diodes for the perception of externality: within the border, all externalities are important; without, they are not. The degree to which group members become aware of the existence of externalities within the border in turn depends on the geographic information nexus: how quickly and comprehensively interpersonal communication transmits news over space. Finally, whether people perceive recognized externalities within the border as threats, windfalls, or inconsequential things is influenced by the collective socialization that has transpired in the area.

The algorithms presented above (and, with more precision, in the appendix to this chapter) provide a framework for testing quantitatively these various roles of the social neighborhood. Numerous potential research questions come to mind. What is the relationship between the spatial density of social networks[39] and the area's accordance and generality? If, as Albert Hunter has suggested,[40] neighborhood perceptions vary between categories of individuals, which specific groups (age, sex, race, socioeconomic status, etc.) manifest the least degree of accordance?[41] Does an observed intergroup dearth of accordance persist over various types of externality spaces?

Neighborhood as a Visual and Physical Construct

Urban designers and architects have written much about the visual-physical dimension of neighborhood. In classic works published over a half century ago,[42] Kevin Lynch and Jane Jacobs have shown how people mentally map their urban surroundings, and how the visual character of the physical environment influences the clarity and interpersonal consistency of these maps. Albert Hunter has found that 80 percent of Chicago residents' descriptions of neighborhood boundaries involved streets. Of these streets, 63 percent were within one block of vacant land and 55 percent were within one block of a railroad.[43] Richard Grannis discovered that social interactions were most dense in "T-communities," networks of pedestrian-friendly tertiary streets within which people need not cross major thoroughfares.[44] Such T-communities might well form the basis of meaningful neighborhood boundaries.

In the context of the present model, one can interpret these findings in two ways. First, distinctive physical features can serve as a rough-and-ready referent for individually judging the proximity of externalities, much as social symbolism functions: are they beyond this physical border or not? Second, certain physical barriers may impede certain types of externalities. An intervening rail line, for example, may effectively isolate disreputable and dangerous behaviors. An intervening hill may abate noise, air, and visual pollution generated by an industrial facility.

Perhaps of more interest is the potential for testing these propositions empirically. For example, do areas of high "imageability," in Kevin Lynch's terms,[45] possess larger degrees of accordance and generality? Can the creation or modification of what he calls "edges," "paths," "landmarks," and "nodes" dramatically augment these measures and, in essence, *create* neighborhood?

Spatial Levels of Neighborhood

My notion of generality relates to Gerald Suttles's groundbreaking observation that people are cognitive of four distinct spatial levels of neighborhood.[46] I would posit that these results stem from individuals' categorization of various potential physical, demographic, and social-interactive changes into a hierarchy of externality spaces. At each spatial level, the appropriate subset of externalities would indicate high generality for each individual *and* high accordance across individuals. This is, of course, consistent with my aforementioned formulation of a neighborhood being associated with a nested set of spatially based attributes. The veracity of this interpretation awaits further empirical tests. What are the groups of externalities that cluster with high degrees of generality and accordance at different spatial levels?

Neighborhood Typologies

The foregoing analysis suggests that neighborhood is a concept that varies in three distinct dimensions: congruence, generality, and accordance. One may thus array actual urban spaces within a three-dimensional matrix according to their scores on these dimensions, analogous to a social area analysis or other types of categorizations employing principal components and cluster analyses.[47] Such an array provides the potential means for integrating disparate views of neighborhood appearing in the literature. Cases where we get high accordance, generality, and congruence in an area (e.g., clustered people with similar ethnic and socioeconomic backgrounds, little intergenerational mobility, dense spatial social networks, and high "imageability" of the physical environment) have been called "urban villages."[48] At another extreme, areas characterized by low scores on these three measures (e.g., people of diverse backgrounds, beliefs, and preferences who move frequently, have spatially dispersed networks, and inhabit a visually undifferentiated space) have provided grist for what Barry Wellman and colleagues have termed "the death of neighborhoods."[49] One might refer to places with values of accordance, generality, and congruence between these two poles as "generic neighborhoods."

The quantitative estimation of the frequency of neighborhoods at different points in the array and the intertemporal and cross-sectional variations in these distributions provides a fertile area of future research. What's more, the meaning and significance of different degrees of these indices deserves investigation. What kind of social, economic, and political reality is hidden behind a certain constellation of congruence, generality, and accordance? Such a question leads inexorably to the next area of discussion.

Prediction and Policy Evaluation in a Neighborhood Context

My formulation of neighborhood as externality space provides implications for researchers and planners who want to be able to predict and, if necessary, alter spatial change. As I will amplify in succeeding chapters, alterations in the physical, demographic, socioeconomic, and social-interactive character of an area result from change in the flow of households and financial resources into that area. The aggregation of individual mobility and investment decisions of the residents, property owners, real estate agents, and financial institutions with interests in that space govern these flows. Price signals generated across the entire metropolitan housing market provide the central information guiding these flows. The alteration of an individual residential mobility or investment behavior affects a particular dwelling with which the individual is affiliated, thereby potentially producing externalities for other residents and investors within whose externality space the dwelling is located. Further behavioral responses can ensue for those whose externality space has been penetrated.

Hence, understanding the *degree* to which neighborhood *exists* over a particular space is a prerequisite for comprehending and predicting *changes in that space*. For example, if the racial composition of a certain block's residents changes, how many residents on adjacent blocks will perceive this as a change in their neighborhood? If there is a wide disparity among residents on these adjacent blocks as to their cognizance of the change, their sense that it is in their neighborhood, and the degree to which it affects their well-being, there would be less likelihood of the spasmodic tipping of the area from one racial group to another. Thus, the accordance of an area becomes important for predicting responses to a particular externality generator. Similarity in the pattern of such responses across different externality types will depend on the generality extant in the area.

The measurement of the degree of congruence, generality, and accordance in an area is also crucial for assessing the impact of various public policies designed to alter the physical or demographic dimensions of the local context. Suppose, for instance, planners were considering renovating a certain block face or putting in a new park. Some relevant questions would then be: Who will view such a change as an alteration in *their* neighborhood? Over what geographic area are these people spread? How large a portion of all residents and owners in this area do they represent? In terms of my externality space formulation, such policy decisions should be guided initially by an examination of the neighborhood mapping produced by the maximizing-congruence algorithm (described above) as applied to the particular externality generator being contemplated in the policy (renovation, park, etc.). It is noteworthy that these boundaries may differ considerably from those typically employed by planners, based on the implications of several case studies.[50] Having established such boundaries, the planners could then measure accordance within these areas in order to gain a proxy for one measure of the efficacy of the policy.

A final way in which the above concepts may be relevant to contemporary programmatic concerns relates to the issue of local community political power. A prestigious panel of urbanists once claimed that "a central problem in micro-community control of the environment is the absence of any authoritative way in which residents can appeal to a single set of boundaries."[51] If, for political reasons, one wanted to "build community," the existing levels of accordance and generality within congruence-maximizing boundaries would provide an indicator of where such community organizing efforts might be most propitious. Furthermore, one could assess the success of such efforts to mobilize collective sentiment and common symbolism by estimating increases in accordance and generality over time.

Conclusion

My concept of neighborhood as externality space overarches and advances the conventional views on neighborhood in several ways. Instead of conceiving of neighborhood as an unambiguously defined geographic place, I specify three distinct dimensions over which the degree of neighborhood varies across space: congruence, generality, and accordance. For example, an archetypical neighborhood with unambiguous boundaries from the viewpoints of all decision-makers of relevance for all important spatial attributes would register high values on all three dimensions. Other neighborhoods can exhibit low values on one or all dimensions, however. In an extreme case, it is possible that no meaningful neighborhood exists in this geographic space beyond the idiosyncratic one that each individual resident might perceive. Measurement of the degree of congruence, generality, and accordance present in urban spaces not only would allow one to quantify the degree of neighborhood present, but also improve the ability to predict how residents and property owners will react to perceived changes in that space.

Formal Expression of Aspects
of Neighborhood

In this appendix, I define the concepts of congruence, accordance, and generality more formally and precisely in terms of formulae. Start with an individual designated n, with a predetermined set of personal characteristics, who is residing at a particular address. The first dimension of this person's externality space, individual *congruence* (C_{en}), is the degree to which individual n's perceptual boundaries of the externality space (Y_{en}) for a particular externality (e) correspond to some predetermined geographic boundaries defined by streets, topographical features, or administrative fiat that delineate an unambiguously bordered space (X) containing the property in which the *n*th individual resides. Formally, I specify the congruence between this individual's particular externality space and the area under investigation as

(1) $$C_{en} = (X \cap Y_{en})/(X \cup Y_{en})$$

where $\cap$ and $\cup$ signify intersection and union, respectively, in set terminology. Heuristically, $X \cap Y_{en}$ represents the area of the region where person *n*'s perceptual map for the impact of externality *e* overlaps the map of the predetermined area, and $X \cup Y_{en}$ represents the sum of the nonduplicated areas of X and Y. The value of C_{en} ranges from a minimum of zero to a maximum of one.

The second dimension that can be specified for an individual, *generality*, is the degree to which individual *n*'s externality spaces (Y) correspond across E number of *different* externalities, with all permutations considered. Formally, individual *n*'s generality is

(2) $$G_{En} = \left[\Sigma_{e=1}^{E} \, \Sigma_{f=1}^{E} \left[\frac{(Y_{en} \cap Y_{fn})}{(Y_{en} \cup Y_{fn})} \right] - E \right] \Big/ 2\Sigma_{e=1}^{E-t} e$$

Heuristically, G_{En} represents the mean ratio of overlapping to footprint areas of externality spaces specified for a variety of potential externalities, for all possible permutations of externality combinations excluding identities ($e = f$). The value of G_{En} ranges from a minimum of zero to a maximum of one (which is scaled by dividing the grand sum by $2\Sigma_{e=1e}^{E-t}$).

Now consider the three dimensions of neighborhood that one may compute across aggregations of individuals. As above, I begin by taking as given some predetermined geographic area of a city with clearly specified cartographic boundaries: area X. This spatial set will demarcate a particular number (I) of residents who live in X, (J) owners of residential property in X, and (K) others with financial interests in these properties in X, such as real estate brokers or financial institution officers. One may select from this group all or some subset as the basis for analysis. Let this group consist of N members.

Now the *aggregate degree of congruence* for the space X for an externality e over N members of the group is the summation of individuals' congruence as defined in equation 1:

(3) $$C_{eN} = [\Sigma_{e=1}^{E}(X \cap Y_{en})]/(X \cup Y_{en})/EN$$

where $N = I, J, K$, or combinations or subsets thereof. Thus, one can specify aggregate congruence for a particular externality in terms of a group mean of the ratios of overlapping to footprint areas of X versus the members' externality spaces for externality e. Maximum aggregate congruence is obtained ($C_{eN} = 1$) when each group member's perceptual space for the particular externality corresponds to the predetermined geographic area; minimum congruence is obtained ($C_{eN} = 0$) when there is no correspondence whatever.

If, however, one wished to define an even more aggregated level of congruence, one could easily expand equation 3 to include summations across all individuals in area X and all E externality types:

(4) $$C_{EN} = \left[\Sigma_{e=1}^{E} \Sigma_{n=1}^{N} \frac{(X \cap Y_{en})}{(X \cup Y_{en})}\right]/EN$$

where $0 < C_{EN} < 1$ and $N = I + J + K$.

Moreover, one could in principle expand aggregate congruence further by considering the views of those prospective households, residential and nonresidential property owners, and public and private institutional investors who might consider living or investing in the area being considered. The only modification required in this case would be to use the *potential location* that each entity was considering moving to or investing in as the point upon which the externality space was defined (e.g., census tract centroid). Having done so, the addition of another summation term in equation 4 involving these M prospective entities is straightforward. Of course, with this aggregation across two types of entities—current and prospective residents and investors—the issue of weighting will arise. Which (if either) group's perceptions of externality spaces are more important in defining the aggregate congruence of this space? As a practical matter, this issue may not arise, because the analyst is likely to be interested in computing aggregate accordance separately for these two sets of perceivers.

Next, we can consider the second dimension of the aggregate neighborhood—*generality*, the aggregate degree to which the individuals' externality spaces coincide for E different externalities, as given by equation 2, summed over N individuals:

$$(5) \qquad G_{EN} = \left[\Sigma_{n=1}^{N} \Sigma_{e=1}^{E} \Sigma_{f=1}^{F} \left[\frac{(Y_{en} \cap Y_{fn})}{(Y_{en} \cup Y_{fn})} \right] - NE \right] \Big/ 2N \Sigma_{e=1}^{E-1} e$$

$N = I$, if residents; J, if owners; K, if others; or combinations of I, J, and K. Aggregate generality is thus the mean of the ratios of overlapping to footprint areas of all possible two-way externality space comparisons, summed over all group members in area X. The generality of area X over a variety of E different externalities would be maximized ($G_{EN} = 1$) for a particular group in X if each individual in the group were to perceive the same boundaries for all externalities (although these boundaries need not coincide from individual to individual). Generality would be minimized ($G_{EN} = 0$) if each and every individual's externality space for any particular externality did not overlap with that for any other externality.

The final *aggregate dimension* is *accordance*: the degree to which all N individuals' externality spaces for a particular externality e overlap. I specified it as

$$(6) \qquad A_{eN} = [\Sigma_{n=1}^{N} \Sigma_{h=1}^{N} [(Y_{en} \cap Y_{eh})/(Y_{en} \cup Y_{eh})] - N]/2\Sigma_{n=1}^{N-1} n$$

where $N = I$, J, K or combinations thereof; $0 < A_{eN} < 1$. Accordance for a particular externality is thus the mean of the ratios of overlapping to footprint areas of all possible two-way interpersonal comparisons of e externality space for N group members in area X.

It should be apparent at this point that C_{EN}, G_{EN}, and A_{EN} as specified are interval measures of three distinct dimensions of the aggregate relationships between externality spaces existing for some predefined geographic area. As such, they are not comparable in a cardinal sense. Certain logical connections do exist among them, of course. For instance, A_{EN} and G_{EN} maximization is a necessary (but not sufficient) condition for C_{EN} to be maximized. In other words, for everyone in an area to agree that its predetermined boundaries accurately reflect their externality space for all externalities, they must also agree that their externality space is the same across all people and all externalities. The converse is not true, however; there may be complete accordance and generality, but the common space thus specified may have little congruence with the predetermined boundaries of the area established by the public sector. Through analogous logic, it can be demonstrated that A and G minimization is neither a necessary nor a sufficient condition for C_{EN} minimization. Finally, A_{EN} and G_{EN} serve as constraints on the maximum C_{EN} level attainable for a particular spatial set X. Although no precise mathematical relationship can be specified at this level of generality, it is intuitively clear that if, for example, A_{EN} and G_{EN} were low, C_{EN} would also tend to be low. That is, if there were little overlap of externality spaces across various individuals and across various externalities, there could not be much consistent overlap between these spaces and area X.

PART 2

Making Our Neighborhoods

THREE

The Origins of Neighborhood Change

As I suggested in chapter 1, a holistic diagnosis of why neighborhoods manifest particular physical, demographic, economic, and social characteristics
and why these characteristics may change over time requires a multilevel,
mutually causal approach. Nevertheless, as an expositional matter one must
start somewhere, taking something as predetermined. In this chapter, I take
as a starting point for a particular metropolitan area under investigation
its distributions of (1) households, which have predetermined financial resources, preferences, and household compositions; (2) owners of existing
residential properties, who have predetermined financial goals and capacities and a stock of dwellings with predetermined physical characteristics;
and (3) developers of new residential properties, who have predetermined
financial goals and production capacities. I also assume for the period under
investigation that the spatial arrangement of transport infrastructure, employment, local political jurisdictions, and environmental conditions in the
metropolitan area remains constant.

In the following exposition, I will discuss forces first from a bottom-
up perspective, then from a geographically top-down one, and then back
again, as a way of emphasizing circular causal patterns at multiple spatial
scales. Specifically, I will demonstrate how market interactions between
individual households seeking to occupy dwellings and owners of existing
dwellings seeking financial rewards will establish prices and rents ("market
valuations") across the metropolitan area for dwellings in different ranges
of quality ("submarkets"). These valuations will affect how households sort
themselves into different qualities of dwellings. Over time, the aggregate
rates of return earned by owners of properties in these various quality submarkets will guide the individual, longer-term investment decisions of both
owners of existing dwellings and developers of new ones. In aggregate, these

decisions will govern how the existing housing stock evolves, and what sorts of new housing are built over the ensuing years. These aggregate changes in the profile of dwellings will, in turn, alter market valuations and subsequent allocations of households via further rounds of residential mobility. Because dwellings are linked to places, however, their physical characteristics and those of their occupants will in aggregate become neighborhood characteristics. These neighborhood characteristics become characteristics of local political jurisdictions when further aggregated spatially, with associated implications for fiscal capacity and service demands.

The Housing Submarket Model of Neighborhood Change: Overview

The goal of this chapter is to advance a model explaining why neighborhoods change in the dimensions that typically matter most to residents and property owners: the physical conditions of the dwellings and the demographic and economic profiles of its residents. Like all models, it abstracts from reality; yet it is powerfully explanatory, despite its simplifying assumptions. In subsequent chapters I will progressively relax several simplifying assumptions and explore their implications for a more nuanced understanding of neighborhood change processes.

I start by stipulating that the essential conditions of a neighborhood are governed by the flows of resources into and out of that place. By "resources" I mean residents; owners of residential and nonresidential properties; for-profit, nonprofit, and governmental institutions; and the money, labor, and social capital they invest in this place. If the flow of in-moving residents were to evince a higher share of a certain ethnic group than in the pool of existing residents, the overall ethnic composition of the neighborhood would shift toward the in-moving group. If property owners were to decide it was profitable to invest heavily in the rehabilitation of their properties, the visual appearance of the neighborhood would be enhanced. If a local religious organization were to allocate new staff to an after-school enrichment program, the cultural and recreational landscape of the neighborhood would be altered. If the municipal fire and emergency medical service were to open a new facility near the neighborhood, its safety would be improved.

Sobering features of these resource flows arise, however. They are finite, competed for by neighborhoods, and often zero-sum in their allocation. Households are the clearest example; at any moment they are finite in number, and can only live in (and pay for housing, stores, and taxes in) one neighborhood at a time. Similarly, local tax revenues and the services they provide are limited; giving to one neighborhood likely will mean giving less to another. This is often the case for financial flows, which are limited by how much income and wealth the metropolitan area's potential housing investors possess, and their ability to borrow funds for those investments.

Thus, it is useful to think of neighborhoods in the context of a pipeline metaphor. Picture neighborhoods within a particular metropolitan area as being enmeshed in a complex web of pipes that connect each of them to one another, the outside world, and major sources of resources like corporations, nonprofit institutions, and governments. Through these pipes flow the aforementioned resources, with the volume in each controlled by the appropriate set of valves. Within this framing, if we want to understand why a neighborhood changes we must understand why the resource flows into it have changed—that is, why its valves were adjusted. In a market-dominated economy such as the United States, we know why: price changes signaled the adjustment. The Housing Submarket Model builds on this framing and shows how the market works via price signals across a quality-segmented, metropolitan-scale housing market to alter flows of the most significant resources: residents and the financial investments by residential property owners, nonresidential property owners, and the local government.

In overview, the model is based on the premise that the metropolitan housing market is the cockpit from which the directions of its constituent neighborhoods are steered.[1] Housing leads; other aspects of neighborhoods follow. Economic, demographic, technological, ecological, political, and other forces operating across the metropolitan area set the behavioral context for current and potential households and for owners and developers of residential property. Key elements of this metropolitan context are the costs of building and maintaining dwellings in different qualitative categories (what I will call "quality submarkets"), the technical, financial, and legal abilities to convert dwellings from one submarket to another, and the aggregate distribution of households by financial means and housing-related preferences. The context in play at the moment leads current owners of residential property to offer their dwellings for rent or sale at certain market values appropriate to the submarket in which it is categorized, thereby providing a price signal. The metropolitan context, in conjunction with these price signals, leads households to select a certain submarket where they will try to occupy a dwelling offered by its owner. Dwellings categorized within a particular quality submarket may constitute quite different combinations of structural, lot, and neighborhood attributes, yet by definition they are seen by households and owners as being close substitutes for one another, or of equivalent "quality," and hence worth the same in the market.

The interplay between property owners seeking financial returns ("suppliers of housing") and households seeking residential satisfaction and stability at the acceptable cost ("demanders of housing") yields market valuations (rents, sales prices) in each housing quality submarket.[2] These market valuations, in turn, establish financial rates of return for those who currently own property, and signal financial prospects for those who might build new housing or transform nonresidential structures into dwellings. The comparative cross-submarket pattern of prospective profitability also signals owners of existing housing, who may find that it is more profitable to change intentionally the quality submarket category of their dwelling by investing or disinvesting in it.

Over time, the aggregate decisions of both creators of new housing and the owners of existing housing will gradually transform the distribution of the stock of dwellings across the array of quality submarkets, with the more profitable submarkets gaining more dwelling units. Accompanying these physical changes in the housing stock will be changes in the demographic and economic profile of households that will continue to sort themselves across residential opportunities largely on the basis of their willingness and ability to pay for occupancy in one submarket versus another close substitute one. Because both the housing stock and the residential occupancies are attached to particular spaces, however, these market-guided behaviors produce differential flows of resources across metropolitan space.

It is this joint evolution of the physical characteristics of the metropolitan housing stock and the associated sorting of households into that stock that fundamentally drives changes in neighborhoods. Not only are the flows of people and dwelling investments into neighborhoods directly determined by this quality-segmented metropolitan housing market, but these flows indirectly shape the flows of other resources from the local retail and public sectors. Note that this model abstracts from any social interactions among households or owners, a simplification that I shall soon drop in forthcoming chapters. Nevertheless, this admittedly unrealistic and limiting assumption of autonomous decision makers should not detract from the numerous insights this model provides about the cross-metropolitan market forces that fundamentally drive neighborhood change.

Housing quality submarkets are not synonymous with neighborhoods; dwellings categorized in the same quality submarket typically are located in a number of locations across the metropolitan area under study, and within a particular neighborhood there may be several housing quality submarkets represented. Nevertheless, to the extent that a particular neighborhood has a sizeable share of its dwellings in the process of being converted from their original submarket to a new one, this place will experience visible, on-the-ground changes in the physical character of its dwellings and in the demographic and/or economic character of its residents. These are changes that have been colloquially described as neighborhood "decay," "gentrification," "blighting," and "invasion and succession."

A provocative and central feature of my model is that an external shock impinging initially on one housing quality submarket will eventually reverberate (though with progressively damped force) to other submarkets. The mechanism through which the shocks are transmitted between submarkets involves behaviors of households changing which submarket they will occupy based on relative desirability and affordability, owners of existing dwellings converting them to another submarket in search of better profitability, and developers of new dwellings diverting their preferred submarket targets in search of better profitability. All respond to intra- and inter-submarket price signals, as we will see. A corollary insight is that the dynamics of neighborhoods are the aggregated product of the individual behaviors of households, residential property owners, and developers that are based on the relativistic evaluations of prospects in alternative submarkets. Changes in a neighborhood's relative attractiveness lead to changes in the flows of resources into and out of it, thus altering its absolute attractiveness.

In sum, the housing submarket model sees metropolitan-wide forces generating new, varying potentials for profit across the array of that metropolitan region's housing quality submarkets. Suppliers—owners of existing dwellings, builders, and developers—respond to the price signals of these altered potentials by adjusting the quality composition of the housing stock over time so that it is more heavily weighted toward the submarkets that were initially signaled as most profitable. Households demanding housing sort themselves among this evolving stock according to their willingness and ability to pay the prevailing price signals, in turn signaling by their actions what further profitable changes suppliers might undertake in the future. As this transformative process occurs in particular submarkets, neighborhoods where such dwellings are primarily located are changed in physical and occupancy terms. These changes, in turn, spawn changes in the local retail and public service realms, thereby generating second-round effects on neighborhoods.

The Housing Submarket Model of Neighborhood Change

In this section I develop in more detail the Housing Submarket Model intended to shed light into the "black box" of neighborhood change by grounding it in microeconomic behaviors of housing demanders and suppliers. This parsimonious yet robust and unifying framework allows one to see why neighborhood change occurs, how the process unfolds, and what its outcomes are for households, property owners, neighborhoods, and local political jurisdictions. The presentation assumes that the reader has familiarity with basic economic concepts and can manipulate elementary supply-and-demand graphs.

Housing Quality Submarkets

"Fruit" is not a terribly useful concept when one is shopping at the grocery. Anyone can tell you that apples are not the same as oranges, though they are both fruit; they differ in their costs of production, their taste when consumed, and likely in their price per pound. So too in the case of housing: all things we call "dwellings" are not equivalent. We therefore need to disaggregate housing into different "products," with each of these housing products being demanded and supplied in distinct markets, though they undoubtedly are connected because in some degree they can be substitutes for each other, like apples and oranges.

On this intuitive basis, I posit that the metropolitan housing market should be treated analytically as a segmented, interconnected array of *housing submarkets*. Each submarket represents a set of exchange possibilities for the purchase or rental of all dwellings in the metropolitan area whose myriad structural and locational attributes (building, parcel, neighborhood condition and status, environment, public services, etc.), though different, are evaluated *as a bundle* by demanders and suppliers as reasonably *close substitutes*. The unidimensional metric for summarily collapsing all these attributes of the housing package I call *quality*. Note that one must distinguish my usage from the colloquial use of this term. By quality I mean the market's summary evaluation of the dwelling's entire multidimensional bundle of attributes, including but not limited to what might generically be called quality (of upkeep, materials, and construction).

The notion of housing quality as I use it here is akin to what property tax assessors refer to as "assessed value." It is a summary valuation of the property (in this case, in monetary units) based on a formula that translates all the physical characteristics of the building and parcel into an estimated dollar value, *within the context of the specific neighborhood and local political jurisdiction in which the dwelling is located*. It is more precisely related to what real estate economists call "hedonic value": a market-based assessment of how much pleasure generic households would derive were they to live in this dwelling.[3] Economists have probed extensively the implicit formula that the market employs when judging a dwelling's hedonic value. They have estimated statistical regression models revealing how the sales price or rent of a property can be disaggregated into the implicit prices of its individual attributes (such as age, number of bathrooms, square footage of lot, air pollution index, and median income of neighborhood).[4] These implicit prices represent the relative weights needed to aggregate the individual housing attributes into a common index value. Once analysts establish these weights from the model, they can subsequently apply them to the characteristics of any particular property to estimate readily its housing quality.

This process can be used (either theoretically or in practice)[5] to array the stock of dwellings in a metropolitan area along a spectrum of quality. Ranges within this spectrum denoting a relatively narrow band of quality specify dwellings within a submarket. Returning to the earlier analogy, each submarket is equivalent to a different type of fruit. Precisely how one might partition such a quality spectrum into discrete submarkets is a somewhat arbitrary choice by the analyst with which all market actors may not agree. Nevertheless, there is a behaviorally revealed market consensus that certain categories of dwellings are closer substitutes than others, in terms of the satisfaction they provide to their occupants and the costs they incur for their suppliers. For the purposes of understanding neighborhood change, a tripartite partitioning of the metropolitan housing market into "low-," "middle-," and "high-quality" submarkets suffices. It is also a useful simplification here to suppress the distinctions between owner-occupied and absentee-owned sectors; for our purposes it is easier to view households as only demanders (renter occupants), and owners only as suppliers (nonoccupants).

It is vital that one distinguishes housing quality and market evaluation (that is, selling price or contract rent); though related, they are not synonymous. One would expect in a well-behaved housing market that a dwelling's quality and market valuation would be highly positively correlated, though not necessarily perfectly. Regardless of how related these concepts are, however, a dwelling's quality and market valuation may change independently over time. An owner may invest heavily to improve the physical quality of a property, yet the property may still fall in market valuation if the metropolitan area economy falls into recession. Conversely, a booming local economy or rampant real estate speculation spawned by easy mortgage credit may boost market valuations of dwellings even as they are being downgraded to lower-quality submarkets through undermaintenance.

Another important aspect of my definition of dwelling quality is that it encompasses not only characteristics of the dwelling and the parcel upon which it sits, but also the myriad of attributes associated with its neighborhood and local political jurisdiction, as discussed in chapter 2. This specification creates three important implications regarding dwelling quality: endogeneity, heterogeneity, and externality vulnerability. Endogeneity here means that a neighborhood's population profile (especially along racial, ethnic, and class dimensions) both contributes tautologically at any moment to a dwelling's current quality submarket designation, and responds over time to these and the full gamut of dwelling and neighborhood attributes present in this and competing neighborhoods. Heterogeneity here means that a neighborhood's population profile (especially along racial, ethnic, and class dimensions) may not be consistently viewed by all residents in terms of how it contributes to "quality." For example, those who have strong preferences for their own race or class group as neighbors may view the in-migration of households of a different race or class group as reducing the neighborhood's quality, and thus the submarket designation of their dwelling. I will probe this aspect more deeply in chapter 7. Externality vulnerability means that residents and owners will potentially be influenced by the mobility and dwelling reinvestment behaviors of other households and owners nearby in the neighborhood. I will explore the implications of this in chapter 9. It means that dwellings can change in their quality designation not only by the intentional actions of their owners that physically modify their dwellings, but also through the actions of neighbors that may be not only unintended but also undesirable from the perspective of the residents and owner of any particular dwelling. I call this form of externally induced, unintended change in the quality submarket designation of a dwelling "passive downgrading/upgrading."

The quality segmentation of the housing market has two important features. First, within each submarket there is room for independent adjustment of demand and supply because of the imperfection of substitution with dwellings in other submarkets. Second, submarkets also are interrelated because there is some substitutability among them; households may switch between them, owners of existing dwellings may convert their units from one to another, and builders of new dwellings may view them as competing destinations for their construction. As shown below, housing submarkets respond to changes in demand or supply in their own and other submarkets in systematic ways, but the pattern and magnitude of response is not uniform across quality submarkets. The closer the substitutability between any two submarkets (that is, the smaller the quality difference), the greater will be the repercussion of changes in one on the other; the more remote the substitutability (that is, the greater the quality difference), the smaller will be the repercussion. Differences in cross-price elasticities (that is, sensitivity of demanders in one submarket to price changes in another) for households that consider switching to different submarkets, and differences in supply responses (especially associated with upgrading versus downgrading costs and the mix between new construction and conversion) are the key sources of this nonuniformity.

To understand what transpires in a submarket, we need to consider two sets of actors and two periods. The two sets of actors are households ("demanders") and dwelling owners, converters, builders, and developers ("suppliers"). The "market period" is an interval so short that suppliers have insufficient time to bring converted or newly constructed dwellings to market. Such supply responses become relevant only in the "medium-run period." I will discuss the behavior of demanders and suppliers during these two intervals in the next section.

Market-Period Demand

For any particular metropolitan housing submarket comprising all dwellings of quality range X, there will be an implicit function relating the number of such dwellings that households will be willing and able to occupy and the prospective market valuation charged for them (that is, purchase price or rent)[6] over some relatively short "market period" (say, a month). This "aggregate demand for submarket X" function reflects an aggregation of the choices that will made by individual households in the housing market under alternative hypothetical market valuation scenarios. The demand function may be thought of as a summary representation of how households would respond in a variety of contingencies framed as "We would be willing and able to occupy this many dwellings of quality X if the owners were to charge us this amount." Each household is assumed to select a quality submarket in order to obtain the most desirable mix of housing and nonhousing goods consumption (based on their preferences), within the financial constraints imposed by their household income and wealth. Because financial constraints require that, ceteris paribus, households will consume a smaller quantity of an item as its price rises, the aggregate submarket demand function will be characterized as an inverse relationship between market valuation per dwelling in the submarket (MV_X) and the quantity of such dwellings that households are willing and able to occupy (Q_X). I show a representative aggregate submarket X demand function as D_{X1} in figure 3.1.

Factors determined outside the housing market (income and preference distributions, prices of nonhousing goods) and by factors determined within

it (market valuations of financially feasible substitute submarkets) will determine the demand for dwellings in a particular quality submarket. First,
the metropolitan-wide numbers of households of various financial means
(income and wealth) will be a determinant of demand. If, for example,
many immigrants with an income appropriate for consuming submarket
X housing were to enter a metropolitan area, it would increase demand in
submarket X. Graphically, it would shift the demand function from D_{X1} to
D_{X2} in figure 3.1. A similar effect would be produced if X were a high-quality
submarket and many middle-income households in the metropolitan area
got much wealthier due to a robust job market raising their wages. Second,
the metropolitan-wide numbers of households of various housing-related
preferences determines demand. These preferences are typically related to
familial status and age: young singles wish to devote a smaller share of their
income to housing; middle-age couples with children wish the opposite and
so tend to choose higher-quality housing for their children's sake, ceteris paribus. A metropolitan area dominated by young or elderly childless singles
is likely to evince stronger demands for modest-quality submarkets than
an otherwise similar one dominated by child-rearing couples. Third, the
prices of all other (i.e., nonhousing) goods and services that the household
might consume determines housing demand. Inflating prices of all other
goods and services relative to the price of housing, for example, will enhance the demand for higher than originally demanded submarkets. Fourth,
the market valuations of other housing submarkets that households see as
reasonable substitutes for X will determine the demand for X. If, for example, the market valuations in a near-substitute submarket Y should rise
and remain substantially higher, some households that previously chose
to occupy housing in submarket Y will change their decisions and instead
try to occupy submarket X because "it offers better value for money." The
magnitude of these induced household reallocations will be larger the closer
is the substitutability (that is, the smaller the quality difference) between
the pair of submarkets in question. This fourth determinant of demand is
particularly important for understanding dynamic processes, for it provides
one of the two mechanisms by which market signals are transmitted from
one submarket to others.

   These determinants of demand for a particular submarket are of course
fundamentally connected to the process of residential mobility discussed
in chapter 1. As I noted, there is a broad consensus among the theories of
intrametropolitan mobility that households make relativistic judgements
about the suitability of their current place of residence and others that they
see as being financially feasible alternatives. In terms of the demand deter-

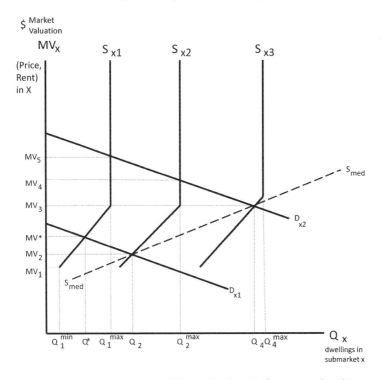

Figure 3.1. Representative market-period demand and supply functions and medium-run supply function

minants above, they make a residential choice of a submarket based on their current income, their housing preferences, and the relative market valuation per unit of quality. If this preferred choice is a different dwelling than the one currently occupied, a move will ensue. Seen in another way, households may eventually view what was originally the preferred choice of dwelling and neighborhood package as no longer so. This could be due to internal changes in the household (such as alterations in income or family circumstances affecting preferences), external changes in the current neighborhood (that degrade its quality in an undesirable way from the household's perspective), or external changes in alternative neighborhoods (that improve the quality/cost ratio in a desirable way from the household's perspective). Thus, as emphasized in chapter 1, the residential mobility of individual households is affected by relative conditions in both the currently occupied neighborhood and submarket and prospectively occupied ones; once such mobility choices have been made, they get aggregated to determine the market-period demands across the submarket arrays. The price signals that such demands provide in conjunction with market-period supplies will drive future changes in neighborhood conditions, as we will see below—potentially spurring a subsequent round of adjustments by households.

Market-Period Supply

I model owners of existing dwellings as if they attempted to maximize the rate of return on their housing investments. The notion of a market-period supply function embodies their resulting aggregate behavior over a short period. I define the "market period" for suppliers as that time interval too short to permit any substantive modifications of dwellings that would alter their quality submarket designation, or for new dwellings to be built or converted from nonresidential dwellings. By definition, then, the market period restricts owner behavior only to the choice of whether to offer a dwelling for occupancy at some current market valuation.[7] The market-period supply function for any particular submarket X (S_X) defines the relationship between various potential market valuations in X (MV_X) and the number of existing dwellings currently in X that owners will offer to the market for intended occupancy (Q_X). This function may be thought of as a summary representation of how owners as a group would respond in a variety of contingencies framed as "We would be willing to offer for occupancy (and hopefully have occupied in fact) this many dwellings of quality X if we were to reap this financial return on each."

Central to the determination of the nature of this market-period supply function is "reservation price"—the minimum market valuation that will induce the owner to put a dwelling on the market. Reservation prices within any submarket likely will vary across owners, depending on the cost characteristics of the dwelling units they own and their expectations. The crucial cost determinant is the relative current cost of having a dwelling occupied versus that of holding it vacant until the next market period. Some costs associated with owning a dwelling depend little on whether it is occupied or not: property taxes, insurance, preventative maintenance and replacements, and perhaps mortgage payments. Other costs may vary greatly, depending on occupancy. Security costs may be higher for vacant dwellings; cost associated with management, repairs, and utilities may be higher for occupied ones. The higher the holding costs of a vacant dwelling compared to the occupancy costs, the greater will be an owner's willingness to offer the dwelling to the current market for occupancy—that is, the lower their reservation price will be. Expectations of future market valuations may also influence reservation prices: optimism is associated with higher reservation prices. Owners will be more desirous to hold their dwelling off the market for a while if they expect market valuations in the relevant submarket to rise substantially in the near future, and do not wish to lock themselves into an inferior financial deal.[8]

During any market period, each owner will have established a reservation price for each dwelling owned. Should the market valuation MV_X be low, only those dwellings with low reservation prices will be offered to the submarket with the intent of being occupied, and thus the aggregate number offered (Q_X) will be low. If MV_X were to rise progressively, it would successively exceed the reservation prices of more and more dwellings, and Q_X will increase in accordance. Thus, over a substantial range of potential market valuations, there will be a direct relationship between Q_X and MV_X; see the range between MV_1 and MV_3 on the market-period supply function S_{X1} in figure 3.1.

There is, however, a limit to both the maximum and the minimum number of dwellings that owners can offer for occupancy during the market period. The minimum is defined by the number of dwellings in X (Q_1^{MIN}) held by the owner in the submarket having the lowest reservation price (MV_1 in figure 3.1). If the market valuation were to drop below MV_1, no one would offer any dwellings for occupancy during that market period. As for the maximum number of dwellings, the market-period supply function must be constrained by the preexisting submarket stock (Q_1^{MAX}) since the market period is defined so as to disallow any alterations in the housing stock. Thus, even if owners were to enjoy extremely high market valuations above MV_3 on the market-period supply function S_{X1} in figure 3.1, they would be unable to offer more than the dwellings they currently own in submarket X (Q_1^{MAX}).

The minimum stock of dwellings, the array of reservation prices (determined by relative holding and occupancy costs and expectations), and the maximum stock together determine the market-period supply function for the submarket. As shown in figure 3.1, the function S_{X1} indicates zero quantities supplied for all market valuations below MV_1 (from 0 to MV_1). Finite numbers of dwellings offered for occupancy begins at (Q_1^{MIN}). This next segment is defined by adding to (Q_1^{MIN}) the cumulative number of dwellings that will be offered for occupancy in the particular submarket at various hypothetically higher market valuations in the range between MV_1 and MV_3. The distribution of reservation prices across owners in X and the number of dwellings each controls determine the precise upward slope of S_{X1}. Finally, S_{X1} becomes perfectly inelastic at Q_1^{MAX} when market valuations exceed MV_3.

Market-Period Equilibrium

Based on market-period demand and supply D_{X1} and S_{X1}, the submarket will gravitate toward an equilibrium position indicated in figure 3.1 by (Q^*, MV^*). This market-period equilibrium is defined by the market valuation MV^*, for which the number of dwellings in submarket X that households wish to occupy equals the number of dwellings in X that owners wish to have occupied. This equilibrium not only specifies the number of dwellings that will actually be occupied in the submarket and their corresponding market valuations, but also delineates the number of dwellings that will be vacant during the market period—the total stock less the occupied stock, $Q_1^{MAX} - Q^*$ in figure 3.1. This has strong intuitive appeal, because one would expect that in "hotter" housing markets there would be fewer vacancies. Such could be represented in figure 3.1 by the combination of market-period demand and supply D_{X2} and S_{X1}, which would yield an equilibrium of (Q_1^{MAX}, MV_5) and no vacant dwellings in the submarket.

It is important to recognize that equilibrium is not simply an abstract combination of a number of dwellings and their market valuation, or a visual representation of the intersection of two lines. Rather, it is a state toward which the behaviors of households and owners themselves will drive the submarket. Consider what would transpire if all owners in submarket X were to erroneously guess that they could get all of their dwellings occupied if they charged MV_4 if market-period demand and supply were D_{X1} and S_{X1}. The result would be that no households would be willing or able to occupy dwellings in this submarket, and this would manifest itself in no prospective occupants agreeing to consummate rental or sales agreements. Owners would eventually adjust to this untenable situation by competing with each other by reducing market valuations in an effort to attract occupants and thereby earn revenues. Once the submarket valuation dropped sufficiently, some households would start to occupy the submarket, but some landlords would still have undesired vacancies and would be willing to undercut their competitors because MV was still above their reservation price. This process would cease only when MV^* was reached consensually by all owners. At this point, all owners who would wish to have their dwellings occupied at MV^* would have done so. One could articulate an analogous scenario in which all owners in submarket X erroneously charged less than MV^*. In this case, the resulting shortages would be manifested in desperate households that could not find a dwelling trying to outbid each other for the scarce vacancy, thus signaling to the happy owner that the market could bear a higher valuation.

Note that I have described equilibrium as a market valuation toward which the submarket gravitates, having specified a set of parameters governing demand and supply that have produced the functions portrayed in figure 3.1. Precise equilibrium is unlikely to be manifested at any moment, because the underlying parameters determining demand and supply are often in flux and the households and owners have imperfect information—a point I shall discuss at length in chapter 5. Nevertheless, the concept is a useful one for our purposes in understanding neighborhood dynamics. As upsets, manifested as demand or supply shifts, alter the equilibrium target toward which households and owners are groping, a different set of market price signals (*MV* changes) will ensue. As I will further explain below, these signals will trigger longer-term adjustments in the quality distribution of the housing stock, which in turn will produce changes in the physical and residency landscape of neighborhoods where these housing adjustments occurred.

Medium-Run Supply Adjustments

Things get more interesting in metropolitan housing markets and their constituent neighborhoods when we allow more time to pass than is permitted in the market-period context. At any moment in a particular submarket, the market-period equilibrium specifies a market valuation and thereby specifies an absolute rate of return that property owners earn from their dwellings. This rate of return may be superior or inferior to rates of return in other submarkets or to those gained from investments outside of the housing sector altogether. It is these relativistic comparisons of profitability that guide longer-term housing supply decisions, since we view suppliers as usually attempting to improve (risk-adjusted) rates of return on their portfolio of assets. Owners of existing dwellings may intentionally wish, for example, to modify the dwellings to convert them into a different quality submarket where prospective rates of return, considering the initial cost of making the conversions and differential ongoing maintenance costs, are superior to those in the original one. Some may be unable to secure even minimal prospective rates of return from their dwelling regardless of its potential submarket, whereupon they may seek to convert it to nonresidential uses or, failing this, to retire it from the housing stock via abandonment.[9] Builders of new dwellings may perceive rates of return in certain submarkets that exceed those potentially attainable in stocks and bonds, and may therefore add to the housing stock in those submarkets. These various actions, which over time modify the distributions of dwellings across the quality submarkets of a metropolitan area, constitute longer-term supply changes.

I refer to the period during which these changes occur as the "medium run."[10] I discuss the two most fundamental types of medium-run supply adjustments—new construction and conversion—below.

As for new construction, the model assumes that a builder will choose the number of dwellings to construct in every potential submarket in order to enhance the overall rate of return on the builder's net assets. In estimating rates of return, the builder must weigh the prospective financial benefits and costs of construction in each submarket. Benefits per dwelling (MV_x) consist of the discounted present value of the expected sales price (or of the expected net rental streams) of a dwelling in the relevant submarket X. It is realistic to assume that no single builder represents such a sizable part of any submarket (existing plus new dwellings) that they have power to set market valuations differently from current submarket equilibrium. Costs per dwelling (C) consist of land and construction costs, the discounted present value of the cost of maintaining a new dwelling in submarket X indefinitely, and the opportunity cost of builders' capital (that is, the rate of return from nonhousing investments). I assume that both MV and C are monotonic (presumably nonlinear), increasing functions of submarket quality X.

The builder attains a superior rate of return for a new housing investment by choosing among the submarkets to identify the one in which the difference between benefits and costs (expected rates of return) is greatest. The builder should construct at least one new dwelling so long as the rate of return in this optimal submarket is greater than zero (the opportunity cost of capital, as noted above, being already included in costs). Organizational capacity and credit constraints will limit the total amount of housing investment undertaken by a builder. In particular locales they also may be constrained by various zoning and housing code regulations or limits on building permits.

Owners of existing dwellings face considerably different constraints and costs when considering longer-term supply decisions. Unlike builders, who have much more flexibility to assemble the components of a housing package most efficiently to produce the quality appropriate for the targeted submarket, the residential capital of current owners is already bound up in a particular set of structural attributes associated with their existing dwellings. Some of these attributes may not be feasibly modified, others may only be modified at great cost, and yet others may not fit well with other aspects of the residential bundle over which the owner has no control. For example, an owner of a dwelling in a very rundown neighborhood may reap only small prospective gains in submarket quality (and thus market valuation) even when substantial sums are invested in rehabilitating the structure itself.

I discussed extant theories of the property reinvestment behavior of dwelling owners in more detail in chapter 1.

Despite these challenges, owners of existing dwellings potentially have a number of options with respect to their property in each quality submarket X_i:

1. Maintain it as the same submarket X_i, with associated costs C_i (discounted present value of maintenance expenditures in X_i, plus opportunity cost of embodied capital in dwelling).
2. Upgrade it from X_i to a better-quality submarket X_j (via additions, improvements, and consolidations), with associated costs C_{ij} (out-of-pocket conversion costs, discounted present value of maintenance expenditures in destination submarket X_j, and opportunity costs).
3. Downgrade it from X_i to a lower-quality submarket X_k (via passive under-maintenance or subdividing larger dwellings into smaller units), with associated costs C_{ik} (out-of-pocket conversion costs, discounted present value of maintenance expenditures in X_k, and opportunity costs).
4. Convert it to a nonresidential property (e.g., an office or retail outlet), with associated cost C_N (out-of-pocket conversion costs plus opportunity costs).
5. Abandon it (ceasing ownership rights, removing it from the dwelling stock that may potentially be occupied), with associated cost C_A (opportunity cost of embodied capital).

A prospective rate of return is associated with each of the above options. For the best choice among options 1 through 3, the owner should compare the marginal benefits (change in MV) and marginal costs (change in C as above) for all potential conversions to different submarkets. If the greatest marginal net benefit associated with converting to another submarket is positive as compared to maintaining the dwelling in the current submarket, the owner will have an incentive to convert the dwelling. Conversion to nonresidential use will be a better option if the rate of return from such use is superior to that from any continued use as housing, even in the submarket with the highest potential rate of return. Abandonment will be optimal if the rate of return from using the structure plus any complementary resources is less for any potential use whatsoever (residential or nonresidential) than the opportunity rate of return of the minimally needed operational resources alone to keep the dwelling in the housing market. Incentives notwithstanding, these supply behaviors by owners of existing dwellings may be constrained by personal skill, time, and financial resources and by various zoning and housing code regulations.

Up to this point I have only discussed the active, intentional decision to convert a dwelling into a different-quality submarket designation. Such conversions may also happen without the efforts or intentions of the owner, however; I call this *passive conversion*. Passive conversion occurs when some force external to and beyond the control of the owner changes one or more attributes of the housing bundle, thus tautologically changing its aggregate quality rating. If the attribute alterations in question are substantial enough to change the quality submarket designation of the dwelling, it has been "passively converted." Examples include an antipollution campaign that substantially improves the air quality around a dwelling, many neighboring owners who allow their properties to become severely blighted, or the construction of a new rapid transit stop nearby.

Aggregate Medium-Run Supply and General Equilibrium

The aggregation of active supply adjustments of both builders and converters defines a medium-run supply function for each submarket, holding constant all potential passive conversions. The derivation of this function depends upon the notion of "metropolitan housing market general equilibrium"—a situation where in the aggregate there are no incentives for households to change submarkets, or for owners or builders to alter the overall distribution of the housing stock across submarkets. I shall demonstrate heuristically how medium-run supply adjustments bring about general equilibrium, and then how subsequent adjustments to a new general equilibrium, triggered by demand alterations, indicate the medium-run supply function.

Suppose that at some moment we have a market-period supply function for quality submarket X as S_{X1}, and a corresponding market-period demand function as D_{X1} in figure 3.1. Also suppose that the current market-period equilibrium (Q^*, MV^*) is associated with a prospective rate of return to conversion and new construction into this submarket that is superior to those available in other submarkets. This situation would induce some owners of existing dwellings in other submarkets to modify their dwellings in order to convert them to quality level X. Analogously, builders of new housing would add to the stock in X via construction, assuming that no housing codes or other legal strictures prevent it, and assuming that no other submarket offers superior returns. As shown in figure 3.1, these conversion and construction responses would be portrayed as a shift in the original market-period supply function for quality submarket X from S_{X1} toward S_{X2}, with a corresponding increase in the total available stock of such dwellings from Q_1^{MAX} toward Q_2^{MAX}.

Because of this increasing supply, market-period equilibrium market valuations would be progressively competed down, thereby reducing the rates of return in submarket X. As the conversion of dwellings into X continues, there would be inexorable reductions in the supply in the submarket(s) in which these converted dwellings originate, thereby boosting market valuations and rates of return in these submarkets. Concomitantly, as the most malleable (that is, inexpensively modified) units are converted, the costs of converting the marginal unit from these origin submarkets would rise progressively. These adjustments in market valuations in both submarket X and in close substitute ones (and adjustment in costs in the case of conversion) simultaneously act to slow and eventually terminate the incentives for adding to the stock of dwellings in X through both forms of supply. All the while during this medium-run scenario, households have been altering their choices of optimal submarket in response to the changing differentials in market valuations. (For simplicity, I do not portray such comparatively modest shifts in D_{X1}).

General equilibrium would be attained in the metropolitan housing submarket array when the point has been reached where (in the aggregate) there are no further incentives for households to change submarkets (in search of a better housing bargain) or for owners or builders to alter the overall distribution of the stock across submarkets (in search of a better rate of return). Let this point be denoted in submarket X by (Q_2, MV_2) in figure 3.1, with the relevant (postadjustment) market-period supply indicated by S_{X2}. Since the submarket array has had sufficient time in this scenario to adjust completely, this market-period equilibrium (Q_2, MV_2) is also a point of general equilibrium, and thus is a point on the medium-run supply function.

To delineate the entire medium-run supply function, suppose that an in-migration of households with income appropriate for consuming X-quality housing upsets this general equilibrium. This would increase the demand for submarket X housing from D_{X1} to D_{X2} as shown in figure 3.1 (all other submarkets unchanged initially). As vacancies fall and market valuations rise to MV_4, rates of return would rise to extraordinary levels in submarket X, thereby inducing similar sorts of housing stock supply adjustments, as described above. Let the new general equilibrium be established in figure 3.1 as (Q_4, MV_3), with the stock increment as embodied in the new market-period supply function S_{X3} (that is, the occupied stock between these two general equilibriums has risen from Q_2 to Q_4 and the total available stock from Q_2^{MAX} to Q_4^{MAX}). It is the locus of such general equilibrium pairs of market valuations and quantities generated by alternative exogenous demand shocks in submarket X (holding initial market valuations in all other submarkets constant), such as are represented by (Q_2, MV_2) and (Q_4, MV_3), that constitute the medium-run housing submarket X supply function, shown in figure 3.1 as S_{MED}.

Several factors determine the particulars of this function.[11] The costs of the various forms of medium-run supply adjustment—new construction, downgrading, and upgrading—influence the aggregate supply responsiveness to the particular submarket X, or "elasticity." For example, if there is little submarket specialization among builders and they do not significantly bid up construction costs in the urban area as they increase building in X, the medium-run new construction component to S_{MED} would be highly *elastic*. Elastic means that a relatively small percentage increase in market valuations will yield a relatively large percentage increase in the stock of housing. By contrast, if the metropolitan area in question has very high prices for construction labor, material, and land, coupled with anti-rowth development regulations, S_{MED} will be less elastic, and thus demand pressures will produce greater increases in market valuations even after the market has had adequate time to respond with new submarket supplies. Similarly, if the stock of existing units initially of lower quality than X can be cheaply upgraded to X, and the stock initially of higher quality than X can be cheaply downgraded to X (both on average), the aggregate conversion component to S_{MED} will be relatively elastic. These conversion costs, in turn, depend on the idiosyncrasies of the existing housing stock, as noted before. A metropolitan area dominated by detached, single-family frame units built many decades ago will evince a different medium-run supply elasticity than an otherwise comparable area dominated, say, by multistory, multiunit structures recently built with steel-frame construction and energy-efficiency certifications.

The mix of new construction and conversion modes of medium-run supply will likely not be the same in all submarkets. Rather, conversion will tend to predominate in lower-quality submarkets, since downgrading is relatively inexpensive for most existing dwellings while housing codes and zoning laws effectively make it too costly (if not legally proscribed) to build new housing at the low market valuations typically prevailing there. Conversely, new construction will tend to predominate in upper-quality submarkets, since it is generally more expensive to upgrade existing units than to build new units with the latest technologies that embody the combination of dwelling attributes desired in current housing preferences. Because S_{MED} implicitly embodies different proportions of conversion and construction responses depending on the submarket, the elasticity of medium-run supply will vary across the submarket array within a metropolitan area.

Dynamics of Intersubmarket Adjustment

It is important to highlight the properties of intersubmarket dynamics in the model, because such dynamics are crucial for comprehending the systemic nature of neighborhood change. I summarily describe this phenomenon as "systematic nonuniformities" of responses. That is, one can predict how repercussions from some exogenous shock in one submarket propagate systematically throughout the submarket array, and the magnitude of these induced repercussions will be systematically uneven throughout the array. Allow me to describe the process using the analogy of a "calm pond" (that is, general housing equilibrium). The Housing Submarket Model sees a "stone dropping into the pond" as the disequilibrium generated by a change in either demand or supply in the submarket where the "stone" hit. This event propagates "ripples"—that is, it generates further responses by households and owners of existing dwellings that change both demand and supply in other submarkets. These ripples systematically move across the pond's surface, but with ever-diminishing force. That is, they first affect submarkets most similar in quality to the originally impacted one, then sequentially affect with ever-decreasing power those of quality increasingly dissimilar to that of the original one. Finally, the ripple stops at "the edge of the pond." The entire array of submarkets has been affected, even if only slightly.

This special dynamic process results from both demand-side and supply-side features of a quality-segmented metropolitan housing market. On the demand side, some households will be induced to switch from their current submarket (or to choose differently, if they are just entering the market) to modestly higher- or lower-quality substitute submarkets in response to altered market valuations in their initial submarket. This means that a disequilibrium in submarket X will change market valuations in X and lead to a corresponding change in demands in other, close-substitute (similar-quality) submarkets, thus triggering disequilibriums there in turn. The induced shifts in demand in near-quality submarkets will likely produce smaller perturbations in market valuation than were present initially in the submarket bearing the brunt of the exogenous shock.[12] These successively more modest perturbations will, in turn, induce further shifts in demand in still other sets of submarkets farther removed from the point of initial impact.

On the supply side, owners of existing dwellings will respond to the initial disequilibrium in submarket X by recalculating their choice of whether to convert from their existing submarket and, if so, into which destination submarket. If the initial disequilibrium were to raise rates of return in submarket X, more owners in other submarkets will choose to convert their dwellings into X to compete for this newly attractive financial gain. These conversions reduce the supply available in the submarkets from which they originated, however, thereby creating disequilibrium there. Recall, however, that owners find the cost of potential conversion positively related to the quality differential between origin and destination submarkets. Thus, an upset of equilibrium in one submarket will lead owners to convert primarily either out of it to near-quality submarkets or into it from near-quality ones; there will be progressively smaller such responses for submarkets more remote in quality from the initial submarket. In either case the resulting alterations in market valuations in the submarkets to which converters in the initially affected submarket flow (or from which converters flow) would be more modest than under the initial disequilibration, and similarly progressively damped with remoteness in quality. This damping effect would be magnified to the extent that part of the reequilibrating response in a submarket comes from new construction.

Thus, intersubmarket repercussions in both quantities and valuations are fundamentally nonuniform inasmuch as they dampen progressively relative to the initially shocked submarket as they are transmitted to submarkets of increasingly dissimilar quality. Moreover, they are nonuniform because neither the responsiveness of households to changes in market valuations of substitute submarkets nor the responsiveness to owners of existing dwellings to alternative profit potentials is equal across the submarket array.[13] Cross-submarket variations in the incomes and preferences of their archetypical occupants explain the former. Idiosyncrasies (especially structural age and attributes) of the existing housing stock at each point in the quality array that affect conversion costs for all submarkets, and the different proportions of conversion and new construction responses, explain the latter source of nonuniformity.

Linking Housing Submarket and Neighborhood Dynamics

Having built the foundations of the Housing Submarket Model, I turn to an explanation of how this model provides insights into the origins of neighborhood change.[14] What I must clarify first is the distinction between housing submarket and neighborhood within a metropolitan area. The fundamental distinction is that a submarket is an abstract, nonspatial categorization of all dwellings in a metropolitan area whose bundles of attributes on net make them closely substitutable. It is in the submarket "space" where the housing market operates, and where aggregations of the metropolitan area's households, dwelling owners, and developers interact dynamically to establish market valuations, rates of return, and occupancy patterns across the submarket array. These market valuations and rates of return comprise the signals that guide households to reside in certain quality submarkets, and owners and developers to revise the number of dwellings in each submarket; these flows are what affect neighborhoods. As we saw in chapter 2, neighborhood is a tangible, place-specific bundle of spatially based attributes associated with clusters of dwellings, sometimes in conjunction with other land uses. As such, dwellings grouped within a common submarket typically are located across many neighborhoods in a metropolitan area. Neighborhoods often (though certainly not always) have within them dwellings that fall within different submarket categories. Even though they are distinct, however, the two concepts are inextricably linked. The myriad of spatially based attributes of the neighborhood in which a dwelling is located (accessibility, environmental quality, public tax/services package, topography, aggregate profiles of residents, dwellings and nonresidential structures, etc.) constitute important attributes in defining the quality submarket of that dwelling. Inasmuch as dwellings within the same neighborhood share roughly the same bundle of spatially based attributes, they will more likely register tautologically a similar overall metric of quality.

Having discussed these distinctions, I provide an overview of how alterations in submarket demand and supply functions send out price signals that alter choices of households, dwelling owners, and developers which, in turn, translate into changes in neighborhoods by altering the flows of households and dwelling investments across metropolitan space. The key for understanding this translation from *submarket space* into *neighborhood space* is to recognize that household demanders tabulated in a particular submarket abstract space are potentially leaving and moving into dwellings located in real neighborhoods in particular spaces. Analogously, dwelling owners and developers in this submarket space may be converting the quality of dwellings located in such real neighborhoods, and may be building new ones. These tangible changes on the ground in flows of human and financial resources potentially alter the aggregate economic composition of residents and the physical characteristics and condition of dwellings of a place—the two key dimensions of neighborhood change analyzed in this book. These changes, in turn, will affect the financial health of the encompassing political jurisdiction, a topic I discuss in more depth below. The degree to which these aggregate household and dwelling changes occur in any particular neighborhood will be directly related to its share of dwellings categorized in the housing submarket being strongly affected at the time.

Consider, first, changes in the economic profile of households in a neighborhood. If changes in demand or supply in a submarket were to create a situation in which in-movers to this submarket were primarily from a lower-income group than the current occupants, the particular neighborhoods where there were many dwellings of this submarket designation would experience *downward income succession*. If the opposite submarket changes were to occur, the altered flow of households would produce *upward income succession* in the neighborhoods where there were many dwellings of this particular submarket designation. "Succession" as a general term here means that the neighborhood's profile of currently in-moving households along some dimension (economic, demographic, racial, ethnic, etc.) is considerably different from the corresponding profile of current occupants, eventually creating a situation where, if such persists, the overall composition of the neighborhood will change.

Consider, next, changes in a neighborhood's dwelling stock characteristics. If changes in demand or supply in a submarket were to create a situation where many of the current property owners in this submarket found it more profitable to *downgrade* their dwellings to a lower submarket, this would result in undesirable physical changes in the neighborhoods where this submarket was manifested. Passive undermaintenance, for example, would be reflected in visible deterioration of the structures. Partitioning of a large, single-family home into smaller apartments would potentially yield more foot and vehicular traffic and loitering. If, on the other hand, the submarket were to signal a huge potential profit gain associated with *upgrading*, this would result in physical improvements to the neighborhoods where this submarket had strong representation. Of course, both of these changes would be accompanied by different market valuations for the converted dwellings and thus a different income profile of the households occupying them. Thus, dwelling conversions can sometimes (though not necessarily) be the precursors to income succession.

If changes in demand or supply in a submarket were to create a heightened incentive for new construction, changes in existing neighborhoods might occur, depending on where the building occurs. Building might involve "infill" on vacant lots, or residential demolition and reconstruction located in an older neighborhood. This typically would raise the aggregate physical quality and income profile of the affected neighborhoods, assuming that the new construction was of a higher submarket quality than the prior norm for these places. Alternatively, new construction may involve the creation of entirely new neighborhoods. Examples of this would include a new subdivision development on farmland, residential redevelopment on a swath of abandoned industrial land, or the conversion of a large complex of former nonresidential buildings into housing.

Reinforcing Neighborhood Dynamics in the Local Retail and Public Sectors

Thus far, my presentation has focused on the metropolitan housing market, because I view it as the fundamental driver of neighborhood change, since it creates the price signals directly guiding the flows of the two most important neighborhood resources: people and financial investments in dwellings. At this point, however, is it worth expanding the core model to explain how the metropolitan housing market indirectly guides resources flowing into neighborhoods from two other important sectors: local retail and public jurisdiction. By local retail I mean enterprises that primarily serve proximate residents; examples include dry cleaners, corner bars, small shops, variety discount stores, and hair salons. Although a local retail sector may not be present in every neighborhood, we generally consider proximity to such a desirable attribute in the housing quality bundle. Moreover, we can think of a robust local resource sector as providing yet another valuable attribute of proximate dwellings: easy access to employment. By local public sector, I mean the smallest taxing authority of which the neighborhood is a constituent part; examples include municipalities, villages, and townships. Obviously, the nature of the public services and infrastructure that the local public sector provides and the tax bill it charges for it are also important attributes in the housing quality bundle.

The metropolitan housing market shapes the local retail environment in or near a neighborhood through its impact on the localized density of household disposable income. Density of disposable income is the product of the area's population density and per capita income or wealth. If adjustments in the housing submarket predominantly represented in a particular neighborhood produce a residential landscape occupied by residents with substantial individual incomes and characterized by dwellings constructed at higher density, the local retail sector will likely be multifaceted, upscale in its products and services, physically well maintained, and profitable. By contrast, if adjustments in the housing submarket predominantly represented in a particular neighborhood were to produce there a residential landscape occupied primarily by poverty-stricken residents and characterized by dwellings constructed at low density, many of which were vacant or abandoned, the remnants of the local retail sector will likely take on the opposite traits.

The metropolitan housing market shapes the local public sector servicing a neighborhood through its impact on the jurisdiction-wide density of population, density of disposable income, and taxable values of residential and nonresidential properties. Most local jurisdictions in the United States accrue the bulk of their revenue through property, income, sales, or utility excise taxes and user fees. Revenues garnered through excise taxes and user fees primarily depend on the population density of the jurisdiction. Revenues gained through income and sales taxes depend on the jurisdiction's density of disposable income. Finally, the jurisdiction's property tax base (that is, the aggregate assessed values across all properties within its boundaries) will depend on how many residential and nonresidential properties there are, and what their market valuations command. As in the illustration above, the local public sector's fiscal capacity will be strong if adjustments in the housing submarket predominantly represented in many neighborhoods within the jurisdiction produce a residential landscape occupied by (1) many residents with substantial individual taxable incomes, (2) better-quality dwellings providing higher assessed values, and (3) a robust local retail sector generating sale tax revenues and higher assessed property values. Such a favored jurisdiction would be in the envious position of being able to deliver a diverse, high-quality suite of public facilities and services for a modest rate of taxation. In this indirect fashion, the flows of resources into neighborhoods from the local retail and public sectors is a result of prior flows of residents and residential property investments, both of which have been determined by the operation of the metropolitan-wide array of housing submarkets.

From the above discussion it follows that the flows of households and dwelling investments and the flows of resources from the local retail and public sector are not only related, but are mutually related in a complex web of *cumulatively reinforcing causation*. Figure 3.2 illustrates these relationships in graphic form. It shows that a shock to the array of metropolitan housing submarkets, external to a particular neighborhood, will set in motion a series of responses by households, residential property owners, and developers that will alter the flows of population and financial resources into neighborhoods through the process described previously. In the case shown in figure 3.2, these effects take the form of downward income succession, downgrading of residential properties and, in the extreme, depopulation and residential abandonment. These household dynamics reduce the density of disposable income and degrade the local retail sector (arrow A). The reduction of population, density of disposable income, and residential property values erodes the jurisdiction's excise, sales, income, and property tax bases if it occurs severely enough in constituent neighborhoods (arrow B). Simultaneously, the degradation of the neighborhood and jurisdiction's local re-

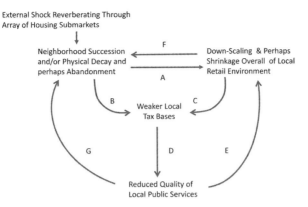

Figure 3.2. Mutually reinforcing cycles of neighborhood downward succession, physical decay, local retail decline, and local jurisdictional service and tax base erosion

tail sector erodes the sales and property tax bases (arrow C). Weaker tax bases, in turn, mean that the local jurisdiction will be forced to reduce the scope, quantity, and quality of its public services and facilities (arrow D), perhaps in conjunction with raising its tax rates to recoup some revenue. Now the feedback effects arise. A weaker public service/facility package, potentially coupled with higher tax rates, makes this jurisdiction a less profitable location for local retailers, thus hastening their decline (arrow E). In tandem, the atrophying of the local retail and public sectors serving the neighborhood will reduce the quality of all dwellings located there, tending to drop them into a lower-quality submarket (arrows F and G). This "passive downgrading" of dwellings was not intended by property owners, but they nevertheless suffer losses in market valuations associated with their new ranking in a lower-quality submarket. This, in turn, will intensify the pressures for active downgrading by owners, and for further downward income succession of households. In extreme cases where the dwellings in question have already been in the lowest-quality submarket, this "vicious cycle" of feedback effects and cumulative neighborhood decline may force some owners to abandon their properties, thus further eroding the quality of all properties in the vicinity.

An Illustration of the Housing Submarket Model of Neighborhood Change

Now that I have explained the conceptual elements and mechanisms within the Housing Submarket Model, we are in a position to analyze a hypothetical,

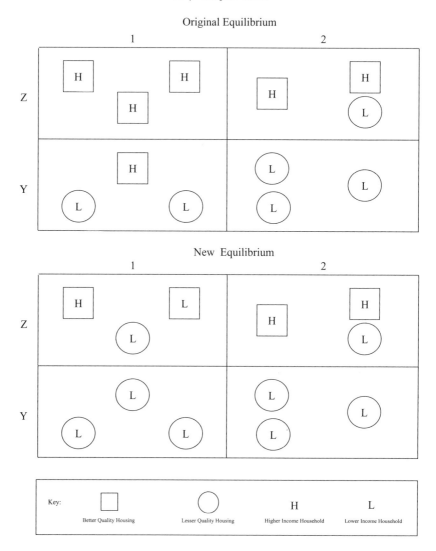

Figure 3.3. Stylized metropolitan area dual housing submarkets, with dwellings and households located in two neighborhoods and two local jurisdictions: (1) original equilibrium, (2) new equilibrium.

simplified scenario and thereby gain better appreciation for the insights the model provides. In this illustration I assume a stylized metropolitan housing market that, for simplicity, has one submarket consisting of six better-quality dwellings and another comprising six lesser-quality dwellings. The two submarkets are of sufficiently close quality that households view them

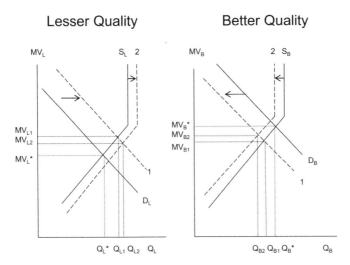

Figure 3.4. Illustration of submarket adjustments in response to loss of higher-income employment

as reasonably close substitutes. This illustration also assumes that there are two neighborhoods in local jurisdiction 1 (neighborhoods Z1 and Y1) and two neighborhoods in local jurisdiction 2 (Z2 and Y2), which together constitute the entire metropolitan area. The twelve dwellings are located across the neighborhoods as shown in the upper panel of figure 3.3. Squares represent the better-quality dwellings and circles the lesser-quality ones. There are twelve households in this metropolitan area: six have higher incomes (H) and six have somewhat lower (L) incomes. In the initial equilibrium portrayed in the upper panel of figure 3.3, these households sort across the neighborhoods according to their willingness and ability to pay for housing: all H occupy better-quality dwellings (primarily located in neighborhoods Z1 and Z2, while all L occupy lesser-quality dwellings (primarily located in neighborhoods Y1 and Y2). For simplicity, also assume that all occupants are renters, all absentee owners reside outside of this metropolitan area, and the income-group composition of a neighborhood is not a valued component of housing quality.

Let's imagine that initially this metropolitan housing market is in general equilibrium; graphically this is portrayed in figure 3.4, with the lesser- and better-quality submarkets each being in equilibrium at (MV_L^*, Q_L^*) and (MV_B^*, Q_B^*). Now we trace what transpires when an exogenous shock to the metropolitan area upsets the aforementioned equilibrium: massive economic dislocations associated with international trade and automation

wipe out half of the higher-income jobs. Assume that these unlucky former H households now find employment that compensates them only at
the lower income level, though they remain in the original metropolitan
area.

Because the income distribution of households is a determinant of submarket demands, the economic dislocations posited in our illustration will
have the joint effect of increasing demand in the lesser-quality submarket
while simultaneously decreasing it in the better-quality submarket. In figure 3.4 this first response is portrayed as shifts in the direction shown by
demand functions labeled 1, raising market valuations and rates of return
in the lesser-quality submarket and lowering them in the other.

Two second-round responses occur. Households adapt in the new market period to the different relative market valuations in the two submarkets.
Recall that the market valuation in a close substitute submarket is a determinant of demand in the submarket under consideration. Here this means
that the initial increase in demand in the lesser-quality submarket will now
be tempered a bit, as some lower-income households originally occupying this submarket find it financially feasible for them to move up to the
now less expensive better-quality submarket. It also could mean that higher
market valuations in the lesser-quality submarket will deter some of the
former higher-income households originally occupying the better-quality
submarket from moving out, since by doing so the rent savings will be reduced. Notice how these household reallocations, in response to relative
market valuations, transmit a disequilibrating shock from one submarket to
the other, and serve to moderate its impact in the original submarket. Both
these effects would moderate the initial shifts in demand due to the income
distribution alteration; for graphic simplicity I suppress distinguishing these
two effects, and instead portray the net demand shifts as the demand functions labeled 1 in figure 3.4, with associated equilibriums in the new market
period (MV_{L1}, Q_{L1}) and (MV_{B1}, Q_{B1}).

The other second-round response occurs over the medium run, due to
actions of housing converters and developers. Since relative rates of return
have shifted in favor of supplying lesser-quality submarket dwellings, some
owners originally holding better-quality dwellings will downgrade them to
compete in the now more lucrative lesser-quality submarket. This has the
effect of reducing the supply in the better-quality submarket while increasing it equivalently in the lesser-quality one, as shown by supply shifts labeled
2 in figure 3.4. Again, market-period equilibriums shift in both submarkets,
with market valuations falling and occupancy rising in the lesser-quality
submarket to MV_{L2}, Q_{L2} (compared to the initial market period MV_{L1}, Q_{L1}),

and market valuations rising and occupancy falling in the better-quality submarket to MV_{B2}, Q_{B2}. If new construction also proves to be profitable and permissible in the lesser-quality submarket, developers would also contribute to the new supply function 2. These medium-run supply adjustments would persist until the rates of return earned by dwelling owners in both submarkets were again equalized in a new general equilibrium. Again, it is worth emphasizing that the housing submarkets respond to shocks that alter relative rates of return by supply adjustments over the medium term which work to restore the original rates of return. When this takes the form of intersubmarket conversions of dwellings, this response serves to mitigate the initial effects in the submarket to which the conversion were destined, but at the same time transmits the shock to a typically near-quality submarket from which the converted dwellings have originated.

We can now relate this series of adjustments to neighborhood change by returning to the hypothetical metropolitan map in figure 3.3 and examining the lower panel. Let us say for illustration that the initial economic dislocation has resulted in three of the six higher-income residents dropping into the lower-income group: two residents of neighborhood Z1 and one in neighborhood Y1. As demands switched from the better- to the lesser-quality submarkets, market valuations fell in the former and rose in the latter. Even with a lower income now, the occupant of the better-quality dwelling in the northeast corner of neighborhood Z1 has decided that the lower-quality submarket was relatively too expensive for what one gets, and has therefore continued to demand the better-quality dwelling, even though it results in more financial strain. Two dwelling owners have responded to the new differential in rates of return between the two submarkets by downgrading two higher-quality dwellings in neighborhoods Z1 and Y1. This downgrading has made it financially feasible for lower-income households to occupy these particular dwellings.

Neighborhoods Z1 and Y1 have clearly changed their occupancy and physical characteristics because of the metropolitan area's economic dislocations. Both have experienced downward income succession of residents, and reductions in the physical quality of their dwelling stock. (They probably suffered a decline in their local retail sectors as well, though I did not graphically portray this here.) Local jurisdiction 1 clearly has lost fiscal capacity. Its property tax base has eroded, as a third of its housing stock was downgraded to the lesser quality submarket, which will exhibit a lower market valuation and assessed value per dwelling than the higher-quality submarket. Moreover, its income and sales tax bases will shrink, as half of its residents' incomes have dropped.

The Proposition of Externally Generated Neighborhood Change

The Housing Submarket Model suggests in several ways a fundamental feature of neighborhood dynamics: Change typically originates outside of the neighborhood. First, the scale of disequilibrating forces is metropolitan-wide, not at the level of neighborhood. Alter the aggregate characteristics of the metropolitan area's households in any one of numerous ways—total number, age, familial status, income—and the demand for one or more quality submarkets will shift. Alter the aggregate characteristics of the metropolitan area's property owners or housing stock in any one of numerous ways—owners' expectations; total number of units; age and type of construction; costs of building, converting, holding, or operating housing—and supply for one or more quality submarkets will shift. All these alterations are measured at the metropolitan level, not the scale of a neighborhood. Dwellings comprising these submarkets are located across the metropolitan area; rarely are they confined to one neighborhood.

Second, the behaviors of households, dwelling owners, and developers are guided by relativistic comparisons. Households may, for example, switch submarkets (and perhaps neighborhoods as well), on the basis of alterations in relative market valuations across submarkets. This implies that some residents may leave a neighborhood not because it has changed any aspect of its quality *absolutely*, but because some other neighborhood has become *relatively* cheaper and is thus "better value for money." Analogously, owners and developers compare relative rates of return among alternative submarkets. This implies that an owner may change the quality of a dwelling in a neighborhood and a developer may no longer wish to build there, not because it has changed any aspect of its quality *absolutely*, but because some other submarket has become *relatively* more profitable. Less abstractly, the hypothetical illustration in the prior subsection makes this point boldly. Neighborhoods Z1 and Y1 did not decline because they "did something wrong." Rather, the wave created by an external economic dislocation washed across them, and this eventually led to their loss of relative and absolute quality.

Other sorts of forces external to the particular neighborhood in question can similarly render it more or less relatively attractive as a destination for people and capital. These external forces are innumerable; a few illustrations suffice. The rapid development of employment in a new suburban "edge city" would change the relative accessibility of many neighborhoods across the metropolitan area, making some more attractive as places to live and invest, and others less attractive. If what previously was a substantial flow of international immigrants into a city's "port-of-entry" neighborhoods were to be stemmed by war or domestic anti-immigration policies, such neighborhoods would see their demands fall. If developers were to construct many new dwellings in suburban subdivisions of quality similar to that of several older neighborhoods, the latter places would likely see a diversion of some of their households. A major natural disaster impinging on certain neighborhoods would displace their households, which would end up disequilibrating other neighborhoods in the area, bidding up market values, reducing vacancies, enhancing rates of return, and thereby encouraging more capital investments in the housing stock there.

All this leads to the first fundamental proposition of this book:

The Proposition of Externally Generated Neighborhood Change: Most forces causing a neighborhood to change originate outside the boundaries of that neighborhood, often elsewhere in the metropolitan area.

Conclusion

What transpires in the housing market, which operates at a metropolitan-wide scale, primarily drives neighborhood change. I model this market as an interconnected array of submarkets segmented by quality; each submarket represents a distinctive type of good within the "housing" rubric. Within each submarket there is latitude for independent adjustments of demand and supply; but crucially, submarkets also are interconnected by the actions of households, owners and converters of existing dwellings, and builders of new dwellings. Exogenous forces and shocks in demographic, economic, ecological, and technical realms impinging initially on one submarket create signals there that eventually lead to systematic but nonuniform repercussions, potentially throughout the entire submarket array. These dynamics of intersubmarket adjustments of demanders and suppliers fundamentally engender the neighborhood change process, which manifests itself in on-the-ground alterations in the demographic and socioeconomic composition of residents, and in the physical character of the residential structures. If such changes are persistent and consistent across a number of neighborhoods, there will be second-round effects that manifest themselves as alterations in the local retail sector and the services delivered by the local public sector. These impacts, in turn, feed back synergistically to magnify the initial impetus of neighborhood change.

FOUR

Neighborhood Downgrading and Upgrading

This chapter applies the metropolitan Housing Submarket Model developed in chapter 3 to demonstrate its power as a diagnostic framework for comprehending the origins, dynamic processes, and consequences of neighborhood decline and revitalization. I consider neighborhood downgrading (a combination of physical erosion of the housing stock and downward income succession of households) and upgrading (the opposite combination) separately, though both are subsumed under the common housing submarket analytical framework. For both processes I start with a stylized theoretical exercise that begins with some external shock to a metropolitan housing market originally in medium-run equilibrium, and then trace how the shock emanates across the submarket array, carrying with it spatial reallocations of households and housing investments that produce changes in neighborhoods and their encompassing local political jurisdictions. These illustrative scenarios employ the same submarket graphic tools introduced in the previous chapter.[1] After these theoretical expositions, I will demonstrate how the predictions of the model comport well with empirical reality, using as archetypes of decline and revitalization Detroit and Los Angeles. I close the chapter with a discussion of limitations of the Housing Submarket Model as a bridge to forthcoming chapters wherein the model's simplifying assumptions are progressively relaxed.

The Origins and Dynamics of Neighborhood Downgrading

The Concept of Downward Filtering

Neighborhood decline has often been associated with the term "downward filtering." Unfortunately, the literature contains almost as many views of

filtering as analysts who employ the term.[2] Scholars have variously seen filtering as changes in dwellings' market valuations, movement of households
across dwelling qualities, and changes in the distribution of dwelling quality. Fortunately, the Housing Submarket Model provides an encompassing
framework within which we can comprehend all these conceptions of filtering and unify them under the umbrella of neighborhood downgrading as
seen through the Housing Submarket Model perspective. In a sense, we can
view all these different formulations of filtering as different facets of neighborhood dynamics revealed by the Housing Submarket Model.

As we saw in the previous chapter, an equilibrium market valuation for
each submarket is established through the interaction of the submarket-
specific market-period demand and supply, and it will change when any of
the determinants of either function are altered. As these market valuations
and associated rates of return change differentially across the submarket
array, several adjustments occur that constitute these aforementioned dimensions of filtering. When, for example, relative market valuations fall in
a particular submarket (due to a decrease in demand, an increase in supply,
or both) some households previously occupying housing in a lower-quality
submarket may be willing and able to move up to this better-quality one.
This has been called "price filtering."[3] Falling relative market valuations will
also induce some owners in this submarket to change the quality of their
dwelling either upward or downward to improve rates of return; this has
been called "dwelling filtering." If the converted dwellings are spatially concentrated, households in the same neighborhoods may "passively filter" as
the quality of their overall dwelling packages (but not the structure component of those packages) is affected by the resultant externalities. These
medium-run demand and supply responses upset the equilibrium in other,
especially nearest-quality, submarkets, thereby triggering further "filtering-
like" dynamics: market valuation and rate-of-return adjustments, household moves, and dwelling quality conversions. The adjustments thus spread
throughout the submarket complex, in successively damped degree with
increasing qualitative dissimilarity. Residents and property owners on the
ground perceive these changes as neighborhood downgrading.

The Mechanism of Neighborhood Downgrading: Individual Responses

To illustrate more clearly the aforementioned multidimensional aspects of
filtering, consider a simplified hypothetical scenario. Start with a representative metropolitan housing market in general equilibrium. Let us then upset this equilibrium by the injection of substantial new construction in the

high-quality end of the submarket array. This new construction may have been induced by a reduction in builders' costs, for example, which has allowed the builders to compete more successfully with owners of existing high-quality dwellings, and which has provided rates of return superior to nonhousing investments (the ever-present opportunity cost of housing investment). Speculative motives by builders also may have produced housing construction, insofar as they have foreseen that their newly built dwellings would hold a marketing advantage over older dwellings of similar quality. Implicit in this scenario is that the metropolitan housing market's elasticity of medium-run supply is relatively high: it takes only a modest increase in market valuation to induce a strong increase in the stock of housing.

The impact of this shock on owners of existing high-quality dwellings is predictable. The intensified competition from builders that owners of existing units face will lead to a reduction in market valuations and associated rates of return, and vacancies will increase. Some owners will have an incentive to downgrade their units to a lower-quality submarket. If this active downgrading is spatially concentrated so that significant negative externalities are generated for nearby dwellings, their owners also may find that their dwellings have been passively downgraded to a lower-quality submarket.[4] As such active and passive downgrading of dwellings ensues, it will depress market valuations in the submarkets into which they converted, and simultaneously will raise them in those from which they converted. Any new construction occurring in the destination submarkets will intensify this depressing effect, of course. For the same reasons as noted above, some owners in these somewhat lower-quality submarkets will also, intentionally or otherwise, downgrade their dwellings. This process of restoring equilibrium at the origin submarket while disrupting it at the destination submarket via conversion responses continues through additional repercussion rounds, with each successive round representing a progressively smaller disruption, ultimately because in each submarket the gross additions to the stock will be greater than the gross losses due to downgrading. This "ripple effect" of successive but ever-damped waves of downgrading behavior from high- to ever lower-quality submarkets eventually, in principle, affects even the lowest-quality submarket, and depresses market valuations there. In such circumstances, some owners in the lowest-quality submarket will inevitably be forced to abandon their dwellings because they have intolerably high costs compared to their meager revenues and will perpetually run operating deficits.[5] Short-term efforts to forestall the inevitable by, for example, deferring property maintenance and payment of property taxes will only hasten the odds of tax foreclosure or building and safety violations.

While this systematic but nonuniform housing conversion response is in process, there will be a concomitant reallocation of households to dwellings. As the shorter-term impact of each successive supply enhancement is felt in a submarket, some households previously occupying somewhat lower-quality submarkets will be induced to move up to the now less expensive better-quality one. The occupancy profiles of the physical downgraded dwellings will also change, as somewhat higher-income households appropriate for consuming the original quality submarket are replaced by somewhat lower-income households appropriate for consuming the quality submarket for which the downward conversion was destined.

Aggregate Impacts across Submarkets: Graphic Exposition

We can analyze the aggregate consequences of the aforementioned behaviors of individual owners and households with the aid of the three-submarket graphic scenario portrayed in figure 4.1. Assume for simplicity that the existing metropolitan area housing stock can be grouped into only three quality submarkets: high (H), middle (M), and low (L). In each, the original market-period (general equilibrium) demand and supply functions are portrayed with the subscript 1. Also assume that the new construction shock has initially increased the stock in the high-quality rental submarket from S_{H1} to S_{H2}. As a result, the market valuations in the high submarket are competed down, vacancies rise, and rates of return fall.

Now we can systematically consider the responses of households and owners of existing dwellings. Some demanders originally occupying the middle-quality submarket now find it desirable and more financially feasible to consume in the high submarket. This switch to a now lower-valued substitute submarket is portrayed in figure 4.1 as a decrease in demand to $D_{M3'}$ and an increase in quantity demanded (i.e., occupancies) along the original demand D_{H1}.

The depressed rates of return in the high-quality submarket trigger some downgrading from high- to middle-quality submarkets, thereby reducing the former's supply to S_{H4} (back toward its original position) and expanding the latter to S_{M4}. This stock adjustment drives market valuations in the high-quality submarket back toward their initial equilibrium, and still further lowers those in the middle submarket. The point where the rate of return in the submarket originally upset by the disequilibrating shock is the signal to the analyst to turn attention to the near-quality submarket that now clearly is no longer in equilibrium.

The market valuation reductions in the middle-quality submarket, in

LOW-QUALITY SUBMARKET   MIDDLE-QUALITY SUBMARKET   HIGH-QUALITY SUBMARKET

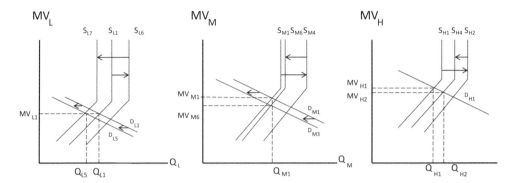

Figure 4.1. Illustration of neighborhood downgrading using the Housing Submarket Model

turn, may induce some tenants originally consuming in the lowest-quality submarket to move up to the middle one, thereby increasing the quantity demanded in the latter and decreasing the demand in the former to D_{L5}. This household adjustment process mimics qualitatively, though probably not quantitatively, the analogous process we previously saw going on in the higher-quality submarket.

With relatively depressed rates of return in the middle-quality submarket, a second, albeit smaller, wave of dwelling downgrading will be generated. This reduces supply in the middle submarket to S_{M6} and simultaneously increases supply in the lowest submarket to S_{L6}. As rates of return in the middle-quality submarket head back toward their original levels, the flow of downward conversion will cease and equilibrium will be reestablished in the middle-quality submarket.

Now the upset has been transmitted to the low-quality submarket. Demand has slackened there at the same time that owners of erstwhile middle-quality units have intensified the competition on the supply side. Though market valuations have dropped now in the low-quality submarket, there are by definition no households currently occupying a yet lower submarket that could now afford to move into somewhat better accommodations.[6] Owners with noncompetitive low-quality units will be forced ultimately to abandon them. This reduces supply to S_{L7} until an equilibrium is reestablished wherein owners of all surviving low-quality dwellings are making returns adequate to keep them in the industry (that is, returns comparable to those for alternative nonhousing investments). Note that this implies that the market valuations in the low-quality submarket must return to approximately their original level if the surviving owners are to stay in operation.[7]

The Consequences of Downward Filtering for Neighborhoods and Local Jurisdictions

The Housing Submarket Model suggests that filtering transpires in ways that affect households' well-being and dwellings' quality. From the perspective of some households that have benefited from the initial declines in market valuation by switching submarkets, they have been able to "filter up" to better dwellings. From the perspective of an individual dwelling unit that was downgraded, it has "filtered down" in terms of both its quality and the economic status of the clientele it now serves. Of more import here, however, are the perspectives from the viewpoints of neighborhoods and local political jurisdictions.

Where the new construction occurred in this scenario influences part of the neighborhood perspective. If, as has been the norm in American metropolitan development, undeveloped land located at the urbanized edge was the site of most new construction, we can say that new neighborhoods emerged there.[8] From the perspective of the older neighborhoods where a sizable number of originally better-quality dwellings were downgraded to a lesser-quality submarket category, they have "filtered down," insofar as they have more of these now lesser-quality dwellings occupied by households with lower incomes than the previous occupants (that is, downward income succession). Other neighborhoods have filtered down even if they did not suffer from dwelling conversions. They also have evinced downward income succession insofar as they were the locations where many of the households with somewhat lower incomes than previous occupants moved in response to the submarket-wide reduction in market valuations. The most severe downgrading of neighborhoods has occurred in places where abandonment was concentrated.

The perspective of the local jurisdictions is highly contingent upon what we assume about the locations of existing dwellings in the three submarkets, and upon where the new high-quality construction has occurred. To simplify the discussion, assume that all existing and newly constructed high-quality submarket dwellings are located in neighborhoods within suburban jurisdictions located on the edge of the urbanized footprint. All existing middle-quality submarket dwellings are located in neighborhoods in older, inner-ring suburban jurisdictions. All existing low-quality submarket dwellings are located in neighborhoods in the central city jurisdiction.

In this scenario, it is easy to discern that the suburban jurisdictions will grow in total population, keeping all their original higher-income residents and adding some of somewhat lower income ones. Such increases in aggregate disposable income should spur the development of the jurisdictions' local retail sector. Some older dwellings will lose assessed value as they downgrade from high- to middle-quality, but more new, high-quality dwellings will be built. The income, sales, and property tax bases of this hypothetical suburban jurisdiction will all grow. This will set in motion a self-reinforcing "virtuous cycle." The improved fiscal capacity of the jurisdiction will allow it to provide a more attractive tax and service package to residents, thus boosting the quality and market valuation of all the housing stock in the jurisdiction, and thereby passively upgrading all its neighborhoods. This more expensive housing will, in turn, attract (or permit to enter) an ever higher income clientele in the future, further spilling over into a stronger retail sector, subsequent improvements in the tax base, and an enhanced status for the jurisdiction's neighborhoods.

The stylized inner-ring suburban jurisdiction will fare less well. It gains no new dwellings, and some of its existing dwellings will downgrade to the low-quality submarket. Lower income succession will occur in some of its neighborhoods as well, but the number of households is unlikely to shrink. The local retail sector may decline somewhat, however, because of the more modest aggregate income profile of residents. Thus, all the forms of tax base in this jurisdiction will likely shrink.

The center-city jurisdiction exhibits the most dramatic declines. Some of its housing stock will be abandoned, with the concomitant passive downgrading of the surrounding neighborhoods. With abandonment will come population loss and a reduction in the jurisdiction's aggregate disposable income. A decline in the local retail sector will follow.[9] The massive erosion of the city's income, sales, and property tax bases is obvious. The "vicious cycle" will set in. The city will be forced to trim back public services and perhaps increase the rate of taxation. Either will reduce the quality and market valuations of the housing submarkets located within its borders and passively downgrade its constituent neighborhoods thereby. The lower rates of return will make it more likely that owners will abandon their properties and households with the means to do so will continue to flee the jurisdiction, thus weakening the tax base further.

The Origins and Dynamics of Neighborhood Upgrading

The Mechanism of Neighborhood Upgrading: Individual Responses

In the foregoing scenario of neighborhood downgrading we saw that the fundamental driver was weak (that is, not very profitable for owners of existing dwellings) metropolitan housing market conditions, in that case spawned by speculative new construction built in excess of projected net household growth. In that circumstance, the search for superior rates of return led some owners of the existing housing stock to downgrade their dwellings to a lower-quality submarket designation. This had the effect of reducing the physical quality and the overall resident income profile of the neighborhoods in which the downgraded dwellings were located. In the extreme case of the lowest quality submarket, some owners were forced to abandon their properties, resulting in severe degradation of neighborhood quality and selective population loss of better-off households.

In the neighborhood upgrading scenario, these dynamics are reversed. The fundamental driver becomes a strong (that is, increasingly profitable, inflating) market for middle- or upper-quality dwellings, coupled with some attractive geographic or dwelling-specific characteristics of the older existing housing stock of low or modest quality.[10] In these demand-driven, tight-market circumstances, owners of these well situated, modest-quality dwellings will have an incentive to upgrade them to make them appropriate for occupancy by a higher-income clientele. Concomitantly, developers of middle- and high-quality submarket dwellings will be incentivized to take advantage of these attractive locations through infill construction (either on vacant land or after demolition of the existing residential or nonresidential structures) or by the conversion of nonresidential structures (e.g., warehouses, retail stores, or factories) into residential use.

Having observed these supply responses, individual households will now sort themselves differently across metropolitan space. Middle- and upper-income households will now have more suitable and desirable housing options in the more attractive locations where the upward stock conversions and infill construction has occurred. Lower-income households, however, will see their options, both in their former locations from which they were displaced and overall (at least in the short-term), as more constrained and more expensive. As always, most lower-income households are confined to the low-quality submarket due to modest finances, but now they must relocate, inasmuch as the geographic distribution of this submarket has evolved. As owners of existing middle- and high-quality submarket dwellings are likely to be content with their ever-increasing rates of return, they will not be looking to downgrade their dwellings to meet demands of lower-income households. Instead, it will likely be certain developers who will see a profit potential by building modest-quality dwellings that barely meet housing codes, located on extremely low-value parcels. These will typically be in heavily polluted core areas with noxious nonresidential land uses, or in peripheral, exurban sites far from employment or amenities.

Aggregate Impacts across Submarkets: Graphic Exposition

We can analyze the aggregate consequences of the aforementioned behaviors of individual owners and households with the aid of the three-submarket graphic scenario portrayed in figure 4.2. As before, assume for simplicity that the existing metropolitan area housing stock can be grouped into three quality submarkets: high (H), middle (M), and low (L). In each, the original market-period (general equilibrium) demand and supply functions are portrayed with the subscript 1. In addition, to make the contrast between this and the prior case even sharper, I assume that this metropolitan area's housing supply elasticity is low. This may be due to large amounts of land that cannot be developed (because of topographic features, public land set-asides, or both) or local public policies that directly or indirectly restrict growth.[11]

In this thought experiment, I posit that equilibrium is upset by a growth in the number of households demanding low- and middle-quality housing, especially if it is located in some older parts of the metropolitan area currently comprising primarily low-quality dwellings.[12] I portray this dual shock in figure 4.2 as increase in submarket demands to D_{L2} and D_{M2}, yielding market valuation (sale price and rent) increases up to MV_{L2} and MV_{M2} respectively. Housing suppliers will likely respond more quickly to the enhanced profit potential provided by the demand from those seeking middle-quality accommodations in desirable locations (often near the core, close to employment and lifestyle amenities) than to demand from lower-income households. In doing so, some owners of low-quality dwellings in these desirable locations will invest in their properties to upgrade them to middle-quality standards. Other developers will find it more profitable to buy such low-quality dwellings, demolish them, and rebuild on the site, often at higher than original density. Both sorts of action have the net effect of reducing the supply of low-quality dwellings, shown in figure 4.2 as a shift to S_{L3}, further inflating the remaining dwellings in the low-quality submarket to MV_{L3}. These actions, coupled with infill construction on vacant or former nonresidential sites in these attractive core locations previously dominated by low-quality housing, will increase the supply available to the middle-quality submarket, shown by S_{M3}. Given a low medium-run supply elasticity, however, the supply response will be relatively tepid, and market valuation will only ease a bit, to MV_{M3}. This low-elasticity assumption is quite reasonable, inasmuch as rehabilitation of older structures and demolition, environmental remediation, and infill construction are typically more expensive options than new building on greenfield sites.

Meanwhile, low-income households have been struggling. The total stock of low-quality housing has shrunk, and what remains is considerably more expensive. Renter households here have several options, all of which are undesirable. If renters can occupy a dwelling, they can expect to pay a larger share of their incomes in rent. Some may double up with roommates or even other families to share rent expenses, albeit now in overcrowded surroundings. Others may cease being independent households, moving in instead with friends or family. Still others may find themselves homeless.

Nevertheless, these modest-income households represent latent profit opportunities for some housing suppliers. As explained above, these are most likely to be builders of new, low-quality dwellings located in the least desirable spatial niches of the metropolitan area. As this new construction proceeds, it will have the effect of increasing the supply of low-quality housing to S_{L4} in figure 4.2. Again, with the assumption of an inelastic metropolitan area housing supply, we would expect this response to be relatively modest, and to only slightly temper market valuations to MV_{L4}.

Although we began this scenario not positing any exogenous demand shock impinging on the high-quality submarket, one is likely to be generated endogenously. As market valuations are pushed up in the middle-quality submarket to MV_{M2}, some households that previously would have chosen to live in middle-quality accommodations now may decide to consume instead in the high-quality submarket. They may view these two submarkets as relatively close substitutes, so they switch to the one that now offers them better "value for money," thereby raising demand to D_{H3}. The improved rates of return available to owners of high-quality housing may induce some new construction of such dwellings, either in desirable suburban neighborhoods or toney core ones, thus boosting supply to S_{H4}.

When all submarkets have re-equilibrated, it is clear that there have been increases in the middle-quality housing stock (mainly in desirable, near-core areas), somewhat smaller increases in the low-quality stock (in less-desirable, peripheral areas), and even smaller increases in the high-quality stock. There has been upgrading of some erstwhile low-quality dwellings,

LOW-QUALITY SUBMARKET   MIDDLE-QUALITY SUBMARKET   HIGH-QUALITY SUBMARKET

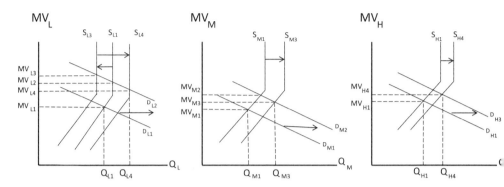

Figure 4.2. Illustration of neighborhood upgrading using the Housing Submarket Model

and new construction at all quality levels (though in different locations depending on quality). Market valuations have risen (though not necessarily equally) across the submarket array, as would be expected from demand increases in an inelastic supply context. This implies higher rates of return for owners of all residential properties than was the case originally.[13]

The Consequences of Upward Filtering for Neighborhoods and Local Jurisdictions

The central neighborhood dynamic produced by the previous scenario is conventionally termed "gentrification." Neighborhoods originally dominated by low-quality housing occupied by modest-income households were redeveloped for use by higher-income residents because these locations, and not others, possessed something rare for which these higher-income households were willing to pay a premium. This could have been proximity to work, transit, recreation, or entertainment, or a historically significant neighborhood design or architectural style. Whatever the source of attraction, these neighborhoods exhibited upward filtering both in terms of the overall physical quality of the residential environment and the overall income profile of its residents. The concomitant result of this neighborhood upgrading is the displacement of the original lower-income occupants, barring any interventions by public policy. This involuntary displacement proceeds both directly and indirectly. Occupants may be directly displaced if their building is vacated prior to rehabilitation or demolition. They may be indirectly displaced if rents or property tax assessments are raised to an unaffordable level to reflect the improvements in dwelling quality that passively redounded to the owner because of the neighborhood improving around the parcel in question. Additional indirect displacement might occur if the local retail sector transforms in ways that make its goods and services less desirable and affordable, or if the neighborhood culture evolves in ways that makes the original residents uncomfortable.

A second neighborhood dynamic produced in this scenario is the creation of new neighborhoods catering to lower-income households. As explained previously, these new neighborhoods are built at basic quality levels in the least desirable interstices and fringes of the metropolitan area. Thus, this scenario of gentrification in the context of strong overall metropolitan housing demands and inelastic supply responses leads to a geographic rearrangement of both where middle-income and lower-income households live.

This geographic evolution produces corresponding changes in the fiscal health of local jurisdictions. Those jurisdictions that ultimately replace lower-income residents living in lower-quality dwellings (and perhaps vacant land or underutilized nonresidential properties) with middle-income households living in middle-quality dwellings clearly will enhance their property, sales, and income tax bases. Fringe jurisdictions bearing the brunt of new construction of modest-quality housing will fare less well financially. The extra tax revenues provided by these new dwellings and residents may prove insufficient to offset the higher costs of associated infrastructure and school improvements and ongoing public service delivery.

Neighborhood Downgrading and Upgrading: The Cases of Detroit and Los Angeles

The predictions generated by the Housing Submarket Model in the two foregoing hypothetical scenarios prove remarkably accurate when compared with data from two metropolitan areas whose contexts and histories closely matched these scenarios over the last quarter century: Detroit and Los Angeles.[14]

Metropolitan Housing Demand and Supply Conditions

Detroit-area residential developers have been only too willing to build a surfeit of high- and middle-quality dwellings, thereby triggering a downward filtering process as shown in stylized form in figure 4.1. The region's

featureless but well-watered plain, fragmented, pro-growth political jurisdictional structure and its impotent regional planning institutions have
been permissive—if not downright encouraging—of unbridled speculative
development.[15] Emmanuel Saiz estimated that the region's medium-run
housing supply elasticity was a substantial 1.24: for every 1 percent increase
in housing prices, the region historically has produced 1.24 percent more
dwelling units.[16]

During every decade since 1950, the Detroit region's developers have
built many more dwellings than the net growth in households required. For
example, from 1990 to 2010, new housing construction in the Detroit metropolitan area represented a gross expansion of the 1990 stock by 20.1 percent, despite the fact that over this same period the number of households
increased only by an anemic 4.3 percent. Detroit developers built this excess
supply because they could make a profit; their new suburban subdivisions
could typically win the competition for middle- and (increasingly) upper-
income occupants when pitted against most of the older housing stock. Because the region's number of households grew more slowly than the number
of new dwellings produced, residents previously housed in older housing
inevitably occupied some of these new homes. As they moved out, they were
replaced by other households that perceived the newly available dwellings
as preferable to the ones in which they currently resided. As this downward
filtering process proceeded, it inevitably resulted in households moving out
of the least competitive dwellings in the metropolitan area, with literally no
one left to occupy those dwellings regardless of how far their market valuations dropped. This excess regional housing supply rendered redundant
almost an equivalent number of dwellings, minus those relatively few lost
due to highway construction or retail and industrial development. Owners
converted some of these redundant dwellings to nonresidential uses, but
the bulk became vacant, undermaintained, and eventually abandoned by
their owners. Typically, after years of increasing deterioration, many of these
abandoned dwellings were demolished or left to arson or rot.[17] In metropolitan Detroit, 9.4 percent of the housing stock present in 1990 had disappeared by 2010. As one would expect in this context of weak demand and
high supply elasticity, Detroit regional home price appreciation from 1991
to the 2006 peak before the Great Recession was modest. Though the area's
home prices increased smartly during the late 1990s economic boom, during the twenty-first century they grew slower than the national average and
much slower than prices in Los Angeles during both pre- and post-recession
years; see figure 4.3.

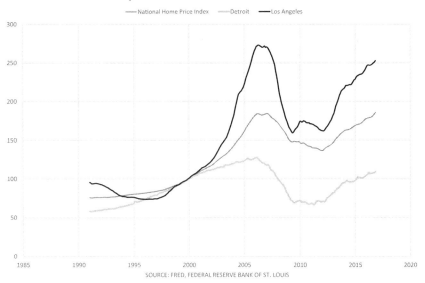

S&P/CASE-SHILLER HOME PRICE INDEX

——— National Home Price Index ——— Detroit ——— Los Angeles

SOURCE: FRED, FEDERAL RESERVE BANK OF ST. LOUIS

Figure 4.3. Home price appreciation, 1991–2016, Detroit metro, Los Angeles metro, and national average. Each area's repeat sales home price index is standardized to base 100 = January, at 2000 prices. Source: Federal Reserve Economic Data, https://fred.stlouisfed.org.

The regional context in Los Angeles was considerably different in many respects. Unlike the Detroit area, the Los Angeles metropolitan area exhibited a robust 18.3 percent growth in the number of households from 1990 to 2010. Sarah Mawhorter provides an in-depth analysis of these demand pressures.[18] Unlike in previous eras when international immigration was the primary driver of growth, during this period it was the emergence of millennials as new households that dominated Los Angeles's housing demographics. This cohort had two distinct components that shaped the cross-submarket pattern of housing demand growth: those without college degrees (more likely to be nonwhite) and those with degrees (more likely to be white). Those in the former group suffered substantial declines in real income. Thus, as in the stylized scenario above, these demographic pressures raised demands for lower- and middle-quality submarkets simultaneously.

As context for understanding the supply-side response to this rising demand, the Los Angeles region has faced considerable topographical constraints on developable land for new construction, including oceans, deserts, and steep mountains.[19] Moreover, some local jurisdictions have adopted limitations on housing construction, and higher-density infill construction projects in older neighborhoods have often generated considerable opposition.[20] According to Emmanuel Saiz, the elasticity of housing supply in the Los Angeles region varies by county but remains inelastic overall: Los Angeles County's elasticity of 0.63 is the second lowest in his ninety-five-region sample, Ventura County's elasticity of 0.75 is the eighth lowest, and Riverside-San Bernardino County's elasticity of 0.94 is the eighteenth.[21] Over the 1990–2010 period, the housing stock expanded on net by 18.5 percent, just enough to keep pace with surging demand. With inelastic supply, however, developers created this new housing only after considerable increases in price, as demonstrated in figure 4.3. Even at the nadir of the recession in 2011, home prices in the Los Angeles metropolitan area remained 63 percent higher than they were in 2000. By contrast, in 2011 average home prices in the nation were only 37 percent higher than in 2000; in the Detroit area they were 30 percent lower than in 2000. By the end of 2016, home prices had rebounded in Los Angeles to 153 percent more than they were in 2000; the comparable figures for the nation and Detroit were only 86 percent and 9 percent.[22] The differences produced by a strong housing demand-inelastic supply response context in Los Angeles and a weak housing demand-elastic supply response context in Detroit are dramatic.

Consequences for Neighborhoods and Local Jurisdictions

The aforementioned metropolitan-scale housing market dynamics of Detroit have produced a stunning example of neighborhood downgrading, most emphatically in the neighborhoods where the least competitive housing was located. The perpetual excess supply of new, middle-, and high-quality dwellings drove older dwellings in these submarkets to filter down in price (and eventually in quality, as their owners actively downgraded them) at the same time that some households could filter up. As they entered neighborhoods that they previously could not have afforded (because prices of existing homes had deflated sufficiently, or because some had been downgraded to a lower quality and value), they created downward income succession from the perspective of the original residents. In this fashion, this "chain of moves" ultimately linked new construction of better-quality dwellings in suburban fringe neighborhoods, deterioration of older dwellings in moderate-quality existing neighborhoods, and vacating of inferior dwellings located in the most dangerous and deteriorated neighborhoods, which were overwhelmingly located within the city of Detroit. As owners of such properties in Detroit found the value of their homes eroded by the lack of buyers, and as the rents collectible from their apartments atrophied as vacancies rose, they quite sensibly chose to invest less in maintaining and improving their properties. Eventually, no matter how much they lowered the asking price or rent, how little they spent on upkeep, and how long they avoided paying property taxes, they lost more money the longer they stayed in operation. At some point the financially rational property owners walked away from their properties. Many of these properties were set on fire, often victims of arson for entertainment or profitable insurance fraud.[23] Erica Raleigh and I found that vacant dwellings and abandoned dwellings were a major contributor to neighborhood crime in Detroit.[24] Thus, the passive downgrading of neighborhoods accelerated as blight and crime intensified. Eventually, the city was left to demolish the abandoned hulks: the stock of dwellings in the city of Detroit has fallen by 14.8 percent since 1990.

In 2009, the city completed a survey of all 343,000 residential parcels within its borders. The results quantified what was obvious to the casual observer: vacant land comprised 27 percent (over 90,000) of the residential parcels in the city.[25] A follow-up survey in 2014 found more than 40,000 structures in blighted condition, another 38,000 with indicators of decay signaling future blight, and 72,000 requiring immediate demolition.[26] Thus, the decades-long process of continuous neighborhood downgrading caused by excess housing construction at the suburban fringe has literally wiped out many of Detroit's neighborhoods, comporting well with predictions of the Housing Submarket Model.

The portrait of neighborhood change in the city of Los Angeles could not be more different, in light of its distinctive metropolitan-wide housing market demand pressures and housing supply elasticities. Instead of losing a quarter of its households and 15 percent of its dwellings since 1990, like Detroit, Los Angeles's neighborhoods swelled with 8.3 percent more households and 8.8 percent more dwellings. As predicted by the Housing Submarket Model analysis, upgrading was the dominant pattern of neighborhood dynamics in Los Angeles during the first decade of the twenty-first century. Robert Sampson, Jared Schachner, and Robert Mare explored decadal changes in Los Angeles County neighborhoods ranked by how their median resident income scored according to national income quintiles.[27] They documented that 31 percent of neighborhoods in the lowest income quintile in 2000 were upgraded to the point where by 2010 they ranked in a higher quintile. For neighborhoods originally in the second, third, and fourth quintiles, the respective percentages upgraded according to this measure were 39 percent, 36 percent, and 24 percent. All such neighborhoods clearly experienced upward income succession.

With many homegrown, college-educated millennials forming house-holds and the resultant turnaround in regional housing price trajectories beginning in 1997, developers found profitable opportunities to build new, high-density accommodations and convert existing nonresidential struc-tures into use for middle-quality housing near the Los Angeles downtown area. In less splashy developments, they also renovated buildings in middle-quality core neighborhoods that had good access to employment and public transit and exhibited stronger socioeconomic and educational profiles. Sarah Mawhorter showed that it was in these neighborhoods where upward succession focused, with college-educated millennials replacing those with-out college degrees.[28] The latter group ended up disproportionately occupy-ing modest-quality neighborhoods in the eastern periphery of the region.

The local retail sectors in Detroit and Los Angeles responded in under-standable ways to changes in the density and income profile of residents in their constituent neighborhoods. Downward filtering in Detroit caused a loss of population in the core and a selective out-migration of better-off households, producing collateral casualties in the local retail and commer-cial sector. There are few more dramatic and depressing aspects of Detroit's landscape than the seemingly interminable miles of abandoned retail stores and vacant lots lining most of the city's erstwhile main commercial corri-dors, from the downtown area almost to the city limits. From 1992 to the brink of the Great Recession in 2007, Detroit lost 13 percent of its retail establishments and 41 percent of its retail employment. By contrast, neigh-borhood infilling and upgrading proved a retail boon for Los Angeles. From 1992 to 2007, its retail establishments increased by 3 percent and its retail employment rose by 7 percent.[29]

The aforementioned changes in the density of population and employ-ment in neighborhoods, the market valuations of housing they held, and the income profile of their residents produced predictable changes in the fiscal capacity of our case study cities. Declining aggregate residential and nonresidential property values, retail employment, and residents with siz-able disposable incomes imposed an ever-tightening financial constraint on Detroit, which relies on revenues from property taxes, income taxes, and utility fees.[30] Despite raising tax rates, Detroit's total revenues have fallen dramatically. The inflation-adjusted aggregate assessed value of its property has fallen 79 percent since its peak in 1958, and the value of its income tax revenues has fallen 76 percent since its peak in 1972. This chronic revenue shortfall has forced Detroit to trim the quality, quantity, and scope of ser-vices that it provides. The strategy to scale back services while simultane-ously raising tax rates has not been enough to avoid insolvency, however. In

July 2013, the city of Detroit became the largest municipality in US history to declare Chapter 9 bankruptcy.[31]

By contrast, the city of Los Angeles has experienced growth in all aspects of its vital property and sales tax bases: aggregate residential and non-residential property values, retail employment, and resident disposable incomes. This strengthening of its fiscal capacity has provided Los Angeles the luxury of spending more on its citizens and keeping their individual taxes relatively low while maintaining fiscal solvency. A comparative portrait of key municipal financial indicators is illuminating. In 1992, Los Angeles's per capita spending was 8 percent less than Detroit's, but by 2014 it was spending 10 percent more than Detroit.[32] Los Angeles's property tax in 2014 raised 42 percent more revenue per citizen than Detroit's, even though its effective property tax rate was only 28 percent as large.[33] Changes in relative outstanding municipal debt per capita summarizes the changing financial fortunes of these two cities. In 1992, Los Angeles's debt per capita was 40 percent more than Detroit's, but by 2014 it was 42 percent less than Detroit's.

Neighborhood Downgrading and Upgrading: Summary and Implications

The Housing Submarket Model partitions the metropolitan area's housing stock into quality submarkets wherein dwelling package quality as adjudged by the market reflects spatial features such as neighborhood physical conditions, residents' socioeconomic status, and public services, as well as features of the structure itself. It then models the behaviors of households, owners of existing dwellings, and developers of new housing as they relate to and ultimately shape this submarket array. The model portrays the process of downward or upward filtering of housing as involving three distinct components: changes in relative market valuations among quality submarkets, changes in submarket occupancy patterns by households of different incomes, and changes in the supply behavior of owners of existing dwellings involving their intentionally downgrading or upgrading them to different-quality submarkets.

In a classic downward filtering scenario, a spurt of new construction of middle- to upper-quality dwellings (in excess of new household demand there) will partially replace existing stock with new stock at targeted-quality submarkets, create (nonuniform) incentives to intensify downgrading throughout the submarket array, and ultimately encourage abandonment of the least competitive stock. In the short run, this process will deflate market valuations in submarkets that have a net increase in housing stock through conversion and construction, and thus potentially will allow some households to occupy better housing there. Both this reduction in market valuation of a particular quality of housing and the downgrading of extant dwellings to a lower quality will produce downward income succession in the affected neighborhoods.

In a classic upward-filtering scenario, growing demand for middle- to upper-quality dwellings well-located near employment and center city amenities bids up housing prices there, leading to a housing supply modification process. Owners of existing lower-quality dwellings in such favored neighborhoods will find it in their financial interest to upgrade the quality of their stocks to serve the needs of a new, higher-income clientele. So will developers of infill housing projects or conversions of formerly nonresidential structures. The result will produce a transformation not only of physical and financial character of the housing stock in the neighborhood, but also of the income (and perhaps age and racial) profile of its residents and the nature and scope of the associated local retail sector. This upward income succession in selected core neighborhoods is associated with the spatial reallocation of lower-income households that either were previous residents of these places or would have been residents there in the absence of intensified competition from some higher-income households. Continuing housing demands from such lower-income households will also produce supply-side adjustments, either in the form of the downgrading of existing dwellings in some other, less desirable neighborhoods or the construction of low-quality dwellings in the least desirable locales of the region.

These analytical predictions hold important implications for local planners and policy makers. As I will show more fully in chapter 9, the processes of neighborhood change and the end states that they ultimately yield are neither efficient nor equitable from a societal standpoint. In the case of neighborhood downgrading dynamics, the results are physical deterioration of housing, loss of housing market valuation, and downward income succession across a wide range of existing neighborhoods across the metropolitan area, with the most severe examples accompanied by residential abandonment in the least competitive neighborhoods in the region. This yields concomitant weakening of fiscal capacity for all jurisdictions where such degradation occurs without the offset of new construction. The implications for the stability of older neighborhoods, and indeed for the quality of life and financial viability of entire municipalities, are manifest, as the case study of Detroit vividly illustrates.[34] In the case of neighborhood upgrading dynamics, the results are physical renovation of housing, infill construction, and former nonresidential conversions; inflated housing market valuations and upward income succession in a selected set of well-located core neighborhoods; and the concomitant strengthening of fiscal capacity for the encompassing jurisdiction, as the case of Los Angeles exemplifies. However, the process also produces displacement and deflection of where lower-income households live in the metropolitan area, inducing other sorts of adjustments in existing neighborhoods (and perhaps the construction of new neighborhoods) whose consequences are not nearly as felicitous.

Amendments to the Housing Submarket Model

The Housing Submarket Model, developed in chapter 3 and applied in this chapter, makes many simplifying assumptions about housing markets, the behavior of actors within it, and noneconomic influences on neighborhood trajectories. Such is appropriate so that we can highlight its structure and operation before we add complications that may prove obfuscating. Bill Rohe and Ken Temkin[35] have offered, however, a nuanced series of valuable amendments and addenda to my pared-down approach that we should acknowledge. Indeed, these constructive suggestions provide guideposts for how I will enrich the core analytical perspective in subsequent chapters.

First, the model does not distinguish owner occupants from absentee landlords and tenants. Clearly, tenure composition matters for neighborhoods. Owner occupants and tenants have different mobility behavior; owners move less because they have security of tenure and higher transaction costs if they move. Owner occupants are, ceteris paribus, more likely to invest dollars and time in the dwelling and be less "market investment-oriented" than landlords, because for them the home is source of consumption as well as investment. Moreover, social pressures within the neighborhood to conform to good upkeep behavior may exert more influence on owner occupants.[36]

Second, the model did not emphasize local political forces, though they sometimes can impinge strongly on neighborhood dynamics. As I acknowledged in the discussion surrounding figure 1.3, local governments—and thus local political forces—are an important source of public services, facilities, and regulations that directly and indirectly affect the flow of resources into a neighborhood. The larger-scale, political-economy root of that flow is beyond the scope of my model.[37] Of course, both top-down forces and grassroots politicking shape these resources flowing from the local public sector. The degree to which a neighborhood can organize to influence the allocation of amenities (such as better public services or a new facility) or disamenities (such as the siting of noxious, pollution-generating institutions) in the area will affect its stability and quality.

Third, the model did not consider either for-profit or nonprofit institutions outside the housing market, although they can be an important component of neighborhood health, again as noted in the context of figure 1.3. The degree to which, for example, mortgage lenders, insurance companies, religious groups, charitable foundations, and other major institutions direct the flow of resources into neighborhoods can be decisive.[38]

Fourth, the model overlooked social and subcultural forces that may operate in neighborhoods. Social networks, mutual levels of place attachment by residents, history, and symbolism of place may provide "noneconomic" dimensions to household propensities for out-mobility, property upkeep, crime prevention, and other actions valuable for neighborhoods. Below I will provide extensive discussions of the roles played by social forces in neighborhoods related to information-gathering and interactive decision-making (chapter 5) and the social mechanisms through which a neighborhood affects behaviors and outcomes for its residents (chapter 8).

Fifth, the model did not distinguish households in any regard except by their incomes and their housing preferences. Yet we know that other characteristics related to gender, race, ethnicity, religion, disability, familial status, marital status, and sexual orientation influence where households may reside. For instance, racial and ethnic minorities will be less likely to move in response to market signals if discrimination in housing transactions and financing impedes them. In chapter 7 I will probe in depth the forces that lead to economically and racially segregated neighborhoods.

Sixth, the model glossed over the imperfect nature of adjustments to market signals. The model implicitly assumed that residents, property owners, and other decision makers had good information about and comparative ease in responding to new market signals, thus creating a smooth adjustment process within and between submarkets. I will relax this assumption in chapter 5, where I will show how housing market decisions typically are made on basis of imperfect information, gaming behaviors, and self-fulfilling prophecies. In chapter 6 I will probe how such processes can produce nonlinear, discontinuous, and threshold-like adjustment processes.

How Does the Housing Submarket Model Compare to Others?

Now that I have presented the core components of the Housing Submarket Model and demonstrated how we can use it to analyze real-world changes in neighborhoods such as those emblematically represented in Detroit and Los

Angeles, it is appropriate to compare this model to alternative perspectives on neighborhood dynamics. The three most famous approaches purporting to explain neighborhood change can be labelled "invasion and succession," "life-cycle" and "filtering."[39]

The invasion-succession approach traces its roots to faculty in the University of Chicago's Department of Sociology, who in the 1920s and 1930s systematically investigated patterns of neighborhood socioeconomic and demographic change and posited causal elements that drew analogies from plant ecology.[40] In their view, change across the entire array of urban neighborhoods was fundamentally driven by the in-migration (or "invasion") of lower-income households from abroad or rural areas into lower-quality quarters near the core of the city. The resultant physical shortages of accommodations in these quarters pushed longer-tenured, better-off residents into somewhat higher-quality neighborhoods located at the periphery of the core port-of-entry neighborhood. Over time, this process would lead to the "succession" of the new group pushing out most of the original inhabitants of the core neighborhood. Of course, like ripples spreading across the surface of a pond, each displaced group in turn would "invade" and eventually "succeed" in neighborhoods forming an ever-expanding set of concentric rings (or pie-shaped wedges, if the residential exit process assumed a direction) centered on the core. In this view, neighborhood change resulted from rising population pressure from a different socioeconomic or demographic group emanating from an adjacent neighborhood, which manifested itself as that group dominating the inflow into housing vacancies that occurred in the neighborhood under consideration.

The life-cycle theory claims that neighborhoods are in key ways analogous to all living organisms insofar as they go through sequentially predictable stages.[41] From this perspective, new neighborhoods are built ("born"), remain vital and vibrant for a considerable period ("youth"), start to lose attractiveness as they show signs of aging ("maturity"), become decayed and obsolete ("elderly"), and finally move into a stage of abandonment ("death"), which sets the stage for demolition and rebuilding ("rebirth"). Each stage in this neighborhood life cycle is distinguished by a set of descriptors of the residents, dwelling conditions, and investments by property owners and others, but the causal forces are not explicitly considered. A more contemporary version of this approach, the "vintage model," is more economically oriented, and argues that the natural tendency for buildings to decay and become obsolete will require increasing amounts of compensatory investment by owners to forestall it, thus rendering the properties less likely to be maintained and more likely to be demolished in favor of newer infill construction.[42] From this perspective, the age profile of the dwellings within a neighborhood inexorably drives its destiny.[43]

Finally, traditional filtering models see dwellings losing value because they age and are rendered less competitive by new high-quality housing built elsewhere in the metropolitan area.[44] Groups with successively lower income than the previous occupants occupy those dwellings as their values fall relative to household incomes.[45] In this view, neighborhood change results primarily from new construction outside and perhaps far from the neighborhood in question, with which the older stock of dwellings there cannot compete successfully.

Compared to the Housing Submarket Model, these classic theories are more myopic in three vital ways: the direction of neighborhood change, its cause, and the market. All these models see neighborhood change as a unidirectional process leading inexorably to decline (in the value or quality of housing and/or the socioeconomic status of its residents), until the place is abandoned and eventually rebuilt. Similarly, each of the three theories sees neighborhood change as having a single cause: low-income population growth, aging of dwellings, and new housing construction, respectively. Finally, all perspectives take only a partial view of market processes. Invasion and succession focuses on the demand side, and the other two on the supply side. None gives sufficient consideration of how housing market prices are determined by the interplay of demand and supply and how, in turn, individual households and investors respond to the existing array of prices and rates of return.

Because of this myopia, the classical theories are less robust in their ability to explain the complex patterns of neighborhood change that we can easily observe across American metropolitan areas today. Invasion-succession models may provide a reasonable description of what happens to residential patterns in cities undergoing a massive influx of lower-income residents, but they offer little in understanding what will occur when a city draws many high-income migrants (like San Francisco), or is bleeding middle-income population (like Detroit). Life-cycle models may well describe a general trajectory for some neighborhoods, but they are silent about how long various stages last, what might affect the time a neighborhood spends in a particular stage, and whether stages are reversible before "death." This approach cannot explain the many neighborhoods that consistently remain vital, high-quality places a century or more after they were built (like Beacon Hill in Boston or the Gold Coast in Chicago). Neither does it predict "middle aged," decent-quality neighborhoods that are upgraded to luxury quarters by gentrifiers who view their housing stock not as obsolete but as "rich in architectural character" and close to amenities and jobs. Filtering models might do an acceptable job of explaining neighborhood decline in the context of a metropolitan area characterized by new housing construction in excess of household formation, but they cannot address many alternative contexts. This includes scenarios of rapid population growth outstripping new construction (like Los Angeles), vast numbers of new employment opportunities arising in core locations near older neighborhoods (like Seattle), or wholesale reductions in the incomes of large swaths of a metropolitan area's households (like Youngstown). By contrast, I have demonstrated that the Housing Submarket Model can comfortably handle a wide range of real or projected contexts describing essential features of both the demand and supply sides of the metropolitan housing market, producing predictions about which sorts of neighborhoods will change their physical quality and their socioeconomic occupancy profiles.

Conclusion

The metropolitan Housing Submarket Model, though simplistic in some regards, provides a powerful explanatory framework for comprehending the fundamental origins, dynamic processes, and consequences of neighborhood decline and revitalization. This model is much less myopic than prior approaches to understanding neighborhood dynamics. As such, it offers more robust explanatory power for the wide variety of changes we are witnessing today. It shows how individual mobility and investment behaviors by households and residential property owners, when aggregated, lead to neighborhood downgrading (a combination of physical erosion of the housing stock and downward income succession of households) and upgrading (the opposite conditions), based on their responses to forces impinging on the entire metropolitan housing market. An application of the model to understanding the cases of Detroit and Los Angeles not only demonstrates the model's usefulness but reinforces its central insight: understanding what is happening to a particular set of neighborhoods requires examining the external forces that are impinging on the entire set of neighborhoods and their constituent housing submarkets at the metropolitan scale. Using the Housing Submarket Model as a foundation, I will show in subsequent chapters how we can enrich our powers for analyzing neighborhoods by relaxing some of the simplifying assumptions I made to keep this core model tractable in introduction.

FIVE

Expectations, Information, Search, and Neighborhood Change

In chapter 2 I defined neighborhood as the bundle of spatially based attributes associated with a proximate cluster of occupied residences, sometimes in conjunction with other land uses. Here it is important to draw out implications from the fact that these spatially based attributes vary considerably in their durability. Some, like certain topographical features, are permanent from the perspective of human time, save major cataclysms. Sewer and water infrastructure and buildings typically last generations. Others, such as tax and public service packages and demographic and socioeconomic status profiles of an area, can change noticeably over the course of a few years. The area's social interrelationships can also change quite rapidly. This means that although some of the key features defining a desirable neighborhood from the perspective of current and prospective households and residential property investors can be counted on to remain constant (and therefore predictable) for extended periods, many others cannot. This implies that decision makers' *expectations* about future changes in these less durable features will play a major role in determining choices about mobility, financial investments, and psychological investments in neighborhoods over the long term.

Unfortunately, these expectations about less durable features of the neighborhood are inherently fraught with a great deal of *uncertainty*, for at least five reasons. First, what happens to a neighborhood is a function of potential changes in numerous malleable attributes, each of which has an indeterminate future to varying degrees. The thoughtful decision maker must form expectations about a wide array of distinct aspects of neighborhood, and then form some summary expectation about how the predicted individual attribute changes will yield net changes in the aggregate.

Second, many households and residential property owners of different types and motivations are present in the typical neighborhood. Their aggregate behavior is crucial for shaping many future neighborhood attributes, yet it is exceedingly difficult to anticipate that behavior accurately, especially given the degree to which it may be influenced by social interactions such as strategic gaming, which I will explore later.

Third, uncertain metropolitan area–wide shocks related to the regional economy, technological innovation, population, immigration, government policy, and vagaries of nature will influence the flow of resources across all neighborhoods in a metropolitan area. Thus, raw data useful in forming expectations about the future of a particular neighborhood should extend over a much wider set of substantive domains, and not be confined to indicators about this neighborhood alone. I summarized this point above in the Proposition of Externally Generated Change.

Fourth, the Proposition of Externally Generated Change provides a corollary reason for uncertainty on the part of an existing resident or owner: the evaluation of their neighborhood by prospective in-movers, investors, and developers will typically be based on a comparison of attributes in competing neighborhoods, not only on the intrinsic, absolute characteristics of the particular neighborhood's attribute set.[1] Perhaps the most obvious example is the status dimension. The absolute income levels of households in a particular neighborhood may rise. Yet, if they are rising at least as much in all other neighborhoods in the metropolitan area, there likely will be no change in outsiders' evaluations of that neighborhood's status attribute, because its relative ranking has not improved. One can make analogous arguments regarding other attributes such as proximity, school quality, and public safety. The upshot is that the relative attractiveness of a particular neighborhood can change when new neighborhoods arise through large-scale construction or rehabilitation projects, and when existing competing neighborhoods are transformed by substantial investments or disinvestments by their owners. This increases uncertainty for households and investors there because different *relative* market evaluations will alter flows of resources across space, while *absolute* changes will occur in the neighborhood under consideration. Thus, as a basis for forming expectations about the future of a particular neighborhood, the relevant information pertains to a much wider geographic scale than this neighborhood alone.

Fifth, decision-makers cannot blithely rely on market valuations established in the housing market to capitalize present and future trends in neighborhood attributes accurately. The spatially based attributes comprising neighborhood vary in the degree to which the market can evaluate them accurately. In order for potential consumers to make informed bid offers for a commodity, they must have some modicum of information about the quantity and quality of that commodity and what likely benefit they would receive from its consumption. Real estate markets may meet this criterion for a large number of spatially based attributes like structural size and features, accessibility, tax/public service packages, demographic and socioeconomic status composition of residents, and pollution.[2] However, current owneroc-cupiers likely have "inside" information about local trends in some of these conditions, which they can exploit to their market advantage.[3] Moreover, the market cannot accurately price most social-interactive dimensions of neighborhood because they are hard for prospective bidders to assess ex ante. The idiosyncratic and personalized nature of neighborhood social interactions means that prospective in-movers will only be able to ascertain how they will "fit in" after an extended period of residence. One implication is that long-term resident-investors may have considerably different market evaluations ("reservation prices," in the terminology of chapter 3) for their neighborhood than prospective residents or investors, because the former have capitalized (positively or negatively) their assessments of the social interactive dimension. Thus, the former may be highly resistant to external market forces when they assess a positive social environment, and may be more easily outbid and eventually supplanted by new owners and residents when they assess a negative one. Another implication is that neighborhoods are particularly prone to forms of insider dealing, with privileged informa-tion communicated to preferred buyers and in-movers by current residents, owners, and their market intermediaries.

The crucial importance of accurate expectations, coupled with their great uncertainty, translates into substantial long-term risk because, once made, decisions about mobility and financial investments in neighborhoods are not easily or cheaply reversible. Choosing to occupy or own a dwelling in-volves substantial out-of-pocket and perhaps psychological transactions costs, which most households and investors are loathe to incur frequently. Many large-scale investments in structures and infrastructures have long projected life spans and are spatially fixed. The high-uncertainty/high-risk nature of neighborhood choice and property investments holds important implications for some of the characteristics associated with neighborhood change, such as threshold effects discussed in chapter 6.

Because of its obvious importance to understanding neighborhood change, this chapter explores how households, property owners, and resi-dential developers go about acquiring information, forming expectations, assessing risks and ultimately making choices under terms of uncertainty. Next, I present a conceptual model of this process.[4] I then synthesize empirical research findings about how people form expectations and make decisions to draw implications for neighborhood change processes.

A Model of Neighborhood Information Acquisition

Overview

I base my model on a holistic view of human behavior: that it results from both external forces (such as social status and cultural norms) and internal forces (such as drives and needs). Both types of forces mold the degree and manner in which people process sensory data about themselves and the world, form beliefs, and arrive at some behavioral decision. People act based on the meaning they assign to an object or an event, and these meanings are both unique because of individual perceptions and common because of social interaction.[5] Thus, while all people can be seen in a general sense as "data acquirers and processors," the method of gathering, interpreting, evaluating, and responding to data is not the same for all, nor is it even constant for the same individual in all circumstances. In some instances, people undertake considerable deliberation in an effort to find the near-optimal decision; they try to become well-informed about a situation and dispassionately weigh the evidence. In other circumstances, people quickly make decisions based what externally might be viewed as insufficient information that is evaluated informally and with passion. In the words of Daniel Kahneman, people at some times "think slow" and at other times "think fast."[6] Though both types are likely involved to some degree with forming expectations about neighborhoods, the significant risks associated with residential mobility and investment behaviors are so large that most people would employ a great deal of "slow thinking" in the process. Regardless, people's beliefs and behaviors are not capricious; they demonstrate underlying consistencies that are verifiable empirically, in principle. The model presented below provides a framework for understanding these regularities amid the human variety.

I summarize the foregoing introductory discussion diagrammatically with figure 5.1. It suggests that the nature of information that key decision makers (households or investors) have regarding both the local and the metropolitan-wide housing market will shape their beliefs and expectations about a variety of neighborhoods. These beliefs and expectations will, in turn, influence their decisions about whether to move and, if so, where; whether to maintain or change the quality of the current dwelling while retaining ownership; whether to sell the current dwelling; whether to abandon the current dwelling; whether to choose a dwelling in a different neighborhood; and whether to invest in a newly constructed dwelling or a conversion of a former nonresidential structure. The aggregation of these behaviors will determine the patterns of household and financial resource flows across metropolitan space, creating a cascading series of neighborhood changes and concomitant alterations in individuals' quality of life and opportunities, housing investors' rates of return, and the financial health of local retailers and political jurisdictions, as we saw in chapters 3 and 4.

Housing market search holds a prominent place in this schematic portrayal. I define housing market search as

> active, intentional acquisition of data regarding multiple characteristics of a metropolitan housing market (that is, currently or prospectively occupied neighborhoods, currently or prospectively owned or occupied residential properties, or other potential external shocks that may affect part or all of the metropolitan housing market).

We can parse previous formulations of the housing market search process into "neoclassical" and "behaviorist" views. In simplest terms, the former view posits fully informed optimizing by the searcher based on predetermined and fixed housing preferences, whereas the latter sees searchers practicing partially informed, rule-of-thumb, heuristic behaviors with preferences being malleable depending on what is discovered during the search process.[7] My formulation attempts to synthesize aspects of both views, though it proceeds primarily from the latter perspective. I expand the realm of information acquisition beyond intentional, active housing search, emphasizing the crucial role of *passively acquired information* in not only forming beliefs and expectations but also triggering and spatially shaping the search process itself. In this sense, I consider the housing market search endogenous in the larger processes of information acquisition; hence the double-headed arrow in figure 5.1.

Conceptual Model

I present the conceptual model proposed for an individual's information acquisition, processing, and behavioral response in figure 5.2.[8] It starts with the distinction between actively and passively acquired data that the individual may have at her disposal as the basis for a decision. One produces by definition actively acquired data through the search process; passively

Figure 5.1. Housing search, information acquisition, mobility, investment, and neighborhood change: overarching framework

acquired data are all others acquired unintentionally during the course of life. One can gain both actively and passively acquired data through a variety of means, as amplified below.

As a matter of course, a sentient being is exposed to a tremendous amount of raw material consisting of sensory inputs. Before such data can possibly change beliefs and expectations, one must subject them to three stages of cognitive processing: *syntactic, semantic and pragmatic.*[9] See the upper portion of figure 5.2. One first assesses in the syntactic component whether the data are worth paying attention to; do they potentially convey information or are they just "noise?" The "datum" of an object is not the object itself; people's perception and interpretation of the object is the datum. The person's "definition of the situation" is thus both subjective and relational because it is socially formed—a key point to which I will return. The syntactic stage not only serves as an interpretive filter for data, but also serves as a regulatory filter adjusting the amount and type of data that one can perceive. People try to strike a balance between being open to receiving new data that potentially provide variety, learning, and innovation and closing off those that might threaten the memory, tradition, and cohesion needed for maintaining individual identity.[10] The relationship between being open or closed to additional data varies contextually with personal circumstances, the nature of the perceived content, and the form of its transmission.

A person will judge data to be potentially useful if they pass the syntactic stage, then assess their credibility in the semantic stage. Credibility is a function of the discrepancy between the individual's assessed probability that something is true and the new data's assessment of such, mediated by a set of facilitating factors involving characteristics of the data, their source, and the individual.[11] If discrepancy were zero, the individual would view new data as valid since they merely reconfirm prior beliefs. At the other extreme of maximum discrepancy, the individual may view data as invalid because they provide such an "outlandish view of reality" compared to the individual's previous view. At any degree of discrepancy, the perceived veracity of data will be influenced by the logic of the order in which they are conveyed, the emotions to which they appeal (e.g., affirmation vs. fear), whether their content is implicit or explicit, and whether they apply to beliefs that are more salient from the individual's perspective. Similarly, perceived veracity will depend on the medium through which it is communicated, as I will expand upon below. Finally, characteristics of the individual receiving the data may affect its acceptance, such as intelligence, credulity, and self-esteem.

If data are assessed as valid, one then proceeds to inquire pragmatically about whether they alter the individual's prior beliefs and expectations—that is, whether the data convey useful information. A change could occur either by expanding the relevant belief set (adding possibilities or new attributes that were unknown previously) or by altering the strengths of the individual's beliefs within the set. Two outcomes are possible. One is that acceptance of valid information reinforces strongly held convictions or strengthens what previously were only weak beliefs. In this case, the pragmatic result is a reduction in uncertainty associated with a belief set. In such circumstances, people are unlikely to seek further corroborating data; instead, they turn to discerning the implications of their reinforced beliefs on their intentions and behaviors.

The other possible pragmatic outcome is that the new, valid information weakens prior beliefs and/or raises new possibilities in a way that increases uncertainty. In this instance, the decision maker must question whether the resultant uncertainty is tolerable. If not, the person undertakes active search; see the lower portion of figure 5.2.[12] The individual then subjects data actively acquired to semantic and pragmatic processing, analogous to passively acquired data. Should such new data prove either not credible or not effective in changing or solidifying beliefs, the decision maker will need to consider continuing the active search and perhaps altering the search strategy. Only when the active search finally produces a tolerable reduction in uncertainty because it sufficiently supports a set of beliefs and expectations will the individual discontinue it.

At this point, the decision maker may feel supported in the current course of action, so there is no intention to change course. On the other hand, a new set of beliefs and expectations may alter an intention, but not an associated behavior, if the decision maker is constrained in undertaking the

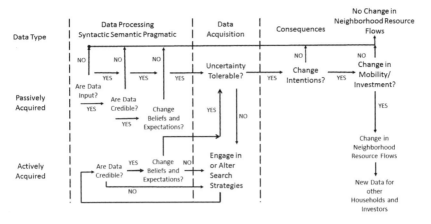

Figure 5.2. Conceptual model of an individual's acquisition and processing of information and behavioral response

desired choice because of financial, physical, psychological, legal, or other limitations. The individual will alter a residential mobility or investment decision only if the intended change can be actualized. Such a decision alters on the margin the conditions in both the origin and the destination neighborhoods of the individual in question; and, if replicated by others, it will alter the aggregate resource flows governing the overall conditions of these places. Once executed, of course, these altered decisions and flows provide new data for other decision makers to process, potentially leading to knock-on effects. See the right-hand side of figure 5.2.

Multiple Dimensions of Information

With this framing, it is now appropriate to consider more deeply the multiple potential sources through which people gain data, because this leads to the notion of a multidimensional portrait of information acquisition; see figure 5.3. This representation suggests that we can usefully categorize data along four independent dimensions: who acquires it and how it is acquired, through what media, and in what spaces. Two dimensions have already been introduced: households residing in the neighborhood and owners of dwellings in the neighborhood constitute the two key sets of actors who passively and actively acquire information.

The third dimension represents the not mutually exclusive media through which data potentially are conveyed. An individual can make firsthand observations of the world. Alternatively, an individual may gain

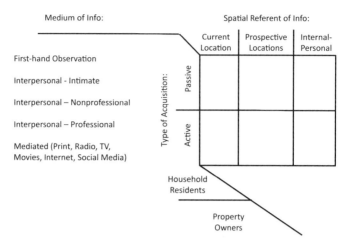

Figure 5.3. The multidimensional nature of information

relevant data from interpersonal contacts with intimate acquaintances (kin or friends), nonprofessionals (known associates and anonymous interpersonal contacts), and real estate professionals (not only brokers, developers, and landlords, but all those with expertise in the particular subject). These contacts can take the form of face-to-face conversations or those transmitted via telephone or electronic media. Finally, an individual typically gets data from a range of impersonal print or electronic media, such as newspapers, television, radio, and the internet. Each of these data sources may differ considerably in their perceived veracity depending on the individual data-gatherer in question. People typically assess information as valid when "it was right before their eyes"; so, too, is that provided by trusted experts. The power of other sources' data will depend on their perceived credibility.

The fourth dimension represents the spatial referent of the information gained. The new data could apply to the individual or her household and inform her about an internal change that would have potential impacts on residential mobility or investing calculus, such as a change in housing preferences or ability to pay for housing. Alternatively, the data could be relevant for particular places: the current dwelling and neighborhood and other dwellings and neighborhoods that could be alternative destinations for moving or investing are of primary interest here. These latter two, spatially related categories of data are of particular relevance for neighborhoods.

Although these four dimensions are conceptually distinct and independent, it is likely that in practice people observe only certain combinations. For example, most internal-personal information is gained passively, via firsthand observation (e.g., when your boss informs you of a substantial raise in salary), though in some cases it might involve active search involving contact with a professional (e.g., a medical doctor). Similarly, active search that involves securing the services of a real estate professional likely will provide information about current and prospective neighborhoods.

To posit that information relevant for understanding neighborhood change has features that vary across four dimensions is not to imply that an individual seeks information using only one combination of those dimensions. On the contrary, the formulation summarized in figure 5.2 emphasizes that it is passively acquired information that ultimately spurs actively acquired information. Moreover, various media likely deliver both passively and actively acquired information in a typical information acquisition episode.

Spatial Biases in Information Acquisition and Neighborhood Effects

Having introduced figure 5.3, I can now tease out its provocative implications regarding spatial biases that characterize information acquisition. First, the spaces to which the individual is exposed during the common course of daily life will form the geographic locus of passively acquired data through firsthand observation. Thus, individuals typically will become better informed about neighborhoods that comprise their routine activity spaces: their current place of residence, of course, but also neighborhoods in which are located their venues of employment, socialization, worship, entertainment, and recreation. Because passively acquired information must yield an intolerable degree of uncertainty before people actively acquire additional information, that subsequent search will also focus on the same spaces as a means of reducing this uncertainty. A long-standing empirical literature has indeed confirmed that most active household residential searches within the same metropolitan housing market are relatively close to their prior residence and are otherwise anchored to their routine activity spaces.[13]

Second, both passively and actively acquired information through intimate and nonprofessional interpersonal contacts will be spatially selective insofar as those people will replicate in part the routine activity spaces of those whom they contact. That is, kin, close friends, work colleagues, and members of organizations to which the individual belongs will provide the richest information about their respective places of residences.[14] The degree to which these two processes yield information about a limited sample of neighborhoods is variable, of course, depending on the spatial extent of the routine activity spaces of the individual under consideration and her primary set of interpersonal contacts. At one extreme, the "cosmopolitan" individual who regularly travels around the metropolitan area and surrounds himself with equally well-travelled associates is unlikely to have his range of neighborhood options constrained by limited, spatially selective data. At the other extreme, "parochial" people who spend the vast amount of their lives within the confines of their own neighborhood and socialize only with their neighbors will possess little information about residential opportunities elsewhere. Stefanie DeLuca and colleagues have found this limited sociospatial world to be especially important in spatially constraining the housing market searches of low-income minority households.[15]

Geography enters into the information acquisition process in yet another deeper way. The individual's social interrelationships within the current neighborhood can affect the syntactic and pragmatic processing of both actively and passively acquired data. Neighbors may socialize residents to accept collective norms about what sources of data are trustworthy and the degree to which any particular datum has veracity based on whether it confirms or denies deeply held beliefs of the group. For example, neighbors may be quick to challenge an individual's firsthand observation of a change in a salient feature of the neighborhood (by discounting its generality or providing contrary observations) when the new data contradict a long and firmly held belief about that aspect of the neighborhood. Alternatively, neighbors may suggest that an individual actively search using information sources that they have employed in the past, thereby biasing the data that the individual will glean from searching in ways that will confirm the group's perceptions. In other instances, individuals may find comfortable certainty in conforming to the "herd mentality" of the neighborhood instead of undertaking an independent assessment of the credibility and potential import of new data confronting them.

The foregoing demonstrates the first way in which "neighborhoods make us": through molding the information we have about the world. The neighborhood supplies a crucial though variable component comprising the routine activity spaces in which we passively acquire information. Social interactive processes within the neighborhood can further shape what sources we trust when acquiring information passively and actively, and what sorts of standards we apply when assessing whether new information is sufficient to warrant altering our beliefs and expectations. Thus, neighborhoods are both a cause and an effect of human action; they shape the beliefs and expectations driving decisions that guide the flow of people and financial resources across space that, in turn, shapes neighborhoods.

Implications of Behavioral Economics for Information and Neighborhood Change Processes

At this point it is appropriate to ask: After passing the syntactic, semantic, and pragmatic stages of the model, what types of information are most likely to generate altered behaviors by residents and investors? Evidence gathered from behavioral economics provides two strong suggestions: (1) information about one's current neighborhood should be more powerful than equivalent information about other prospective neighborhoods; and (2) information indicating that one's current neighborhood is declining should be more powerful than equivalent information that it is improving.

Alex Marsh and Kenneth Gibb have contributed a valuable synthesis of empirical findings from the field of behavioral economics that can aid our understanding of housing search and neighborhood dynamics.[16] Of salience here are:

- *status quo bias*: People prefer what they know, even if the prospect offers greater gain.
- *loss aversion*: People place more absolute value on a loss of well-being or money than on an equivalent gain.
- *experienced versus prospective utility*: People discount the well-being associated with not-yet-experienced alternatives because it is more subject to variation.[17]
- *anchoring*: People underrate the differences between two alternatives when an absolute value is associated with one of them, as opposed to neither of them being benchmarked.
- *downward trend aversion*: People prefer a progressively more desirable sequence of outcomes than a progressively less desirable sequence, even when both have equivalent aggregate values.

Status quo bias, experience versus prospective utility, and anchoring work jointly to make information about one's current neighborhood a more powerful predictor of altered mobility or investment behavior than equivalently valid information about an alternative neighborhood. Hypothetical residence or property investment in a different neighborhood will inherently appear more risky, since the current and future conditions appertaining there will appear less certain than they are for the current neighborhood. Thus, only if a new alternative promises to be a hugely superior option will its risk-adjusted premium be sufficient to induce a household to move there or an investor to buy a property there. Yet people will partly discount this premium due to anchoring based on relevant status quo values, further disempowering information about an alternative neighborhood from triggering a move or an altered investment.

Aversion to loss and downward trends together imply that information indicating current neighborhood decline will be more powerful behaviorally than equivalent information that it is improving. If current households and investors now perceive, because of new information, that residents of a somewhat higher socioeconomic status are moving in and property values are rising, they may be delighted. They will not, however, alter their earlier decisions to continue residing or reinvesting in the neighborhood. Conversely, equivalent new information about eroding status and values is more likely to trigger intentions to move elsewhere, and to divest and buy elsewhere, before losses in satisfaction and rates of return mount.

The Proposition of Asymmetric Informational Power

If we combine these two lessons from behavioral economics on what sorts of information are likely to be most powerful in altering intentions and behaviors we can deduce the second major proposition of this book:

> *The Proposition of Asymmetric Informational Power*: Information about the absolute decline of the current neighborhood will prove more powerful in altering residents' and owners' mobility and investment behaviors than information about its relative decline or its absolute improvement.

To put this proposition differently, information about contextual changes (i.e., information external to the individual's personal circumstances) is more powerful to the degree that it works to "push" people to move out and/or disinvest in their neighborhood. By contrast, new information about prospectively superior options in other neighborhoods that render the current neighborhood only *relatively* less desirable is, all else being equal, less likely to "pull" people out. Of course, new information that the current neighborhood is improving absolutely will have no impact on either mobility or investment behaviors. This proposition suggests that households will be more likely to leave in response to information about the absolutely deteriorating external conditions in their neighborhood than to do so in response to information that physical conditions in another equally expensive neighborhood nearby have improved to the point where they are now superior. Property owners will be more likely to disinvest by downgrading the quality of their dwellings if they expect, based on new information, that their absolute rates of return are soon to fall, than they are likely to do in response to new information of even better rates of return elsewhere. Note how this proposition adds nuance to the Housing Submarket Model employed in chapters 3 and 4, which did not refer to asymmetries in adjustment processes. This proposition suggests that submarket forces that work to "push" households and property owners out of one submarket into another will likely be more frequent and quantitatively significant than those that work to "pull" them from one to another.

Unfortunately, there is only a smattering of evidence supporting this proposition. A long-standing literature on residential satisfaction and intraurban mobility provides suggestive support. This research leaves no doubt that households become dissatisfied, develop moving intentions, and often move from neighborhoods that they perceive as deteriorated, unsafe, and inhabited by those of inferior socioeconomic status.[18] However, these studies typically do not measure changes in conditions in the current neighborhood (only levels), nor do they compare indicators across competing neighborhoods. With two exceptions, they also do not consider the role of expectations in shaping residential satisfaction and triggering decisions (a topic to which we turn below). Clarence Wurdock found that white households were more likely to plan moving out when they expected the neighborhood to become 50 percent or more black-occupied within five years.[19] Garry Hesser and I found that greater pessimism about property value appreciation in the future was associated with plans to leave the neighborhood sooner.[20]

Key Indicators for Forming Expectations about Neighborhood Change

I argued above that there were many powerful reasons why people's expectations about the neighborhood inevitably shape household and investor decisions governing the flow of resources across neighborhoods. In succeeding sections of this chapter, I provided a model of how people gather data in an effort to inform these expectations, and the implications that follow from these efforts about what general sorts of information pertaining to what geographies are likely to be most salient. Now we examine whether any particular data domains seem to be especially powerful in predicting the future of neighborhoods.

Evidence from Statistical Models of Predictive Neighborhood Indicators

The vast majority of the previous empirical work related to building predictive statistical models of neighborhood change have employed census data to model decennial changes in particular census tract characteristics of interest. These regression-modeling efforts specified how neighborhood indicators measured at the beginning of a decade correlated with subsequent decadal changes in neighborhood outcome indicators.[21] By far the most sophisticated and convincing example of this genre is the work of John Hipp, who found that higher violent or property crime rates in a neighborhood led to more concentrated poverty, more residential turnover, a weaker retail sector, and a higher share of black population ten years later.[22]

As valuable as these pioneering efforts have been in building our understanding of long-tern neighborhood changes, data points separated by ten years impose many limitations when thinking about dynamics over a finer grain of time. One cannot precisely ascertain the degree to which decadal changes have been constant throughout the period. This is especially crucial when the phenomenon in question exhibits threshold points or other nonlinear adjustments, as I will explore in the next chapter. Moreover, these works make the untenable assumption that the neighborhood indicator measured at the beginning of the decade was indeed an exogenous predictor, as opposed to an endogenous one or a spurious correlate of previous trends in the neighborhood manifested before the period under analysis.[23]

By contrast, recent efforts have attempted to exploit newly available annual, quarterly, or even monthly observations of neighborhood indicators in building more dynamic models. Peter Tatian and I developed the first predictive statistical hazard model of gentrification: consistent, substantial home price appreciation in disadvantaged neighborhoods in the District of Columbia.[24] We found that the key predictors of the onset of neighborhood housing appreciation were (1) the income levels, denial rates, and Hispanic shares of those taking out mortgages to buy homes and condominiums in the neighborhood *two* years earlier; (2) adjacency to neighborhoods that were rapidly appreciating during the prior *two* years; and (3) the rate of home and condominium sales in the neighborhood *one* year before.

Jackelyn Hwang and Robert Sampson also modeled gentrification, using a rich dataset for Chicago neighborhoods during 2007 to 2009.[25] They found that, past a threshold point, the concentrations of black and Hispanic residents in a neighborhood deterred the inflow of higher-income, predominantly white households. Perceptions of disorder had a similar deterrence effect, though objective measures of disorder did not. Complementary findings emerged from modeling of the Los Angeles housing market undertaken by John Hipp, George Tita, and Robert Greenbaum.[26] They found that increased neighborhood property and violent crime rates predicted increased housing turnover (and, in the case of violent crime, lower home values) in the subsequent year, but not vice versa.

Three sophisticated longitudinal econometric analyses have demonstrated that crime may not be the ultimate predictive neighborhood indicator, however; home foreclosures lead to more crime nearby, after some lag. Ingrid Ellen, Johanna Lacoe, and Claudia Sharygin (2012) found that a marginal increase in foreclosures in New York City resulted in 3 percent more total crimes, almost 6 percent more violent crimes, and 3 percent more public nuisance crimes on the block face in the subsequent quarter.[27] Charles Katz, Danielle Wallace, and E. C. Hedberg revealed that for every additional foreclosure in Glendale, Arizona, there was a cumulative impact over the next three or four months of twelve more property crimes and three more violent crimes per thousand population.[28] Sonya Williams, Nandita Verma, and I discovered in our analysis of Chicago that home foreclosures temporally preceded a variety of other neighborhood indicators (property and violent crime, total and mean home purchase mortgage loan amounts, small business loans) but that the reverse did not occur. By contrast, all other indicators exhibited complicated temporal patterns of interrelationships, implying that they often were mutually causal.[29]

In sum, statistical modeling efforts that carefully establish temporal sequences (and thus, implicitly, direction of causation) point consistently to two candidates for neighborhood indicators that hold strong predictive power for subsequent flows of resources into neighborhoods: foreclosed homes and crime. Unfortunately, only by inference can we deduce from these studies that decision makers controlling these flows were using information that they acquired about foreclosures and crime to shape their perceptions, expectations and, ultimately, behaviors.

Survey Evidence about Formation of Perceptions and Expectations in Neighborhoods

Other research has probed more directly through personal surveys what domains of data households and investors focus upon when forming perceptions and expectations about their neighborhoods. In the only study to investigate neighborhood expectations explicitly, Garry Hesser and I interviewed homeowners in Minneapolis and in Wooster, a small Ohio town; we measured their separate expectations about future changes in both their neighborhoods' property values and quality of life, and then statistically related their relationships with other perceptions and objective neighborhood indicators. We found that current levels of objective indicators of the physical, demographic, and socioeconomic characteristics of neighborhoods generally were weak predictors of both types of expectations compared to homeowners' own subjective impressions about recent trends in the neighborhoods. These two types of expectations proved quite independent; moreover, they exhibited distinct sets of predictors. For example, though some white homeowners viewed a higher proportion of black neighbors as a basis for a more pessimistic outlook on property-value appreciation, this did not affect their expectations regarding general neighborhood quality of life.[30] These findings suggest that new information about neighborhoods may trigger adjustments in owners' investment behavior without changing households' satisfaction or intentions to move, and vice versa. Importantly, the social-interactive dimension of neighborhood context proved crucial in shaping homeowners' expectations. Both the individual and collective degrees of neighborhood identification and social integration were strong contributors to optimism about property-value changes. This perhaps indicates that homeowners closely identifying with a cohesive neighborhood believe that, collectively, the area will be successful in warding off elements that could erode values or will be less susceptible to strategic gaming—a topic I will discuss in chapter 10 in the context of policy proposals. Finally, elderly homeowners were much more pessimistic in their expectations about property-value appreciation than any other age group, all else being equal. This result is consistent with the hypothesis that those who are least likely to obtain large amounts of reliable, contemporary housing market information, and who thus are less certain about the future, exhibit a bias toward greater pessimism.

Several other survey-based studies investigated the basis of perceptions about current conditions in neighborhoods. Though distinct from expectations, it is likely that perceptions and expectations will be highly correlated.[31] Richard Taub, Garth Taylor, and Jan Dunham interviewed homeowners in the Chicago area and elicited their perceptions and expectations about the neighborhood and their likelihood of reinvesting in their properties.[32] They discerned that perceptions of increasing crime or increasing percentages of black residents led homeowners to worry about the market competitiveness of their neighborhood, which in turn reduced their likelihood of investing in their properties but strengthened their intention to move out. They found clear evidence of racial encoding by not only white but also black and

Hispanic homeowners: perceived higher percentages of black residents were positively associated with greater perceived crime problems.

Lincoln Quillian and Devah Pager uncovered complementary relationships between perceived crime and racial composition in their analyses of surveys from Chicago, Baltimore, and Seattle.[33] They observed that respondents assessed their neighborhoods' safety on the basis of what the foregoing model would predict: information gleaned from personal experience (that is, victimization) and official police statistics about crime. What was more significant is that the respondents also viewed their neighborhoods as less safe when they had higher percentages of young black males as neighbors, even after controlling for official crime rate, the socioeconomic composition, the percentage of Latino residents, the neighborhood's physical appearance, and measures of disorder in the neighborhood, along with respondents' personal characteristics. Remarkably, this racialized perception of safety held for whites and blacks alike.

Probing further into the perceptions of safety, we see that perceptions of disorder, such as graffiti and groups of loitering youths, are key predictors of perceptions of crime. Wesley Skogan's Chicago study identified strong relationships between residents' perceptions of neighborhood disorder, their beliefs that the neighborhood was unsafe, and their ensuing behaviors of disinvesting and moving out, all leading to a cumulative spiral of neighborhood decay.[34] Robert Sampson and Stephen Raudenbush pushed deeper into the information used to shape these beliefs by employing other Chicago survey data.[35] They discovered that, as expected, residents' perceptions of disorder positively correlated with objective observers' visual ratings of several indicators of disorder. What was startling was that the percentages of black and poor residents of the neighborhood proved to be even more powerful predictors, for both black and white residents.

Finally, an innovative survey study employing videos of neighborhood vignettes with different class and racial dimensions revealed the depth of how whites in Detroit and Chicago negatively stereotype neighborhoods with black residents, though it did not focus on crime and disorder in particular. Maria Krysan, Mick Couper, Reynolds Farley, and Tyrone Forman found that whites perceived neighborhoods as much more "desirable" when only white neighbors appeared in the videos, in comparison to scenarios where racially mixed groups or only black neighbors appeared.[36]

The Proposition of Racially Encoded Signals

The aforementioned findings provide a consensual portrait about how many urban residents gain information about their neighborhoods' disorder, safety, and competitive prospects: they use the share of black residents as a proxy indicator.[37] Crucially, more than simple racial prejudice appears to produce this phenomenon, since blacks are often as likely as whites to be influenced by black population composition in shaping their perceptions of neighborhoods. These findings strongly suggest that prior beliefs involving stigmatization of concentrations of black poverty supplement both white and black residents' observational data regarding their current neighborhoods' "objective" indicators of disorder and crime. Put differently, social constructs related to race inform perceptions of key features of neighborhoods that clearly influence mobility and financial investments.

Several other studies support the notion that racial composition serves as a convenient proxy for a variety of other aspects of neighborhoods that may be harder to evaluate. David Harris shows that the percentage of black population in a neighborhood is associated with lower property values primarily because it serves as a proxy for a lower-income, poorly educated population.[38] In another study, he draws similar conclusions about why residents are less satisfied in neighborhoods with higher percentages of black residents.[39] Ingrid Gould Ellen analyzes this issue comprehensively.[40] She finds that white homeowners are less satisfied with, more likely to leave, and less likely to move into neighborhoods with recently growing black populations, even when the neighborhood's physical conditions, socioeconomic composition, and overall percentage of black and other minority residents is controlled.[41] She deduces that white homeowners employ substantial recent black population growth as a predictor of future neighborhood decline.

All this evidence leads to the third proposition of the book:

> *The Proposition of Racially Encoded Signals*: Key types of information shaping perceptions and expectations about the neighborhood will influence the behaviors of residents and property owners; a significant amount of such information lies encoded within the share and the growth of the black population in the neighborhood.

Conclusion

Understanding why neighborhoods change fundamentally requires an understanding of how households and property owners form their perceptions and expectations about neighborhoods. This implies that we must probe the nature of how people acquire and process data and form beliefs. Social psychology and behavioral economics yield notable insights here.

First, since passively acquired information provides the foundation of active search for housing market and neighborhood information, decision makers' amount of information and the certainty of their beliefs will take on distinctive spatial configurations. These geographic configurations will roughly correspond to an individual's routine activity spaces.

Second, the neighborhood itself supplies a crucial (though variable) component comprising the routine activity spaces in which we passively acquire information. Social interactive processes within the neighborhood can further shape what sources we trust when acquiring information passively and actively, and what sorts of standards we apply when assessing whether new information is sufficient to warrant altering our beliefs and expectations. Thus, the neighborhood helps to "make us" in terms of what we believe, which in turn influences the residential mobility and investment decisions we make that collectively "make the neighborhood."

Third, evidence suggests that (1) information about one's current neighborhood should be more powerful than equivalent information about other, prospective neighborhoods; and (2) information indicating that one's current neighborhood is declining should be more powerful in altering behaviors than equivalent information that it is improving. I summarize this as the Proposition of Asymmetric Informational Power.

Fourth, statistical studies show that increases in home foreclosures and crime powerfully predict future declines in various indicators of neighborhood health. Resident surveys similarly show the power of perceived crime and disorder in shaping beliefs about and satisfaction with the neighborhood. However, not only "objective" data like official statistics, but also the perceived racial context of the neighborhood shape these perceptions. A significant amount of information for both white and black residents lies encoded within the share of the black population in the neighborhood and the change in this share, a point I summarize as the Proposition of Racially Encoded Signals.

SIX

Nonlinear and Threshold Effects
Related to Neighborhood

How neighborhoods respond when we intervene in them is of central concern to planners and policy makers in the realms of community development, residential integration by economic and racial status, residential quality of life, and assisted housing. If all neighborhoods responded in a linear (that is, proportionate) fashion, the decisions of planners and policymakers about where, how, and how much to intervene would be comparatively simple. In such a scenario, each unit of some sort of programmatically induced input (for example, one more dollar of housing rehabilitation subsidy, one more household of a particular economic and racial status, or one more affordable dwelling unit) would be expected to yield a constant amount of programmatic outputs—both desirable (for example, privately funded housing rehabilitation, enhanced economic independence of households) and perhaps undesirable (for example, reductions in proximate property values, induced out-moving of households). This would be true regardless of the scale of the intervention or the context of its particular location. Unfortunately, the world is not so simple.

Multiple domains related to neighborhoods are characterized by nonlinear or threshold effects. Nonlinear and threshold relationships are exhibited both by the effect of the neighborhood on individuals and by the forces that cause neighborhood changes in the aggregate. Nonlinear effects are causal relationships wherein the size of impact (on some outcome variable of interest) produced by a marginal change in some causal variable depends on the value of that variable. Figure 6.1 shows a visual manifestation of an illustrative nonlinear relationship OF. In this case, the marginal positive impact of X is greater at low values of X, diminishes as X gets larger, and eventually becomes negative if X is sufficiently large. Threshold effects are a particular sort of nonlinear relationship in which the magnitude of the causal influence changes dramatically past some critical point(s). A threshold relationship can be a continuous mathematical function, as in lines *OEB* or *OED* in figure 6.1, or a discontinuous relationship, as in line segments *OE* and *AC*. Point *X'* indicates the critical point, with point *X''* portraying a second critical point for relationship *OED*.

Threshold effects related to neighborhoods are not simply an intellectual curiosity. On the contrary, their existence holds powerful implications for the social rationale for neighborhood revitalization and resident diversification policies, and for their strategic formulation. For example, if the relationship between the percentage of a "disadvantaged group" living in a neighborhood and the aggregate incidence of socially problematic behaviors were linear (that is, proportional), the spatial redistribution of the disadvantaged population would not in itself lead to any net changes in the aggregate incidence of such problematic behaviors across society. Instead, it would merely result in a zero-sum geographic redistribution of the problematic behaviors from one neighborhood to another. If, however, this relationship were characterized by negative social behaviors ensuing only after a critical mass of disadvantaged populations were exceeded in the neighborhood, a different conclusion would follow. This would imply that net gains in aggregate social well-being on utilitarian grounds (that is, Pareto improvements) likely result from policies that aimed to keep the compositions of neighborhoods below this threshold through a neighborhood "social mix" strategy. That is, one neighborhood could be "revitalized" without dragging down other neighborhoods. As another illustration, the existence of critical points for private reinvestments in dilapidated neighborhoods implies that scarce public revitalization resources should be strategically targeted so that these critical points can be exceeded, thus leveraging private investments with the public ones. I will amplify and analyze these points with more precision in later chapters.

The individual mobility and investment behaviors of households and residential property owners often manifest nonlinear and threshold effects that, in turn, likely generate aggregate nonlinear responses in neighborhood dynamics. Conversely, changes in the neighborhood's characteristics often reflect back to influence a wide range of behaviors of individual residents in nonlinear and threshold-laden ways. In this chapter, I first provide a variety of behavioral mechanisms that in theory should yield nonlinear responses of individuals to external stimuli in particular contexts. This provides a foundation for understanding how neighborhood conditions might affect individual behaviors in nonlinear way, and also how such behaviors might in turn produce nonlinear changes in aggregate neighborhood indicators.

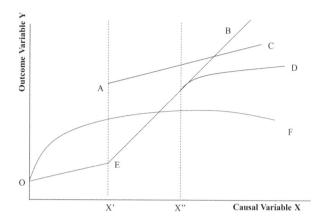

Figure 6.1. Illustrations of nonlinear and threshold effects

I synthesize the existing empirical research demonstrating that the ways in which neighborhoods shape individual behaviors related to residential mobility, investments in property, educational attainment, fertility, employment, and a variety of other domains often manifest themselves as threshold-like relationships. I then consider the nonlinear effects associated with dynamics of neighborhood racial composition, poverty and disadvantage, and how these changes are associated with neighborhood-wide changes in crime and property values. I review the evidence on threshold effects on neighborhood property values and crime resulting from the location of assisted housing. Finally, I advance the Proposition of Linked Threshold Effects as a means of synthesizing this literature..

Behavioral Mechanisms of Nonlinear and Threshold Effects

A change in an aggregate population characteristic in a neighborhood must imply tautologically a change in one or more of three constituent groups occurred: the number and composition of out-movers from the neighborhood, the number and composition of in-movers to the neighborhood, and the characteristics of residents who remain in the neighborhood during the period. Analogously, the aggregation of individual owners' investment behaviors will determine the physical condition profile of the dwellings in the neighborhood. According to several models—socialization, gaming, tolerance, contagion, and diminishing returns—the behavior of the individuals comprising these groups may be influenced in ways that manifest nonlinear and/or threshold effects. One can analyze out-migration behavior through collective socialization, gaming, and tolerance models; in-migration be-havior through gaming and tolerance models; behavior of residents who remain through collective socialization, gaming, contagion, and diminish-ing returns models; and investment behaviors of owners through collective socialization and gaming models.

Collective Socialization Models

Collective socialization models focus on the potential role that social inter-actions exert on shaping an individual's attitudes, values, and behavior.[1] The tenet of this collective socialization approach is that a sufficiently powerful social group can influence others to conform to its customs, norms, and behaviors. Such an effect can only occur, however, to the degree that (1) the individual comes in social contact with the group and (2) the group can exert more powerful threats or inducements to conform to its positions than can competing groups. These two preconditions imply the existence of a critical point. Presuming the importance of interpersonal contact in enforc-ing conformity, if the individuals constituting the group in question are scat-tered thinly over urban space, they are less likely to be able either to convey their positions effectively to others with whom they might come in contact, or to exert much pressure to conform. It is only when a group reaches some critical mass over a predefined neighborhood that it is likely to be effective in shaping other residents' behavior. Past this critical point, as the group re-cruits more members, its power to sanction nonconformists probably grows nonlinearly. This is especially likely when the position of the group becomes so dominant as to become normative in the area. A sociological illustration of the collective socialization logic is William Julius Wilson's contention that, as a critical mass of middle-class families leaves the inner city, low-income blacks left behind become increasingly isolated from the positive role models that the erstwhile dominant class offered.[2] I developed a model of how both economic and collective socialization forces shape owner oc-cupants' dwelling investment behavior.[3] Homeowners who identify closely with the other residents in a socially cohesive neighborhood will face strong collective pressures to adjust their home investment decisions in confor-mity with group norms about acceptable home upkeep, else face poten-tial social sanctions. However, this influence will only manifest itself after critical points of both collective cohesion and homeowner identification with neighborhood have been exceeded.[4]

A variant of this collective socialization process can also produce thresh-old relationships when one views it as the loss of collective social control.

For example, in a neighborhood exhibiting increasing amounts of public disorder and violence, residents may become fearful to intervene in or even be present in public spaces, whereupon the deterrence supplied by collective efficacy wanes and the rate of antisocial behaviors accelerates.[5] Up Lim and I developed a formal model of how this process could lead to nonlinear neighborhood crime dynamics.[6]

Gaming Models

The tenet of gaming models is that, in many decisional situations, the costs and benefits of alternative courses of action are uncertain and depend on how many other decision makers choose various alternatives. That is, an individual's expected payoff varies depending on the number or proportion of others who make a decision before that particular individual does. Thus, the concept of critical amount of observed prior action is central in this type of model. The well-known prisoner's dilemma is the simplest form of gaming model. Thomas Schelling developed a more sophisticated model of collective behavior that results from what he called the multiperson prisoner's dilemma. Expanded to a situation with more than two decision-makers (say n), Schelling contends that there is some number k such that if at least k individuals choose their nonpreferred alternative and the rest do not, those who do are better off than if they had all chosen their preferred alternative. If the number is less than k, this is not true. Thus, k can be interpreted as a critical point—that is, the smallest size of the group that can be profitable for those who join, though they may be resentful of free riders who follow their own preferences without regard for the group.[7]

Mark Granovetter devised a different gaming model of collective behavior that results from the aggregation of the distribution of individually defined critical points in the population.[8] He contended that for a particular decision maker there is a critical point where net expected benefits begin to exceed net expected costs. Beginning with a frequency distribution of such points, Granovetter derived the ultimate or "equilibrium" number making each decision. Slight modifications in one or more of these distributions produced large changes in the aggregate behavior of individuals in a neighborhood.[9]

I developed a model of owner occupant's home reinvestment behavior that leads to a prediction of various sorts of gaming behaviors depending on context.[10] The model begins with the homeowner's preferences for both consumption and asset aspects of the home, the initial quality in the neighborhood, and whether the homeowner's expectations involve qualitative changes in the neighborhood or merely property price changes. It assumes that all homeowners place value on the consumption aspect of the home, and view the quality of the neighborhood as an important contributor to livability. As a result, the perceived consumption value of home upkeep and optimism about changes in neighborhood quality will be directly related. It further assumes that the weight placed on the asset aspect of the home grows immensely when homeowners perceive that they can expect a much smaller capital gain from selling the home than they thought would be forthcoming when they purchased it. If the homeowner were to reside in a neighborhood where there was a discrepancy between currently expected capital gain and originally expected capital gain, one can predict unconventional responses. Optimism about property inflation may make homeowners confident that they can attain their capital appreciation goals easily, even with little extra home upkeep effort. Pessimism about property appreciation may lead them to intensify their upkeep efforts, to salvage some minimal gain. In higher-quality neighborhoods, however, homeowners may feel confident that their minimal capital gain expectations will be met, regardless of short-run vagaries of the housing market. As a result, their property value expectations in such circumstances may have little impact on their upkeep behavior.

Tolerance Models

The tenet of tolerance models is that decision makers in a residential environment will respond if the aggregate observed behavior of neighbors (or an exogenous event) raises an undesirable neighborhood attribute above the level they find tolerable. Unlike in gaming models, uncertainty does not play any significant role here. The simplest tolerance model as applied to residential mobility implies the existence of a threshold-like relationship. As I summarized in chapter 1, several theories of mobility rely upon the notion that when a scalar describing the household's psychological state (variously labeled as dissatisfaction, stress, or disequilibrium) exceeds a critical value, intentions to move or an active housing market search will ensue in an abrupt, discontinuous fashion.

A more sophisticated version of the tolerance model shows how an endogenous, self-sustaining out-migration process occurs once the negative neighborhood attribute in question reaches a critical point. The trigger occurs if households in a neighborhood have different levels of tolerance for the triggering attribute, with the least tolerant responding first by leaving the neighborhood when its personal critical point is exceeded. If additional changes in the causal neighborhood attribute result from the course of action taken in response to the initial event by those with the lowest tolerance, the new level of the neighborhood attribute may now be above the tolerance critical value of the least tolerant remaining households. For example, this could take the form of lower-income or minority households occupying the dwellings of the least tolerant who have recently left the neighborhood. The process may continue with new rounds of attribute change and household adjustments via out-mobility until the process is completed. At the extreme, the process may end when all the original residents in a neighborhood have responded by moving away. The theoretical development of tolerance models has focused on changes in a neighborhood's racial composition,[11] though extensions to tolerances for other sorts of neighborhood attributes associated with population composition are straightforward.

Contagion Models

The basic tenet of contagion models is that if decision makers live in a community where some of their neighboring peers exhibit nonnormative behaviors, they will be more likely to adopt these behaviors themselves. In this way, social problems may be contagious, spreading through peer influence. Randall Crane proposed a formal contagion model to explain the incidence and spread of social problems.[12] The key implication of his contagion model is that there is a critical point in the incidence of social problems in a specified population. If the incidence remains below the critical point, the prevalence of the problem will fall toward some relatively low-level equilibrium. However, should the incidence surpass this point, the problems will spread explosively, in "epidemic" fashion, as more and more individuals engage in the problematic behavior. Crane postulated two conditions determining the susceptibility of a neighborhood to epidemics of social problems: the distribution of individual residents' risk of developing social problems and their susceptibility to peer influence.[13]

Diminishing-Returns Models

The core premise of this model is that the perceived net benefits, and thus the likelihood, of engaging in a behavior is related to one or more forces that change endogenously as the aggregate characteristics of the neighborhood change. Insofar as perceived net benefits and collective socialization forces in the neighborhood are related, these models overlap.[14] Nevertheless, there may be additional forces that are independent of collective socialization. For example, the likelihood that an individual will engage in property crime may rise as neighborhood poverty rates rise, due to an erosion of collective efficacy. However, it may rise at a diminishing rate if at the same time the number of suitable targets for property crime (houses, stores, individuals) starts to wane or the competition from other criminal becomes more intense. Both forces could lead to a perception of diminished marginal returns from crime, thereby retarding the increase in such behaviors.[15]

Heterogeneity of Relationships across Individuals

A theoretical discussion of nonlinear neighborhood-related relationships would be incomplete without considering whether these relationships in general, and critical points in particular, are similar in different contexts. Theory suggests that the answer is no because of (1) compositional differences in the individuals being exposed to the particular feature of neighborhood context, (2) exposure to other features of the neighborhood context being simultaneously applied that may be synergistic or contrary, and (3) potential buffering actions by individuals.[16]

Careful consideration of the aforementioned intraneighborhood social-interactive mechanisms of nonlinear effects on individuals suggest that relationships are likely heterogeneous by gender, income, age, education, ethnicity, and perhaps other characteristics. The socialization, tolerance, and contagion mechanisms have effects only to the extent that people (1) spend a substantial amount of time in the neighborhood, (2) are locally oriented in their social interactions, and (3) do not marshal sufficient resources to insulate themselves from these effects. The aforementioned characteristics of residents can potentially influence all of these three conditions. We would expect, for example, local social control in areas with more traditional, patriarchal norms to produce strict monitoring of the behaviors of women, thus potentially insulating them from some neighborhood socialization or contagion effects and negating their greater time spent in the neighborhood.[17] Such would imply a higher critical point for them. Women with child-care responsibilities, the elderly, and lower-income residents would be more likely to develop a denser network of relationships more focused on the neighborhood.[18] Such would imply a lower critical point for them inasmuch as they would be more vulnerable to socialization and contagion forces. The evidence from nonexperimental and experimental studies indeed suggests that different neighborhood effect mechanisms may have varying salience across different groups,[19] though researchers have rarely investigated explicitly the implied differences in measured thresholds.[20]

A second reason for deducing that nonlinear responses and critical points will be dissimilar in different contexts is that people do not experience a particular neighborhood attribute in isolation from other neighborhood attributes; neighborhood exposures are inherently "bundled" along many dimensions. Simultaneous exposures to other neighborhood treatments may intensify the particular exposure's expected response through synergistic interactions. Put differently, different dimensions of neighborhood influence may be not additive but multiplicative. An analogous possibility is that there may be antidotes to the neighborhood influence under consideration: exposures to other aspects of neighborhood that counteract the particular exposure's expected response.

The final reason for predicting heterogeneity in nonlinear relationships is potential buffering forces in the neighborhoods. People, their families, or their communities may respond to the neighborhood characteristic under consideration in ways that counteract its expected response. Because residents individually and collectively potentially have agency, they may engage in compensatory behaviors that offset negative neighborhood effects. For example, parents may keep their children in the home when youngsters who are bad role models are using the local playground.[21] Such buffering actions would serve to increase critical points of thresholds.

Evidence on Nonlinear Individual Behavioral Responses to Neighborhood

Considerable empirical research demonstrates that thresholds often characterize how neighborhoods shape individual behaviors related to residential mobility, investments in property, educational attainment, fertility, employment, and a variety of other domains. Unfortunately, none of these studies directly test which of the aforementioned mechanisms are primarily at work. Deductive reasoning suggests that different mechanisms may come into operation depending on the behavioral domain.

Household Mobility Behaviors

The longest-standing body of evidence here—what has been called the "racial tipping" literature— relates to the mobility responses of white households when the number or share of black neighbors increases. Though racial transition of neighborhoods has often been investigated,[22] there have been few studies of individual white households that isolated racial composition as the main driver of mobility in comparison to other potential causes, and which also tested for nonlinear relationships. In a notable exception, Kyle

Crowder found that the percentage of minority households in the neighborhood during one year and the probability of a white household leaving the neighborhood during the following year were strongly related in a distinctly nonlinear fashion, even when controlling for neighborhood mean income and shares of families with children and long-term residents.[23] The typical white household had a baseline probability of .07 of moving out of an all-white-occupied neighborhood. This probability rose steadily to .10 as the percentage of minority residents rose to 30 percent, stayed roughly constant in the range of 31 to 60 percent, and then rose steadily again to .12 in the neighborhood with 99 percent minority residents. Whites were more likely to move away at any percentage of minority neighbors if they had higher incomes and resided in a metropolitan area with more exclusively white neighborhoods providing options for where to move. Interestingly, the composition of the minority households (mix of black, Hispanic, or Asian) did not affect this basic relationship, nor did prior growth in the percentage of black residents. These findings offer support for the tolerance model of nonlinear relationships.

Several other studies have investigated how the racial composition of potential destination neighborhoods affected choices in nonlinear ways, while controlling for other features of this destination. Ingrid Ellen analyzed whether whites or blacks would occupy a vacant dwelling based on the current percentage of black population in the neighborhood.[24] She identified a highly nonlinear relationship, regardless of whether a black (instead of white) home seeker moved into a vacant rental or sales dwelling. The probability of black occupancy rose significantly as the neighborhood percentage of black residents rose from zero to 10 percent, then rose very little in the range from 11 to 50 percent, and rose substantially again at higher percentages. The nonlinearity in the relationship was particularly dramatic for homebuyers in neighborhoods with 10 percent black residents if a white household previously occupied the vacant dwelling, whereas it was particularly dramatic in neighborhoods with 50 percent black residents if the vacant dwelling was previously occupied by a black household. This latter finding is consistent with that of Yannis Ioannides and Jeffrey Zabel. They found that, controlling for other neighborhood characteristics like median income, homeownership rates, and educational attainment, higher percentages of nonwhite residents increasingly attracted nonwhite households as in-movers, and this marginal attractiveness as a moving destination grew even stronger once a neighborhood exceeded 50 percent nonwhite households.[25] Lincoln Quillian recently confirmed the nonlinear racial mobility patterns observed by Ellen, Ioannides, and Zabel, though he noted that they are less nonlinear when distance between origin and destination neighborhood is controlled.[26] He also found that the probability of selecting a neighborhood was strongly inversely related to the absolute difference between the household's income and the median income of the neighborhood, though at a diminishing marginal rate. These findings from mobility destination studies also offer support for the tolerance model of nonlinear relationships.

Dwelling Owner's Investment Behaviors

Richard Taub, Garth Taylor, and Jan Dunham interviewed homeowners in the Chicago area, eliciting their perceptions and expectations about the neighborhood and their likelihood of reinvesting in their properties.[27] They discerned what they termed "investment thresholds" for individual homeowners: the percentage of other residential property owners in the neighborhood who would need to be visibly investing in their properties before the owner in question would be willing to do the same. These investment thresholds varied by household circumstances and neighborhood context. Higher-income and larger-family households had lower thresholds; those in older, more deteriorated neighborhoods had higher thresholds. However, within the latter category of neighborhoods there was a pronounced differentiation by race of the homeowner and the neighborhood. Even when whites perceived their deteriorated neighborhood to be predominantly white-occupied, on average they would demand that more than half their neighbors would reinvest in their homes before they would do so; the corresponding figure for black and Hispanic homeowners in such contexts was only a third. Interestingly, all races exhibited much higher investment thresholds when they perceived the neighborhood to be racially mixed: three-fourths for whites and half for blacks and Hispanics, on average. They also discovered that only 36 percent of sample homeowners had improved their homes substantially in the prior two years when they perceived that no one else on their block was doing so, whereas 65 percent had improved their homes when they perceived that others on their block were doing so.

Evidence that Garry Hesser and I gathered from homeowners in Minneapolis and in Wooster, Ohio, provides strong support for the existence of thresholds produced by intraneighborhood collective socialization dynamics.[28] The homeowner's degree of identification with neighbors held immense explanatory power for home upkeep behavior, but only when that homeowner lived in a cohesive neighborhood where most neighbors shared the same solidarity sentiments. Compared to average homeowners in noncohesive neighborhoods, owners in the most cohesive neighborhoods who identified most closely with their neighbors spent 28 percent to 45 percent more annually on upkeep, and exhibited a 66 percent lower likelihood of exterior home defects. Of most relevance to the topic of threshold relationships, however, is that neither the homeowner's own sense of identification with neighbors nor the neighborhood's collective degree of solidarity influenced behavior independently. Rather, individual and collective identification simultaneously needed to exceed a critical value before home upkeep efforts increased.[29] All these findings and those of Taub et al. are consistent with the Granovetter gaming threshold model.

Employment, Education, Fertility, and Cognitive Outcomes

Research by Thomas Vartanian and by Bruce Weinberg, Patricia Reagan, and Jeffrey Yankow provides consistent evidence of thresholdlike relationships between neighborhood poverty rates and the probabilities of various outcomes for individual residents.[30] The independent positive impact of neighborhood poverty rates on undesirable outcomes, like duration of poverty spells and welfare dependency, appeared to be nil unless the neighborhood exceeded about 20 percent poverty, whereupon the externality effects grew rapidly until the neighborhood reached approximately 40 percent poverty; subsequent increases in the poverty population had no substantial marginal effect. Analogously, the independent impact of neighborhood poverty rates in discouraging positive outcomes like hours of work, hourly wages, and total income was nil unless the neighborhood exceeded about 15 percent poverty, whereupon the effects grew rapidly until the neighborhood reached roughly 30 percent poverty; subsequent increases in poverty appeared to have no marginal effect. This evidence indicates a dual threshold relationship; I portray a generic summary version in figure 6.2. The existence of the lower threshold supports the social contagion and collective socialization models; the second threshold suggests that marginal impact of these forces wane as the behaviors become normative in the neighborhood.[31]

As far as thresholdlike relationships between individual outcomes and neighborhood percentages of affluent residents, the work of Randall Crane, of Greg Duncan et al., and of Lindsay Chase-Lansdale et al. is revealing.[32] Unfortunately, though they all identify a critical point of neighborhood affluence, they differ on its value. Crane's analysis found strong evidence of contagionlike effects on both secondary school leaving and teenage childbearing in the share of affluent (that is, employees in professional-managerial occupations) neighbors. For whites and blacks there was a critical point, at 5 percent affluent neighbors, below which dropout rates skyrocketed in epidemiclike fashion. These threshold effects were more dramatic for black males than for females. He observed a similar critical point at a low percentage of affluent neighbors for both black and white teen women's childbearing rates.[33] Duncan et al. found a quantitatively different nonlinear neighborhood effect on educational attainment from the percentage of affluent neighbors.[34] They observed that the positive effect of the affluent became dramatically stronger when the neighborhood percentage exceeded the national mean. Chase-Lansdale et al. examined how the percentage of affluent neighbors related to a variety of intellectual and behavioral development test scores for youth. They discovered, controlling for family influences, that the percentage of affluent neighbors was positively associated with higher intellectual functioning scores for black children and female children only when the percentage exceeded the 25th percentile and was less than the 75th percentile; for other children the effect was linear. All these studies are consistent with two interpretations: (1) an epidemic-like contagion process takes hold when the share of affluent professional neighbors drops below a critical point, or (2) collective social norms discouraging certain negative behaviors and encouraging positive ones take hold only after the share of this group surpasses a critical point in the neighborhood. The primary distinction is whether this critical point is low (5 percent, as per Crane), moderate (25 percent, as per Chase-Lansdale et al.), or considerably higher (50 percent, as per Duncan et al.).

Other studies of neighborhood effects on individual outcomes also have provided support for the notion of a threshold relationship, but because they do not employ neighborhood poverty or affluence rates as indicators, they are not directly comparable to those above. Ruth Lopez Turley analyzed how behavioral and psychological test scores for youth were related to the median family income of the neighborhood.[35] She determined that youths' self-esteem was positively associated with median neighborhood income, but at a diminishing marginal rate. Anna Santiago, Lisa Stack, Jackie Cutsinger and I analyzed the relationship between an index of neighborhood social vulnerability on the secondary school performance of low-income Latino and black youth.[36] We found a positive relationship between a youth's hazard of repeating a grade and the degree of neighborhood social vulnerability to which they were exposed, which became much stronger when this index exceeded its mean value. The findings of Turley and my colleagues imply that improving the economic environment of youth has a much greater impact for those initially in disadvantaged (that is, lower-income, fewer affluent residents) neighborhood circumstances. As such, they are generally consistent with those of Crane and of Chase-Lansdale

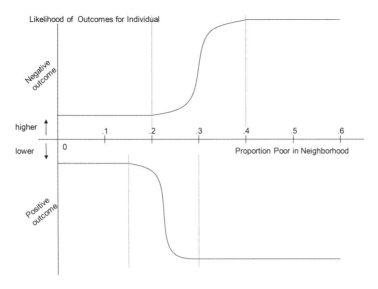

Figure 6.2. Summary of evidence on neighborhood poverty effect on individual economic outcomes. Source: author, based on Vartanian 1999a, 1999b; and Weinberg, Reagan, and Yankow 2004. See text.

et al. However, because both studies only tested for distinct relationships below and above mean values for the neighborhood indicators employed (like Duncan et al.), they do not provide guidance as to the precise value of a critical point.

Evidence on Nonlinear Neighborhood Dynamics

In the section above, I reviewed studies that identified nonlinear effects of neighborhood characteristics on observed individual behaviors and developmental outcomes. Now I turn attention to studies that investigate whether forces that change the aggregate characteristics of neighborhood proceed in a nonlinear fashion. Scholars have observed nonlinear neighborhood dynamics in the domains of racial composition, poverty rates, crime rates, and property values.

Racial Tipping

Several studies test for nonlinear relationships between the characteristics of census tracts measured during one census year that predict changes in a variety of tract characteristics during the ensuing decade.[37] In the realm of racial dynamics, many empirical studies have found that thresholdlike relationships characterize neighborhood racial transition, though no universal tipping point exists.[38] For example, David Card, Alexandre Mas, and Jesse Rothstein searched for distinctive breaks in the relationship between the decadal change in whites' share of a neighborhood population and the percentage of minorities at the beginning of the decade—what they called "tipping points." They found that the mean point of discontinuity was 13 percent minority composition, though it ranged from 5 to 20 percent across the 114 largest metropolitan areas. They found that these tipping points did not appreciably change between the 1970–1980 and 1990–2000 periods analyzed, nor did the composition of the minority population in the neighborhood influence these points. They did discern, however, that tipping points were higher in metro areas with white populations who were more racially tolerant based on their responses to the General Social Survey.

I found complementary results for Cleveland indicating that tipping points not only varied across metropolitan areas but also within cities, based on the characteristics of the neighborhood's white population. [39] The critical value of the percentage of black residents in a predominantly white-occupied neighborhood that would trigger large upsurges in the rate at which white households moved out during the ensuing decade varied from 2 to 47 percent black population, depending on the socioeconomic and demographic profile of white residents that was correlated with their racial attitudes. These aggregate studies and the aforementioned studies of individual mobility in response to racial composition offer strong support to the tolerance model of nonlinear responses.

Neighborhood Gentrification

There is some evidence that one may characterize the dynamics of upward income succession of neighborhoods by one or more nonlinear processes. Jackelyn Hwang and Robert Sampson investigated the determinants of gentrification in Chicago neighborhoods during 2007 to 2009, employing an unusually rich set of predictors.[40] They found that if a neighborhood's rate of black occupancy exceeded 40 percent, its chances of gentrifying were substantially reduced.

Neighborhood Disinvestment

Several studies have probed different aspects of private resources flowing into neighborhoods' residential sectors and have uncovered threshold effects. Lei Ding investigated home mortgage originations across Detroit neighborhoods during the Great Recession.[41] He found that nearly a third of Detroit's neighborhoods faced significant challenges in obtaining mortgage credit due to information externalities associated with a paucity of previous mortgage-financed sales and the concentration of foreclosures. When the number of mortgages in a census tract was five or fewer in the previous year, the odds of a mortgage application being denied increased 32 percent. Jenny Schuetz, Vicki Been, and Ingrid Gould Ellen found strong threshold relationships in New York City during the 2000 to 2005 period between the concentrations of foreclosures and negative impact on property values in the vicinity.[42] Impacts were exhibited only when three or more foreclosed properties were within a distance of 250 to 500 feet (loss of 3.3 percent of value), and when six or more were within 501 to 1,000 feet (loss of 2.8 percent of value). Hye-Sung Han examined the effect of abandoned residential properties on proximate property values in Baltimore from 1991 to 2010.[43] There was an observed impact on nearby property values only when the number of abandoned properties within 250 feet was more than two, though the marginal impact dropped significantly when the number exceeded fourteen.

Neighborhood Poverty Rate Growth

Roberto Quercia, Alvaro Cortes, and I probed for nonlinear relationships in predicting decadal changes in neighborhood poverty rates.[44] We identified a distinct threshold effect when neighborhoods exceeded a poverty rate of about 54 percent. For neighborhoods above that critical point, there was a rapid growth in poverty rate over the ensuing decade, though for neighborhoods with lower poverty rates the pattern was one of relative stability.[45] We also found that the percentage of workers not employed in professional or managerial jobs in a neighborhood was a robust predictor of its poverty rate growth when it surpassed a critical point of about three-quarters. The latter finding of a critical point in the range of 20 to 25 percent represents a middle-ground estimate between the aforementioned findings of Crane, Duncan et al., and Chase-Lansdale et al. regarding threshold relationships between neighborhood shares of affluent residents and individual outcomes related to dropping out of school, teen fertility, and cognitive impairment.[46] This is reassuring, as one would expect that neighborhood-wide increases in these undesirable individual outcomes would intensify the selective in-migration of poor and out-migration of nonpoor households such that poverty would be concentrated over time in such neighborhoods.

Crime Rates and Neighborhood Poverty

Several studies probe the relationship between crime and measures of neighborhood poverty and disadvantage. Focusing first on violent crime, Lauren Krivo and Ruth Peterson investigated the correlates of crime rates across three categories of neighborhoods in Columbus, Ohio: low poverty (less than 20 percent), high poverty (20 percent to 39 percent), and extreme poverty (40 percent and higher) rates.[47] They identified distinctive, but sometimes inconsistent, nonlinear relationships depending on the crime predictor. In the case of a multi-item index of neighborhood disadvantage, there was an ever-increasing positive relationship between violent crime rates and three disadvantage categories of neighborhoods. In the case of poverty rates, there was a constant positive relationship in the range between zero and 39 percent poverty, but no further association once poverty exceeded 39 percent.

Lance Hannon investigated the determinants of neighborhood homicide rates in New York City.[48] Like Krivo and Peterson, he found an accelerating marginal positive relationship between homicide rates and a neighborhood disadvantage index, which was particularly strong for predominantly black-occupied neighborhoods.[49] Also like them, Hannon found evidence of a critical point neighborhood poverty rate of 20 percent past which violent crime rose as poverty rose. Unlike Krivo and Peterson, however, he found that homicides increased at an ever-increasing rate as neighborhood poverty rate increased, even when it exceeded 40 percent.

John Hipp and Daniel Yates offered a potential resolution of these sometimes contradictory results in their study of crime patterns and poverty rates across neighborhoods in twenty-five cities.[50] They found that homicide rates indeed had a critical point (about 10 percent) of neighborhood poverty and crime rates accelerated up to about 25 percent poverty, but the relationship became virtually nil in neighborhoods above 40 percent poverty. An index combining all violent crime, however, exhibited a positive but marginally diminishing relationship at all levels of neighborhood poverty, essentially with no relationship in neighborhoods above 40 percent poverty.

The aforementioned studies also probed property crimes, with somewhat different results. Krivo and Peterson's findings for property crime indicated a distinct nonlinearity suggestive of thresholds.[51] There was no significant difference between 20–39 percent and over 39 percent poverty neighborhoods, but both had at least 20 percent higher property crime rates than low-poverty (under 20 percent) neighborhoods, suggesting a critical value around the 20 percent neighborhood poverty rate. When they employed the neighborhood disadvantage index, the same result emerged.

Hipp and Yates did not replicate this threshold relationship for property crime and neighborhood poverty, however.[52] Instead, they found that property crime rates rose at a steadily decreasing rate as neighborhood poverty rose until poverty exceeded 40 percent, whereupon the relationship essentially disappeared. This finding was consistent with that of Lance Hannon's for Austin and Seattle.[53]

In sum, the research on the aggregate relationship between neighborhood-level crime rates and deprivation is conclusive that nonlinearities are present, but is inconsistent on their exact nature, depending on which type of crime is measured and whether one measures neighborhood conditions by poverty rates or by a broader disadvantage index including poverty and other indicators. It seems likely that there is a critical value of poverty (in the range of 10 to 20 percent) past which violent crime, especially homicides, will start to rise dramatically, consistent with the collective socialization model. At extremely high neighborhood poverty rates, however, the relationship with either violent or property crimes becomes very weak, suggesting the diminishing returns model.

Property Values and Neighborhood Poverty Growth

Jackie Cutsinger, Ron Malega, and I investigated how residential property markets across all metropolitan areas responded to increases in neighborhood poverty over the course of a decade.[54] The first core finding was that the response depended crucially on the beginning-of-decade poverty rate in the neighborhood: declines in home values and apartment rents started after a smaller increment in poverty, and thereafter dropped more rapidly the higher the beginning level of poverty. The second core finding was a consistent critical point in the range of 10 to 20 percent poverty rates where property values and rents began to fall. A neighborhood with no poor individuals at the start of a decade did not evince any declines in values until its poverty rate exceeded 11 percent, or any decline in rents until its poverty rate exceeded 18 percent. Neighborhoods starting at 5 percent poverty must have exceeded 10 percent before any noticeable decline in values occurred, and an even higher percentage for rents to decline. Finally, neighborhoods starting at 10 percent poverty began suffering value and rent declines with any subsequent increase in poverty. These results are consistent with the theoretical predictions of the gaming model of dwelling owners' maintenance behavior presented above. The evidence further showed, however, that this housing market response to rising neighborhood poverty past the critical value was subject to diminishing returns. Neighborhoods that already had at least 20 percent poverty rates at the start of the decade exhibited further acceleration of value and rent decreases with further poverty increases. This began to abate, however, as the poverty concentration solidified, such that by the time the neighborhood reached a 40 percent poverty rate, the marginal negative impacts on property values and rents were declining. I show a summary visual portrayal of these results in figure 6.3. The final core result was that values of the owner-occupied stock were more sensitive to poverty rate increases than rents.

Complementary cross-sectional analysis of UK property markets conducted by Geoffrey Meen revealed a remarkably similar nonlinear response mechanism.[55] He found a negative logit-shaped relationship (portrayed in figure 6.3) between a neighborhood's mean housing prices and its level of deprivation (a multi-item index of economic, social, and physical problems). The ratio of mean housing prices in a neighborhood to the price of the highest-priced neighborhood in that same metropolitan area varied little across areas with low levels of deprivation, but began to decline rapidly within one standard deviation of the mean deprivation. However, once a neighborhood became extremely (say, in the highest decile) disadvantaged, there were few subsequent declines in relative property values; it had reached the bottom of the hierarchy.

Both Meen's and my analyses indicate that property markets clearly negatively capitalize increases in neighborhood poverty and disadvantage once they exceed a critical point,[56] though past this point the responses are nonlinear, with decreasing marginal impacts eventually at very high levels of deprivation. We cannot be sure from these two studies exactly what neighborhood conditions are producing these price effects. Based on other evidence presented in this chapter, however, it is reasonable to posit that three factors jointly produce this "dual threshold" result. These are (1) nonpoor households' aversion to lower-income neighbors (on the grounds of status discrepancy); (2) households' aversion to problematic behaviors triggered by such neighborhoods (e.g., not working, welfare dependency, violent crime, etc. as discussed above); and (3) owners reducing the maintenance of, actively downgrading, and in extreme cases abandoning their properties. I would argue that the second factor probably has primacy here, due to the remarkable consistency in findings across studies of how neighborhood poverty relates to individual economic outcomes, neighborhood rates of violent crime, and property values. One can visualize this point by comparing the lower panels of figure 6.2 and figure 6.3. Recall that in all these realms there is a clear indication of a critical value of poverty rate past which a variety of "neighborhood problems" are likely to emerge visibly, whereupon they are

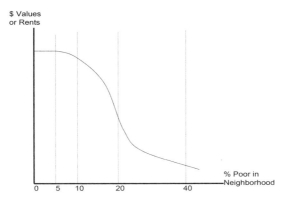

Figure 6.3. Relationship between neighborhood property values and poverty rates (not drawn to scale). Source: author, based on Galster, Cutsinger, and Malega 2008; and Meen 2005. See text.

negatively capitalized into property values and rents. Moreover, to the degree that neighborhood poverty is inversely related to the percentage of residents employed in professional/technical occupations, surpassing poverty critical values is also likely to yield higher incidences of dropping out of school, teen parenting, and other cognitive and behavioral problems, as per the above discussion. However, all these problematic behaviors by individual residents, plus the aggregate patterns of violent and property crime (which may or may not be committed by residents), apparently evince diminishing marginal relationships at very high levels of neighborhood poverty. Again, this corresponds well with the observed pattern of housing prices and rents summarized in figure 6.3.

Assisted Housing and Neighborhood Property Values and Crime

Several methodologically rigorous statistical studies have examined whether the addition of different sorts of affordable housing into neighborhoods affected proximate property values in nonlinear ways.[57] Amy Schwartz, Ingrid Gould Ellen, and Ioan Voicu focused on newly constructed affordable housing projects in New York City. They identified evidence consistent with substantial positive price impacts from these developments, which decayed over distance up to two thousand feet.[58] Higher concentrations of new dwellings generated larger positive spillovers, but with diminishing returns. Context also mattered, however: the marginal positive impact of each new unit was greater in poorer neighborhoods.[59]

With colleagues Anna Santiago, Robin Smith, and Peter Tatian, I studied

Table 6.1. Summary of statistical estimates of threshold property value impacts of assisted housing

Neighborhood Context	Dispersed Public Housing (Denver)	Housing Choice Voucher (Section 8) (Baltimore County)
Higher-value, less vulnerable	POSITIVE impact if not more than five sites are within 1,000 to 2,000 feet	POSITIVE impact if not more than three sites are within 500 feet
	NEGATIVE impact if more than one site is within 1,000 feet, or more than five sites are within 1,000 to 2,000 feet	NEGATIVE impact if more than three sites are within 500 feet (maximum number observed = 4)
Lower-value, more vulnerable	Small POSITIVE impact if not more than four sites are within 1,000 to 2,000 feet	NEGATIVE impact if any sites are within 2,000 feet. Size of impact grows with number of sites.
	NEGATIVE impact if more than four sites are within 1,000 to 2,000 feet	Impact slightly mitigated if the same number of Section 8 tenants are in fewer sites

Source: Galster et al., 1999; Galster, Tatian and Smith, 1999; Santiago, Galster and Tatian, 2001; see text.

the price impacts of scattered-site public housing in Denver, Colorado, typically developed through the acquisition of single-family dwellings at foreclosure sales and their subsequent rehabilitation.[60] Proximity to such sites in the range of one to two thousand feet generally resulted in higher home prices than would have been predicted otherwise. The magnitude and direction of implied impact clearly proved contingent, however, on the concentration of scattered-site facilities in the neighborhood and on the neighborhood's submarket position. There was a threshold pattern whereby home price impacts became negative when more than a critical mass of public housing sites or dwelling units was located in a neighborhood. This vulnerability from "reconcentration" was most acute in lower-value neighborhoods, especially where homeowners perceived a vulnerability to their quality of life. I present the details of these nonlinear results in the left column of table 6.1.

We also investigated the home price impacts of the Housing Choice Voucher (formerly Section 8) rental subsidy program in Baltimore County, Maryland.[61] In-moving tenants using vouchers had no impact on single-family home prices within two thousand feet in the average neighborhood in which they were located. Once more, however, the magnitude and direction of relationships were contingent on the interaction between neighborhood context and voucher-holder concentration. The in-migration of households using vouchers into a higher-valued neighborhood resulted in higher home prices nearby (arguably due to the structural rehabilitation that participation in the county's voucher program required), unless the concentration exceeded three households within a five-hundred-foot radius. In lower-valued, higher-poverty neighborhoods where owners felt more vulnerable to forces of decline, however, *any* additional voucher households had a harmful influence on home prices. I present these nonlinear, contingent results in greater detail in the right column of table 6.1.

A pair of careful recent studies explored how voucher holder concentrations affected neighborhood crime rates.[62] Susan Popkin and colleagues probed the criminogenic consequences of using vouchers to relocate former public housing tenants in Chicago and Atlanta whose original dwellings were demolished as part of redevelopment efforts.[63] They found strong evidence of threshold effects from concentration, which differed by type of crime and city. In Chicago, a neighborhood with between two and six relocated voucher households (per thousand households) at the beginning of a quarter had 5 percent higher rates of violent crime and property crime during that quarter than a neighborhood with no relocated households, other things being equal. Relocated households using vouchers had no effect on gun-related crime in Chicago, or on either property or violent crime in Atlanta, until they reached a higher critical point of between six and fourteen relocated households per thousand, however.

Leah Hendey, Susan Popkin, Chris Hayes and I conducted a complementary study of the crime impacts of the generic Housing Choice Voucher program in Chicago.[64] We discovered that growth in the rate at which voucher holders moved into a neighborhood during a quarter only became positively associated with increases in property crime rates during the subsequent quarter if the starting concentration of voucher holders exceeded sixty-eight per thousand households (that is, about 7 percent of the population). By contrast, we could not identify any critical points or other nonlinear patterns involving changes in voucher holder concentrations and subsequent changes in violent crime rates in Chicago neighborhoods.

In sum, the evidence from studies of the impact of assisted housing provides further confirmation for the patterns I have previously described. Negative neighborhood reactions like higher crime rates and lower property values are only likely to occur once a critical rate of poverty has been exceeded. In the case of more disadvantaged households added to a neighborhood through assisted housing policy, the greater the initial level of poverty in the neighborhood, the lower the extra number of disadvantaged households that can be added before the critical value is exceeded.

Proposition of Linked Threshold Effects

In this chapter, I have demonstrated that nonlinear, typically thresholdlike relationships are exhibited in many realms of neighborhood dynamics.[65] A holistic synthesis of this evidence suggests that a neighborhood's conditions will only change rapidly and substantially if certain critical points for its residents and property owners are exceeded; but for these altered neighborhood conditions to affect residents' behaviors, they must themselves exceed other critical points. I summarize this in the fourth major proposition of this book.

> *Linked Threshold Effects*: Individual mobility and housing investment decisions are triggered discontinuously once perceptions and expectations regarding the neighborhood have exceeded critical values. Aggregations of individual actions typically lead to large changes in neighborhood conditions only after these causal forces exceed a critical point. Once begun, aggregate changes in neighborhood conditions progress over time in a nonlinear fashion once they exceed another critical point. Many effects of neighborhood conditions on residents and property values only occur once critical values of conditions are exceeded, but eventually the marginal impacts of these conditions may wane at extreme values.

Conclusion

Nonlinear and threshold relationships are common in the neighborhood context, relating both to the effect of neighborhood on individuals and the causes of neighborhood changes. An amalgam of often reinforcing processes related to socialization, gaming, tolerance, contagion, and tolerance generate these relationships. At the individual level, the evidence shows that the likelihood of white households moving out of a neighborhood increases dramatically after a critical value of the percentage of minorities and/or the growth in this percentage is exceeded. The odds that a household of any race will move into a neighborhood are also related to the racial composition of that destination in a highly nonlinear way. Analogously, dwelling owners are unlikely to reinvest in their properties unless critical values of neighboring owners are already doing so. Neighborhood disadvantage, rates of poverty, and rates of affluence often influence in nonlinear ways the likelihood that individuals will engage in various economic and social behaviors. Not surprisingly because of these individual behavioral foundations, neighborhood-level changes in the poverty rate exhibit nonlinear dynamics, in turn generating nonlinear reactions in neighborhood crime rates and property values. The existence of nonlinear and threshold effects holds powerful implications for both the social rationale for and strategic formulation of neighborhood revitalization and resident diversification policies, presented in chapters 9 and 10.

SEVEN

Neighborhood Segregation
by Class and Race

Some of the most obvious and enduring features of the American metropolitan landscape are the stark differences in who lives where. The residential populations inhabiting a neighborhood typically consist of one predominant racial or ethnic group ("race" hereafter) and represent a narrow range of incomes and wealth ("class" hereafter). This homogeneity, as viewed within neighborhoods, translates into a geographic pattern of segregation when viewed among neighborhoods. As I will demonstrate in chapters 8 and 9, this segregation by race and class is as pernicious in its impact as it is clear-cut in its existence. My first purpose here is to document the status of neighborhood segregation by race and class, and to explain how neighborhoods transition from occupancy primarily by one group into occupancy by another. Second, I aim to develop a conceptual model of metropolitan structures and causal forces within which one can perceive the causes of neighborhood segregation by race and class holistically.

At the outset, it is useful once more to consider this topic from the perspective of adding more realism to my Housing Submarket Model of neighborhood change. In this chapter, I relax the prior assumptions that (1) preferences for the neighborhood population components of housing quality are homogeneous among households; (2) housing search outcomes are race neutral; (3) willingness and ability to pay for housing can always be freely exercised, subject to information constraints; and (4) suppliers of housing can develop wherever in whichever quality submarket category they find most profitable. As for the first point, the current neighborhood racial, ethnic, and income group composition is potentially assessed as "quality" differently, depending on the race, ethnicity, and income of the particular household. Thus, sorting within a generically defined housing quality submarket may occur by those seeking more homogeneity of households occupying the housing stock in the neighborhood in question. As for the second and third points, here I allow for the possibility of illegal discriminatory acts constraining the housing and neighborhood options available to minority home seekers. Finally, I will consider the role of local governments in limiting via land-use regulations the types and qualities of dwellings that can be developed within the jurisdiction, thereby producing more homogeneous spatial clusters of submarkets, and ultimately income groups, than would have been produced by an unfettered market.

Segregation by Class and Race: Trends and the Current Situation

Segregation by Class

National trends in rising inequality in household income and wealth, which academic work and the popular press have documented well, are mirrored by increases in the degree to which households in different income groups live apart from each other.[1] No matter how economic segregation is measured, trends show dramatic if uneven growth in the degree of segregation by income since the 1970s.[2] Sean Reardon and Kendra Bischoff, for example, used the proportion of families living in neighborhoods that have median income at least 50 percent above the metropolitan area median income ("extremely affluent") or 50 percent below area median income ("extremely poor") to reveal changes in the degree to which American families are residing in communities stratified by economic status.[3] They found that in 2012, 34 percent of American families lived in neighborhoods that were either extremely affluent or extremely poor, a rate that is more than double the 15 percent rate observed in 1970.[4] The magnitude of income disparity between neighborhoods is substantial, even when not considering the income group extremes. To illustrate, Stuart Rosenthal and Stephen Ross showed that the median income of neighborhoods in the 75th percentile of the national metropolitan neighborhood distribution was 55 percent more than the median income of neighborhoods in the 25th percentile.[5]

Despite the overall upward trend in neighborhood segregation by income, there remains considerable diversity of incomes in the average American neighborhood, though less so at the extremes noted above. With colleagues Jason Booza and Jackie Cutsinger, I probed the economic composition of metropolitan neighborhoods in 2000, categorized by various median income ranges.[6] In very low-income neighborhoods (that is, those with median incomes below 50 percent of the area's median income), 59 percent of the residents had incomes below 50 percent of the area median, 19 percent were between 50 and 80 percent of the area median, 8 percent were between 80 and 100 percent of the area median, and only 14 percent earned more than the area median income. At the other extreme, in very high-income neighborhoods (that is, those with median incomes above 150 percent of the area's median income), 62 percent of the residents had incomes above 150 percent of the area median, 11 percent were between 120 and 150 percent of the area median, 7 percent were between 100 and 120 percent of the area median, and only 20 percent earned less than the area median income. In moderate-income neighborhoods (that is, those with median incomes between 80 and 100 percent of the area's median income) there was considerably more diversity: each of the six income groups specified by US Department of Housing and Urban Development guidelines comprised at least 12 percent of the population, and none exceeded 22 percent. We also identified a rapidly growing phenomena we called "bipolar neighborhoods:" those whose populations are jointly dominated by families earning less than 50 percent and those earning more than 150 percent of the area's median income.[7] At the same time, we also highlighted a distinctive reduction in neighborhoods having the greatest diversity of income groups: those with median incomes in the middle ranges.[8]

Although the growth of more homogeneously affluent neighborhoods is an important contributor to the rise of economic segregation,[9] most of the public concern about the issue stems from the rise of spatially concentrated disadvantage. Paul Jargowsky documented trends in the proportion of Americans living in neighborhoods with a poverty rate of 40 percent or greater in a series of reports. He demonstrated that there was substantial growth in concentrated poverty from 1970 to 1990, a decline of such neighborhoods during the prosperous 1990s, but then a substantial rebound in concentrated poverty since 2000, due largely to the Great Recession.[10] Since 2000, the number of extreme poverty neighborhoods swelled by more than 75 percent and the number of Americans living in such neighborhoods rose from 7.2 million to 13.8 million people, a remarkable increase of more than 90 percent.[11]

Neighborhood Class Transitions

A related important issue is the degree to which patterns of neighborhood income segregation are stable over time across geography. That is, does the economic profile of a neighborhood typically remain constant over long periods, or are upward and downward income succession common? The answer depends on how one measures neighborhood economic status and its change, and what period and which type of neighborhood one considers.[12] The general pattern is that there is considerable flux in neighborhood status, though there is more stability at both extremes of neighborhood affluence and disadvantage, however measured. How much flux there will be varies according to the decade, the metropolitan scale, and the overall economic circumstances in the particular metropolitan area during that decade.

Looking across all metropolitan neighborhoods from 1970 to 2000, Stuart Rosenthal found the greatest stability among neighborhoods with less than 15 percent poverty rates, on average: 81 percent of them in that category in 1970 remained in the same category by 2000.[13] Among neighborhoods with over 45 percent poverty, 43 percent remained in the same category between 1970 and 2000. Those with intermediate levels of poverty were less stable: roughly 60 percent of these neighborhoods failed to retain their 1970 absolute poverty status by 2000. Analyses of Los Angeles County neighborhoods by Robert Sampson, Jared Schachner, and Robert Mare suggest that relative stability at the extremes is contingent upon metrowide economic conditions. During the 1990 to 2000 period, 97 percent of neighborhoods in the poorest quintile measured by median income remained in that category, but from 2000 to 2010 only 68 percent of these neighborhoods remained in this category. The comparable figures for neighborhoods starting in the richest quintile were 70 percent and 87 percent.[14] Using changes in finite categories of income understates the variability of neighborhood status over time, however, especially in the extreme poverty categories. With colleagues Roberto Quercia, Alvaro Cortes, and Ron Malega, I employed absolute decadal changes of five percentage points or more in the poverty rate to identify a change in neighborhood status. By this measure, we found that roughly equal thirds of neighborhoods that had 40 percent or higher poverty rates remained stable, experienced upward succession, or experienced downward succession during the ensuing decade.[15]

Stuart Rosenthal has taken the longest-term view of this topic, analyzing neighborhood changes over half a century across thirty-five metropolitan areas.[16] He concluded that change is the norm over this period: on average, a neighborhood changed its median income (relative to the full sample) by 12 to 15 percent in absolute value per decade from 1950 to 2000. Remaining in the same relative median income quartile was still more common at the extremes, however. Thirty-four percent of neighborhoods in the lowest income quartile and 44 percent of those in the highest income quartile in 1950 remained so in 2000; the contrasting figures for the middle two quartiles were only 26 to 27 percent. Of those neighborhoods substantially changing their relative position, most neighborhoods in the lower half of the income distribution tended to move up in status, while most neighborhoods in the upper half tended to move down.[17]

Perhaps the highest-profile type of neighborhood class transition is termed "gentrification": a process by which many households of greater socioeconomic status move into neighborhoods occupied predominantly by lower-income households.[18] Though scholars have employed the term gentrification in different ways, Ingrid Ellen and Lei Ding provide an appealing formulation that provides a clear portrait of the significance of this phenomenon in US metropolitan areas over the last three decades.[19] They examine the degree to which low-income central-city neighborhoods (census tracts having median household incomes placing them below the 40th percentile of their metropolitan area's neighborhood income distribution) have exhibited substantial increases in their neighborhood's standing relative to that of their metropolitan area (that is, an increase in the ratio of the neighborhood mean to the metropolitan mean of the particular indicator by more than ten percentage points) during a decade. During the 1980s, about 9 percent of these neighborhoods experienced such a substantial increase in their relative median incomes; during the 1990s and 2000s this figure rose to 14 percent. Changes appear even more prevalent when measured by shares of college-educated people. During the 1980s, about 27 percent of low-income neighborhoods saw their relative share of college-educated residents rise substantially; this dropped slightly to 25 percent during the 1990s, but rose to 35 percent during the 2000s.

Beyond describing the frequencies of various types of neighborhood class transitions, several researchers have probed the predictors of such changes using sophisticated multivariate models. Stuart Rosenthal showed that the older the housing stock in a neighborhood, and the more that stock represented subsidized housing, the greater its chances of experiencing a decline in its economic status.[20] Several analyses of patterns from the 1970s and 1980s indicated that higher percentages of black residents predicted subsequent declines in the average income levels of the neighborhood, though this relationship may have reversed itself more recently; moreover, the relationship appears not to be the same for Hispanic neighborhood composition.[21] More home foreclosures and higher percentages of renter-occupied dwellings also are predictive of the declining economic status of neighborhoods.[22]

Segregation by Race

Economic inequality across American neighborhoods often overlaps with racial and ethnic inequality.[23] According to a variety of commonly used measures,[24] the residential segregation of blacks and non-Hispanic whites continues to be extremely high in many metropolitan areas, although black/white segregation has declined steadily since 1970.[25] The average metropolitan black household in 2010 lived in a neighborhood that was 41 percent black and 40 percent white. Measures of evenness in the spatial distribution of both Hispanics and Asians relative to whites show, on the contrary, slight increases in segregation over time, though they still do not approach the geographic dissimilarity of blacks and whites in most areas. The residential isolation of Hispanics and Asians also has increased over time, consistent with the rapid population growth of both groups. The average metropolitan Hispanic household in 2010 lived in a neighborhood that was 42 percent Hispanic and 40 percent white; the comparable figures for Asians were 18 and 52 percent.[26]

As stark as these figures are, they are even more dramatic for children, who are more residentially segregated by race than adults are. Ann Owens has documented that, in the one hundred largest metropolitan areas in 2010, the average black child lived in a neighborhood where only 22 percent of children were white and over half were black, whereas the average black adult lived in one where 33 percent of adults were white and only 46 percent were black.[27] The average Hispanic child lived in a neighborhood where 55 percent of children were Hispanic and 25 percent were white; the average Hispanic adult lived in one where 45 percent of adults were Hispanic and 35 percent were white.

Neighborhood Racial Transitions

Though it is clear that American neighborhoods' racial compositions typically are not representative of their corresponding metropolitan area's composition, there certainly are examples of diverse neighborhoods. In an encouraging trend, they appear to be both growing in number and becoming more stable in their diversity over time. Ingrid Ellen, Keren Horn, and Katherine O'Regan examined metropolitan neighborhoods from 1990 to 2010 and found that the share they considered integrated (that is, those in which the group in the minority comprised at least 20 percent of the population) rose from slightly less than 20 percent to slightly more than 30 percent during this twenty-year period.[28] This increase was due to both a small increase in the number of neighborhoods becoming integrated for the first time and a more sizable increase in the share of integrated neighborhoods that remained so during the period. Indeed, stability of integration was the hallmark: between 1990 and 2000, 77 percent of integrated neighborhoods remained so; from 2000 to 2010, this percentage rose to 82 percent. Neighborhoods that experienced a larger growth of minority residents during the prior decade, were located closer to areas of minority concentration, and had more homeowners with children were less likely to remain stably integrated.[29]

The typical residential mobility dynamic fueling integration was minority households moving into neighborhoods predominantly occupied by whites. The predominantly white-occupied neighborhoods that ultimately became more integrated began the decade with slightly lower percentages of white residents, homeownership rates, and median incomes, and were somewhat closer to minority-dominated areas. Ellen, Horn, and O'Regan also showed that white in-migration was most likely to be the force integrating lower-income, primarily renter-occupied, center-city minority neighborhoods. This latter mobility pattern appears to be rapidly accelerating. Ellen and Ding demonstrated that in recent decades a growing number of low-income central-city (predominantly minority-occupied) neighborhoods witnessed large increases (i.e., more than ten percentage points) in their percentages of white residents relative to their metropolitan area's percentage.[30] During the 1980s, only about 5 percent of such low-income minority neighborhoods saw their relative share of white residents rise substantially; this rose slightly to 7 percent during the 1990s, but jumped to 16 percent during the 2000s.

The Dynamics of Neighborhood Change by Class and Race

The foregoing descriptive portrait of neighborhood class and race profiles makes it clear that, while segregation is the norm in aggregate, many individual neighborhoods experience considerable flux in the composition of their populations. Why this process of neighborhood population change occurs and why it sometimes yields a wholesale replacement of one group by another instead of a stable mix has been the subject of considerable investigation. On the one hand, the process of neighborhood class or racial change is deceptively simple: if the composition of the in-movers does not match the composition of the out-movers, the neighborhood's aggregate composition must change. What makes this process fascinating is that the aggregate composition of the neighborhood will partly influence the composition of both in- and out-movers. Thus, these flows of people are endogenous because people react to neighborhood composition and, by doing so, change it. The fact that the groups competing for housing in the neighborhood many not similarly value its aggregate class or racial composition is the reason why a mixture of groups may not prove stable. In this section, I present a simple model of the neighborhood transition process that makes these points clear and demonstrates their import.[31]

To understand why neighborhoods change their population composition, one must focus fundamentally on who is moving in, instead of who is moving out.[32] A simple thought experiment suffices to make this vital point. Imagine some hypothetical neighborhood, with a mix of groups X and Y currently in residence. Now if only members of group X were to occupy every vacancy opening up in the neighborhood for the indefinite future, the neighborhood must inevitably change to represent a greater and greater share of X residents, so long as some vacancies are generated by members of group Y. The *rate* at which the neighborhood will change its composition will be influenced by whether the in-flow and out-flow profiles match, but its ultimate fate will not. It follows, then, that one must ultimately base a model of neighborhood population transition on which group(s) will most likely comprise the stream of in-movers.

The Willingness to Pay Model offers a simple but powerful way to accomplish this.[33] In simplest form, it assumes that two distinct class or race groups are competing for housing in a particular hypothetical neighborhood containing housing of a homogeneous quality. Purchasing power and preferences for housing and the residential composition of the neighborhood are assumed to be homogeneous within, but not across, both groups. In a world of perfect information and no discrimination, any housing vacancy in this neighborhood will be allocated to any member of the group who is willing to pay more.[34] Each member of the homogeneous group may be thought of as having an implicit "willingness to pay" function that indicates how much the household is willing and able to pay to occupy a vacant dwelling in the neighborhood in question, for each alternative class or race composition of that neighborhood. The variations in willingness to pay across these alternative compositions are a manifestation of the common preferences among households in the group: they will manifest greater willingness to pay for the preferred compositions in direct relation to the strength of this preference. Holding constant for the moment the neighborhood composition, the aggregate supply-and-demand characteristics present in the housing quality submarket represented in the hypothetical neighborhood will influence the amount that a typical member of the particular group is willing to pay. If, for example, the group's population has been growing rapidly and the target

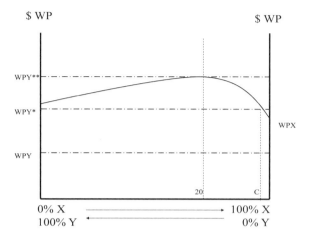

Figure 7.1. The Willingness to Pay Model of neighborhood composition, and its stability. Source: author's adaptation based on Schnare and MacRae 1978; Colwell 1991; and Card, Mas, and Rothstein 2008.

submarket in question has been inelastic in its response across the metropolitan region, the level of willingness to pay for any such vacant dwellings in this neighborhood will ratchet upward.

A graphic exposition of the Willingness to Pay Model demonstrates the insights it provides for explaining neighborhood change and the tenuousness of diverse populations in neighborhoods. Start with a hypothetical neighborhood containing housing of a homogeneous quality, which remains so throughout this illustration. The two household groups competing for this neighborhood are X and Y. I show the possible combinations of these two groups residing in the neighborhood along the horizontal axis of figure 7.1; the willingness to pay is measured on the vertical axis. Assume that all members of group X prefer "modest integration:" 20 percent Y and 80 percent X neighbors, with marginally less desire to have ever greater or ever smaller percentages of their own group as neighbors. By contrast, assume that all members of group Y are indifferent to the race or class composition of their neighbors: X and Y neighbors are perfect substitutes. These last two assumptions imply that members of X will be willing to pay the most if the neighborhood exhibits 80 percent of X, but there is no variation in the willingness to pay by members of Y regardless of the neighborhood's composition.

Suppose that group X was initially the sole occupier of the neighborhood. In this situation, there may be little competition from group Y because perhaps they are few in number in the region, have insufficient incomes to consider bidding for housing in the neighborhood, or happily occupy housing elsewhere. In this initial circumstance, whenever a vacancy appears, the higher bidder will emerge from group X because its willingness-to-pay function (shown as *WPX* in figure 7.1) dominates that of group Y (shown as *WPY*). The in-movers will all be members of group X indefinitely, and the neighborhood composition will remain homogeneously X.

Now suppose that time has passed, and the circumstances of group Y have changed such that they have intensified their competition for this neighborhood, embodied in *WPY**. In this case, a vacancy occurring in the all-X neighborhood will be filled by a member of group Y, since *WPY** is greater than *WPX* at 100 percent X. Y will also fill the next vacancy, and so on, until the neighborhood eventually assumes a mixture of *C* percent X and 100 – *C* percent Y residents. If the aggregate personal circumstances, demographic and economic conditions, and housing market context shaping both *WP* functions remain constant, the neighborhood will remain stably mixed at this composition indefinitely. Both X and Y have equal odds of winning the competition for any vacancy occurring in a neighborhood with *C* percent X population. Should the in-mover randomly turn out to be a member of group X, the neighborhood percentage of X will exceed *C* and a member of group Y thus will win the bid for the next vacancy, restoring stability at *C*. The opposite will occur should the in-mover be a member of group Y. However, should the level of *WPY* continue to rise, the neighborhood's share of Y will as well. Eventually this share will reach 20 percent with *WPY***, the threshold of instability (that is, the tipping point) in this particular case. Any further shifts upward in *WPY* will mean that the neighborhood will tip inexorably to occupancy solely by group Y members, as they will continue to outbid group X for any future vacancies, regardless of its composition.[35]

Despite its many simplifying assumptions, the Willingness to Pay Model illuminates several realistic generalizations regarding the prospects for stable diversity of groups in neighborhoods. The chances of a substantial diversity of groups in a particular neighborhood remaining stable over time will be enhanced the degree to which one or more of the groups manifest certain characteristics. These include (1) being unwilling to pay substantially more for larger shares of their own group, (2) being willing to pay substantially more for diverse neighborhoods instead of those where one group predominates, (3) not rapidly changing the number of households competing for the housing submarket(s) predominant in the particular neighborhood, and (4) not being systematically underrepresented in the bidding process for dwellings in the neighborhood due to spatial biases (discussed in chapter 5) or illegal discriminatory barriers.

There have been numerous attempts over the last half century to develop conceptual and simulation models trying to explain how segregation of groups can be an equilibrium outcome of an unfettered housing market allocation process driven only by preferences for composition of the neighborhood.[36] The latest generation of agent-based (cellular automata) computer models has shown how complex aggregate patterns of residential segregation can arise from a small set of simple, agent-level social dynamics operating within stylized metropolitan contexts.[37] This outcome is not inevitable, however; it depends on the nature of stylized preferences specified. This has been convincingly demonstrated by Elizabeth Bruch and Robert Mare, who show that considerable segregation results when simulated individuals equally prefer all options when they are in the majority over all options where they are in the minority.[38] However, when one employs alternatives involving finer gradations of preferences for own-group neighbors, much less segregation is simulated. Finally, when preference structures are simulated that match as closely as possible the range of racial preferences revealed in American public opinion surveys, virtually no segregation emerges.[39]

It is clear that the interactive dynamics that come into play when households are sorting themselves across metropolitan space are much more multifaceted and nuanced than simulations based on stylized preferences can simulate, or than only one aspect of this complex choice problem can explain. In what follows, I advance a conceptual model that attempts to synthesize all the primary causal forces behind neighborhood class and racial composition, and to elucidate how they are interconnected, often in mutually reinforcing ways.

A Structural Model of Neighborhood
Segregation by Class and Race

When viewed independently, multiple and disparate causal forces determine residential segregation by class and segregation by race. When viewed holistically, many of these forces are the same for both types of segregation, and some are distinct but interrelated. More fundamentally, some explanatory forces are endogenous, that is, they are themselves influenced by the degree of segregation extant in the metropolitan area, and the two forms of segregation are themselves mutually reinforcing.[40] I begin presenting this holistic model by delineating each of the proximate causes of class and racial segregation that scholars have forwarded before synthesizing them in a common framework.[41] I believe that this original, holistic framing is powerful

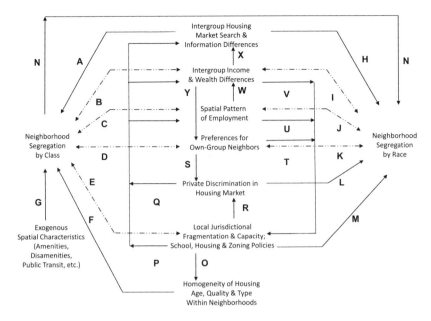

Figure 7.2. A structural model of neighborhood segregation by class and race

because it helps explain why both forms of segregation have been such a durable feature of American neighborhoods.[42]

Proximate Causes of Class Segregation

There are seven distinct proximate causes of the residential segregation of households distinguished by their economic status.[43] First, households will choose locations partly based on their relative valuation of work commuting time and consumption of housing. When confronting a geographic pattern of employment clusters where the value of land per acre is bid up, households making a residential location choice must trade off commuting time with housing expense (and thus the quantity they can consume). If there are substantial differences in the ways that different income groups relatively value these two elements, they will tend to sort spatially according to proximity to employment.[44] See path C in figure 7.2. Of course, this first proximate cause takes no heed of preexisting patterns of housing development, location-specific amenities and disamenities, and overlays of local political jurisdictions. I emphasize these dimensions below.

A second proximate cause is class sorting according to the age of housing stock, a position advanced by Jan Brueckner and Stuart Rosenthal. Assuming that, all else being equal, older housing is generally of lower quality (smaller size, obsolete systems and amenities, health and safety hazards, poorer up-keep, etc.) and is more expensive to maintain at a constant quality, higher income groups will outbid lower-income groups for locations with newer dwellings. Inasmuch as housing typically has been built in a consistent tem-poral pattern from a city's historic core outward, such newer dwellings are more likely to be located nearer the fringes of the urbanized area. The ex-ception is core redevelopment areas that might have witnessed wholesale demolition or rehabilitation of older housing.[45] See path F in figure 7.2.

The third proximate cause is that different classes of households will have different willingness to pay for a wide variety of natural and human-made attributes that vary geographically, often in idiosyncratic ways, across any particular metropolitan area, These attributes are predetermined in the sense that which groups ultimately live near them exert no influence over them. Natural amenities such as scenic waterfronts and desirable topographical features, and human-made attractions such as parks and concentrations of historically significant architecture may serve as magnets for upper-income settlement because of the greater income elasticity of demand for such luxuries.[46] Conversely, areas characterized by undistinguished natural features, few public amenities, and heavy concentrations of pollution will be avoided by higher-income groups, and will be left as residual spaces to households that can only afford the cheapest accommodation.[47] Locations close to public transportation links are also relevant here, though it is less clear whether this amenity is relatively more attractive to the rich who place a higher value on their time, or the poor who may not own a vehicle.[48] See path G in figure 7.2.

The fourth proximate cause is amenities and disamenities associated with neighborhoods that arise endogenously as particular households oc-cupy them.[49] Households with homophily preferences will be more willing to pay to live in neighborhoods where their own income group is domi-nant than in otherwise identical neighborhoods where their group is under-represented, and they will make intraurban mobility choices accordingly.[50] Related preferences to have appropriate peer groups for their children may drive upper-income parents to cluster with parents of similar class status in the same neighborhoods and schools.[51] If lower-income groups are thought to generate negative externalities (such as crime) in the neighborhood, thereby eroding the quality of life and perhaps encouraging socially prob-lematic behaviors by other residents—topics that I will explore in detail in chapter 8—higher-income households will try to avoid neighborhoods where they live in noticeable concentrations.[52] See path D in figure 7.2.

The fifth proximate cause relates to the fragmentation of most US metropolitan areas into many local political jurisdictions such as municipalities, townships, and school districts. To the extent that different classes possess different preferences about how much they are willing to be taxed for locally supplied public services and facilities and the particular composition of those services and facilities, Charles Tiebout has argued that groups will sort across jurisdictions according to the intensity and variety of tax/service package offered.[53] This may be especially important for parents of school-age children who are concerned about peer effects.[54] The greater the number of such jurisdictional variations, the greater the intrajurisdictional class homogeneity and the greater the segregation of classes across metropolitan space.[55] Other local policies related to schools, such as whether to merge districts, develop magnet schools, or permit enrollment across district lines, may also contribute to class segregation by strengthening or weakening the link between neighborhood and school economic composition. See path E in figure 7.2.

The sixth proximate cause is that the existing housing stock in any particular neighborhood is typically quite homogenous in quality (in the broadest sense of quality that I began employing in chapter 3). This homogeneity arises because of location-specific differences in the feasibility and costs of building certain types of housing (such as the availability of bedrock to support high-rise construction), economies of scale in the development of homogeneous subdivisions, and geographic niche specializations of builder-developers.[56] Due to interclass differences in the willingness and ability to pay for different housing quality submarkets (as explained in chapter 3), one would expect that if a neighborhood is dominated by a dwelling stock comprised of only one quality submarket, it will be occupied by a narrow range of income groups. In a special case, large-scale developments of public or other subsidized housing complexes can create spatial dwelling homogeneity occupied only by households within a limited range of incomes because of income-eligibility limits.[57] See path F in figure 7.2.

The last proximate cause is spatial biases in housing market information, which I discussed in length in chapter 5. These biases imply that, once established in a particular geographic pattern, income groups will tend to move between dwellings and neighborhoods in ways that perpetuate current residential patterns of segregation. See path A in figure 7.2.

Of course, all the prior discussions have assumed that there is a nontrivial degree of variability in economic wherewithal among households in the metropolitan area. Obviously, the degree of income and wealth inequality among households is neither constant across metropolitan areas, nor is it constant over time within a metropolitan area. The greater inequality among classes, the more powerful all the above forces are likely to be in producing residential segregation. See path B in figure 7.2.

Proximate Causes of Racial Segregation

There are six proximate causes of racial segregation; five are closely related to their counterpart causes discussed in the context of class segregation.[58] Indeed, the first is class segregation itself. Because of residential segregation by income groups (regardless of its causes) and distinctive interracial differences in the distribution of income and wealth, class segregation will produce de facto racial segregation.[59] See paths N and I in combination in figure 7.2.

The second proximate cause of racial segregation is interracial differences in the spatial distribution of employment. If, for the moment, one takes as fixed both the location of jobs within a metropolitan area and the particular individuals comprising the work force at each such location, one can deduce that workers will tend to cluster around their respective predetermined places of employment to reduce the out-of-pocket and time costs associated with commuting. Because a much higher proportion of all minorities are employed in central cities than are whites, it follows that residential patterns should reflect this disparity, assuming that members of both races are equally averse to commuting.[60] See path J in figure 7.2.

The third proximate cause is preferences for neighborhood racial composition. Both public opinion polls[61] and statistical studies of willingness to pay for housing[62] consistently reveal that most black and Hispanic households most prefer neighborhoods with roughly equal racial proportions, whereas whites generally prefer ones that are predominantly white-occupied. What is less clear is how and the degree to which this combination of preferences dynamically translates into segregation, as discussed at length above.[63] Moreover, whites' expressed aversion to predominantly black-occupied neighborhoods may be related to the freighted stereotypes they hold about such places, as I discussed in chapter 5. See path K in figure 7.2.

The fourth proximate cause is discriminatory acts by private housing market agents, such as property owners and real estate agents, or by private mortgage lenders. Housing market discrimination been documented at the national level in an ongoing series of matched-tester studies by Margery Austin Turner and colleagues.[64] These practices can cause segregation if they serve to exclude minority home seekers from nonminority neighborhoods into which they otherwise would be willing and able to move, or if they render occurrences of neighborhood integration more transitory.[65] The former set of acts includes actions such as "steering" and "exclusion";[66] the latter includes "blockbusting" and "panic peddling."[67] Indeed, it appears that minorities' chances of encountering discrimination are much higher when they attempt to secure housing in majority white-occupied neighborhoods.[68] Denial of mortgage finance (or its provision only on less favorable terms) may also hinder minorities' ability to move into predominately owner-occupied neighborhoods that might be primarily occupied by whites.[69] See path L in figure 7.2.

The fifth proximate cause is racially discriminatory acts and policies by public institutions and governmental bodies. Douglas Massey and others have documented the sordid mid-twentieth century history of segregationist policies promulgated by federal mortgage guarantors and public housing agencies.[70] Explicitly discriminatory local government actions of various sorts also reinforced segregation across the country.[71] Though the contemporary extent of this factor is difficult to quantify, the periodic filings of federal legal suits directed at localities' fair housing violations suggests that this issue has not been relegated to history. Even in the absence of illegal actions, local policies related to schools, such as whether to merge districts, develop magnet schools, or permit enrollment across district lines may contribute to racial segregation by strengthening or weakening the link between neighborhood and school racial composition. See path M in figure 7.2.

The last cause of racial segregation is misinformation about housing opportunities extant in neighborhoods where few members of one's own racial group reside.[72] Due to the aforementioned spatial biases in one's information acquisition process, minority households may have insufficient, inaccurate, and biased information about the quality of life and relative expense of housing in neighborhood inhabited primarily by whites, and vice versa.[73] If their ambient level of information leads both groups to underestimate systematically the quality of life and overestimate the expensiveness of housing in the other group's neighborhoods, they may not bother to search there for housing options. See path H in figure 7.2.

Interactions among Proximate Causes

Thus far, I have listed proximate causes of segregation as if they were independent. Clearly, they are not. Consider first the role of local jurisdictional public policies regarding affordable housing and land use zoning patterns. In the extreme, a jurisdiction may forbid any public and other forms of subsidized housing and require single-family detached homes to be built on large plots of land, thus generating a high housing cost range across the jurisdiction. Though less exclusionary than this extreme case, jurisdictions that establish large-scale zones exclusively for one particular type of housing structure will increase the homogeneity of housing values within any particular neighborhood.[74] See path O in figure 7.2. Cross-locality variations in nonresidential land use zoning and business attraction policies (development fees, tax abatements, environmental regulations, etc.) will also shape the spatial pattern of employment in the metropolitan area. Interlocal differences in public service quality, especially as related to health, education, recreation, and safety, will produce differences in children's ability to develop human capital that ultimately will contribute to intergroup income and wealth differences in the region. See path P in figure 7.2. Finally, such differences in local public service quality can promote racial discrimination because real estate agents can use such invidious distinctions as a basis for steering white home seekers away from racially diverse jurisdictions by using the subterfuge that "they have inferior services and schools."[75] See path R in figure 7.2.

Discrimination in the housing and mortgage markets imposes direct penalties (in the form of information and money) on minorities whom it victimizes. As John Yinger has demonstrated, discrimination reduces minorities' net benefits from searching in the housing market because it erodes the quantity and quality of information that search provides, yielding thereby an estimated annual penalty of billions of dollars in foregone consumers' surplus.[76] There will be additional financial penalties exacted from minorities when they face discriminatory terms in renting accommodations or securing mortgage credit.[77] Thus, in this manner discrimination contributes to interracial disparities in both information and economics; see path Q in figure 7.2.

Preferences for neighbors predominantly of one's own economic or racial group also influence other proximate causes. Real estate sales agents may be loath to show minority home seekers vacancies in neighborhoods where their current or prospective white customer base resides if they perceive that customer base as having strong racial prejudices that might motivate retaliation against any agents who attempt to break unwritten color lines.[78] Analogously, landlords of large apartment buildings who perceive their current white tenants as willing to pay a greater premium for a homogenous clientele than prospective minority tenants will have strong economic motives to cater to their white customers' preferences and exclude any minority renters. See path S in figure 7.2. Strong preferences for homophily on class or race grounds can stimulate the formation and preservation of fragmented local political jurisdictions, since they can more effectively achieve homogeneous communities through the exclusionary school, housing and zoning policies enacted by such entities. See path T in figure 7.2.

The residential preferences of their residents and other proximate causes of segregation jointly influence features of local governments. Jurisdictions with the good fortune to have a high-income resident profile and a strong nonresidential tax base will find themselves with an enviable fiscal capacity; see paths V and U in figure 7.2.

The spatial pattern of employment in a metropolitan area may have an impact on interracial differences in income and wealth. According to John Kain's well-known "spatial mismatch hypothesis," the spatial separation from where most minorities live and where most appropriately skilled employment growth is located, coupled with informal, spatially constrained job search techniques typically employed by minority job seekers, reduces minority employment opportunities.[79] See path W in figure 7.2.

Finally, intergroup differences in economic wherewithal will influence the nature, extent and modes of housing market search undertaken. Higher-income households have better access to more sophisticated real estate professionals and electronic sources of information. Income groups also differ in the spatial patterns of housing market information they gather passively, due to their differences in social networks and routine activity spaces, as explained in chapter 5. See path X in figure 7.2. Moreover, greater intergroup differences in income and wealth will translate into magnified gaps in socioeconomic status that will foment stronger homophily preferences. The larger the intergroup differences in consumption patterns, the less the groups will perceive they have in common. See path Y in figure 7.2.

Mutually Reinforcing Causal Relationships

Not only are the various proximate causes of segregation interrelated, the segregation outcome itself influences many of these factors in turn. It is this complex, mutually reinforcing pattern of relationships, "cumulative causation," that helps explain the durability of segregation in our society. I portray the key mutually reinforcing relationships in my formulation as dashed, double-headed arrows in figure 7.2.

First, not only do predetermined intergroup income and wealth differences generate class and race segregation as a result, but both forms of segregation work over time to perpetuate and magnify these differences, even across generations. See paths B and I. The multiple mechanisms through which these segregation "neighborhood effects" operate and the evidence showing that these effects are substantial will be the subjects of chapters 8 and 9.

Second, not only do the geographic patterns of employment affect where employees choose to live, but the spatial distribution of employment will shift in response once segregated neighborhoods have been established. It is patently clear that the amount and nature of local retail activity, and its associated employment, will evolve in consonance with the economic profile of residents living nearby, as discussed in chapter 3. Neighborhoods exhibiting downward income succession will undergo an unmistakable transformation of the proximate retail environment, with banks replaced by cash-checking outlets, fine dining by fast food, wine shops by liquor stores, dress boutiques by dollar stores, and so on. With extreme concentrations of poverty, the local retail environment may virtually disappear, as we saw in the case of Detroit in chapter 4. This sector may also adapt as a niche market serving a minority racially concentrated environment.[80] More broadly, employers of all sorts may relocate their operations in ways that improve the prospects that their more "desirable" (that is, well off and white) customers and employees will be attracted and retained.[81] In a more subtle way, neighborhood class and racial composition can affect the likelihood that successful entrepreneurs will emerge from a local community because it will shape the financing, training, and potential market they can expect to access, as demonstrated by Timothy Bates.[82] See paths C and J in figure 7.2.

Third, preferences for neighborhood class and racial composition not only lead individuals to make certain residential choices, but the original development and continued reinforcement of such preferences are themselves byproducts of the residential environment. Segregation is fundamental in both shaping and preserving social preferences. One must understand whites' preferences for predominantly white neighborhoods, for example, as a contingent product of twentieth-century urban racial history. More than a century of racial residential separation—explicitly enforced by a host of private and public discriminatory actions, institutional practices and statutes, coupled with unprecedented growth in the (especially Northern) urban black populations—characterizes this history. This residentially constrained but growing black population tended to focus its housing demands on the few neighborhoods bordering the ghetto that were "opened" to blacks, typically through the unscrupulous actions of "blockbusters." The deluge of pent-up black demand, coupled with the scare tactics of blockbusters, steering by real estate agents, and redlining by lenders, quickly tipped neighborhoods from all-white to all-black occupancy.[83] No wonder, then, that many whites still view integration with suspicion. These suspicions are abetted when, in extreme cases of race-class segregation documented by Kenneth Clark, a "ghetto subculture" emerges with distinctive ways of speech, dress, and social interaction.[84] More generally, one is less likely to question or alter homophily preferences if one lives in a segregated environment where the residential contact with other groups is limited, as demonstrated by Gordon Allport and Thomas Pettigrew.[85] See paths D and K in figure 7.2.

Finally, the actions and capacities of local political jurisdictions not only contribute to class segregation but in turn are driven by it. As William Fischel has shown, the school, housing and land use zoning policies promulgated by local political jurisdictions will reflect the political interests of their dominant group and will work in ways that preserve if not enhance their influence. Higher-income residents will contribute more per capita to local property, sales, and income tax bases than those with lower incomes, and are also likely to impose lower municipal costs per capita. Therefore, for instance, upper-income suburbs will be prone to enact strong exclusionary zoning policies to preserve their homogeneity, political dominance, and fiscal capacity.[86] See path E in figure 7.2.

Conclusion

It has been conventional to view residential segregation by economic class and segregation by race or ethnicity as separate features of neighborhoods in America. Though both have evolved in distinctive ways, I have tried to demonstrate in this chapter that these aspects of neighborhoods are fundamentally linked. This is because they share several common proximate causes, influence each other directly, and are both key nodes in a complex web of mutually reinforcing causal links. This cumulative causation model of class and race segregation represents in the most powerful way the central theme of this book: We make our neighborhoods, and then they make us. This holistic portrayal has a clear empirical implication: metropolitan areas that exhibit more class segregation should also exhibit more racial segregation, a result that has been borne out by recent empirical work.[87]

PART 3

Neighborhoods Making Our Selves

EIGHT

The Effects of Neighborhoods on Individual Socioeconomic Outcomes

In chapter 5, I explained one major way that neighborhood affects us: shaping our perceptions and expectations that ultimately shape our residential mobility and housing reinvestment behaviors. Here I turn to an even more significant way in which neighborhoods make us: how neighborhoods directly and indirectly shape adults and children in ways that affect their socioeconomic prospects. I first present a conceptual model showing the relationship between neighborhood context; individual residents' attitudes, behaviors, and attributes; and opportunities for social advancement. I next provide a detailed analysis of the theory and evidence related to the issue of the mechanisms through which neighborhood context exerts its impact on us. Finally, I briefly review the evidence arising from the latest sophisticated statistical evidence that plausibly measures the causal magnitudes of neighborhood effects on a wide variety of individual outcomes contributing to socioeconomic prospects.

A Conceptual Model of How Variations in Spatial Context Generate Inequalities in Socioeconomic Outcomes

In overview, my conceptual model contends that variations in geographic context across multiple scales (neighborhood, jurisdiction, metropolitan region)—what I call "spatial opportunity structure"—affect the socioeconomic outcomes that individuals can achieve in two ways by altering

1. the payoffs that will be gained from the attributes that individuals possess during the period under study, and
2. the bundle of attributes that individuals will acquire, both passively and actively, during their lifetimes.

In the case of the first mechanism, the spatial opportunity structure serves as a mediating factor, translating a person's bundle of individual attributes into achieved status depending on the geography of the individual's residence, work, and routine activity spaces. In the case of the second mechanism, the spatial opportunity structure serves as a modifying factor affecting the bundle of attributes that individuals develop over time in three ways. First, it directly influences the attributes of individuals over which they may exercise little or no volition, such as exposure to environmental pollutants or violence. Second, it directly influences the attributes of individuals over which they exercise considerable volition by shaping what they perceive is the most desirable, feasible option. It does so by influencing (1) what information about the individual's options is provided, (2) what the information objectively indicates about payoffs from these options, and (3) how the information is subjectively evaluated by the individual. These decisions early in life lead people into various path-dependent trajectories of achieved socioeconomic status and subsequent life decisions, in cumulatively reinforcing processes that can stretch across lifetimes and generations. Third, in the case of children and youth, the spatial opportunity structure indirectly influences their attributes through induced changes in the resources, behaviors and attitudes of their caregivers.

Overview and Definitions

Here I focus on understanding how the spaces in which individuals are embedded influence their socioeconomic outcomes. I conceptualize this aspect of space as *spatial opportunity structure*, the panoply of markets, institutions, services, and other natural and human-made systems that have a geographic connection and play important roles in peoples' socioeconomic status achievements.[1] The spatial opportunity structure includes labor, housing, and financial markets; criminal justice, education, health, transportation, and social service systems; the natural and built environment; public and private institutional resources and services; social networks; forces of socialization and social control (collective norms, role models, peers); and local political systems. By achieved socioeconomic status I mean earnings, wealth, and occupational attainment.

Various elements of the spatial opportunity structure operate at and vary across different spatial scales, as I introduced in chapter 1. This variation occurs over at least three distinct spatial scales. Across neighborhoods, variations in safety, natural environment, peer groups, social control, institutions, social networks, and job accessibility occur. Across local political jurisdictions, health, education, recreation, and safety programs vary. Across metropolitan areas, the locations of employment of various types and the associated wages, working conditions, and skill requirements vary, and there are differences in housing and other market conditions that affect individuals' opportunities for advancement.[2] Of course, since the smallest neighborhood scale is nested in all the larger ones, the attributes of all of these spaces become attached to each particular residential location, as I explicated in chapter 2. Thus, we can consider all of them *neighborhood effects*. It is in that sense that I employ this term here.

I view the spatial opportunity structure as affecting socioeconomic outcomes via "structuring opportunity" both directly and indirectly. It directly affects how, during a particular span of time, a set of personal attributes will pay off in terms of socioeconomic status achievements. Over a longer span of time, the spatial opportunity structure indirectly affects the set of attributes that individuals bring to the opportunity structure. Some of these indirect effects require little or no individual volition to acquire. This would include aspects of mental and physical health that may be passively acquired by living in the natural, built, and social environment, and the collective norms and local networks that influence what information people receive and how they evaluate it. In the case of children and youth, other indirect effects transpire through influences on the caregivers that affect the resources and parenting behaviors brought to bear in the household. A final indirect effect occurs by molding individual volition involved in decisions related to cognitive skill development and educational achievement, risky behaviors, marriage, fertility, labor force participation, and illegal activities. Decisions regarding these domains are so crucial in determining socioeconomic outcomes in our society that I label them *life decisions*. Below I amplify and illustrate these concepts and relationships with the aid of a heuristic model.

A Heuristic Model of Achieved Socioeconomic Status

In figure 8.1 I present a visual portrayal of my conceptual framework for understanding how neighborhood effects provide a foundation for inequalities in achieved status. Starting with the most basic and obvious relationship, an individual's attributes will play a fundamental role in producing markers of achieved socioeconomic status; this is represented by path A in figure 8.1. If the individuals in question are adults, one would expect that interpersonal variations in their current bundles of achievement-influencing attributes would explain substantial variation in their contemporaneously measured achieved socioeconomic status; in the case of children, current attributes

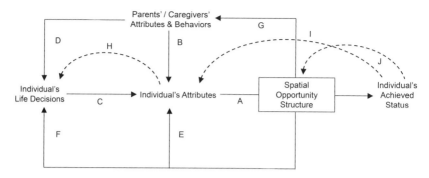

Figure 8.1. Heuristic model of the foundational role of the spatial opportunity structure in achieved socioeconomic status of individuals

would be predictive (though with less precision) of future achieved socio-economic status at some point when they became adults. Some personal characteristics are essentially fixed over the lifetime of the individual, inasmuch as they are associated with the vagaries of conception and birth. Such fixed attributes would include, for example, genetic signature, place and year of birth, and many (though not all) characteristics of the individual's parents and ancestors. Other personal characteristics are potentially more malleable over a lifetime. Some may be acquired passively, such as through childrearing activities of one's parents, as is portrayed in path B in figure 8.1. Other malleable attributes will be the product of previous decisions and actions by the individual even though, once acquired, these attributes may no longer be malleable (e.g., a physical disability or criminal record); this is portrayed as path C in figure 8.1. Some decisions are especially important in establishing a trajectory for achieved status outcomes, what I have previously called life decisions.[3] These would include actions related to employment, crime, childrearing, cognitive and vocational skills, educational credentials, smoking, drinking, substance abuse and other aspects of health, and social networks. Of course, the norms, aspirations, information, and resources that individuals bring to bear in a particular life decision–making situation are substantially influenced by multiple inputs supplied by their parents or caregivers, both currently and perhaps earlier in their lives, as represented by path D in figure 8.1.

Spatial opportunity structure as mediator between personal attributes and achieved status. At this point in my exposition, I take all these fixed and malleable attributes as predetermined so I can isolate one crucial role played by the neighborhood space in which the individual is currently embedded. I posit that the spatial opportunity structure serves as a *mediator* between individuals' current characteristics and their socioeconomic status outcomes; see path A in figure 8.1. The spatial opportunity structure varies dramatically within metropolitan areas in the ways that it evaluates personal attributes in the process of translating them into achieved status. This means that one's chances for such achievements will be enhanced or eroded depending on one's place of residence, work, and routine activity space. Several illustrations serve to make my point. Even the most attractive attributes from an employer's perspective may not yield a high income if the potential employee in question resides far from potential workplaces and cannot find a suitably fast and reliable form of commuter transportation. Underresourced, poorly administered schools with weak teachers and a cadre of disruptive, violent peers will be less likely to leverage students' curiosity and native intelligence into literary and numerical competence and, ultimately, marketable educational credentials for those who have decided to get a diploma. Those who have accumulated little to no labor force experience may find that neighborhoods dominated by illegal or underground markets will favorably evaluate some of their attributes (e.g., present orientation, predilection for violence) that were discounted in mainstream labor markets. Women embedded in neighborhoods dominated by patriarchal norms and collective socialization into rigid gender roles will be less able to convert even the most productive personality attributes and educational credentials into socioeconomic achievements in the larger society.

Spatial opportunity structure as a modifier of personal attributes. As potent as the aforementioned effects of the spatial opportunity structure as mediator may be, it also exerts a powerful influence in three distinct ways through the passive and active acquisition and/or modification of personal attributes over time. First, through environmental exposure it directly influences some attributes of individuals over which they may exercise little or no volition. Second, it directly influences the attributes of individuals over which they exercise considerable volition by shaping what they perceive is the most desirable, feasible option in the process of making life decisions. Third, in the case of children and youth, the spatial opportunity structure indirectly influences their attributes through induced changes in the resources, behaviors, and attitudes of their caregivers. Diagrammatically, I am now turning our attention to explicating paths E, F, and G portrayed in figure 8.1.

The neighborhood's physical and social environment constantly molds an individual's personal attributes, even if such molding has not been consciously chosen and may be unobserved by the individual; this is represented by path E in figure 8.1. Several examples from the physical and social scientific literature illustrate my point. We know, for example, that variations in air pollution are associated with a range of health outcomes.[4] Lead associated with neighborhoods with older housing stock causes permanent damage to children's cognitive functions and attention spans.[5] Exposure to violence (either as a victim or as a witness) creates physical, mental, and emotional responses that, among other things, have been shown to interfere with academic performance.[6]

As noted above, individuals can modify their attributes through their own life decisions. The spatial opportunity structure affects such decisions by shaping an individual's perceptions of what is the most desirable, feasible course of action; I portray this relationship in path F in figure 8.1. The spatial opportunity structure shapes these decisions by influencing (1) what information about the individual's options is provided, (2) what the information objectively indicates about payoffs from these options, and (3) how the information is subjectively evaluated by the individual. I explained these processes in detail in chapter 5 in the context of information used by households and property owners to form attitudes and expectations driving residential mobility and investment behaviors. Analogous processes also work when it comes to information related to the spatial opportunity structure. Therefore, for example, local networks can affect the quantity and quality of information that an individual can access regarding the opportunity set.[7] William Julius Wilson's notion of "social isolation" associated with minority neighborhoods of concentrated disadvantage is illustrative of local networks bereft of information about employment opportunities.[8] The collective norms operating within these networks can also shape which media of information transmission are considered more reliable sources of data about the opportunity structure. Neighborhood or school-based peers, role models, and other collective socialization forces can shape one's norms and preferences, thereby altering the perceived prospective payoffs associated with various life decisions.

Finally, the spatial opportunity structure indirectly affects the attributes that children and youth will exhibit by shaping the resources, attitudes, health, and parenting behaviors of their adult caregivers; this portrayed as path G in figure 8.1. In my discussion of paths E and F, I described the various mechanisms of how spatial context can affect a person's attributes; my point here is simply to note that when such persons happen to be caregivers, they become the medium through which the spatial opportunity structure transmits its impacts to those under their care. As illustration, there is ample evidence that the health (mental and physical) and resources (economic and social) of parents have a profound effect on how children develop in multiple domains.[9] Thus, should the spatial opportunity structure have an impact on any of these domains through any of the causal processes previously modeled, the indirect causal link to the succeeding generation will be made. A variant of this connection is that researchers have observed caregivers altering their parenting styles in response to their perceptions of the spatial context in which their children must operate.[10]

Feedback effects. To complete my conceptual model, I consider several feedback effects, designated with dotted lines in figure 8.1. Once an individual makes a particular life decision, the associated attribute becomes part of the individual's "resume" (path H in figure 8.1). This change in the portfolio of attributes will affect the individual's opportunities in the future, perhaps irreversibly, depending on the life decision in question. Certainly the acquisition of educational credentials provides a lifelong change in one's set of feasible opportunities; so does being convicted of a felony. Less obviously, prior life decisions may reshape individuals' aspirations, preferences, and evaluative frames. For example, the prior decision to raise children may intensify one's aversion to risky entrepreneurial ventures or participation in illegal activities. Similarly, if prior choices to seek long-term employment have consistently been frustrated, one's willingness to invest in human capital development for the future and respect for civil authority may wane, leading to a pessimistic reevaluation of feasible options in the opportunity set. The previous decision to participate in gang activities may expose those individuals to different attitudinal and aspirational norms that likely alter their assessments of many options in the life decision set.

What one has achieved up to a particular moment in terms of markers of socioeconomic status (income, wealth, and occupation) also generates two feedback effects. The first is that the degree of achieved status shapes the bundle of attributes the person will develop in the future by altering the degree of financial constraint on obtaining certain attributes; I represent this by path I in figure 8.1. For example, greater accumulated wealth by a certain time in life permits people to buy superior training and credentials, maintain better health, and free themselves from constraints on employment by offloading some child-care responsibilities on to hired caretakers. One will be exposed to different sources of information, collective norms, peer effects, and role models in the workplace, depending upon occupation.

Finally, and perhaps most fundamentally, achieved status affects what spatial opportunity structure one confronts, as portrayed by path J in figure 8.1. Clearly, for most households in the United States that do not receive subsidies for housing, the neighborhood and associated characteristics of the spatial opportunity structure they will experience will depend on their ability to pay for housing. Residential sorting on the bases of income and wealth is to be expected in an economy where the market performs the main resource allocation functions, as modeled in chapter 3. Ability to pay for products and services will determine degree of exposure to other aspects of the spatial opportunity structure via interfaces with schools, transportation systems, retail shopping, and workplaces. Households with the greatest financial means select what they perceive as the most desirable niches within the spatial opportunity structure in which to live and undertake their routine activities, which are ceteris paribus the most highly priced, of course. The financial exclusivity of these spaces can be abetted by a variety of zoning codes and other development restrictions, if the well-heeled can politically dominate a local jurisdiction to serve their interests, as I explained in chapter 7. At the other extreme of achieved status, households with little to no market power are relegated by default to the least expensive residual pockets of the spatial opportunity structure: slums, ghettos, and the streets.

Cumulative causation and path dependencies. The foregoing model should make it obvious that I view the processes involved in achieving socioeconomic status as cumulative, path-dependent, and typically mutually reinforcing over time. One's stock of attributes measured at any time will be shaped by the neighborhoods one has experienced in the past, both directly and indirectly through their influence on previous life decisions and actions by caregivers. Going forward, this current set of attributes will constrain (to a greater or lesser extent, depending on the attribute bundle and past socioeconomic achievements) the perceived life-decision options and associated expected payoffs. As illustration, a person who has dropped out of high school and served jail time for committing a felony will have far fewer options in the future for attaining higher socioeconomic status than a person who has a graduate degree and no brushes with the law. In addition, the expected financial payoffs associated with any similar life decision options they share (like working full-time) will differ significantly. In turn, these current interpersonal differences in opportunities will lead both people down different paths of life decisions in the future. Abetting this mutually reinforcing sequence of decisions over the life course is the aforementioned financial effect on which neighborhoods one can afford to access. Those whose paths have resulted in substantial achievements in status early in life can afford to occupy more privileged niches in the spatial opportunity structure, thereby providing themselves and their offspring with even better attributes and opportunities, which in turn will spawn even more productive life decisions.

The evolution of the spatial opportunity structure. The foregoing description has taken the housing market, a prime driver of the spatial opportunity structure, as predetermined. From the perspective of an individual decision maker, this is reasonable. From a longer-term general equilibrium perspective, of course, the housing market in particular and the spatial opportunity structure in general is constantly evolving, partly in response to how the population has been sorting themselves as housing demanders across the metropolitan area. As I have documented and analyzed in chapter 7, this sorting process has produced a great deal of racial and class segregation. In the next chapter I will document wide interneighborhood variations in many other contextual indicators. It is beyond the scope of this model to consider all these forces shaping the spatial opportunity structure; nevertheless, a few illustrative comments are in order.

Some of the alterations in the spatial opportunity structure may be exogenous to the actions of households, such as industrial restructuring produced by new technologies or international trade. However, the aggregate behaviors of households within a metropolitan area produced by a previous period's opportunity structure may endogenously influence other alterations. For example, the poor quality of a neighborhood's public school may constrain children's ability to gain good skills and credentials. Yet, if many parents decide to participate in a political process, the result may be a reallocation of fiscal resources to improve the local school. The educational background of the parents of students living in the district also comprises an important element of constraint on school outcomes. Inasmuch as better-educated parents create more intellectually stimulating home environments, better monitor the completion of homework, and demonstrate more interest in what goes on in school, the quality of the classroom environment will improve for all students. So if, in response to inferior public education, better-educated parents move out of the district or enroll their children in private schools, the constraints on all parents who remain in the public school system become tighter. As another example, housing developers may cater to parents who have substantial status achievements by building new, high-quality subdivisions that create exclusive niches in the spatial opportunity structure. After incorporation, these niches may provide a wide range of attractive amenities and public services that encourage the success of the children living there.

Thus, those who are successful in one round of spatial status competition are in a better financial position in the next round to occupy superior neighborhoods within the evolving spatial opportunity structure, thereby improving their and their children's odds of perpetuating this success and generating market forces that alter the structure itself over time. Conversely, those who evince few status achievements early in life are relegated to the multidimensionally inferior, least expensive neighborhoods, where they are induced by the resultant opportunity set to make life decisions that tend to perpetuate their inferior status. When some of these decisions viewed by the larger society as "social problems" become concentrated in the niches low-status people occupy, the larger opportunity structure will morph in many ways. Those with financial means move away from neighborhoods and schools of concentrated disadvantage, weakening the local retail sector and the entry-level job opportunities they provide. These same moves may strain the financial capacity of the local political jurisdiction, forcing a retrenchment in public services. In this fashion, a self-reinforcing spiral of spatial decline and individual impoverishment can be generated in certain locales, as I explained in chapters 3 and 4.

Summary of a Heuristic Model of the Spatial Opportunity Structure

Within the framework I have portrayed in figure 8.1, is it easy to comprehend how space plays a vital role not only as a foundation for current inequality, but for the perpetuation of intergenerational inequality as well. Through cumulative causation and path dependency, those with the greatest status attainments achieved early in adulthood can spatially nest in a neighborhood segment of the opportunity structure that enhances their prospects for continued success and provides their offspring with improved chances for replicating this success themselves. Over time, the spatial opportunity structure in turn evolves in ways that further benefit those with the greatest achieved status. By contrast, those who start with little typically are "stuck in place," both geographically and socioeconomically, as powerfully documented by Patrick Sharkey.[11]

The Mechanisms of Neighborhood Effects

We may now probe more deeply the precise means through which the various dimensions of neighborhood context affect their residents, using the overarching model portrayed in figure 8.1. There have been many scholarly treatises about the potential causal connections between neighborhood context and individual behavioral and health outcomes.[12] Though often in these works the potential mechanisms differ in labeling and categorizations, there is a broad consensus about how the underlying causal paths operate in theory. Unfortunately, there is no consensus about which mechanisms demonstrate the strongest empirical support. Perhaps this is because which mechanism dominates is contingent on the type of person and outcome being investigated. In this section, I list fifteen potential causal pathways between neighborhood context and individual behavioral and health outcomes, synthesizing both sociological and epidemiological perspectives. I provide a new conceptualization of dimensions of neighborhood effect mechanisms that uses a pharmacological "dosage-response" analogy to clarify the empirical challenges of this field of enquiry. I then review empirical studies related to neighborhood effect mechanisms and draw provisional conclusions about the dominant mechanisms operating.

How Does Neighborhood Transmit Effects to Individuals?

My synthesis of the disparate literatures in social science and epidemiology identifies fifteen distinctive types of linkages. I think it most useful to group these fifteen mechanisms of neighborhood effects under four broad rubrics: social-interactive, environmental, geographical, and institutional.[13]

Social-interactive mechanisms. This set of mechanisms refers to social processes endogenous to neighborhoods.

· *Social contagion*: Contact with peers who are neighbors may change behaviors, aspirations, and attitudes. Under certain conditions, these changes can take on contagion dynamics that are akin to "epidemics."
· *Collective socialization*: Individuals may be encouraged to conform to local social norms conveyed by neighborhood role models and other social pressures. Achieving a minimum threshold or critical mass before a norm can produce noticeable consequences for others in the neighborhood characterizes this socialization effect.
· *Social networks*: Information and resources of various kinds transmitted through neighbors may influence individuals. These networks can involve either "strong ties" or "weak ties."
· *Social cohesion and control*: The degree of neighborhood social disorder and its converse, "collective efficacy,"[14] may influence a variety of behaviors and psychological reactions of residents.
· *Competition*: Under the premise that certain local resources are limited and not pure public goods, this mechanism posits that groups within the neighborhood will compete for these resources among themselves. Because the outcome is a zero-sum game, residents' access to these resources and their resulting opportunities may be influenced by the ultimate success of their group in "winning" this competition.
· *Relative deprivation*: This mechanism suggests that residents who have achieved some socioeconomic success will be a source of disamenities for their less well-off neighbors. The latter may view the successful with envy or make them perceive their own relative inferiority as a source of dissatisfaction.

· *Parental mediation*: The neighborhood may affect (through any of the mechanisms listed under all categories here) parents' physical and mental health, stress, coping skills, sensed efficacy, behaviors, and material resources. All of these, in turn, may affect the home environment in which caregivers raise children.

Environmental mechanisms. Environmental mechanisms refer to natural and human-made attributes of the neighborhood that may affect directly the mental or physical health of residents without affecting their behaviors. As in the case of social-interactive mechanisms, the environmental category can also assume distinct forms:

· *Exposure to violence:* If people sense that their property or person is in danger, they may suffer psychological and physical responses that can impair their functioning or sensed well-being. These consequences are likely even more pronounced if the person has been victimized.
· *Physical surroundings:* Decayed physical conditions of the built environment (e.g., deteriorated structures and public infrastructure, litter, graffiti) may impart psychological effects on residents, such as a sense of powerlessness. Noise may create stress and inhibit decision-making through a process of "environmental overload."
· *Toxic exposure:* People may be exposed to unhealthy levels of air-, soil-, or water-borne pollutants because of the current and historical land uses and other ecological conditions in the neighborhood.

Geographical mechanisms. Geographic mechanisms refer to aspects of a neighborhood that may affect residents' life courses solely due to its position in space relative to larger-scale political and economic elements, such as

· *spatial mismatch:* Certain neighborhoods may have little accessibility (in either spatial proximity or as mediated by transportation networks) to job opportunities appropriate to the skills of their residents, and thereby may restrict their employment opportunities.
· *public services:* Some neighborhoods may be located within local political jurisdictions that offer inferior public services and facilities because of their limited tax base resources, incompetence, corruption, or other operational challenges. These, in turn, may adversely affect the personal development and educational opportunities of residents.

Institutional mechanisms. The last category of mechanisms involves actions by those typically not residing in the neighborhood who control important institutional resources located there, or points of interface between neighborhood residents and vital markets:

·   *Stigmatization:* Neighborhoods may acquire stigma based on public stereotypes held by powerful institutional or private actors about its current residents. In other cases this may occur regardless of the neighborhood's current population because of its history; its environmental or topographical disamenities; the style, scale and type of its dwellings; or the condition of its commercial districts and public spaces. Such a stigma may reduce the opportunities of its residents in various ways, such as job options and self-esteem.
·   *Local institutional resources:* Some neighborhoods may have access to few high-quality private, nonprofit, or charitable institutions and organizations such as benevolent associations, subsidized day care facilities, human welfare agencies, and free medical clinics. The lack of these institutions and organizations may adversely affect the personal development opportunities of residents.
·   *Local market actors:* There may be substantial spatial variations in the prevalence of certain private market actors that may encourage or discourage certain behaviors by neighborhood residents, such as liquor stores, fresh food markets, fast food restaurants, and illegal drug markets.

Conceptual Issues in Uncovering and Measuring Mechanisms of Neighborhood Effects

I find it revealing to employ a pharmacological metaphor of *dosage-response* here and frame the conceptual issues as follows: What about a particular "dose of neighborhood" might be *causing* the observed individual "response?" The challenges in answering this deceptively simple question are legion, and my purpose here is to present some of the major ones.[15] If we are to understand deeply why aspects of the neighborhood context affect residents, we ultimately must answer seventeen questions arrayed under three overarching rubrics regarding the *composition, administration, and response to the neighborhood dosage.*

The composition of the neighborhood dosage. What are the "active ingredients" that constitute the dosage? What is it about this space in terms of internal social interactions, environmental conditions, geographic attributes, and reactions of external institutional drivers that is the causal agent, and how can it be measured precisely? If neighborhood is a multidimensional package of causal attributes, as is likely, we must identify and measure directly each part of the package.

The administration of the neighborhood dosage. In this realm, several questions must be addressed.

· *Frequency: How often is the dosage administered?* For example, does a particular form of social interaction occur only rarely or, as in the case of air pollution, does the exposure occur during each inhalation?
· *Duration: How long does the dosage continue, once begun?* Certain social interactions can vary dramatically in their length, whereas the dosage of unresponsive public services and nonexistent facilities can be omnipresent.
· *Intensity: What is the size of the dosage?* How concentrated are the toxins? How weak are the local services? In the case of social interactive causes, the answers to the frequency, duration, and intensity questions will be related to the amount of time the individual spends in the neighborhood and outside the home in "routine activities."
· *Consistency: Is the same dosage being applied each time it is administered?* Do pollutants or the threat of victimization vary daily on the basis of meteorological conditions or time of day?
· *Trajectory: Is the frequency, duration, and intensity of dosage growing, declining, or staying constant over time for the resident in question?* Do the individuals in a rising trajectory context evince fewer effects because they become "immune," or evince stronger effects because their resistance is "weathered?"
· *Spatial extent: Over what scale does the dosage remain constant?* How rapidly do the frequency, duration, intensity and consistency of dosage decay when the subject travels away from the residence? Do any of these gradients vary according to the direction of movement away from the residence?
· *Passivity: Does the dosage require any cognitive or physical action by residents to take effect?* Do residents need to engage in any activities or behaviors, or even be cognizant of the forces operating upon them, for the effect to transpire? In the case of endogenous local social interactions, the answer is probably yes, but not in the case of the other categories of mechanisms.
· *Mediation: Does the resident in question receive the dosage directly or indirectly?* For example, parents directly affected by the neighborhood may mediate neighborhood influences indirectly borne by children.

The neighborhood dosage-response relationship. Again, in this realm we must raise several issues:

- *Thresholds: Is the relationship between variation in any dimension of dosage administration and the response nonlinear?* Are there critical points at which marginal changes in the dosage have nonmarginal effects?

- *Timing: Does the response to the dosage occur immediately, after a substantial lag, or only after cumulative administration?* For example, you might acquire stigma as soon as you move into a certain neighborhood, but eroded health due to lack of local recreational facilities may not show up until much later.

- *Durability: Does the response to the dosage persist indefinitely? Or does it decay slowly or quickly?* The developmental damage done by lead poisoning is, for illustration, indelible.

- *Generality: Are there many predictable responses to the dosage administration, or only one?* Peers may influence a wide variety of adolescent behaviors, whereas certain environmental toxins may have rather narrowly defined health impacts.

- *Universality: Is the relationship between variation in any dimension of dosage administration and the particular response similar across children's developmental stages, demographic groups, or socioeconomic groups?* The same dosage of neighborhood may yield different responses, depending on the developmental or socioeconomic status of those exposed.

- *Interactions: Are dosages of other intra- or extra-neighborhood treatments also being administered that intensify the dosage's expected response?* Different dimensions of neighborhood may be not additive, but multiplicative in their consequences.

- *Antidotes: Are dosages of other intra- or extra-neighborhood treatments also being administered that counteract the dosage's expected response?* For example, efforts to improve residents' health by building new clinics and outreach facilities in the neighborhood may appear to founder if environmental pollution in the area gets worse.

- *Buffers: Are people, their families, or their communities responding to the dosage in ways that counteract its expected response?* Because residents individually and collectively potentially have agency, they may engage in compensatory behaviors that offset negative neighborhood effects, such as when parents keep their children in the home while certain violent youngsters are using the local playground.

Past Investigative Responses and Their Limitations

There are two broad sorts of approaches that social scientists have employed in an attempt to answer the above questions and uncover the dominant neighborhood effect mechanisms at work. The first consists of field-interview studies of people's social relations and networks within neighborhoods and nonresidents' opinions about neighborhoods, involving both quantitative and qualitative analyses of the data collected thereby. The second consists of multivariate statistical studies estimating models of how various neighborhood indicators correlate with a variety of individual outcomes for children, youths, and adults.

Field-interview studies try directly to observe potential mechanisms. In this vein, there have been numerous sociological and anthropological investigations, but they are often limited in their ability to discern the relative contributions of alternative causes because of their qualitative nature and their typical focus on only one set of mechanisms to the exclusion of others. Nevertheless, several have been revealing and remarkably consistent in their findings that allow us to rule out certain potential causes. Moreover, this style of investigation is more appropriate for probing many of the questions noted above, such as active ingredients, passivity, mediation, and buffering of dosages.

The multivariate statistical approach tries to draw inferences about neighborhood effect mechanisms from the statistical patterns observed. It has its own challenges, akin to a physician making a differential diagnosis based on a patient's symptoms and only a partial, poorly measured medical history. One inferential notion that has been used is that if particular descriptors of a neighborhood prove more statistically and economically significant predictors of resident outcomes, they may hint at which underlying process is dominant. For example, imagine that the variable "percentage of residents in the neighborhood who are poor" did not prove statistically significant, but that the variable "percentage of residents in the neighborhood who are affluent" did prove so in a regression predicting outcomes for low-income residents. This would suggest that a positive social externality from the affluent group (such as role modeling), not a negative social externality from the poor group (such as peer effects), was present. Unfortunately, an overview of the research record typically does not produce such unambiguous results for coefficients. Moreover, most of this statistical literature is of little help to us here because it does not disaggregate findings by economic or demographic group. For example, how is one to interpret the finding from a regression model estimated over youth sampled from a variety of income groups that there is a negative correlation between the percentage of poor households in the neighborhood and an individual's chances of dropping out of high school? One cannot make the deduction that nonpoor youth are positively influencing poor youth through role modeling. A second inferential notion often employed draws upon the assumption that different types of neighborhood social externalities yield distinctive functional forms for the relationship between the percentage of disadvantaged or advantaged residents in a neighborhood and the amount of externality generated. For example, collective social norms and social control likely come into play only after a threshold scale of the population group thought to be generating this effect has been achieved in the neighborhood, as I explained in chapter 6. We can use this logic to draw out implications for underlying mechanisms of neighborhood effects if the statistical procedures used to investigate the relationship between neighborhood indicators and individual outcome permit the estimation of nonlinear relationships. Unfortunately, as I documented in chapter 6, few extant empirical studies test for nonlinear relationships between neighborhood indicators and various individual outcomes. Moreover, even if we observe thresholds and other distinctive nonlinear relationships, it need not uniquely identify only one causal mechanism.

In what follows, I will organize the review in subsections corresponding to the foregoing mechanisms of neighborhood effects,[16] bringing to bear evidence from the two approaches as relevant. Before turning to this empirical evidence, however, I note as preface that no definitive, comprehensive study of neighborhood effect mechanisms exists; none examines more than one or two of the above questions for an array of potential causal mechanisms.[17] Indeed, scholars have not addressed most of the questions explicitly in the theoretical or empirical literature. Thus, one should treat my conclusions regarding neighborhood effect mechanisms as provisional.

Evidence on Social-Interactive Mechanisms of Neighborhood Effects

Social contagion and collective socialization. Numerous statistical studies have examined in detail the social relationships of youth from disadvantaged neighborhoods.[18] They have identified links between deviant peer group influences and adolescents' grade point average, mental health, antisocial behavior, school attainment, and substance abuse.[19] Anne Case and Lawrence Katz's investigation of youth in low-income Boston neighborhoods is notable because of its sophisticated efforts to avoid statistical bias.[20] They find that neighborhood peer influences among low-income youth are strong predictors of a variety of negative behaviors, including crime, substance abuse, and lack of labor force participation. Stephen Billings, David Deming and Stephen Ross found with natural experimental data from North Carolina that peer effects on youth criminal behavior arise when school peers of the same race and gender reside less than one kilometer away from each other.[21] This body of scholarship suggests that peer effects and role modeling among disadvantaged young neighbors often generate negative social externalities.[22]

However, the extent to which such negative socialization would diminish in the presence of higher-income youth is unclear. James Rosenbaum and his colleagues have provided a series of studies related to black families living in public housing in concentrated poverty neighborhoods who were assisted (with rental vouchers and counseling) in finding apartments in majority white-occupied neighborhoods of Chicago and its suburbs as part of a court-ordered remedy for the *Gautreaux* public housing discrimination suit.[23] Though he provides one of the most optimistic portraits of the benefits that such moves can provide to black adults and their children, he does not find a great deal of social interchange or networking between these new in-movers and the original residents. Rosenbaum concludes by stressing instead the importance of role models and social norms in middle-class suburban environments for generating positive outcomes for those participating in the Gautreaux program.[24] However, this optimistic conclusion has been challenged by recent qualitative case studies revealing limited role modeling between upper-income and lower-income blacks in gentrifying neighborhoods,[25] and in mixed-income neighborhoods built on redeveloped public housing sites.[26]

The threshold notion embedded implicitly in both the social contagion and collective socialization mechanisms potentially allows them to be identified by regression-based studies that allow for nonlinear relationships between the measure of neighborhood context and the probability of the individual outcome being investigated. My review of this evidence in chapter 6 provides further support for the social contagion and collective socialization processes.

Social networks. Several qualitative studies based on field evidence investigate the social networks of blacks in US urban areas.[27] They find that, controlling for personal income, those in areas of concentrated poverty typically are more isolated within their households and have fewer close external ties, especially with those who are employed or well educated. Black females' volume, breadth, and depth of social relationships in poor neighborhoods are especially attenuated. Because job seekers in US high-poverty areas often rely upon neighbors for potential employment information, the situation appears ripe for neighborhood effects in such disadvantaged places, manifested as resource-poor social networks.

Statistical studies provide further support to the hypothesis that the social network mechanism of neighborhood effect has veracity when it comes to finding employment in the United States. Welfare participation appears to be enhanced by geographic proximity to others on welfare, especially if these proximate others speak the individual's language.[28] People who live on the same census block also tend to work on the same census block because they interact very locally when exchanging information about jobs, even when one controls for personal characteristics.[29] Consistent with sociological field evidence above, interactions are stronger between individuals who share a common education.[30]

Evidence also suggests that the social networks established in disadvantaged US neighborhoods may be so influential that they are difficult to break even after people move away. Xavier de Souza Briggs examined the social networks of black and Hispanic youth who participated in a court-ordered scattered-site public housing desegregation program in Yonkers, New York, during the 1990s.[31] He found few differences in the network diversity or types of aid provided through networks between youth who moved to developments in white middle-class neighborhoods and those who remained in traditional public housing in poor, segregated neighborhoods. The former group did not leverage any benefits of living in more affluent and racially diverse areas, and their social ties typically remained within the common race and class confines of their scattered-site developments. Other studies found that families participating in the Moving to Opportunity demonstration in Chicago were likely to maintain close social ties with their former poverty-stricken neighborhoods even after they moved a considerable distance away to low-poverty neighborhoods.[32] More than half of those families indicated that their social networks were located somewhere other than their new neighborhood.

A large number of US-based field studies provide a complementary view. They consistently show that the social interaction among members of different economic groups is quite limited, even within the same neighborhood or housing complex.[33] Members of the lower-status group often do not take advantage of propinquity to broaden their "weak ties" and enhance the resource-producing potential of their networks, instead often restricting their networks to nearby members of their own group.

Social cohesion and control. In a number of studies, Robert Sampson and his colleagues emphasize the importance of the social control mechanism.[34] To understand the effects of disadvantaged neighborhoods, they argue, one must understand their degree of social organization, which entails the context of community norms, values, and structures enveloping residents' behaviors—what Sampson has labeled "collective efficacy." Sampson's work has empirically demonstrated that disorder and lack of social cohesion are associated with greater incidence of mental distress and criminality in neighborhoods.[35] There also has been work suggesting that social control and disorder potentially have effects on an array of youth outcomes.[36]

Finally, Anna Santiago and I provide a unique perspective on the issue by asking low-income parents what they thought the main mechanisms of neighborhood effects upon their children were.[37] The dominant plurality (24 percent) cited lack of norms and collective efficacy. By contrast, they cited peers (12 percent), exposure to violence (11 percent), and institutional resources (3 percent) much less often. Of interest is that one-third reported that their neighborhoods had no effect, either because their children were too young or because they thought they could buffer the impacts.

Competition and relative deprivation. The US statistical evidence (already cited) overwhelmingly suggests that affluent residents convey positive externalities to their less well-off neighbors in most outcome domains; in the realm of secondary education there is, however, cautionary evidence that more intensive competition from better-off students can produce some negative outcomes for lower-income students.[38] The qualitative evidence is inconsistent, with some case studies indicating that upper-income gentrifiers can sometimes mobilize and compete in ways that can work to the detriment of the original lower-income residents.[39]

Parental mediation. Few would disagree that parents' mental and physical health, coping skills, sensed efficacy, irritability, parenting styles, and sociopsychoeconomic resources loom large in how children develop. Thus, if any of the above elements are seriously affected by the neighborhood, by whatever causal mechanism, child outcomes are likely to be affected—though in this case the neighborhood effect for children is indirect.[40] For example, as I will explore in the following section, certain neighborhoods expose parents to much higher stress, which in turn adversely affects children.[41] Such neighborhoods may also vary, however, in their degrees of social support that might serve to defuse the negative effects of stress. As another example, parenting styles related to responsiveness and warmth and to harshness and control vary across aspects of neighborhood disadvantage.[42] Such variations, in turn, are associated with adolescent boys' psychological distress, among other outcomes.[43] Finally, riskier neighborhoods are associated with lower-quality home learning environments in many dimensions, thus resulting in lower reading abilities, verbal skills, and internalizing behavior scores.[44]

Evidence on Environmental Mechanisms of Neighborhood Effects

Social scientists have extensively studied exposure to violence as an environmental effect mechanism. The Yonkers (New York) Family and Community Survey and Moving to Opportunity demonstration have strongly supported the importance of this factor as perceived by parents, since most public-housing families cited safety concerns as a prime reason for participating in these programs.[45] One of the most significant results of the Moving to Opportunity demonstration was the substantial stress reduction and other psychological benefits accrued by parents and children who moved from dangerous, high-poverty neighborhoods to safer ones.[46] Other work has demonstrated that youths and adults exposed to violence as witnesses or victims suffer increased stress and decline in mental health.[47] Exacerbated stress, in turn, can produce a variety of unhealthy stress-reduction behaviors such as smoking,[48] and over the long term can reduce the efficacy of the body's immune system.[49] Studies also have linked exposure to violence with aggressive behaviors and reduced social cognition, though these relationships appear to be substantially mediated by the stress levels of parents.[50]

Researchers have highlighted the negative health impacts of several aspects of the physical environment of the neighborhood, such as deteriorated housing[51] and ambient noise levels.[52] Others have argued that the physical design of neighborhoods (absence of sidewalks, local land use mixes, cul-de-sacs, etc.) can affect the amount of exercise that residents get, which in turn affects obesity rates and other health outcomes.[53] Results from the Moving to Opportunity demonstration found that those moving from disadvantaged to low-poverty neighborhoods had reduced rates of obesity, which supports the view that some unspecified physical features of the neighborhood environment were at play.[54]

Finally, a variety of toxic pollutants potentially present in a neighborhood can generate a variety of physiological responses that impair the health of residents.[55] As illustrations of how widespread these health consequences can be, epidemiological studies have identified strong associations between air pollutants and lower life expectancy, higher infant and adult mortality risks, more hospital visits, poorer birth outcomes, and asthma.[56] Air pollution has been shown to degrade students' performance on examinations and, over the longer term, lower their postsecondary educational attainments and earnings.[57] Proximity to hazardous waste ("brownfield") sites has been associated with higher rates of mortality from cancer and other diseases.[58] Studies have demonstrated that even small amounts of lead poisoning (typically produced by residue from deteriorated lead-based paint formerly used in homes or in nearby industrial sites) produces harms to infants and older children in the realms of mental development, IQ, and behaviors.[59]

Evidence on Geographical Mechanisms of Neighborhood Effects

Numerous studies have investigated the issue of racial differentials in accessibility to work (the "spatial mismatch" hypothesis).[60] Ethnographies have shown that low-income youths can benefit greatly from part-time employment (by gaining resources, adult supervision, and routinized schedules), yet their neighborhoods typically have few such jobs.[61] Nevertheless, there is considerable statistical evidence that this spatial mismatch is of less importance to economic outcomes in most metropolitan areas than the social-interactive dimensions of neighborhoods.[62]

Evidence on Institutional Mechanisms of Neighborhood Effects

Many studies have documented the vast differences in both public and private institutional resources serving different neighborhoods.[63] Though there has been considerable debate on this subject, the current consensus seems to be that measurable educational resources and several aspects of student performance are highly correlated.[64] Shortages of high-quality child care facilities are acute in many low-income neighborhoods, despite their proven effectiveness in building a variety of intellectual and behavioral skills in young children.[65] Lower-income communities are also at a disadvantage in terms of access to medical facilities and practitioners.[66] Still other studies have shown how the internal workings of institutions serving poor communities shape expectations and life chances of their clientele.[67] Moreover, it is clear that many low-income parents believe that a paucity of local resources can adversely affect their children,[68] and often try to compensate for this lack by seeking such resources outside their neighborhoods.[69]

There is also substantial evidence regarding the large spatial variations in many sorts of market actors whose proximity may affect health-related behaviors of neighborhood residents. Several studies, for example, have documented distinctive race and class patterns in the locations of supermarkets[70] and liquor outlets.[71] Quantifying a convincing causal link between such contextual variations and individuals' diets, consumption patterns, and health has proven more challenging, however.[72] In a similar vein, several qualitative studies have recounted incidences of place-based stigmatization of areas;

but it is difficult to quantify the extent and power of this mechanism, because scholars have not yet related it statistically to individual outcomes.[73]

A Synthesis Regarding Evidence on Neighborhood Effect Mechanisms

What does the foregoing evidence suggest about the relative importance of various neighborhood effect mechanisms? With the mandatory caveat that firm conclusions are elusive here due to the underdeveloped state of scholarship and the complexity of the topic, my evaluation provisionally suggests the following nine conclusions.

First, research has consistently linked high concentrations of poverty (which typically are heavily Hispanic-occupied and especially black-occupied neighborhoods) statistically to weaker neighborhood cohesion and structures of informal social control. This situation is associated, in turn, with negative consequences like increased youth delinquency, criminality, and mental distress, although scholars have not yet linked it to other important outcomes like labor market performance. In this research, however, the aforementioned concentrations of poverty retain their relationship with a variety of child and adult outcomes even after intraneighborhood levels of social control and cohesion are taken into account. Clearly, more than this mechanism is at work.

Second, the fact that neighborhood poverty rates appear consistently related to a range of outcomes in a nonlinear thresholdlike fashion further suggests that the social contagion (peers) or the collective socialization (roles models, norms) forms of causal linkage are transpiring. There may also be some selectivity involved, as some socially disadvantaged groups seem more vulnerable to these contexts than are advantaged ones. I do not believe that the evidence can clearly distinguish the respective contributions made by the latter two alternatives.[74]

Third, the presence of affluent neighbors appears to provide positive externalities to their less well-off neighbors, seemingly working via the mechanism of social controls and collective socialization. Social networks and peer influences between the affluent and the poor, by contrast, do not appear as important in this vein. The outcomes for individuals that are most strongly related to affluent neighbors seem to be different from those most strongly related to disadvantaged neighbors. There is consistent evidence to suggest thresholds here as well, though the precise threshold is unclear and likely varies by outcome under consideration. Finally, most evidence indicates that the influence on vulnerable individuals of advantaged neighbors is smaller in absolute value than the influence of disadvantaged neighbors, whatever the mechanisms at play.

Fourth, there is little evidence suggesting that the competition or relative deprivation mechanisms operate in a meaningful way for lower-income individuals, with the possible exception of the secondary education domain.

Fifth, studies have consistently found relatively little social networking between lower-income and higher-income households or children within a given neighborhood, and this lack is compounded if racial differences are involved. Thus, there is little to support the version of neighborhood effects in which advantaged neighbors create valuable "weak ties" for disadvantaged ones.

Sixth, local environmental differences appear substantial, and likely produce important differentials in mental and physical health. Exposure to environmental pollutants and violence has the clearest consequences for the health of children, youths, and adults. Scholars have not adequately explored the longer-term consequences of these health impacts on educational, behavioral, and economic outcomes.

Seventh, it is unclear how much geographic disparities related to accessibility to work play an important role in explaining individual labor force and educational outcomes in all metropolitan areas.

Eighth, differences undoubtedly exist in in local institutional quality (especially related to public education), and local market actors. Unfortunately, convincing statistical models of the relationship between measured variations in these potential institutional causal mechanisms and a wide range of individual outcomes are rare.

Finally, there is probably a substantial indirect effect on children and youth that transpires through the combined effects of the social-interactive, environmental, geographic, and institutional dimensions of the neighborhood context on their parents. This is likely to affect a broad range of outcomes, though there have been no attempts to measure them comprehensively.

In sum, it is most sensible to conclude that many sorts of neighborhood effects are in operation simultaneously, but their relative importance is contingent on the particulars of the situation. Which mechanism dominates likely depends on the domain of outcome in question, and on the age, gender, and economic resources of the individuals under investigation.[75]

Evidence on the Magnitude of Neighborhood Effects on Socioeconomic Outcomes

Obtaining unbiased, meaningful estimates of the independent, causal effect of an individual's neighborhood context is a notoriously challenging enterprise.[76] Perhaps the most contentious aspect in this realm of scholarship, however, is the issue of geographic selection bias.[77] The central issue here is that individuals or their parents typically move from and to certain types of places with an aim of improving their household's prospects. Researchers can readily measure, and thus statistically control, many of these household predictors of residential choices, as I discussed in chapter 1. Concerns arise, however, because households likely have *unmeasured* motivations, behaviors, and skills related to their own socioeconomic prospects or those of their children, and make neighborhood selections as a consequence of these unobserved characteristics that by definition cannot be statistically controlled by researchers. Any observed relationship between neighborhood conditions and outcomes for adults or their offspring may be biased because of this systematic spatial selection process.[78] Skeptics may rightly argue that unmeasured individual attributes drive the observed relationship, not the independent causal impact of the neighborhood in which the individual resides.

Three Approaches to Estimating Causal Impacts of Spatial Context

There have been three general empirical approaches adopted in response to the challenge of geographic selection bias. The most common approach consists of a variety of econometric techniques applied to observational (non–experimentally generated) longitudinal datasets involving individuals and their spatial contexts. The two other, less common approaches use natural or experimental designs to generate quasi-random or random assignments of households to neighborhoods.

Econometric models based on observational data. Most studies of spatial context effects have used observational data collected from surveys or administrative records of individual households residing in a variety of places because of mundane mobility factors associated with normal housing market transactions. The subset of studies that has tried to overcome geographic selection bias employs one or more of the following approaches:[79]

· *Difference models based on longitudinal data*: Measuring differences between two periods in both outcomes and spatial contexts reduces the biases from unobserved, time-invariant individual characteristics.[80]

- *Fixed-effect models based on longitudinal data*: Dummy variables for each individual observation serve as proxies for all unobserved, time-invariant characteristics of individuals that may lead to both geographic selection and outcomes.[81]
- *Instrumental variables for spatial context characteristics:* The researcher devises proxy variables for geographic characteristics under investigation that, though correlated with these characteristics, only vary according to attributes exogenous to the individual, and thus are uncorrelated with their unobserved characteristics.[82]
- *Residents of same block*: If little sorting on individual unobserved characteristics occurs at the census block level, then the impacts of networks among these very localized neighbors should be free of geographic selection bias.[83]
- *Timing of events*: Individuals moving into certain well-defined places (such as public housing developments) after an event being investigated (such as a school achievement test) are likely to share common unobservable characteristics with individuals moving into the same places just before the event, so the short-term effect of the place can be measured by comparing the two groups' outcomes.[84] Analogously, one can address the selection bias problem by exploiting the variation in the timing of discrete neighborhood events compared to interview assessments for a sample of children in families that have previously selected the same neighborhood.[85]
- *Propensity score matching*: Individuals who are closely matched on a wide variety of observable characteristics that predict their similar residential mobility behavior are likely to be well-matched on their unobservable characteristics as well; comparisons between matches of differences in their spatial contexts and individual outcomes should thus provide unbiased causal evidence.[86]
- *Inverse probability of treatment weighting (IPTW)*: Like propensity score matching, IPTW uses a model of selection into the treatment status to predict the probability that an individual is in the observed treatment state. The investigator then constructs a weighted pseudosample in which the treatment and control groups are balanced on as many observable characteristics as possible. IPTW models selection into treatment status at multiple time points, allowing for unbiased estimates of treatment effects over time in the presence of observed confounders that vary over time and may be endogenous to the treatment.[87]
- *Nonmovers*: Analyzing how exogenous neighborhood changes induce different outcomes for individuals who do not move during the analysis period arguably avoids part of the mobility selection issue.[88]
- *Sibling comparisons*: Researchers can reduce biases from unobserved, time-

invariant parental characteristics by measuring differences in outcomes and neighborhood experiences between siblings, who presumably are affected by the same set of unmeasured household characteristics.[89]

None of these econometric fixes to observational datasets is without challenge. As illustration, difference models reduce statistical power by shrinking variation in the outcome variable, and they assume that change relationships are independent of starting conditions. Fixed-effect models assume that the individual dummies adequately capture the bundle of unobserved characteristics for all times during the panel, and that the effect of this bundle remains constant during the panel. Instrumental variables must be both valid and strong, requirements that are not easily met. Microscale investigations are limited to neighborhood effect mechanisms than operate only at the small geographic scales, and they assume that there is no residential sorting on unobserved characteristics at that scale. Relying on the timing of moves immediately before and after an event assumes that context effects operate quickly after exposure. Propensity score matching and IPTW require assumptions about the strong relationship between unobservable and observable characteristics of individuals. Those individuals who do not move may be exhibiting residential selection based on unobserved characteristics. Variations in neighborhood exposures across siblings may be minimal, thus eroding statistical power.

Quasirandom assignment natural experiments. It is sometimes possible to observe nonmarket interventions into households' residential locations that mimic random assignment. In the United States, such experiments typically have been based on court-ordered public housing racial desegregation programs,[90] regional fair-share housing requirements,[91] or scattered-site public housing assignments.[92] In Canada and Europe, they have involved allocation of tenants to social housing,[93] or placement of refugees in particular locales.[94]

Although these natural experiments may indeed provide some exogenous variation in locations, researchers are unlikely to avoid the geographic selection problem completely. In most cases, program staff makes assignments, and participants have some nontrivial latitude in which locations they choose, both initially and subsequent to original placement. Moreover, if the programs involve the use of rental vouchers, there will be selectivity in who succeeds in locating rental vacancies in qualifying locations, and in signing leases within the requisite period. These various potential selection processes raise the possibility that low-income families who succeed in living persistently in low-poverty neighborhoods have been especially motivated, resourceful, and perhaps courageous—traits measured poorly by researchers, but which likely would help the families succeed irrespective of their spatial contexts. Additional empirical problems can arise if sampled subjects move quickly from their quasirandomly assigned dwellings to other locations, thereby minimizing their exposure to measured context, and potentially confounding consequences because moving itself can be disruptive. As time passes, the randomness of location can erode, as selection of who stays in initially assigned places and who moves away comes into play. Finally, there may limitations in the range of places to which study participants move or are assigned, because of the location of available private rental or subsidized housing, thereby reducing the power of statistical tests to discern context effects.

Random assignment experiments. Many researchers advocate a random assignment experimental approach for best avoiding biases from geographic selection. Producing data on outcomes by an experimental design whereby individuals or households are randomly assigned to different geographic contexts is, in theory, the preferred method. In this regard, the Moving to Opportunity (MTO) demonstration has been touted conventionally as the study from which to draw conclusions about the magnitude of neighborhood effects.[95] The MTO research design randomly assigned public housing residents who volunteered to participate in one of three groups: (1) controls that got no voucher but stayed in public housing in disadvantaged neighborhoods, (2) recipients of rental vouchers with no restrictions, and (3) recipients of rental vouchers and relocation assistance who had to move to census tracts with less than 10 percent poverty rates and remain there for at least a year.

There has been substantial debate over the power of MTO as an unambiguous test of spatial context effects.[96] The debate focuses on five domains. First, although MTO randomly assigned participants to treatment groups, it randomly assigned neither characteristics of neighborhoods initially occupied by voucher-holders (except maximum poverty rates for the experimental group) nor characteristics of neighborhoods in which participants in all three groups later moved. Thus, there remains considerable question about the degree to which geographic selection based on unobserved characteristics persists. Second, MTO may not have exposed any group to neighborhood conditions long enough to observe much effect. Third, MTO overlooked the potentially long-lasting and indelible developmental effects upon adult experimental group participants who spent their childhoods in disadvantaged neighborhoods. Fourth, it appears that even experimental MTO movers rarely moved out of predominantly black-occupied neighborhoods near those of concentrated disadvantage, and achieved only modest changes in school quality and job accessibility. Thus, they may not have experienced sizable enhancements in their geographic opportunity structures. For these reasons, MTO may not have provided definitive evidence about the potential effects on low-income minority families from prolonged residence in multiply advantaged neighborhoods, despite its theoretical promise and notwithstanding conventional wisdom.

In summary, none of the three broad approaches to measuring effects of spatial context has proven limitation-free and unambiguously superior. Nevertheless, they as a group offer the strongest plausibly causal evidence to date on the topic at hand. Therefore, in the review that follows I will synthesize findings only from these methodologically rigorous studies that employ one or more of the aforementioned approaches.

A Synthesis of the Scientific Literature on Neighborhood Effects on Individuals

I organize the review by outcome domains that are closely related to socioeconomic opportunity: (1) risky behaviors, (2) cognitive skills and academic performance, (3) teen fertility, (4) physical and mental health, (5) labor force participation and earnings, and (6) crime.[97] I emphasize at the outset that the scope, diversity, and complexity of the relevant literature is vast, so I limit my synthesis to only those studies that employ one of the aforementioned techniques for producing estimates of plausibly causal effects. Moreover, I do not attempt to review findings in any detail, reconcile conflicting results, nor attempt any formal meta-analysis. Instead, my aim is basic: in each outcome domain I will tally the number of these methodologically rigorous studies that find substantial, statistically significant effects of at least some aspect of spatial context (for at least some set of individuals) and those that do not.

Risky behaviors. As for risky behaviors, six studies of context effects involving the aforementioned econometric approaches to overcoming geographic selection have been undertaken, and most identified effects on a variety of risky behaviors.[98] There are two examples of either the random or quasirandom neighborhood assignment approaches relevant to risky behaviors. Strong context effects on risky behaviors appear in both studies, but they are contingent on gender, ethnicity, and timing. Early MTO findings suggested that residence in lower-poverty neighborhoods led to substantial reductions of girls' rates of risky behaviors and boys' drug use. However, after initial declines in risky behavior, boys living in lower-poverty neighborhoods four to seven years after their first move were more likely to reengage in risky behaviors.[99] By the end of the demonstration project, girls assigned to low-poverty neighborhoods were less likely to have serious behavioral problems. There were no significant group differences in more serious antisocial behaviors, however. Anna Santiago and colleagues' analysis of data from a Denver natural experiment revealed that cumulative exposure to multiple dimensions of neighborhood context (especially safety, social status, and ethnic and nativity composition) affected the hazard of adolescents running away from home, using aggressive or violent behavior, or initiating marijuana use, though with substantial ethnic heterogeneity of relationships.[100]

Cognitive skills and Academic Performance. A recent meta-analysis of the international literature and a comprehensive review of the US literature conclude that there are nontrivial neighborhood effects on the development of cognitive skills, academic performance, and educational attainment.[101] My assessment of the methodologically sophisticated literature reaches a similar conclusion, though I hasten to note that the magnitude of the neighborhood effect likely varies across individuals and groups.

Over the past twenty years, researchers have frequently used measures of cognitive skills to assess evidence for neighborhood effects,[102] but only a smaller number of these studies have taken steps to address the problem of selection bias. Two studies have modeled selection into poor neighborhoods and then used inverse probability of treatment weighting to identify the impact of long-term exposure to neighborhood poverty on cognitive skill development. Using data from Chicago, Robert Sampson, Patrick Sharkey, and Stephen Raudenbush found that living in neighborhoods of concentrated disadvantage leads to substantial declines in reading and language skills assessed years later.[103] Patrick Sharkey and Felix Elwert used national data from the Panel Study of Income Dynamics, and found that family exposure to neighborhood poverty over consecutive generations reduces children's performance on tests of broad reading skills and applied problems skills by more than half of a standard deviation.[104] Sharkey found that exposure to a recent homicide near one's home reduced the performance of black children on tests of reading, language, and applied problems by more than a third of a standard deviation.[105] In a later study, Sharkey and colleagues found similar effects of recent exposure to nearby homicides on children's performance on vocabulary assessments, as well as effects on assessments of impulse control and attention.[106]

Experimental evidence from the MTO demonstration shows mixed and complex results. Several years after the experiment began and ten to fifteen years later, there were no effects of the intervention for the full sample on assessments of cognitive skills.[107] However, the experiment generated positive effects on the reading assessments of black children across all cities four to seven years after implementation.[108] There were improved reading and math scores for the full sample of boys and girls among families that remained in low-poverty neighborhoods for longer durations of time.[109] Finally, there were strong positive cognitive effects for children in the Baltimore and Chicago sites, though these persisted over ten to fifteen years only for the Chicago sample.[110]

The research literature on academic outcomes and educational attainment also is large. Many studies have employed one or more of the econometric techniques above to obtain plausibly causal estimates from observational data sets.[111] They found strong residential neighborhood effects on variously measured educational outcomes, with only two exceptions.[112]

Numerous studies based on natural experiments also are relevant in this outcome domain. These include data based on the Gautreaux and Yonkers court-ordered public housing desegregation programs,[113] public housing revitalization efforts,[114] inclusionary zoning mandates,[115] combined assisted housing-education programs,[116] and public housing assignments.[117] These numerous natural quasi-experiments provided only one example of no observed neighborhood effects,[118] though several of the observed effects in other studies were contingent on gender and ethnicity.

Recent evidence from MTO on college attendance is relevant for the discussion of neighborhood effects on educational attainment. Raj Chetty, Nathaniel Hendren, and Lawrence Katz reanalyzed MTO data and found that moving to a lower-poverty neighborhood significantly increased college attendance rates for children who were below the age of thirteen when their families moved to low-poverty neighborhoods, as compared to experimental group children who moved when they were older, or children in the other MTO study groups.[119]

Teen fertility. Only two studies have used any of the aforementioned statistical techniques to account for potential geographic selection bias confounding observational data on the fertility patterns of youth and their neighborhood contexts, and they come to contrary conclusions about the importance of neighborhood effects.[120] The evidence from natural and random assignment experiments is more consistent. Anna Santiago and I found that hazards of teenage childbearing and fathering were greater in neighborhoods with higher property crime rates, lower occupational prestige, and higher percentages of Latinos, though strength of effect was contingent on gender and ethnicity.[121] Results from the MTO demonstration showed that girls in the experimental group whose parents moved to low-poverty neighborhoods felt safer and less pressured to engage in early sexual activity (and thus, by implication, early pregnancy and childbearing) in their new neighborhoods.[122] The aforementioned Chetty, Hendren, and Katz analysis of the subset of MTO experimental children who moved to low-poverty neighborhoods before they were thirteen years old concluded that they, indeed, were less likely to become single parents.[123]

Physical and mental health. A handful of studies used the aforementioned statistical techniques applied to observational data producing results that, though somewhat inconsistent, do not uncover strong context effects on health.[124] Three studies based on propensity-score matching methods demonstrated no or barely discernable effects on minority infant mortality using different measures of neighborhood.[125] Based on inverse probability weighting methods, however, other research found that neighborhood poverty and mortality were related in a strong nonlinear way,[126] but had no consistent effects on self-assessed health and disability.[127] Finally, a study using the fixed-effect modeling approach ascertained no impact of neighborhood disadvantage on self-rated health, mental health, and physical functioning, or on the amount of physical activity, instead finding evidence of selection of those with poorer health into more disadvantaged neighborhoods.[128]

The random assignment experimental evidence from MTO is also mixed, but it shows impacts on some health outcomes. Results showed no significant differences in child asthma rates among groups assigned to neighborhoods differing in their poverty rates, although there were effects on adult obesity and diabetes rates, and stress levels among adults and children were much lower among those assigned initially to low-poverty neighborhoods.[129] Findings for mental health suggested neighborhood effects, but their size and direction varied, depending on lag of measurement after assignment, gender, and age.[130] Health benefits appear to be much larger, however, for the subset of MTO experimental households that resided for substantial periods in low-poverty neighborhoods.[131]

The few natural experiments involving health outcomes consistently found neighborhood effects, at least on selected health indicators. Deborah Cohen and colleagues employed exogenous shocks in the density of neighborhood alcohol outlets associated with the 1992 Los Angeles riots as a causal identification strategy, and found strong impacts on neighborhood gonorrhea rates.[132] Mark Vortuba and Jeffrey King analyzed data from the Gautreaux public housing relocation program.[133] They found that when young, low-income black men relocated to neighborhoods with better-educated residents, their all-cause mortality and homicide mortality rates dropped, as compared to corresponding rates of those moving to more poorly educated areas. Finally, Anna Santiago and I found strong neighborhood effects on the diagnoses of several child and adolescent health problems (asthma, obesity), using data from the Denver public housing natural experiment, though the relationships were often contingent on gender and ethnicity and in some cases manifested nonlinear thresholds.[134] Asthma problems, for example, arose sooner for low-income minority children residing in neighborhoods that had more property crime, lower occupational prestige, and higher concentrations of air pollution. We also found that several aspects of neighborhood context (especially safety, prestige, nativity and ethnic mix, and neurotoxin pollution) proved strongly and robustly predictive of low-income black and Latino children being diagnosed with neurodevelopmental disorders (retardation, learning disabilities, developmental delays, autism, ADD-ADHD).[135]

Labor force participation and earnings. Most investigators find neighborhood effects on labor market outcomes when using one of the aforementioned econometric techniques on nonexperimental observational datasets.[136] Several researchers also have probed these effects exploiting the quasirandom assignment occurring in natural experiments.[137] All but one[138] find evidence of strong neighborhood effects on several measures of adult and teen labor market outcomes in their analyses.

Virtually all investigations using MTO data uncovered no substantial short- or long-term context effects on teen or adult labor market outcomes.[139] There are three notable exceptions, however. Susan Clampet-Lundquist and Douglas Massey, and Margery Turner and colleagues, analyzed the subset of MTO experimental households that resided for substantial periods in low-poverty neighborhoods, and identified their adult employment and earnings outcomes as being substantially better than those of households in the control group.[140] In their aforementioned study, Chetty, Hendren, and Katz observed that MTO experimental children who moved to low-poverty neighborhoods before they were thirteen years old later exhibited significantly higher earnings as young adults than either experimental group children who moved after age thirteen or children from the other study groups.[141]

Crime. Six recent studies provide consistent and persuasive causal evidence concerning the strong (if heterogeneous by gender) causal impact of neighborhood context on criminality. Mark Livingston and colleagues used temporal lags and neighborhood fixed effects to identify the effect of the share of criminal offenders resident in Glasgow, Scotland, postal code areas.[142] They found that higher neighborhood shares of residents committing offenses during a quarter strongly predicted the probability of first-time violent and property offending among residents in the subsequent quarter.

Four natural experiments are relevant here. Exploiting the quasirandomness of assignment to public housing in Denver, Anna Santiago and I found that low-income Latino and black youth had greater hazards of engaging in violent behavior in neighborhoods with lower occupational prestige and higher property crime rates, though with gendered impacts.[143] Anna Piil Damm and Christian Dustmann used the Danish dispersed settlement policy for refugees to identify the causal impact of municipal characteristics on youth criminality.[144] They found that the share of those between the ages of fifteen and twenty-five who were convicted of a crime in a municipality during the year the family was assigned there strongly raised the probability of young male (but not female) refugees being convicted of a crime (especially for violent crimes and younger teens) in later years. Gabriel Pons Rotger and I employed exogenous assignment to social housing in Copenhagen to identify strong causal effects of the prior drug offending characteristics of the housing development's residents at time of assignment on the odds of individuals aged fifteen to twenty-five committing property and drug crimes over the next two years.[145] Stephen Billings, David Deming, and Stephen Ross used natural experimental data on fourteen-year-old students in Mecklenburg County, North Carolina, to demonstrate that context effects on their criminal behavior only arise when school peers are neighbors residing less than one kilometer away from each other, and that the effects are stronger when neighbors are enrolled in the same grade in school.[146]

Finally, there is some modest evidence of context effects on male criminality from MTO. Early impact evaluations indicated that minority males from families randomly assigned to low-poverty neighborhoods evinced fewer arrests.[147] These effects diminished and even reversed over time, however.[148]

A tabulation of the findings. Table 8.1 summarizes the foregoing findings on the number of methodologically rigorous studies that have found substantial, statistically significant effects of spatial context for at least some category of individuals, and on those that have not, by outcome domain. The tally makes it clear that the preponderance of evidence in every outcome domain is that multiple aspects of neighborhood context exert important causal influences over a wide range of individual outcomes related to socioeconomic opportunity, though which aspects are most powerful are contingent on the outcome, and on the gender and ethnicity of the individuals in question.[149]

Table 8.1. Summary of conclusions from causal* analyses of neighborhood effects, by domain of individual outcomes

Studies identifying significant effects on at least one outcome	Studies identifying no effects
Risky behaviors	
Ahern et al. 2008; Cerda et al. 2010; Nandi et al. 2010; Sanbonmatsu et al. 2011; Cerda et al. 2012; Gibbons, Silva, and Weinhardt 2013; Santiago et al. 2017	Novak et al. 2006; Jokela 2014
Educational performance and attainment	
Rosenbaum 1995; Duncan, Connell, and Klebanov 1997; Vartanian and Gleason 1999; Crowder and South 2003; Clampet-Lundquist 2007; Fauth, Leventhal, and Brooks-Gunn 2007; Galster et al. 2007a; DeLuca et al. 2010; Schwartz 2010; Sharkey and Sampson 2010; Jargowsky and El Komi 2011; Sharkey et al. 2012, 2014; Casciano and Massey 2012; Santiago et al. 2014; Gibbons, Silva, and Weinhardt 2014; Carlson and Cowan 2015; Chetty, Hendren, and Katz 2015; Galster, Santiago, Stack, and Cutsinger 2016; Galster, Santiago, and Stack 2016; Tach et al. 2016; Galster and Santiago 2017a, 2017b	Plotnick and Hoffman 1999; Ludwig, Ladd, and Duncan 2001; Jacob 2004; Sanbonmatsu et al. 2006, 2011; Kling, Liebman, and Katz 2007; Gibbons, Silva, and Weinhardt 2013; Weinhardt 2014
Teen fertility	
Harding 2003; Popkin, Leventhal, and Weismann 2010; Sanbonmatsu et al. 2011; Santiago et al. 2014; Chetty, Hendren, and Katz 2015; Galster and Santiago 2017b	Plotnick and Hoffman 1999
Physical and mental health	
Leventhal and Brooks-Gunn 2003; Cohen et al. 2006; Vortuba and King 2009; Glymour et al. 2010; Ludwig et al. 2011; Sanbonmatsu et al. 2011; Do et al. 2013; Kessler et al. 2014; Moulton, Peck, and Dillman 2014; Santiago et al. 2014	Schootman et al. 2007; Hearst et al. 2008; Johnson et al. 2008; Jokela 2014
Labor force participation and earnings	
Rosenbaum 1991, 1995; Rubinowitz and Rosenbaum 2000; Edin, Fredricksson, and Åslund 2003; Weinberg, Reagan, and Yankow 2004; Dawkins, Shen, and Sanchez 2005; Cutler, Glaeser, and Vigdor 2008; Bayer, Ross, and Topa 2008; Clampet-Lundquist and Massey 2008; Galster et al. 2008; Åslund and Fredricksson 2009; Damm 2009, 2014; DeLuca et al. 2010; Galster, Andersson, and Musterd 2010, 2015, 2017; Musterd, Galster, and Andersson 2012; Sari 2012; Sharkey 2012; Turner et al. 2012; Hedman and Galster 2013; Damm 2014; Galster, Santiago, and Lucero 2015a, 2015b; Chetty, Hendren, and Katz 2015; Galster, Santiago, Lucero, and Cutsinger 2016; Chyn 2016; Galster and Santiago 2017a	Plotnick and Hoffman 1999; Ludwig, Duncan, and Pinkston 2005; Katz, Kling, and Liebman 2001; Ludwig, Ladd, and Duncan 2001; Ludwig, Duncan, and Hirschfield 2001; Orr et al. 2003; Oreopoulos 2003; Bolster et al. 2007; Kling, Leibman, and Katz 2007; Propper et al. 2007; Ludwig et al. 2008; van Ham and Manley 2010; Sanbonmatsu et al. 2011; Ludwig 2012
Crime	
Katz, Kling, and Liebman 2001; Ludwig, Duncan, and Hirshfeld 2001; Livingston et al. 2014; Santiago et al. 2014; Damm and Dustmann 2014; Rotger and Galster 2017; Billings, Deming, and Ross 2016	Kling, Ludwig, and Katz 2005; Sanbonmatsu et al. 2011

* Employing a quantitative technique yielding plausibly causal estimates; see text for details.

The Proposition of Multifaceted Neighborhood Effects

I distill the theory and evidence presented in chapter 8 into the fifth major proposition in this book:

> *Multifaceted Neighborhood Effects*: Neighborhood context strongly affects the attitudes, perceptions, behaviors, health, quality of life, financial well-being, and life prospects of resident adults and children through a variety of causal processes and pathways.

Conclusion

Neighborhoods make us by affecting our individual socioeconomic outcomes. They structure these opportunities both directly and indirectly. They directly affect how our personal attributes will pay off in achieved status, and indirectly affect the attributes we embody. Some of these indirect effects require little or no individual volition to acquire, such as exposures to environmental contaminants and violence, or collective norms and local networks that influence what information we receive and how we evaluate it. In the case of children, other indirect effects transpire through neighborhood influences on the caregivers. A final indirect effect occurs by molding the individual volition involved in major life decisions; neighborhood influences what people perceive as feasible and desirable options. The neighborhood exerts these direct and indirect effects on our life chances through a wide variety of not mutually exclusive mechanisms in social interactive, environmental, geographical, and institutional domains. The overwhelming preponderance of empirical evidence arising from studies that convincingly uncover causal effects indicates that the neighborhood exercises a profound influence on our mental and physical health, our cognitive development, and our behaviors related to education, fertility, work, and crime. These effects appear highly contingent, however. Their magnitudes and primary mechanisms of causation vary according to the gender, age, socioeconomic status, and other aspects of the individual, and the outcome domain being considered.

NINE

Neighborhoods, Social Efficiency, and Social Equity

Thus far I have explored what neighborhoods are, why and how they come into being, why they exhibit particular characteristics, why they change over time, and, in turn, why and how they affect individuals and the local political jurisdiction of which they are constituents. Here my analysis turns normative and considers the degree to which the processes of neighborhood change and the outcomes they yield are socially desirable. I ask whether (1) the primarily market-driven processes that neighborhoods undergo as they transition between states (i.e., the dynamic perspective) and (2) the population and housing stock characteristics that neighborhoods exhibit at any moment (i.e., the static perspective) are the best we can hope for from a society-wide perspective. By "society," I mean the population as a whole living in the metropolitan area under consideration, though the normative issues are certainly of relevance to residents of both smaller and larger geographic entities.

My analysis will consider for both static and dynamic perspectives two aspects of social well-being: *efficiency and equity*. I adopt as the social efficiency criterion a conventional utilitarian position: enhancing the self-assessed well-being of the sum total of households in the metropolitan society under consideration. I consider well-being as a function of not only physical consumption but also psychological (e.g., identity, esteem, efficacy, purpose) and sociological (e.g., love, status, affirmation, community) attributes. It is clear that social efficiency cannot be assessed unambiguously in some cases of alternative market outcomes or policy options, because we cannot be certain how the people affected will quantitatively evaluate the alternatives. Moreover, we cannot be certain how decision makers will weigh such evaluations in the process of aggregating them to the societal level.[1] This is problematic, however, only when some gain and some lose from an actual or contemplated situation, and the decision maker must somehow measure and summarize these gains and losses to compute the aggregate change in social well-being. This thorny challenge can be skirted when we can unambiguously judge that certain situations generate losses to some with no compensatory gains for others (thereby reducing efficiency), and different situations generate gains to some with no offsetting losses for others (thereby enhancing efficiency).[2] Fortunately, such unambiguous situations often arise in the context of neighborhoods.

By equity grounds, I mean the degree to which the neighborhood situation under consideration (in either static or dynamic perspectives) disproportionately enhances the well-being of less advantaged citizens, particularly those of color and those with lower incomes. I recognize that this definition of equity is arbitrary, and is unlikely to be proven universally shared. Nonetheless, it is the explicit norm expressed by the American Institute of Certified Planners in their code of professional ethics, and one with which I personally agree. To be clear, a formulation that focuses purely on the disadvantaged implicitly suggests that we would judge as fair a situation wherein disadvantaged households benefited, even if there were absolute reductions in the well-being of more advantaged households. Of course, this need not be the case; there are undoubtedly situations that prove both efficient and equitable: those where the disadvantaged benefit and the advantaged are not harmed (or perhaps benefit as well).

Throughout this book, I have framed neighborhood dynamics as resulting from flows of households and financial resources across metropolitan space. In the United States, market forces and the price signals they produce are the prime determinants of these flows. There is a long-standing belief within the neoclassical economics paradigm—at least since Adam Smith—that a fully informed, highly competitive market context will automatically (as if guided by an "invisible hand") reach the most efficient state for the populace. Within an idealized abstraction of an economy, this may be true. In the case of real neighborhoods, it is patently untrue. I will demonstrate in this chapter why the market processes that drive neighborhood change and the neighborhood conditions that result are both highly inefficient and inequitable.

Social Inefficiencies: Static Perspective

Overview and Key Concepts

Social inefficiencies arise in the distribution of households and financial resources across metropolitan space primarily due to neighborhood externalities and strategic gaming.[3] In the context of neighborhoods, we may define these key factors as follows:

Neighborhood externality. A decision involving an action or inaction attached to a particular location undertaken by an individual, household, firm, or institution that generates benefits or costs to others living or owning property nearby, which are not borne by the decision-maker. The inefficiency arises in such circumstances because the decision is based only on that actor's perceived benefits and costs, not on the aggregation of such benefits and costs across both the decision maker and all relevant neighbors of the property in question. Society as a whole will end up devoting insufficient resources to actions conveying positive benefits spilling over to the neighborhood (e.g., a person volunteering for a block patrol, or a homeowner repairing a deteriorated dwelling). This occurs because the actors controlling these resources will not account for these external benefits in their private decision-making calculus when deciding what is best for them in isolation, unless they are unusually altruistic. Conversely, society will waste resources undertaking too many actions that impose negative side effects on the neighborhood (e.g., a person engaging in disruptive public drunkenness, or a property owner abandoning a dwelling), because the actors will not account for these external costs in their private decision-making calculus. In sum, actions that generate externalities represent a failure of decentralized, autonomous decision making (whether guided by market prices or not) to reach the socially optimal amounts of activities and associated resource allocations. Insufficient resources of all kinds in our society get devoted to pursuing actions generating positive externalities, and just the opposite occurs for those generating negative externalities. Of course, because tautologically individual actions in a neighborhood context occur within close proximity, the setting is fertile for significant externalities of multiple sorts, as I will document below.

Strategic gaming. An action to achieve a future objective based on the predicted but uncertain future action of all others of relevance, in a context where the benefits and/or costs of each of the interrelated actors depend on the aggregation of their actions. Gaming contexts typically yield suboptimal outcomes for the allocation of society's resources because each actor decides in isolation to be conservative and not put themselves in the most vulnerable position of being "out in front" of the others, despite the fact that if all actors were to undertake the common behavior they all would benefit collectively. Thus, for example, a middle-class parent who has recently moved into a gentrifying city neighborhood may in principle wish to enroll her children in the local public school, but may be reluctant without being certain of what other middle-class parents in the catchment area will do. A neighborhood business owner may withhold voluntarily contributing to an initiative to beautify the retail strip if he thinks he can "free ride" on the contributions of others. In both cases, if all parties involved behave in the same conservative strategic way, they will forego a superior situation that could have arisen had everyone been able to coordinate their actions with perfect foresight and assurances of mutuality. In sum, actions that follow from strategic gaming considerations represent a failure of decentralized, autonomous decision making (whether guided by market prices or not) to reach the socially optimal amounts of activities and associated resource allocations. Inasmuch as payoffs of many individual actions in a neighborhood context depend heavily on neighbors' corresponding actions that may be very uncertain, the setting is fertile for significant inefficiencies produced by strategic gaming behaviors, as I will document below.

Inefficiencies in Property Owners' Investment Behaviors: Theory

As I will summarize below, owners of residential properties in a neighborhood could undertake a host of potential actions that have financial consequences not only for the property in question but also for other properties nearby. These positive and negative externalities emanate from decisions related to how much is invested in the dwelling and parcel, whether the owner occupies the premises, and whether the property should be converted to a nonresidential use or abandoned completely. In all cases, the nature of the inefficiency-inducing externality is similar: the individual owners assess what makes most financial sense from their perspective, and largely overlook what makes social sense when we account for all affected parties' benefits and costs.

Two hypothetical examples suffice to illustrate. In the first case, an owner might ask herself whether investing $50,000 in upgrading her dwelling is worth it in terms of enhancing her own property's value; should she assess this prospective increase in discounted future value as only $40,000 she will be unlikely to undertake the investment because it would incur a $10,000 loss. What this self-interested rationality overlooks in this hypothetical example is that each of the ten neighboring homes would gain $2,000 in value were she to upgrade. Thus, from society's perspective she should invest $50,000 in upgrading because she and the other owners in aggregate would reap $60,000 gain in value (that is, $40,000 plus 10 × $2,000). The practical problem here—the failure of decentralized, market-based resource allocation mechanisms—is that the extra $20,000 in social benefit is external to the decision maker, and so she does not "do the right thing" by investing resources in her dwelling. Some sort of collective organizational mechanism must be devised (such as an $11,000 tax on the beneficiaries of $20,000 of externalities, which is then offered to the prospective upgrader in the form of a subsidy) to overcome this misallocation of our resources.

In the second example, an owner is struggling with a long-term cash flow on a rental property. Due to weak conditions in the submarket in which this dwelling is classified, the owner finds he cannot collect enough in rents to cover the minimum costs required to keep the property in operation. If no financial relief is found despite all feasible cost-saving measures, the desperate owner may assess that the current net loss of $1,000 per month is unsustainable, whereupon he suspends all property upkeep and payments on taxes, insurance, and perhaps mortgage, and "milks" the property for whatever he can get until foreclosure and seizure inevitably occur.[4] The social inefficiency of this choice of not to invest rests on the fact that the undermaintenance and eventual abandonment of the dwelling reduces neighboring properties' values substantially, as I will document below. If the aggregate value of these external losses were to prove greater (in discounted present value terms) than $1,000 per month, the social inefficiency is manifest.

Strategic gaming also can play an important role in guiding the investments in property in a distorted fashion. Property owners' expectations about what other investors in the neighborhood are likely to do in the future undoubtedly play a vital role in determining their dwelling investments, because they are aware of the web of interdependent externalities that links them. Clearly, the financial payoffs that one owner can expect to reap from some incremental investing (or not investing) in housing upkeep and improvements are synergistically influenced by the aggregate amount of such investments undertaken by nearby property owners. Unfortunately for the particular owner, the actions of other investors typically cannot be predicted with certainty. The context for strategic behavior is thus established.

What kind of strategies do dwelling owners employ? The long-standing conventional view has been to posit "minimax" motives in a classic game-theory framework: owners avoid options that expose them to major potential losses, attempting always to choose in such a way that even in the worst circumstances their maximum prospective loss will be minimized. In practical terms, such a strategy means one of undermaintaining or refraining from unnecessary repairs and improvements when the local market context is uncertain, because any other strategy leaves one vulnerable to neighbors who also choose to undermaintain. This tendency to "wait and see" what others do before committing is the basis of reinvestment thresholds, as I explained in chapter 6. Of course, if everyone waits for everyone else in the neighborhood to take the risky move of "getting out in front" and reinvesting, it is unlikely that such reinvestments will ever occur. In the more realistic case where owners exhibit a distribution of reinvestment thresholds associated with varying tolerance for risk, it is possible that even if some reinvest, many others will not follow suit. Either result is inefficient, because it is likely that the individual and aggregate returns for all owners would be greatest if all would reinvest collectively. The type of strategic context in which actions that appear rational to each individual decision maker lead to counterproductive group outcomes has been termed in strategic gaming literature as "the prisoners' dilemma."

Inefficiencies in Property Owners' Investment Behaviors: Evidence

Externalities. There is a robust empirical literature quantifying negative and positive neighborhood externalities associated with dwelling owners' behaviors. It has long been observed that deteriorated housing in the neighborhood makes homeowners more pessimistic about future property appreciation,[5] though there have been few studies that relate direct measures of dwelling maintenance to values of homes nearby.[6] Most housing price research has focused on the impacts of tax-delinquent, foreclosed and vacant, or abandoned properties, under the assumption that they manifest visible deterioration that generates negative externalities. The consistent conclusion from this substantial body of work is that the externalities impart serious harm to property values, which is magnified the longer the deteriorated dwelling persists but decays over distance. Studies of tax-delinquent properties' effects indicate a one-to-two percent decrement in a home's sales price for every such delinquent property within about 500 feet.[7] Investigations of foreclosed properties' impact reveal a similar 1 to 2 percent decrement in a home's sales price for every foreclosed property nearby, with effects roughly twice as large within 250 feet as they are within 251 to 500 feet.[8] Negative effects have been registered as far away as 3,000 feet, however, especially if foreclosed dwellings take longer to be resold, and their concentration of exceeds a threshold.[9] Finally, research on the detrimental home price impact of proximate abandoned properties is less consistent on magnitude of impact: within 500 feet, estimates range from 1 to 9 percent,[10] and perhaps as much as 22 percent if the abandoned property is adjacent to the one sold.[11] Though abandonment-generated negative externalities also appear to decay with distance, research has identified nontrivial impacts as far away as 1,500 feet, especially if the property has been abandoned for more than three years.[12]

Several studies identify strong positive externalities associated with improvements in residential properties. Two studies quantify substantial positive neighborhood externalities generated by new infill construction projects involving subsidized housing for first-time home buyers. One study found that property values increased by an average of 8 percent per home within 150 feet of the new construction; within 151 to 300 feet the figure was 2 percent.[13] The other study found even wider-scale impacts, with infill dwellings raising property values within 500 feet by over 6 percent and within 501 to 2,000 feet by about 3 percent.[14] Two independent evaluations of comprehensive neighborhood revitalization strategy in Richmond, Virginia, observed substantial land and housing value spillovers, though the magnitude of these external impacts dropped by about half every 1,000 feet farther from the improved site.[15] Another study estimated that each additional permit to renovate a home increased the final sales price of other homes within 150 feet by 1.8 percent.[16]

Other studies quantify the positive externality value of owners residing within their dwellings. Edward Coulson and colleagues found that the conversion of one house from absentee ownership to occupant ownership increased prices in the average surrounding neighborhood by 5.5 percent.[17] This externality could be even stronger in neighborhoods with less than 80 percent overall homeownership rates.[18] Bev Wilson and Shakil Bin Kashem estimated that a ten-percentage-point increase in a census tract's homeownership rate would lead to an appreciation of property values there by 1.6 percent more.[19]

Another strand of research examines information externalities associated with conducting home sale and mortgage transactions. Greater volumes of home mortgage loans in a neighborhood during the recent past reduce the uncertainty associated with appraising the current value of a property, thereby enabling lenders to distinguish observable risks better, and encouraging them to increase the aggregate supply of loans in this neighborhood.[20] Because the previous home sales enabled by an individual lender's loans become public information and all lenders benefit from it, however, individual lenders have insufficient incentive to help facilitate loan transactions that would help all lenders gain a better understanding of market values. The inefficiency created by this information externality can be especially severe in cases of neighborhoods where extremely few market transactions occur. As illustration, it has been estimated that lending in more than 30 percent of the neighborhoods in the Detroit metropolitan area were adversely affected in the recent post-recession period by the lack of accurate information on neighborhood home sales prices.[21] This lack of lending impedes home appreciation and sales potential, in turn discouraging owners in affected areas from investing in their properties.

Strategic gaming. The empirical literature on strategic gaming in neighborhoods is thinner, but two studies are notable. Richard Taub, Garth Taylor, and Jan Dunham drew revealing inferences regarding strategic gaming behaviors from their surveys of homeowners in Waukegan and Chicago, Illinois, about their home reinvestment behaviors in different contexts.[22] Their Waukegan sample revealed that 14 percent of homeowners did not engage in gaming; they "pioneered" instead, reinvesting during the last two years even though none of their neighbors did. At the other extreme, 30 percent engaged in a "free-rider" strategy: not investing even though all of their neighbors did. The remaining owners exhibited intermediate threshold levels, at which point they switched from a free-riding strategy to a "crowd-following" strategy. Taub et al.'s Chicago results revealed markedly different strategies, what they termed "making the best of a bad situation" and "capitalizing on a good situation,"[23] depending jointly on whether they owned in a deteriorated or well-kept neighborhood, and on whether they were dissatisfied or satisfied with the trend in property values. For those in deteriorated contexts (both blacks and whites), satisfaction with property appreciation increased their propensity to free ride, apparently an indicator that one can reap sufficient capital gains from the dwelling without improving it. However, dissatisfaction with property appreciation decreased the propensity of owners to engage in this strategy; for them, investing made more sense as a vehicle for raising the consumption value of the home to make the best of a bad situation. In better-quality neighborhoods, just the reverse changes in strategies were associated with differing satisfactions with property appreciation. In these contexts, greater satisfaction with appreciation apparently was associated with the owner's increased confidence that they could safely invest because they expected others to invest as well, since the financial returns from such investment were enhanced. In sum, Taub, Taylor, and Dunham clearly demonstrated the contingent nature of strategic gaming practices. In deteriorated neighborhoods, stronger price appreciation raises owners' threshold scores; in well-kept neighborhoods, the relationship reverses.

My research with Garry Hesser on homeowners in Minneapolis and in Wooster, Ohio, revealed an identical contingent pattern in deteriorated neighborhoods.[24] Homeowners in such contexts who were most pessimistic about dwelling capital gains significantly intensified their exterior upkeep investments. We posited that one can comprehend this trend-bucking behavior by positing that the well-being gained from home-asset value increments rises rapidly when capital value is expected to fall below a minimally accepted threshold upon which homeowner wealth accumulation plans were made. Conversely, homeowners in low-value neighborhoods responded to more optimism about property appreciation by adopting a free-rider strategy and deferring external repairs, apparently believing that they could meet their expected wealth targets even while maintaining their home less. Unlike Taub, Taylor, and Dunham, however, we observed no relationship between investment behavior and expectations about home appreciation among homeowners in moderate- and high-quality neighborhoods, plausibly because they were confident that they would reap some minimally acceptable capital gain from their property regardless.

Hesser and I also observed a noncontingent strategic behavior revealed by patterns of investments and differing expectations about the neighborhood's future quality of life.[25] Across all sorts of neighborhoods, optimistic expectations about qualitative neighborhood changes were associated with substantially more home reinvestment. As illustration, compared to the most optimistic but otherwise comparable homeowners, the most pessimistic ones spent 61 percent less annually on their homes and exhibited a .14 higher incidence of exterior dwelling defects. These results clearly suggest a crowd-following variety of strategic gaming. If homeowners perceive the quality of their area as improving, they will flow with the trend and intensify their own reinvestment behaviors. Just the opposite ensues with more pessimism. This conservative "wait and see what others do before I invest" strategy is consistent with the findings from behavioral economics related to loss aversion and status quo bias, as I discussed in chapter 5. It is also consistent with spatial econometric models that uncovered endogenous, mutually reinforcing relationships among proximate owners renovating their properties.[26]

A summary measure of property investment inefficiency. Up to this point, I have argued that the combination of externalities and strategic gaming biases individual dwelling owners towards undertaking too few investments in their properties and too many actions that represent disinvestments in their properties, as compared to what would be desirable from a utilitarian social efficiency perspective. Put differently, the current market-driven processes guiding the physical quality of neighborhoods is likely to produce a pattern of too many lower-quality neighborhoods and too few good-quality ones, in comparison to what our society would be willing to pay for. Jacob Vigdor has provided clear support for this conclusion by measuring households' willingness to pay for neighborhood quality, and comparing it to the actual housing price changes that accompany observed changes in neighborhood quality.[27] He found that price increases associated with neighborhood revitalization were smaller than most households' willingness to pay for such improvements, and that just the opposite relationship held in the case of neighborhood decay.

Inefficiencies in Households' Mobility Behaviors: Theory

Types of mobility-related externalities. When households choose to move into or out of a neighborhood, they likely will generate several types of externalities that transpire both directly (affecting residents' quality of life) and indirectly (affecting behavior of both residents and external parties). Directly, the act of a household occupying a dwelling previously occupied by a household with distinctly different demographic, racial, or class characteristics may provide an external benefit or cost for neighbors who place a value on these characteristics. Existing neighbors who prefer homophily, for example, will perceive the in-migration of a similar household (e.g., of the same race or income) as generating positive externalities for them, because it enhances their self-assessed quality of residential life. On the contrary, if the in-migrating household increases the racial or class diversity of the neighborhood, it may produce a negative social externality in the form of reduced social cohesion and trust among residents who preferred the previous, more homogeneous neighborhood composition.[28]

The indirect externality effects manifest themselves as induced behavioral changes undertaken both by residents of the neighborhood and by external parties. Both residents' mobility choices and life choices may be affected. In the former case, marginally changing the aggregate population attributes of a neighborhood may change the quality-of-life evaluations made by current and potential households (noted above), in ways that may lead some original members to move to another neighborhood. This imposes on them the extra financial, time, and psychological costs associated with this "forced move." In the latter case, the indirect externality effect of household mobility occurs because the neighborhood's composition influences the behavior of adults and children residing there. As I explained in chapter 8, the population of a neighborhood can affect life decisions by its residents (education, fertility, crime, etc.) through numerous social-interactive mechanisms. Yet, once again, the effects that an individual household might have on shaping the social-interactive environment for others in the neighborhood, such as providing a role model or a conduit for employment information, are external to its decision-making calculus. This provides yet another rationale for deducing socially inefficient outcomes associated with changing neighborhood populations.

This population change may also lead to altered evaluations of the neighborhood by external parties such as potential in-moving households, potential property investors, lenders, insurers, and real estate agents, thereby changing resource flows across space. For example, if a wide swath of households and resource controllers in the particular metropolitan housing market view the type of in-migrating household as "undesirable," they will downgrade the perceived quality of the neighborhood in question, and it will suffer concomitant declines in its market valuations. Current property owners in this neighborhood will perceive this as a negative financial externality produced by these extra-neighborhood reactions.

The foregoing discussion of indirect externalities means that demographic and physical attributes of neighborhood are mutually causal over time. Changes in one attribute may change behaviors by one or more types of households and investors that lead, in turn, to reinforcing changes in other attributes, and so on. These behavioral externalities will be especially severe if processes exceed threshold points. Because this atomistic household decision making about neighborhood choice generates longer-term behavioral consequences for others operating or potentially operating in the neighborhood, socially inefficient outcomes are manifested.

Besides their wide variety and direct and indirect impacts, there is another crucial distinction between the externalities that arise from property investment behavior and those arising from household mobility behavior: heterogeneity of effect. Virtually all residents and owners in a neighborhood (and in the larger society, for that matter) will perceive the abandonment of a property as imposing costs on them. Not so for changes in neighborhood household composition. Type X households may evaluate an increase in the share of type X households in the neighborhood as a good thing, but type Z neighbors may have the opposite evaluation. Further complicating the matter is that externalities may flow in both directions between neighboring household groups (depending on their preferences), in which case what may be socially desirable from an efficiency standpoint might be a situation where the countervailing negative and positive intergroup externalities result in a net positive for the neighborhood.

Of course, those who believe they are suffering negative externalities from the in-migration of other neighbors may leave the neighborhood (especially if they exhibit higher incomes and are not constrained by racial or ethnic discrimination). Thus, part of the residential patterns we observe today across our neighborhoods is the result of households seeking to avoid interneighbor negative externalities (and experience positive ones if possible). As I documented in chapter 7, segregation by race and income constitutes the dominant population pattern across most American neighborhoods. This raises the key question here: is this segregated pattern *efficient* from a social standpoint?

The answer depends on the nature of both intergroup externalities within neighborhoods and the indirect externalities that manifest themselves as induced behavioral changes by external parties controlling resource flows into the neighborhood. We must distinguish between these two types of processes for two reasons. First, because efficiency requires us to consider the well-being of residents of all affected groups, a more comprehensive analysis of potential intra-neighborhood social externalities is required. We must consider the possibility that negative social externalities imposed by, for example, disadvantaged individuals on their advantaged neighbors outweigh the positive social externalities that may flow in the opposite direction. If that were the case, it is easy to imagine a social weighting scheme (such as utilitarianism) that would register the highest values when the two groups were completely segregated residentially. Second, if *only* the extra-neighborhood process of place-based stigmatization and resultant resource restriction were operative, we would not need to concern ourselves with the potential zero-sum or negative-sum aspects associated with intra-neighborhood social interactions between disadvantaged and advantaged groups. On the contrary, changing the population composition by reducing the share of disadvantaged people in a neighborhood so that externals ceased their stigmatizing would provide a net gain for the well-being of *all* individuals living in the formerly stigmatized neighborhood, with no offsetting costs being borne by anyone. The next section amplifies and explicates these claims systematically, with a theoretical model of how we can assess the inefficiency or efficiency of segregation.

A model of socially efficient neighborhood population composition. For simplicity of exposition, but with no loss of generality in conclusions, I make several assumptions. First, our hypothetical society consists of households categorized into two groups, generically labeled "advantaged" (A) and "disadvantaged" (D). It is immaterial to this analysis on what basis we classify households into A or D groups: income, race, or immigrant status are most relevant possibilities in the current national context. Second, these characteristics do not change during the period in question when we are assessing externality effects from various mixes of the groups in neighborhoods.[29]

Third, all households within a group are identical in the extent to which they produce or are affected by intraneighborhood externalities. Fourth, "society" consists of two neighborhoods with predetermined boundaries and housing stocks; all housing is equally affordable, adaptable, and desirable to both groups. Last, I assume that there are no spatial spillovers of externalities between neighborhoods; all externalities are intra-neighborhood here.

Let all types of direct and indirect intra-neighborhood externalities (that is, changes in quality of life, financial standing, social relationships, and behaviors) associated with various mixtures of A and D households in the neighborhood under examination be summarized by an index I. This index can assume positive values (good external effects on net) and negative values (bad external effects on net), as compared to the baseline situation (where we normalize index I to zero). The index's total value (I_T) is the sum of the net externalities generated by the allocation of A across both neighborhoods (I_A) plus the externalities generated by D across both neighborhoods (I_D). Without loss of generality, I express the I_T functions in terms of the percentage of households in one neighborhood who are members of group D (%D), which means in this neighborhood the percentage consisting of A households is $(100 - \%D)$. In the other neighborhood, these percentages are reversed. Improvements in social efficiency are associated with improvements in I_T.

The analysis that follows is comparative-static in nature: I consider various de novo allocations of A and D households across these two hypothetical neighborhoods, not dynamic processes of transforming preexisting household allocations. That is, I analyze the comparative social efficiency consequences of various alternative allocations of fixed amounts of A and D households across two identical neighborhoods with fixed and equal total households in all cases. The discussion below proceeds with a reliance on graphic exposition; a parallel mathematical exposition is provided in the chapter 9 appendix. With these bases established, I turn to ten alternative cases that exhaustively represent various types of intra-neighborhood social externalities that I outlined above and in chapter 8.

Case 1: Group D generates constant marginal negative externality β for all neighbors; group A generates constant marginal positive externality φ for all neighbors.

This case describes one form of the "collective socialization" neighborhood effect mechanism whereby impacts are transmitted equally to A and D households alike. Each additional D household (replacing an A household in the particular neighborhood, by definition) may, for illustration, provide another inappropriate role model, try to recruit all neighbors into illegal activities, or engage in publicly violent acts so that all neighbors fear to leave their dwellings. Or they simply may be uniformly viewed as stigmatized residents whose presence reflects poorly on all neighbors' achieved status. By contrast, each additional A household that replaces a D household in the neighborhood may provide a positive socializing influence on all neighbors, such as role-modeling mainstream culture or engaging in acts that promote collective efficacy.

In this hypothetical case, the externality functions for either of the two representative neighborhoods can be portrayed as in figure 9.1, since one is simply the mirror image of the other. Figure 9.1 plots the percentage of this neighborhood's households comprised of group D (%D)—and, implicitly, the percentage comprised of group A (100 – %D)—against the externality index (I) associated with both groups, with I normalized to zero indicative of a baseline situation with no internal neighborhood externalities. The origin indicating zero occupancy by D households is on the left, and the origin indicating zero occupancy by A households is on the right. The externality relationship for group D is shown as I_D: a straight line beginning at the left-hand origin (D cannot generate any externality when they are not present) and negatively sloping ($= \beta$) thereafter, signifying that each added D household reduces the collective well-being in the neighborhood by β. The relationship for A is shown as I_A: a straight line beginning at its origin (A cannot generate any externality when they are not present) and sloping upward from that origin ($= \varphi$) thereafter, thus signifying that each added A household increases the collective well-being in the neighborhood by φ.

Under these assumptions, the perhaps surprising implication is that *any mixture* of groups within and between neighborhoods (that is, ranging from maximum feasible segregation to maximum feasible mixture) will produce exactly the same total amount of externalities, and thus is equally efficient using our standard.[30] The intuition is as follows. Switching any group D household from one neighborhood to another will reduce I_D by β in the origin neighborhood and raise it by β in the destination neighborhood, yielding no net change in aggregate for our stylized society. An analogous argument can be made when switching a group A household: the marginal gain of φ where one is added will be offset by the marginal loss of φ where one is subtracted. Note this conclusion holds regardless of whether A or D is assumed to have positive, zero, or negative externalities; so long as the group's externality is *constant on the margin*, efficiency will not be affected by neighborhood composition.

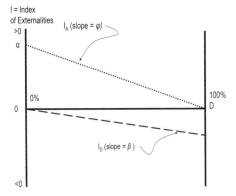

Case 1: A has constant marginal externality = $\varphi > 0$ for all;
D has constant marginal externality = $\beta < 0$ for all

Figure 9.1. Social efficiency of hypothetical constant marginal intraneighborhood
externalities: case 1

*Case 2: Group D generates constant marginal negative externality β for all neighbors
beyond threshold X (expressed as %D).*

Here with the "epidemic/social norm" mechanism, the marginal neighborhood externality effect is not constant, but rather commences once the group generating it exceeds a critical value; see chapter 7.[31] In this instance, the representative group D externality function for a neighborhood will appear as I_D in figure 9.2. Until the percentage of D households exceeds the threshold X, there will be no externality manifested; each additional D thereafter imposes a constant marginal negative externality.[32] Here it is clear that efficiency would be maximized if in every neighborhood %D could be kept at or below X percent of the households, because then there would be no negative externalities anywhere. This may not be possible, however, depending on the relative percentages of threshold X and of D households. If the percentage of the entire population of households represented by D were larger than X, the decline in I_T overall would be minimized by allocating exactly X percent D households to as many neighborhoods as possible, with the remaining D being allocated in whatever manner across the others. Thus, unlike in case 1, here when there is a threshold for the negative neighborhood externality there are very precise implications for a desired neighborhood composition on efficiency grounds, which essentially has a ceiling percentage of the negative externality-producing group manifested in as many neighborhoods as feasible. If both threshold X and the share of D in the overall population were small percentages, it would imply that efficiency

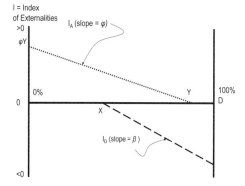

Figure 9.2. Social efficiency of hypothetical intraneighborhood externalities with thresholds: cases 2, 3, and 4

would involve a good deal of segregation manifested as many neighborhoods predominantly occupied by group A, each with only a token share of D. However, if both threshold X and the share of D in the overall population were equal to 50 percent (as D is in this simplified case), efficiency would imply that all neighborhoods should have an equal mix of the two groups.

Case 3: Group A generates constant marginal positive externality φ for all neighbors beyond threshold Y (where Y is defined as maximum %D where φ persists).

Here with the "epidemic/social norm" mechanism we have the converse of case 2, with group A producing positive externalities for all if they exceed a minimum threshold of Y percent (that is, the equivalent condition is that %D falls below [100 – Y] percent). The process of social norm transmission operates here in identical fashion to that described above in case 2, except that past the threshold, socially *desirable* collective socialization processes ensue.

The efficiency analysis follows as above; see the I_A function in figure 9.2. To maximize the sum of positive externalities, we should avoid having neighborhoods where group A households represent less than their threshold. Any A households residing in neighborhoods with less than their threshold concentration would be "wasted" from the perspective of social efficiency, since none would be producing positive externalities at this concentration. Thus, the optimal allocation would have as many A households as possible residing in neighborhoods where their concentrations exceeded the threshold. This means filling up neighborhoods completely with A households until this group is exhausted; any remaining could be allocated across the remaining neighborhoods in whatever manner. This set of assumptions in case 3 implies that an extremely segregated situation would be efficient.

Case 4: Group D generates constant marginal negative externality β for all neighbors beyond threshold X and A generates constant marginal positive externality φ for all neighbors below threshold Y (where Y is defined as maximum D where φ persists) and Y > X.

Here, from the perspective of the "epidemic/social norm" mechanism, I combine cases 2 and 3 to consider implications of the assumption that different household types produce *countervailing* (though not necessarily equal in magnitude) externalities that ensue at different threshold points. Figure 9.2 again applies, with I_D and I_A functions both operative.[33]

The outcome of the efficiency analysis rests on the relative magnitudes of the two externalities being generated. In this situation, inter-neighborhood variations in the household mixture in the range between the two thresholds produce a constant I_T, because the net marginal externality combining both functions is a constant (following the logic of case 1). Put differently, switching group A and D households between neighborhoods that have exceeded *both* thresholds (and continue to do so after the hypothetical reallocation) will lead to no net change in efficiency, because the gains in the destination neighborhood will exactly offset the losses in origin neighborhood. However, whether such a mixed situation will be superior to more segregated options when one or the other threshold has not been exceeded cannot be ascertained without more information about the relative magnitudes of the two externality parameters φ and β.

Consider the following thought experiment. What would happen to efficiency if we were to reallocate some households within some of these mixed neighborhoods (that is, those with %D values between X and Y in figure 9.2) so that we instead produced more segregated neighborhoods (that is, some with %D less than threshold X, and others with %D greater than threshold Y)? If the positive externality produced by group A were much greater than the negative externality produced by group D, the set of neighborhoods with %D less than X would enjoy massive increases in positive externalities associated with now larger percentages of group A residents, with no offsetting negative externalities from group D (because their percentage would be below X). By contrast, the set of neighborhoods with %D greater than threshold X would evince some increase in negative externalities associated with their now larger percentages of D households, and no offsetting positive externalities from group A (because their percentage would be below 100 − Y). If indeed $|\varphi|>|\beta|$, then the gains in the former set of neighborhoods will offset the losses in the latter, and it will be more efficient for society as a whole to convert mixed neighborhoods into those that have more segregation. Following on the logic of case 3, efficiency would be maximized by allocating as many A households as possible to completely segregated neighborhoods, and then (if mathematically possible) allocating D households among any remaining neighborhoods to minimize the number that exceed threshold X.

The conclusion is the opposite if we reverse the assumptions about the relative magnitudes of the externalities and replay our thought experiment. If $|\varphi|<|\beta|$, then the gains in the set of previously below-threshold neighborhoods with a now larger share of group A will not offset the losses in the other set, and it will be more efficient to avoid switching mixed neighborhoods for those that have more segregation. Following the logic of case 2, efficiency here would be maximized by allocating as many D households as possible to neighborhoods with below-X concentrations and then (if mathematically possible) allocating A households among any remaining neighborhoods to maximize the number that exceed threshold Y. It is mathematically possible, of course, that the two parameters are precisely equal in absolute value, such that all allocations are equally efficient.

Case 5: Group D generates growing marginal negative externality for only D neighbors.

The externality modeled here can be considered a "selective socialization" process, wherein the assumed bad influence of one D household is felt only by other D households (not A households) in the neighborhood, perhaps because they are more vulnerable to these influences, or because the social networks of D households are homogeneous within the group and do not include any A households. Here the negative externality produced by the marginal D household increases nonlinearly with the number of D households in a neighborhood because there are more D neighbors to be affected by the externality generated by the marginal D household. Thus, the marginal negative externality can be expressed as $\beta\%D$. Households in group A are assumed irrelevant as either transmitters or receivers of this externality, perhaps because they have few social networks involving group D, or because they have a great social distance from them. I show the nonlinear externality function for group D in one neighborhood, I_D, in figure 9.3. In

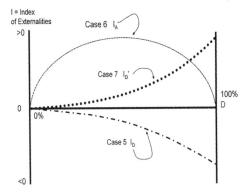

Figure 9.3. Social efficiency of hypothetical variable marginal intraneighborhood externalities: cases 5, 6, and 7

this case, allocating all group D households to neighborhoods in the smallest percentages possible, equally across all neighborhoods, would minimize the total negative externalities that they produce for themselves. That is, because the negative externality grows more than proportionately with the addition of one more group D household, for the most efficient solution, society should disperse these households in the lowest equal concentrations possible—that is, equal to their share in the overall population. If D households represented a small share of the population, this result implies that efficiency would be manifested as every neighborhood being predominantly occupied by A households. On the other hand, if D households represented half of the population (as in the simplified model), this result implies that equally mixed neighborhoods would be most efficient across the board.

Case 6: Group A generates growing marginal positive externality for only D neighbors.

Here with the "selective socialization" mechanism, the externality produced by each A (φ) benefits each D (but not other A households) present in the neighborhood. This could represent a situation wherein each group A household provides a valuable behavioral role model for all group D households present, which is irrelevant for other group A households because they already exhibit this behavior.[34] I show the corresponding I_A externality function for a particular neighborhood in figure 9.3. The I_A function would take on the shape of an inverted U, because eventually more A households in the neighborhood create a negative marginal impact as they reduce the number of D households present to benefit from the externality. Efficiency concerns imply that, as in case 5, the maximum positive externality overall will occur when the mix of group A and D households is identical across all neighborhoods (and equal to their respective shares in the population). The intuition is as follows. Starting with a common mix of A and D, if two neighborhoods were to switch some A and D households, the gain in positive externalities in the neighborhood losing D households would be less than the loss in positive externalities in the neighborhood gaining D households.

Case 7: Group D generates growing marginal positive externality for only D neighbors.

This variant of the "social network" mechanism describes what we might called "group affinity." The notion implicit in this case is that as more group D households cluster in space, they can build stronger social ties within the group and build valuable cultural capital. Such might represent an "ethnic enclave" of newly arrived immigrants, for example. Here the total positive externality increases nonlinearly with the number of D in a neighborhood because there are more D neighbors to both generate and be affected by the externality. Group A households in this case are irrelevant as either transmitters or receivers of externalities. I show in figure 9.3 the group D externality function appertaining as I_D.' Efficiency considerations lead here to the opposite conclusions from those in case 5. In this case, segregation is efficient, regardless of the share of D households in the overall population. By allocating as many D households as possible to homogeneous D-occupied neighborhoods, society will achieve a higher value for I_T than if society allocated D in any smaller percentages across neighborhoods. Because the marginal benefit of an added group D neighbor rises as more of group D are already present, such a household always should be added to the neighborhood with the greatest %D, up to a maximum of 100 percent.

Case 8: Group A and group D generate growing marginal positive externalities, but only for neighbors not like themselves.

This variant of the "social network" mechanism describes what we might call "social cohesion." In this view, there may be nothing intrinsically good or bad about the behaviors and attitudes of either group, but there is a larger societal value in the social interaction between them in a neighbor-

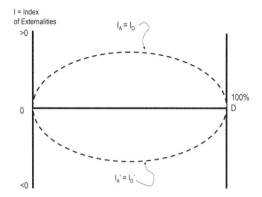

Figure 9.4. Social efficiency of hypothetical selective, variable marginal intraneighborhood externalities: cases 8 and 9

hood context, because it builds intergroup social capital. That is, mutual and equal positive externalities (like tolerance and empathy) are generated for all participants when they reside together; such is the essence of the "contact hypothesis."[35] I present the identical I_D and I_A externality functions that correspond to this case in figure 9.4. From an efficiency perspective, this is analogous to case 6, wherein both A and D produce positive externalities whose marginal benefits are proportional to those of the other group in the area. As before, the implication is that as many neighborhoods as possible should be mixed at equal percentages of group A and D households to maximize efficiency, regardless of their respective shares in the overall population.

Case 9: Group A and group D generate growing marginal negative externalities, but only for neighbors not like themselves.

Here I model the "competition" neighborhood effect mechanism, which is formally equivalent to assuming that both groups have homophily preferences. Each member of both groups in this case receives disamenities from the presence of members of the other group in the neighborhood. Their common I_D' and I_A' externality functions are presented in figure 9.4. This is analyzed as the converse of case 8, wherein both A and D produce negative instead of positive externalities whose marginal benefits are proportional to those of the other group in the area. From the social efficiency perspective, one draws the conclusion that as few neighborhoods as possible should be mixed; rather group A and D households should be completely segregated, regardless of their respective shares in the overall population.

Case 10: Group D generates constant, lump-sum negative externality β for all neighbors (A and D) if D exceeds threshold Z.

This can be seen as the "neighborhood stigmatizing" mechanism. If the external marketplace holds stereotypical views about group D, it may develop negative responses toward anyone from a neighborhood where group D constitutes more than Z percent of the households, and may restrict flows of other resources to that place. Though in some sense it is not the fault of group D households that others stereotype them in this fashion, it is appropriate to model this as if they indeed were the source of this externality, even though it ultimately emanates from outside the neighborhood. I model this as a constant externality of lump-sum amount β that is imposed discontinuously once %D exceeds Z (see I_D in figure 9.5).[36] It is clearly more efficient in case 10 to avoid concentrations of group D households that exceed the stigmatizing threshold Z. If group D represents a small share of all households or Z is large, this well may be mathematically feasible. If not, it is preferable to allocate group D households in such a way that as many neighborhoods as possible do not exceed Z; all allocations of the remaining D will be equally efficient. Whether these efficient allocations produce mainly mixed or segregated neighborhoods will depend on the size of Z and the share of D in the overall population. If both are 50 percent, all neighborhoods should have 50 percent D and A households. If Z is small compared to the percentage of D in the population, many neighborhoods will have a large majority of A households, with only Z% of D households.

In summary, the foregoing makes it clear that the comparative social efficiency of alternative distributions of population groups among neighborhoods crucially depends on the nature of the externalities that they transmit to members of their own group and members of the other groups. See the second column of table 9.1 for a succinct summary of the prior ten cases' implications for the neighborhood population composition having the greatest social efficiency. Both complete segregation and complete mixing to the extent that is arithmetically feasible emerge as potentially socially efficient outcomes, depending on the nature of the intra-neighborhood externalities (as well as the shares of groups in the overall population) being assumed. It thus becomes a critical empirical matter to ascertain which pattern of

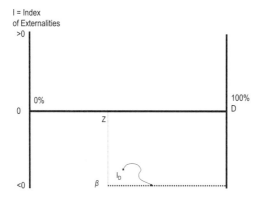

Figure 9.5. Social efficiency of hypothetical constant stigma after threshold neighborhood externalities: case 10

intergroup externalities appears dominant in the contemporary American context.

Inefficiencies in Households' Mobility Behaviors: Evidence

In chapters 6, 7 and 8, I already presented the evidence relevant for assessing which of the prior hypothetical cases most closely matches the reality of most US neighborhoods, so I summarize it only briefly here. Unlike the previous theoretical discussion wherein "advantaged" and "disadvantaged" were generic terms, here it is important to distinguish the evidence related to the economic composition and the racial composition of the neighborhood.

Externalities among different economic groups. My review in chapter 8 of social interactive neighborhood effect mechanisms concluded that there was strong evidence of negative behavioral externalities created among members of economically disadvantaged groups, which manifested themselves through peer effects and collective socialization. Crucially, as I demonstrated in chapter 6, these effects typically take the form of social contagion after the concentration of the poor exceeds a critical threshold (i.e., 15 to 20 percent poverty rates).[37] It is reasonable to assume that many of the behaviors generated past this threshold (such as engaging in violent or illegal activities) have negative external impacts on both economically disadvantaged and advantaged neighbors.

Table 9.1. Summary of neighborhood population composition implications arising from alternative neighborhood effect mechanisms emanating from groups A and D (shown in parentheses)

Neighborhood externality or effect type (shown parenthetically)	Most socially efficient allocation across neighborhoods
1. $D < 0$ for all, $A > 0$ for all; both constant on margin (collective socialization)	Households allocated in whatever manner; alternative allocations with same social efficiency
2. $D < 0$ for all past threshold X (epidemic/social norm)	As many D households as possible to neighborhoods $< X$; allocation of any remaining D irrelevant
3. $A > 0$ for all past threshold Y (epidemic/social norm)	As many A households as possible to neighborhoods $> Y$; allocation of any remaining A irrelevant
4. $D < 0$ for all past threshold X; $A > 0$ for all past threshold Y; (epidemic/social norm)	As many A households as possible to neighborhoods $> Y$ if A's externality $>$ D's; as many D households as possible to neighborhoods $< X$ if D's externality $>$ that of A
5. $D < 0$ other D only; proportional (selective socialization)	All neighborhoods with identical A and D composition (= overall population shares of A and D)
6. $A > 0$ for D only ; proportional (selective socialization)	All neighborhoods with identical A and D composition (= overall population shares of A and D)
7. $D > 0$ other D only; proportional (social networks)	As many D households as possible to neighborhoods with 100%D; highest feasible %D in remaining neighborhood
8. D and $A > 0$ for others; proportional (social networks)	Equal % A and D wherever D is present, if possible; as equal % A and D as possible in remaining neighborhoods
9. D and $A < 0$ for others; proportional (competition; relative deprivation)	As many D households as possible to neighborhoods with 100%D; as many A households as possible to neighborhoods with 100%A
10. $D < 0$ constant for all past threshold Z (stigmatization; institutional resources)	As many D households as possible to neighborhoods $< Z$; allocation of any remaining D irrelevant

Note: Inequality signs indicate whether assumed intraneighborhood externality from advantaged household group A or disadvantaged household group D is positive or negative.

Additional evidence shows that poor individuals will also gain absolutely by residence near more economically advantaged neighbors. Role modeling and social control provided by economically advantaged neighbors (manifested by greater public safety), in conjunction with superior public services and institutional resources, seem more likely mechanisms of positive intra-neighborhood externalities emanating from the advantaged group.[38]

As I showed in chapter 8, several random assignment and natural experiments revealed that these positive externalities can be particularly powerful for younger children from poor families living among economically advantaged households.[39] Evidence I reviewed in chapter 6 indicated that there likely was a threshold concentration of advantaged households in a neighborhood required to generate this positive externality, though the specific threshold parameter was uncertain.

In total, the foregoing evidence strongly suggests that (1) economically disadvantaged households create negative externalities for all neighbors once they exceed a threshold concentration, and (2) economically advantaged households create positive externalities for all neighbors once they exceed a threshold concentration. As such, this evidence points clearly toward a context as portrayed in case 4 (figure 9.2) above, though the dual marginal externalities produced past the thresholds may not be proportional as shown. Unfortunately, it is difficult from available evidence to draw any conclusions about which of the marginal magnitudes of externalities is larger. In my view, the spectrum of problems associated with concentrated disadvantage are some of the most costly we face in American society. The logical implication of this view is unambiguous. The current pattern of many American neighborhoods exceeding a poverty concentration threshold of 15 to 20 percent is socially inefficient; it yields a higher rate of unproductive and problematic behaviors for society as a whole than would be generated by alternative distributions of economic groups across neighborhoods that manifested a radically deconcentrated pattern of poverty.

How large of a social inefficiency is this? With my colleagues Jackie Cutsinger and Ron Malega, I provided a plausible lower-bound estimate using parameters from the econometric model we estimated for the causal relationship between neighborhood decadal changes in poverty rates and subsequent changes in property values and rents.[40] We simulated how property values and rents would have changed in the aggregate for neighborhoods in the one hundred largest metropolitan areas, had populations hypothetically been redistributed such that two conditions were met. First, all census tracts in 1990 exceeding 20 percent poverty had their rate reduced to 20 percent by the year 2000. Second, only the lowest-poverty tracts were allocated additional poor populations, with each increasing their poverty rate by five percentage points maximum. We found in this thought experiment that owner-occupied property values would have been a staggering $421 billion (13 percent, measured in base-year 1990 dollars) greater, and monthly rents would have been $400 million (4 percent) greater in aggregate, ceteris paribus.

Externalities among different racial groups. As I discussed in chapter 7, public opinion polls and statistical studies of willingness to pay for housing consistently reveal that most black and Hispanic households prefer neighborhoods with roughly equal racial proportions. Framed in terms of externalities, this evidence suggests that black and Hispanic households residing in predominantly minority-occupied neighborhoods see new white neighbors as conveying positive externalities, at least up to the point where the neighborhood manifests as substantial diversity of races. This perception of more racially integrated environments providing positive externalities for minorities also receives support from two econometric studies demonstrating plausibly causal relationships between greater residential exposure of blacks to whites (that is, less segregation) and reduced high school dropout rates for black youths.[41] This evidence is most consistent with the selective socialization mechanism, shown stylistically above in case 6 (figure 9.3).

By contrast, the same evidence from chapter 7 indicates that most whites generally prefer predominantly white-occupied neighborhoods. Opinion polls revealing whites' negative stereotypes of individual minorities imply that they perceive more than a modest share of black or Hispanic neighbors as imposing negative externalities on them. This interpretation is also consistent with whites' pessimistic expectations associated with predominantly black-occupied neighborhoods (as I discussed in chapter 5) and their willingness to pay more for neighborhoods that are predominantly white-occupied (as I discussed in chapter 7). Finally, the aforementioned literature on racial "tipping" strongly suggests that the magnitude of the negative externalities imposed by blacks increases on the margin as the tipping point approaches. These strands of evidence all point to a model wherein D households selectively impose increasingly negative externalities on only A households after a threshold %D has been surpassed. This is the analog of case 5 above, with the addition of a threshold.

However, additional evidence suggests that another negative externality process be included as well. Recent work by Anna Santiago and me has indicated that a variety of negative outcomes for low-income black and Hispanic youths associated with being raised in preponderantly minority-occupied neighborhoods do not mainly transpire from the racial composition per se, but rather from the correlated shortcomings in public safety, city services, and institutional investments that flow into such places.[42] I think it reasonable, therefore, to posit that a threshold of disadvantaged (minority) residents is associated with this mechanism of stigmatization and altering resource flows from external forces that harm A and D households alike, so that another appropriate stylized model is case 10.

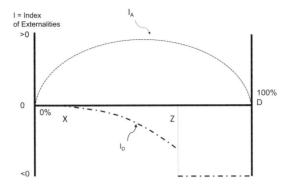

Figure 9.6. Social efficiency with combination of externalities representing current situation

Combining the arguments of the prior two paragraphs yields a synthesized externality function for D (minority) households as portrayed as I_D in figure 9.6. After surpassing threshold X, the function assumes an increasingly negative slope for reasons explained above. After %D exceeds a second threshold of stigmatization Z, however, a lump-sum of negative externality is added to this underlying function. In the range of %D > Z there is little reason from theory or evidence to believe that further increases in D concentration yield increasingly negative externalities; I therefore portray this segment as a horizontal line, for simplicity.

In sum, the evidence points to a model of intra-neighborhood racial externalities as portrayed in figure 9.6. Two conclusions follow. The first conclusion one can draw from figure 9.6 is that a neighborhood with %D < X offers a more efficient (higher net positive externalities) alternative than one with %D > Z. In other words, neighborhoods where D households remain in the minority (assuming X < 50%) are more socially efficient than those where D constitute the overwhelming majority of residents (%D > Z). The second conclusion is that the most efficient allocation of households would be with all neighborhoods having the identical composition (equal the shares of A and D in the overall population), with one possible exception. This remarkable conclusion about the social efficiency of maximum feasible racial mixing holds quite generally within a wide range of the relative magnitudes of the offsetting positive and negative externalities, the values of the thresholds, and the relative population sizes of the two groups. Three alternatives suffice to demonstrate.

First, consider a situation where D is such a small percentage of the metropolitan area's households that it would be mathematically feasible for all neighborhoods to house them at equal concentrations less than X

percent. In this situation, we would conclude, analogously to case 6 above, that all neighborhoods with identical racial compositions would be most efficient. Starting at this distribution, consider the thought experiment of reallocating some D households such that their percentage increased in one neighborhood while decreasing in another. Given the convex curvature of the I_A function, this reallocation would clearly reduce the total positive externalities since the gain in the neighborhood increasing in %D would be smaller than the loss in the one decreasing %D. This gain would be even less (perhaps even negative) were this reallocation to increase %D in the former neighborhood past X.

Second, consider a situation where D is a sufficiently large percentage of the metropolitan area's households such that it would be mathematically feasible for all neighborhoods to house A and D at an identical concentration with %D between X and Z. This situation superficially seems more complicated with the I_D function now operative, but the conclusion is the same: divergence from an identical mix across all neighborhoods reduces overall efficiency. This can be deduced from a similar thought experiment performed as above for both I_A and I_D functions separately, consistent with the logic in cases 5 and 6 above.

Third, consider a situation where D is such a large percentage of the metropolitan area's households that it only would be mathematically feasible that all neighborhoods could house A and D at an identical concentration with %D > Z. Here, a thought-experimental comparison of alternative allocations among neighborhoods, all of which maintain that %D > Z, would again reveal that an identical mix across all neighborhoods maximizes overall efficiency. However, with the discontinuity in the I_D function at Z, one must also compare hypothetical allocations involving some neighborhoods reducing their %D below Z. It is possible that efficiency may be enhanced by replacing two neighborhoods with identical compositions of A and D with one with %D < X and the other with a %D greater than originally, so long as the negative stigmatization externality occurring at Z (the gain the neighborhood lowering its %D) is large relative to the marginal loss in positive externality (the loss of the neighborhood raising its %D). Under such conditions, social efficiency would be maximized by having as many D households as possible allocated to one set of neighborhoods with an identical composition of D and A households (with %D slightly less than Z), and the remaining D households allocated to another set of neighborhoods that also have an identical (though different) composition of D (%D > Z) and A households.

In summary, an empirically grounded analysis based on intraneighborhood racial externalities suggests that the most socially efficient allocation of households would involve a situation in which virtually all neighborhoods in a metropolitan area would have a common racial composition, roughly matching that of the racial groups in the area as a whole. By implication, the predominant pattern of racial segregation we observe across our metropolitan areas must be socially inefficient. Unfortunately, social scientists have not agreed on how this inefficiency should manifest itself and how it should be uncovered, and thus there is far from any empirical consensus on the degree to which segregation imposes penalties on our society. Consider three realms of evidence.

First, two studies taking similar empirical approaches have come to different conclusions about whether whites gain in absolute terms (instead of just relative to minorities) from racial segregation. Ingrid Ellen, Justin Steil, and Jorge De la Roca find that individual white households living in more racially segregated metropolitan areas have higher wages, complete college at higher rates, and attain higher-status occupations than whites in desegregated areas.[43] By contrast, Gregory Acs, Rolf Pendall, Mark Treskon, and Amy Khare find that neither black-white nor Hispanic-white segregation is significantly associated with median household incomes or per capita incomes of white households.[44] Moreover, greater levels of black-white segregation are associated with lower bachelor's degree attainment rates among whites and higher metro-wide homicide rates, which presumably impose costs on all groups. They also find no significant associations between whites' median incomes, per capita incomes, or college graduation rates and *economic* segregation for the metropolitan area.[45] They do find, however, substantial harms to minorities from segregation, as I will amplify below. Their findings thus suggest that segregation is inefficient, since some members of society lose while no one gains.

Second, several studies find that racially diverse neighborhoods score higher on some measures of unfavorable social conditions, which would argue against the inefficiency of segregation. John Hipp, for example, discovers that neighborhoods with similar housing and socioeconomic profiles have higher crime rates if they have greater racial diversity, a result he attributes to heightened senses of relative deprivation.[46] Robert Putnam has observed that there are lower levels of social capital in racially diverse neighborhoods.[47] Unfortunately, these studies' conclusions about causation are not definitive, since they only observe patterns across neighborhoods, which cannot rule out the bias from selective mobility that I discussed in the previous chapter.

The third realm of evidence relevant to the social inefficiency of racial segregation is the question of whether whites' perceptions of negative externalities from their exposure to different racial groups should unquestioningly be accepted as either socially acceptable or immutable.[48] There is considerable evidence that both advantaged and disadvantaged populations may benefit from sharing the same neighborhood if the contact results in a reduction of intergroup prejudices.[49] Many US studies have observed that interethnic group tolerance and subsequent social contacts expand with greater intra-neighborhood exposure, especially when they occur earlier in life.[50] The "contact hypothesis," as it is termed, implies that white's perceptions about the putative negative externalities flowing from substantial racial diversity in neighborhoods are malleable. If indeed whites' prejudices might wane over time from experience with more diverse neighborhoods, this would tip the balance of evidence farther toward the conclusion that racial segregation is a socially inefficient outcome.

Social Inefficiencies: Dynamic Perspective

In the last section, I examined how a static snapshot of our neighborhoods reveals socially inefficient patterns of too little property investments and too much segregation by income and by race, due to strategic gaming and externalities that led to market failures. Here I switch the focus of the inefficiency analysis to consider the *dynamic process* by which neighborhoods transition from one set of demographic, economic, and physical characteristics to another. Again, I will conclude that the autonomous, market-guided dynamics are inefficient from a societal perspective, this time because of *self-fulfilling prophecies*. A self-fulfilling prophecy in a neighborhood context is a process that starts with an individual making a decision related to residential mobility or property investment on the basis of fearful expectations. Unfortunately, if many other decision makers in the neighborhood do the same, this aggregation of actions ushers in the feared event. This is a classic example of collective irrationality: what is sensible action from the perspective of an autonomous individual proves irrational when the collective engages in the same action. Researchers have documented well these self-fulfilling prophecies in the realms of residential mobility and property reinvestment behaviors.

Racial composition-related expectations drive many of these self-fulfilling prophecies. Recall that I reviewed in chapter 5 the strong evidence indicating that whites, and often blacks, view a substantial share or large increase in the black population of a neighborhood as a harbinger of declining quality of life and property values, as summarized in the The Proposition of *Racially Encoded Signals*. When a large number of current residents and owners use this indicator as a basis for underinvesting in their properties and/or leaving the neighborhood, they will encourage the very racial and perhaps class succession of their neighborhoods that they pessimistically expected. Robert Sampson and Stephen Raudenbush provided a dramatic example of this dynamic.[51] They observed that white residents, especially those who were better off financially, perceived more disorder in a neighborhood with larger shares of black residents, even controlling for a myriad of objective indicators of disorder. As a result, they were more likely to disinvest and move away from the neighborhood, thus ushering in more disorder. Richard Taub, Garth Taylor, and Jan Dunham documented an analogous process.[52] They observed that whites' perceptions of growing in-migration of black residents fueled concomitant expectations of eroded public safety and competitiveness of the neighborhood, which led them to cut back their upkeep activities.

Expectations regarding racial change are not required to generate inefficient self-fulfilling prophecies in neighborhoods, however. Owners who hold pessimistic expectations about the future quality of life in their neighborhood will reduce their property upkeep investments, hastening the decline they feared.[53] In sum, the dynamics of neighborhood change often embody collectively irrational behaviors that produce outcomes that none of the individual decision-makers would have desired.

Social Inequities: Static Perspective

The inefficiently low levels of investment in residential properties and high levels of neighborhood segregation by race and income do not impose their costs evenly across all groups in America. On the contrary, these costs are disproportionately borne by those who have traditionally been least advantaged in our society: lower-income and minority households.[54]

Investigating the adverse consequences of residential segregation for ethnic minority people has a long and distinguished social scientific history.[55] Over the last several decades, scholars have developed sophisticated statistical models that permit valid causal inferences to be drawn about the degree to which racial segregation produces a variety of interracial disparities in outcomes.[56] These studies identified substantial and roughly equal socioeconomic and health costs that segregation imposes on blacks and Hispanics. Justin Steil, Jorge de la Roca, and Ingrid Ellen provide recent estimates of the approximate magnitudes of these harms for individual young adult minorities of the ages twenty-five to thirty.[57] For black individuals, a one-standard-deviation increase in the black-white dissimilarity index of metropolitan area segregation is associated with a decline in the probability of completing high school of 1.4 percentage points relative to whites (that is, 20 percent of the difference in means between these groups). A one-standard-deviation increase in the Hispanic-white dissimilarity index is associated with an even larger decline in the probability of finishing high school of 3 percentage points for Hispanic individuals relative to white individuals (that is, 33 percent of the difference between group means). Analogously, such an increase in segregation is associated with a decline in the probability of completing college by 4.8 percentage points for blacks and 4.6 percentage points for Hispanics (representing 21 percent and 19 percent of the respective mean gaps with whites). Both blacks and Hispanics exhibit equally strong relationships between racial segregation and interracial gaps in single motherhood, in being simultaneously out of school and out of work, and in earnings.[58]

By contrast, there is much less causal evidence about the degree to which intermetropolitan variations in economic segregation are responsible for individual differences in socioeconomic outcomes, and how these relationships may vary by race. All the cross-sectional work here is descriptive in nature.[59] Raj Chetty, Nathaniel Hendren, Patrick Kline, and Emmanuel Saez found that children growing up in metropolitan areas with higher levels of economic segregation are less likely to advance from their parents' economic position, controlling for many other characteristics of their metropolitan area.[60] Bryan Graham and Patrick Sharkey come to a similar conclusion using different data sets and measures.[61] Gregory Acs, Rolf Pendall, Mark Treskon, and Amy Khare observed that blacks in metropolitan areas with lower amounts of economic segregation have significantly higher per capita incomes, median household incomes, and rates of attaining bachelor's degrees, controlling for other characteristics of their metropolitan areas.[62] Statistical studies of individual outcomes and neighborhood-level exposures to different socioeconomic groups (the "neighborhood effects" literature I summarized in chapter 8) have given us most of the substantial plausible causal evidence regarding the inequities produced by economic segregation.

Due to the synergistic operation of racial and economic segregation, neighborhood physical decay, economic deprivation, and minority composition exhibit distinctive spatial congruence in American metropolitan areas. Blacks and Hispanics are exposed, on average, to much higher incidences of neighborhood physical and socioeconomic disadvantage than whites, even when they have similar incomes.[63] Several studies employing the latest census data have confirmed this conclusion in complementary ways. John

Logan showed that across all metropolitan neighborhoods, the average black person is exposed to a 77 percent higher neighborhood poverty rate, than the average white person, and the average Hispanic person is exposed to a 62 percent higher poverty rate.[64] The interracial gaps in neighborhood poverty exposure are even greater for poor minorities: 102 percent and 85 percent higher for blacks and Hispanics, respectively.[65] Paul Jargowsky documented that 25 percent of poor blacks and 17 percent of poor Hispanics live in neighborhoods with extreme poverty rates of 40 percent or more, compared to only 7 percent of poor whites.[66] These dramatic neighborhood inequalities extend across the income distribution. Patrick Sharkey found that blacks with household income of $100,000 or more live in and are nearby neighborhoods with higher levels of disadvantage than white families with income of $30,000 or less.[67] Sean Reardon, Lindsay Fox, and Joseph Townsend showed that neighborhood economic conditions are the same for the average white household earning $11,800, the average Hispanic household earning $45,000, and the average black household earning $60,000.[68]

From the foregoing, it is abundantly clear that segregation-induced differences in exposure to neighborhood disadvantage lead ultimately to unequal socioeconomic outcomes for individuals based on their race and class.[69] Yet, what is it exactly about these inequitable differentials that creates these effects? Below I briefly document five categories of unfair burdens that these disadvantaged households bear because of the segregated pattern of physical, demographic, and economic characteristics of American neighborhoods.[70]

Subcultural Adaptations

The spatial isolation of lower-income and racial minority groups can encourage and permit the development of distinct subcultural attitudes, behaviors, and speech patterns that may impede success in the mainstream world of work, either because they are counterproductive in some objective sense or because they are perceived to be so by prospective (typically higher-income, white) employers. Segregation makes it harder for low-income and minority children to acquire the "soft skills" valued in the labor market.[71] These valuable skills, especially styles of communication and interpersonal relationships, arise primarily from social patterns prevailing in white middle-class culture. Instead, these children may develop alterative patterns that may serve them well on the streets (like cool posing and hypersensitivity to perceived disrespect)[72] but hinder them in the conventional workplace.[73]

Reduced Wealth Accumulation via Higher Prices

Wealth is stripped from low-income and minority communities because the nature of the local retail and financial services sector renders it more expensive to live there. These communities pay more for food, primarily due to the lack of large-volume supermarkets.[74] Poor neighborhoods and predominantly black neighborhoods have roughly half the number of supermarkets as do wealthy ones and white ones.[75] The withdrawal of the mainstream financial services industry from disadvantaged neighborhoods has created a vacuum that has been filled by the fringe financial sector, including payday lenders, check-cashing outlets, rent-to-own stores, and pawnshops.[76] Fees paid to payday lenders and check-cashing outlets for services that are normally free in better-banked communities run into the billions of dollars annually.[77] One estimate calculates that average full-time workers regularly using a check cashing service would have gained $360,000 in wealth during their working lifetimes if they had saved those fees by having a checking account.[78] Higher-interest subprime mortgage lending is often foisted upon minority homebuyers even when their credit scores do not justify it.[79] One recent study estimates that, as compared to equally qualified white borrowers in same-quality white neighborhoods, black borrowers in predominantly black neighborhoods in Baltimore paid 6.4 percent higher monthly mortgage costs (resulting in roughly $16,000 more over the life of a thirty-year loan) as a net result of racially disparate patterns of mortgage lending.[80] Insurance coverage for homes and autos is more expensive in low-income and minority-occupied neighborhoods.[81] The combined effect of these excess costs of living in low-income neighborhoods has been estimated to strip away about a quarter of a poor person's income;[82] it is probably even greater if blacks or Hispanics predominantly occupy the neighborhood.

Inferior Public Services and Institutions

Not only are lower-income and minority households separated residentially from their higher-income and white compatriots; they disproportionately reside in distinct municipalities that are more financially stressed because of their combination of economic and population decline and concentrations of poverty. This means that the juxtaposition of inferior public services and high tax rates may be the unenviable situation facing such disadvantaged households. Moreover, lower-income and minority households disproportionately endure not only the worst interjurisdictional inequities in public services and facilities, but intra-jurisdictional ones as well. Many studies have documented the vast differences in both public and private institutional resources serving different neighborhoods both across and within jurisdictions,[83] and there is growing consensus that such institutions serve as important mechanisms through which neighborhood effects transpire. [84] As illustration, measurable educational resources vary dramatically across space and correlate strongly with several aspects of student performance.[85] Black, Hispanic and low-economic-status students generally can access only inferior school resources. The average black or Hispanic public elementary school student in 1999–2000 attended a school where more than 65 percent of students were poor, compared to only 30 percent poor in the average white child's public school.[86] Shortages of high-quality childcare facilities are acute in many low-income and minority neighborhoods, despite their proven effectiveness in building a variety of intellectual and behavioral skills in young children.[87] Lower-income communities are also at a disadvantage in terms of access to medical facilities and practitioners.[88] Furthermore, it is clear that many low-income minority parents believe that the perceived paucity of local institutional resources adversely affects their children,[89] and often try to compensate for this shortcoming by seeking them from outside of their neighborhoods.[90]

Unhealthy Exposures to Pollution and Violence

The physical and social environment can affect health through multiple pathways, resulting in strong disparities in morbidity and mortality across neighborhoods differentiated by race and income.[91] First, undermaintained housing can create issues of physical danger (e.g., overloaded electrical systems, defective heating sources, or broken steps and railings); epidemiological problems related to drafts, mold, vermin infestations, and lead toxins;[92] and a reduced sense of personal efficacy.[93] Second, neighborhoods predominantly occupied by racial minorities or by lower-income households have higher concentrations of air pollution and exposure to toxic waste sites.[94] One recent study found that blacks lived in neighborhoods with concentrations of toxic air pollutants that are 1.45 times greater than whites' and 1.7 times greater than Hispanics', on average. Expressed another way, blacks earning $50,000 or more live in neighborhoods with more air pollution that whites earning less than $10,000 per year.[95] In turn, many international epidemiological studies link air pollutants to lower life expectancy, higher infant and adult mortality risks, more hospital visits, poorer birth outcomes, and asthma.[96] Proximity to hazardous waste ("brownfield") sites is associated with higher rates of mortality from cancer and other diseases.[97] There are strong links between neighborhood minority racial composition and children's elevated blood lead levels.[98] Studies show that even small amounts of lead poisoning, typically produced by residue from deteriorated lead-based paint formerly used in homes, can harm infants.[99] Lead poisoning also harms the mental development, IQ, and behaviors of older children.[100] Third, poor minority communities often possess few recreational opportunities and healthy food sources nearby, thus raising the risks of obesity.[101] Fourth, individuals' stress levels are substantially higher in poor areas,[102] yielding permanent harm to the cognitive and behavioral development of children,[103] reducing the efficacy of the body's immune system,[104] and increasing rates of cardiovascular disease and premature death for adults.[105] It can also produce a variety of unhealthy stress-reduction behaviors, such as smoking.[106] Fifth, exposure to crime and violence is substantially higher in areas of concentrated poverty and minority occupancy.[107] Youths and adults exposed to violence as witnesses or victims suffer increased stress and decline in mental health.[108] Exposure to violence is linked to poorer pregnancy outcomes and low birth weight,[109] poorer educational outcomes,[110] and more aggressive behavior.[111] Violence interacts with other aspects of the environment to erode health synergistically. It contributes directly to higher stress levels. Fear of crime encourages caregivers to keep their children indoors, reducing thereby their options for exercise and aggravating their chances of obesity.[112] Youths exposed to violence smoke more, and run a higher risk of pregnancy.[113] The net effect of all of these environmental mechanisms on health inequalities is stunning. Differences in neighborhood economic background account for a third or more of the variation in midlife health status; for example, a fifty-five-year old raised in a high-poverty neighborhood has about the same health as a seventy-year old raised in a low-poverty one.[114]

Access to Employment

Employment opportunities for minority and low-income workers may become more restricted in light of progressive decentralization of jobs (especially those paying decent wages only with modest skill requirements) in metropolitan areas, because the ability of those workers to learn about and commute to jobs declines as their proximity to them declines. Scholars have long labelled this "the spatial mismatch hypothesis." Suggestive ethnographies have shown that low-income youths can benefit greatly from part-time employment by gaining resources, adult supervision, and routinized schedules;[115] yet their neighborhoods typically have few such jobs.[116] Evaluations of the Gautreaux program in Chicago showed that low-income black youths moving to the suburbs were more likely to hold jobs and earn more money than their counterparts who stayed within the city.[117] Numerous rigorous statistical studies also have investigated this issue.[118] This literature generally confirms that mismatch can be an important aspect of spatial opportunity differentials in at least some metropolitan areas. Distance to generic jobs may be less important than distance to jobs held by one's own racial group, however—thus suggesting that not merely distance but the presence of ethnic-specific networks is crucial in understanding differential access to employment.[119] Even if people can secure jobs, however, the associated transportation costs associated with spatial mismatch can consume up to a third of a moderate-income person's budget, to say nothing of many valuable hours in their day.[120]

In summary, the foregoing evidence indicates a clear case of static inequity. The various manifestations of racial and economic segregation are inequitable because they disproportionately impose costs on black, Hispanic, and lower-income households while disproportionately denying them associated benefits.

Social Inequities: Dynamic Perspective

From a dynamic perspective, we can examine the degree to which the flows of households and financial resources across space lead to neighborhood changes that adversely affect the well-being of lower-income and minority households in disproportionate ways. I consider two domains of these dynamic social inequities: wealth disparities from housing appreciation, and involuntary mobility through residential displacement.

Wealth Disparities from Differential Homeownership and Housing Appreciation Rates

There have been dramatic, long-standing, and expanding interracial differentials in wealth: the median wealth of a white household is twenty times that of a black household and eighteen times that of a Hispanic one.[121] Moreover, asset inequality is crucial in perpetuating racial inequalities in education, occupation, and income for succeeding generations.[122]

Housing constitutes a primary source of this wealth differential, since it is the dominant form in which the vast majority of Americans hold their wealth.[123] We can decompose differentials in housing wealth into two components: intertemporal differences in rates of homeownership, and in appreciation of homes. For most of the twentieth century, minorities' chances for owning homes were extremely limited because blatant discrimination by lenders denied them traditional sources of mortgage finance. This was often abetted by explicit federal regulations that denied mortgage insurance on the basis of even tiny numbers of minority households in neighborhoods.[124] In the twenty-first century, the outright denial of mortgage credit on the basis of race has become rarer, but other discriminatory mortgage practices have arisen that make it less likely that minorities can continue to own the homes they have purchased. These practices include predatory lending: home equity loans foisted upon existing homeowners designed to extract high fees and interest rates and ultimately default, which have been concentrated in poor and minority neighborhoods.[125] By differentially exacerbating the chances of home foreclosure, new forms of racially discriminatory mortgage lending have systematically stripped housing wealth from minority households and the neighborhoods in which they live. As illustration, Jacob Rugh, Len Albright, and Douglas Massey estimated that, in comparison to equally qualified white borrowers owning homes in same-quality white neighborhoods, black borrowers owning in predominantly black neighborhoods in Baltimore experienced a 7.9-percentage-point higher chance of foreclosure over the first decade of the twenty-first century. They also suffered a loss of two million dollars in accrued home equity due to home repossession. The authors traced these severe consequences to the racially disparate patterns of mortgage lending by one major lender alone.[126] Their estimates do not include the substantial externality costs imposed by foreclosures on the value of nearby properties, as I documented earlier in this chapter.[127]

The second component of housing wealth differentials is the different rates at which peoples' homes appreciate over time, based on their distinctive neighborhood contexts. This component is more central to the issue of neighborhood dynamic inequity. Put differently, to what degree do the flows of households and financial resources across space that lead to neighborhood change affect the ability of different racial groups to gain wealth through the appreciation of property they own? The answer is that it affects it to a substantial degree, according to the initial level and subsequent change in the economic and racial composition of the neighborhood.

A substantial and consistent body of evidence makes it clear that properties in neighborhoods with either a higher share of poor households or an increase in such a share experience less appreciation.[128] Chenoa Flippen has documented clear patterns of differential home appreciation for owners across American metropolitan areas according to the poverty composition of the neighborhood at the time the property was purchased and the way in which it then changed, controlling for various other household and neighborhood characteristics.[129] Illustrative of the magnitude of these differentials, she found that dwellings appreciated 30 percent less when the initial percentage of poor residents exceeded 30 percent (compared to those in neighborhoods with poverty rates below 5 percent). They appreciated 15 percent less if the neighborhood's poverty rate increased by more than ten percentage points since time of purchase (compared to those with no increase in poverty).

A similar empirical consensus exists for the negative impact on appreciation of higher or growing shares of black households in the neighborhood.[130] Flippen finds that dwellings appreciated 10 percent less when the initial percentage of black residents exceeded 65 percent (compared to those in neighborhoods with no black residents); they appreciated 7 percent less if their neighborhood's share of blacks increased by more than ten percentage points after time of purchase (compared to those with no increase).[131]

The evidence provides a murkier picture regarding the impact of Hispanic neighborhood composition on home appreciation. Higher initial shares of Hispanic households in the neighborhood are generally associated with substantially lower rates of appreciation.[132] By contrast, growing shares of Hispanics appear to boost home values somewhat.[133] Flippen estimates that dwellings appreciated 28 percent less when the initial percentage of Hispanic residents exceeded 10 percent (compared to those in neighborhoods with no Hispanic residents); they appreciated 13 percent more if their neighborhood's share of Hispanics increased by more than five percentage points since time of purchase (compared to those with no increase).[134]

Though the evidence is strong that home appreciation is decidedly less in neighborhoods with substantial shares of poor, black, or Hispanic residents, it is less clear about why this is the case. Several factors undoubtedly contribute. As I documented in chapter 7 and summarized in the *Principle of Racially Encoded Signals*, most white households are reluctant to shop for housing in neighborhoods with more than trivial shares of black or Hispanic residents, thus reducing aggregate demand for such places. As noted above, discriminatory mortgage terms proffered by lenders may erode effective demands by potential minority homebuyers. Risky loans and concomitant foreclosures differentially are concentrated in minority neighborhoods, thereby generating negative property value externalities. Perceptions of impending racial transitions may inspire "panic selling" of homes by white owners. Other owners, foreseeing such transitions, will cut back on the maintenance of their properties. Such responses produce self-fulfilling prophecies of property value depreciation, as I have explained above. In concert, these forces limiting appreciation in substantially minority-occupied neighborhoods render them more vulnerable to downward succession by lower-income groups, as researchers have documented.[135] Such succession will eventually raise the neighborhood's poverty rates and, as the prior evidence indicates, will thereby further magnify the deflating impact on property values in a synergistic fashion. The net effect of these factors is to constrain the flows of households (especially white, nonpoor ones), of investments by property owners, and of investments by financial institutions in a collective fashion that limits the ability of dwelling owners in minority and low-income neighborhoods to enjoy an amount of property value appreciation equivalent to that enjoyed by owners in other neighborhoods.

This dynamic social inequity clearly is borne disproportionately by black and Hispanic homeowners in racially diverse and predominantly minority neighborhoods. The evidence is unambiguous that black and Hispanic homeowners have indeed experienced, on average, significantly less appreciation than white homeowners, and have suffered greater losses in value when the housing market has declined.[136] Flippen has simulated, for example, that if the average black homeowner were to live in a neighborhood with the same characteristics as the average white homeowner, the home would be worth 39 percent more; the corresponding figure for the average Hispanic homeowner is 76 percent more![137]

It is less certain, however, whether this burden of differential appreciation is disproportionately borne by lower-income property owners. First, there is no definitive information about the income distribution of owner occupiers and absentee owners of residential properties, and how such distributions vary by the racial and economic composition of neighborhoods where their properties are located. Second, the evidence on whether lower-valued or higher-valued properties generally appreciate at a higher rate is conflicting, so even rough inferences are problematic.[138]

Involuntary Mobility through Residential Displacement

The second dynamic social inequity issue is the degree to which the process of upward succession (or "gentrification") of neighborhoods (introduced in chapter 4) imposes severe burdens on the original lower-income (often minority) residents. That is, does the in-migration of higher-income (typically white) households lead to the wholesale and involuntary outmigration (or displacement) of the original residents, and the imposition of other monetary and nonmonetary costs on those who remain?

There is a substantial body of scholarship that addresses this question, which employs investigative strategies ranging from ethnographies conducted in particular case study neighborhoods to multivariate statistical models estimated on nationwide metropolitan datasets.[139] There is no doubt that gentrification is becoming a more prominent feature of American neighborhoods during the twenty-first century.[140] What is more in doubt is the degree to which this dynamic harms the original residents of these revitalizing neighborhoods.

Rents and property values in revitalizing neighborhoods rise due to active dwelling upgrading by owners to serve a higher-income clientele, and to passive upgrading as rents capitalize the higher-valued neighborhood physical conditions and socioeconomic profile for all dwellings, regardless of whether they are structurally improved themselves. In principle, this process could easily "force out" the original tenants who can no longer afford these higher rents.[141] Two empirical challenges bedevil this deceptively simple proposition. First, how much rents increase in gentrifying areas is often difficult to ascertain, because of the lack of detailed, up-to-date, small-area data on rents. Second is the challenge of specifying the counterfactual: How many would have moved even in the absence of these rent increases? Many studies have investigated this question using different data sets and methods of statistical analysis, yet they have reached a common conclusion: Residential turnover in gentrifying neighborhoods is not substantially higher than that in equivalent, lower-income neighborhoods that do not gentrify.[142] That is, *involuntary* displacement may not be very frequent because lower-income households move frequently as a matter of course, for a variety of reasons unrelated to rent increases. Research by Lei Ding, Jackelyn Hwang, and Eileen Divringi, analyzing where people live after they move from gentrifying areas, implies, however, that some involuntary displacement is occurring.[143] They found that lower-income households in gentrifying neighborhoods are more likely to move to lower-income neighborhoods than are similar households moving from areas that are not gentrifying, especially when housing cost increases are greater in the original neighborhood.

Even if higher rents do not force them to move, lower-income residents of gentrifying neighborhoods will often see their rent burdens and the prices of local retail goods and services inflating.[144] Though more difficult to quantify, a variety of nonmonetary costs for original residents also have been documented. These costs take the form of reductions in political power, civic engagement, and "cultural displacement": a change in the aggregate neighborhood norms, preferences, retail sector, and service amenities.[145] These social dynamics often can lead to a rise in social tensions within the neighborhood.[146]

In fairness, however, several sorts of benefits accrue to lower-income residents who remain in gentrifying neighborhoods. There appears to be an improvement in their economic circumstances, as revealed by several measures of income and credit scores,[147] though the evidence on overall employment growth in gentrifying neighborhoods and other processes through which these improvements emerge is ambiguous.[148] Gentrification is typically associated with increased feelings of safety and satisfaction, and more amenities enjoyed by lower-income residents.[149] Finally, homeowners (many modest-income minorities) see more growth in their home equity.[150]

In sum, conclusions about dynamic inequities associated with neighborhood gentrification are not clear-cut. Some lower-income and minority residents have certainly experienced involuntary relocation. As a result, they have borne substantial out-of-pocket and other costs, such as disruption of social ties and residence in worse neighborhoods. However, it is uncertain how many such involuntary moves have been generated by gentrification. The alteration in the well-being of those who remain is even more ambiguous, due to the mixed evidence about the various gains and losses that have been borne.

Inefficiencies, Inequities, and Cumulative Causation

We should now step back and gain a holistic perspective on the issues I have discussed. I visually represent this view in figure 9.7. In chapter 7, I demonstrated how a mutually reinforcing nexus of causal processes encourages the segregation of our neighborhoods and schools by race and economic class, as encapsulated in figure 7.2. I diagrammatically represent these synergistic forces of race and class prejudices, discrimination, local political jurisdiction fragmentation and segregationist policies, and intergroup differences in housing purchasing power on the left-hand side of figure 9.6. In this chapter I have argued that systematic underinvestment in our housing stock and the population flows that yield segregation of neighborhoods are not efficient from the standpoint of society as a whole, and are especially burdensome to lower-income black and Hispanic households. In particular, I have documented how such disadvantaged households bear an unfair burden in the form of subcultural adaptations, reduced wealth accumulation, inferior public and private services and institutional resources, intensified exposures to unhealthy and violent environments, and atrophied access to employment appropriate to their skill levels. I summarily represent these relationships by the dotted arrows in the center of figure 9.7. In chapter 8 I explained how and why the characteristics of neighborhoods influence in-

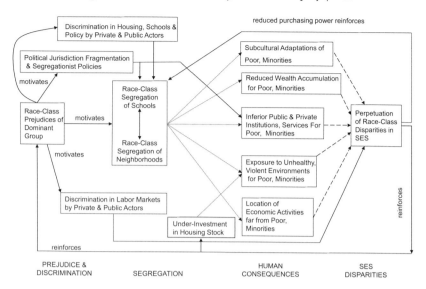

Figure 9.7. Cumulative causation among race, class, segregation, and underinvestment

dividuals and presented evidence about the strength of these neighborhood effects. Here I advance these arguments to reinforce my earlier point, made in chapter 8, that these multidimensionally inferior neighborhood contexts faced by disadvantaged households serve to perpetuate their disadvantaged socioeconomic status, both directly and indirectly, by influencing their life choices. I represent this result by the dashed arrows on the right of figure 9.7.

These interrelationships between inefficient and inequitable patterns in our neighborhoods are even more insidious because they are mutually reinforcing.[151] I represent this diagrammatically by introducing feedback loops into figure 9.7, labeled "reinforces." First, race and class disparities in socioeconomic status contribute to the segregation of neighborhoods by making it less financially feasible for those of more modest purchasing power to afford housing in places where those with higher incomes bid up prices. As I explained in chapter 7, greater spatial clustering of dwellings representing a narrow range of market valuations (often abetted by exclusionary zoning practices) will translate into greater economic segregation when the economic gaps among households are wider. Moreover, such intensified clustering of similarly valued dwellings will generate greater segregation by race as well, because of interracial differences in income and wealth distributions. Second, race and class disparities lead to underinvestment in residential properties. The existence of a large number of poor households, of course, creates a demand for low-quality housing, as I illustrated via the Housing

Submarket Model in chapters 3 and 4. Moreover, expectations strongly influenced by racial change in the neighborhood guide dwelling owners' investments, as embodied in the *Principle of Racially Encoded Signals* presented in chapter 5. Third, race and class disparities reinforce the prejudices held by the dominant group—typically nonpoor whites of European ancestry—as shown by the arrow running from right to left at the bottom of figure 9.7. Many whites perceive blacks and Hispanics as less willing to work, more prone to get involved with gangs and drugs, less intelligent and educated, and less able to speak English well.[152] To the extent that some empirical reality supports these stereotypical beliefs, it is precisely the reality epitomized by the human consequences that emanate from residing in their spatial niche of the metropolitan spatial opportunity structure.

Prejudices, of course, motivate a variety of behaviors by whites, as shown by the arrows labeled "motivates" in figure 9.7. Prejudice directly reinforces segregation in neighborhoods and schools through white "flight" and "avoidance." As I have documented in chapter 6, many whites leave neighborhoods and schools when they exceed a threshold percentage of minorities or poor, and avoid such contexts when searching for alternative residential locations. Prejudice indirectly reinforces segregation in three ways. First, it incentivizes illegal behaviors by private housing market agents and landlords (like exclusion and steering), because agents will see it as more profitable to cater to the prejudices of their white clientele by preserving their homogeneous neighborhoods via discrimination.[153] Similar motivations have led public officials to adopt discriminatory policies related to public housing urban redevelopment, schools, and other public sector domains.[154] Second, it encourages the fragmentation of local governmental jurisdictions so that the forces of local political action and public policies (like exclusionary zoning) can mobilize more effectively to preserve the privileged status of their neighborhoods. In turn, this local political fragmentation is a prerequisite for the interjurisdictional fiscal disparities that, as I noted above, drive much of the inferior public services and schools that disadvantaged neighborhoods must suffer. Third, it leads to discrimination in labor markets related to the employment, retention, compensation, and promotion of minorities. Clearly, this feeds back to intensify further the initial interracial disparities in socioeconomic status.

To summarize the picture of cumulative causation in figure 9.7 more simply: We have created a metropolitan opportunity structure consisting of *warped space*. Its primary linchpin is race-class segregation of neighborhoods and schools, abetted by underinvestment in the housing stock. This opportunity structure directly erodes the mental and physical health of disadvantaged households, reduces their ability to access jobs and accumulate wealth, and degrades the quality of services and institutions with which they come into contact—all because of the neighborhoods in which they must reside. It indirectly induces many lower-income minority households residing in these disadvantaged neighborhoods to undertake behaviors that are rational within their constrained set of options, but which ultimately serve to perpetuate their socioeconomic inferiority. In turn, these behaviors legitimize prejudices held by the dominant group against lower-income and minority households, motivating and justifying in the view of the dominant group legal and illegal acts and structures in housing markets and local political jurisdictions that reinforce segregation and underinvestment in disadvantaged neighborhoods.

The Propositions of Inefficiency, Inequity, and Unequal Opportunity

I succinctly summarize the foregoing analysis in three propositions:

Inefficiency: Private, market-oriented decision makers governing resource flows among neighborhoods usually arrive at an inefficient allocation due to externalities, strategic gaming, and self-fulfilling prophecies, systematically producing too little investment in housing and too much segregation by race and economic standing.

Inequity: Lower-socioeconomic-status black and Hispanic households and property owners typically bear a disproportionate share of the financial and social costs associated with segregation, underinvestment, and neighborhood transition processes while reaping comparatively little of their social benefits.

Unequal opportunity: Because neighborhood context powerfully affects children, youth, and adults—while neighborhood contexts are very unequal across economic and racial groups—space becomes a way of perpetuating unequal opportunities for social advancement.

Conclusion

Our market-dominated system for determining the flows of human and financial resources across neighborhoods has produced a systematic bias toward too little investment in housing and too much segregation by race and economic standing, both of which are socially inefficient and inequitable. Inefficiencies arise primarily due to the presence of externalities of several sorts, strategic gaming, and self-fulfilling prophecies. Inequities arise because disadvantaged residents disproportionately confront neighborhoods that are inferior in many domains. The forces that maintain this inefficient and inequitable neighborhood system are intertwined in a mutually reinforcing system of cumulative causation that serves to perpetuate race and class disparities in America.

If ever there were a classic illustration of pernicious market failure, it is here. Thus, there is a prima facie case for collective intervention in markets through public policy, and planning for rectifying these inefficient and inequitable outcomes. I consider principles and practices for doing so next.

Mathematical Analyses of Most Efficient Social Mix with Different Neighborhood Externality Effects

This appendix provides some precision to the graphical and heuristic arguments made in the preceding chapter. It employs the same simplifying assumptions and symbolism explained in the text, and proceeds in a parallel organizational fashion. For mathematical tractability here, I add two additional assumptions, with no loss of generality in conclusions. First, in our hypothetical society there are two hundred households categorized into two groups of one hundred households each, A and D. Second, society has two neighborhoods containing an identical number of households—one hundred—so that all potential allocations of households can be thought of as either numbers or percentages residing in either neighborhood. The goal is to ascertain which mix of A and D in both stylized neighborhoods maximizes the index of total externalities I_T (or minimizes it when it is negative at all mixes).

Case 1: D Generates constant marginal negative externality β for all neighbors; A generates constant marginal positive externality φ for all neighbors.

$$I_D = \beta(\%D) + \beta(100 - \%D) = 100\,\beta \qquad \beta < 0$$
$$I_A = 100\varphi - \varphi(\%D) + 100\varphi - \varphi(100 - \%D) = 100\varphi \qquad \varphi > 0$$
$$I_T = I_D + I_A = 100\,(\beta + \varphi)$$

Because I_T is not a function of %D, it will not vary by neighborhood mix; I_T is constant across all mixes. Whether I_T is positive or negative depends on relative magnitudes of β and φ.

Case 2: Group D generates constant marginal negative externality β for all neighbors beyond threshold X.

$$I_{\mathrm{D}} = \beta(100 - \%\mathrm{D} - X) \text{ if } \%\mathrm{D} \le X;$$
$$= \beta(\%\mathrm{D} - X) + \beta(100 - \%\mathrm{D} - X) = (100 - 2X)\beta \text{ if } X < \%\mathrm{D} \le 100 - X$$
$$= \beta(\%\mathrm{D} - X) \text{ if } \%\mathrm{D} > 100 - X \qquad \beta < 0$$
$$I_{\mathrm{A}} = 0$$
$$I_{\mathrm{T}} = I_{\mathrm{D}} + I_{\mathrm{A}} = I_{\mathrm{D}}$$

We minimize by considering each segment separately. When $\%\mathrm{D} \le X$, I_{T} is minimized ($=100\beta$) by making $\%\mathrm{D} = X$. When $X < \%\mathrm{D} \le 100 - X$, I_{T} is a constant $[= (100 - 2X)\beta]$. When $\%\mathrm{D} > 100 - X$, I_{T} is minimized by making $\%\mathrm{D}$ as small as possible ($\approx 100 - X$), thus rendering $I_{\mathrm{T}} = (100 - 2X)\beta$. Thus, I_{T} overall is minimized by allocating $X\%$ D households in one neighborhood and $100 - X\%$ in the other.

Case 3: Group A generates constant marginal positive externality φ for all neighbors beyond threshold Y (where Y defined as maximum D is where φ persists).

$$I_{\mathrm{A}} = Y\varphi - \varphi(\%\mathrm{D}) \text{ if } \%\mathrm{D} \le 100 - Y;$$
$$= Y\varphi - \varphi(\%\mathrm{D}) + Y\varphi - \varphi(100 - \%\mathrm{D}) = 2Y\varphi - 100\varphi \text{ if } 100 - Y < \%\mathrm{D} \le Y$$
$$= Y\varphi - \varphi(100 - \%\mathrm{D}) \text{ if } \%\mathrm{D} > Y \qquad \varphi > 0$$
$$I_{\mathrm{D}} = 0$$
$$I_{\mathrm{T}} = I_{\mathrm{D}} + I_{\mathrm{A}} = I_{\mathrm{A}}$$

We minimize by considering each A segment separately. When $\%\mathrm{D} \le 100 - Y$, I_{T} is maximized ($= Y\varphi$) by making $\%\mathrm{D} = 0$ (i.e., $dI_{\mathrm{T}}/d\%\mathrm{D} < 0$). When $100 - Y < \%\mathrm{D} \le Y$, I_{T} is a constant ($= 2Y\varphi - 100\varphi$). When $\%\mathrm{D} > Y$, I_{T} is maximized ($= Y\varphi$) by making $\%\mathrm{D}$ as large as possible (i.e., $dI_{\mathrm{T}}/d\%\mathrm{D} > 0$), thus rendering $I_{\mathrm{T}} = Y\varphi$. Note that, since $Y < 100$, $2Y\varphi - 100\varphi < Y\varphi$. Thus, we maximize I_{T} overall by allocating 100 percent of D households in one neighborhood and none in the other so it can house the maximum number of A households.

Case 4: Group D generates constant marginal negative externality β for all neighbors beyond threshold X, and A generates constant marginal positive externality φ for all neighbors below threshold Y (where Y is expressed in terms of %D and, for simplicity, Y = 100 − X).

If $X < Y$:
$$I_{\mathrm{D}} = \beta(100 - \%\mathrm{D} - X) \text{ if } \%\mathrm{D} \le X;$$
$$= \beta(\%\mathrm{D} - X) + \beta(100 - \%\mathrm{D} - X) = \beta(100 - 2X) \text{ if } X < \%\mathrm{D} \le 100 - X = Y$$
$$= \beta(\%\mathrm{D} - X) \text{ if } \%\mathrm{D} > Y \qquad \beta < 0$$
$$I_{\mathrm{A}} = Y\varphi - \varphi(\%\mathrm{D}) \text{ if } \%\mathrm{D} \le 100 - Y = X;$$
$$= Y\varphi - \varphi(\%\mathrm{D}) + Y\varphi - \varphi(100 - \%\mathrm{D}) = 2Y\varphi - 100\varphi \text{ if } X < \%\mathrm{D} \le Y$$

$$= Y\varphi - \varphi(100 - \%D) \text{ if } \%D > Y \qquad \varphi > 0$$
$$I_T = I_D + I_A$$
$$= \beta(100 - \%D - X) + Y\varphi - \varphi(\%D) \text{ if } \%D \leq X;$$
$$= \beta(100 - 2X) + 2Y\varphi - 100\varphi \text{ if } X < \%D \leq Y$$
$$= \beta(\%D - X) + Y\varphi - \varphi(100 - \%D) \text{ if } \%D > Y.$$

If $X > Y$:
$$I_D = \beta(100 - \%D - X) \text{ if } \%D \leq 100 - X = Y;$$
$$= 0 \text{ if } Y < \%D \leq X$$
$$= \beta(\%D - X) \text{ if } \%D > X \qquad \beta < 0$$
$$I_A = Y\varphi - \varphi(\%D) \text{ if } \%D \leq Y;$$
$$= 0 \text{ if } Y < \%D \leq X$$
$$= Y\varphi - \varphi(100 - \%D) \text{ if } \%D > X \qquad \varphi > 0$$
$$I_T = I_D + I_A$$
$$= \beta(100 - \%D - X) + Y\varphi - \varphi(\%D) \text{ if } \%D \leq Y;$$
$$= 0 \text{ if } Y < \%D \leq X$$
$$= \beta(\%D - X) + Y\varphi - \varphi(100 - \%D) \text{ if } \%D > X$$

Now $dI_T/d\%D = 0$ always when $X < \%D \leq Y$, so society is indifferent to mixes within this range X–Y. However, if $|\varphi| > |\beta|$, $dI_T/d\%D$ will be < 0 when $\%D \leq$ the lower threshold, and $dI_T/d\%D$ will be > 0 when $\%D >$ the higher threshold; the signs will be reversed if the relative magnitudes of φ and β are reversed. Note also that $I_T(\%D = 0) = I_T(\%D = 100) = Y\varphi + \beta(100 - X)$; the former is > 0, the latter < 0. Thus, the only choices for optimum are between 100% D in one neighborhood-zero in the other, or two with mixes in the range of X–Y. Which choice will be preferred we cannot ascertain without more information about the relative magnitudes of φ and β. If the positive externality from A is much more powerful than the negative externality from D—that is, if $|\varphi| > |\beta|$—then the mixed option will be inferior. We should have $\%D = 0$ in one neighborhood and the remainder in the other, if feasible. On the contrary, if the negative externality from D is much more powerful than the positive externality from A—that is, if $|\varphi| < |\beta|$—then the mixed option will be the maximum I_T available, with $\%D < X$ in at least one neighborhood. It is mathematically possible, of course, that the two parameters are precisely equal in absolute value, such that all allocations are equally efficient.

Case 5: Group D generates growing marginal negative externality only for D neighbors.

Here the marginal negative externality increases with the number of D in a particular neighborhood ($= \beta\%D$), because there are more D neighbors to be affected by the externality. The total externality function for D in that neighborhood thus can be expressed as $\beta\%D^2/2$. Group A is assumed irrelevant as either transmitter or receiver of externality. For both neighborhoods:

$$I_D = \beta\%D^2/2 + \beta(100 - \%D)^2/2 \qquad \beta < 0$$
$$= 5{,}000\beta - 100\beta\%D + \beta\%D^2$$
$$I_A = 0$$
$$I_T = I_D + I_A = I_D = 5{,}000\beta - 100\beta\%D + \beta\%D^2$$

In this case, allocating all D to one neighborhood or the other yields $I_T = 5{,}000\beta$, which is a lower (more negative) value than if D were equally allocated in the smallest possible percentage across all neighborhoods (here, 50%), whereupon $I_T = 2{,}500\beta$. Expressed differently, $dI_T/d\%D = -100\beta + 2\beta\%D$, which is minimized at $\%D = 50$.

Case 6: Group A generates growing marginal positive externality only for D neighbors.

Here the externality produced by each A (φ) benefits each D present in the neighborhood, so it can be expressed as $\varphi\%D$. The total externalities produced in one neighborhood by A is thus $\varphi\%DA$, or $\varphi\%D(100 - \%D) = 100\varphi\%D - \varphi\%D^2$. Analogously, in the other neighborhood the total externalities produced by A will be $100\varphi(100 - \%D) - \varphi(100 - \%D)^2$. After simplification, we can write

$$I_D = 0$$
$$I_A = 200\varphi\%D - 2\varphi\%D^2 \qquad \varphi > 0$$
$$I_T = I_D + I_A = I_A = 200\varphi\%D - 2\varphi\%D^2$$

The maximum of I_T occurs here at a 50-50 split of D between neighborhoods, as can be seen by setting $dI_T/d\%D$ ($= 200\varphi - 4\varphi\%D$) to zero.

Case 7: Group D generates growing marginal positive externality only for D neighbors.

Here the marginal positive externality increases with the number of D in a neighborhood ($= \beta\%D$) because there are more D neighbors to be affected by the externality. The total externality function for D in that neighborhood thus can be expressed as $\beta\%D^2/2$. Group A is irrelevant as either transmitter or receiver of externality, by assumption. For both neighborhoods, therefore:

$$I_D = \beta\%D^2/2 + \beta(100 - \%D)^2/2 \qquad \beta > 0$$
$$= 5{,}000\beta - 100\beta\%D + \beta\%D^2$$
$$I_A = 0$$
$$I_T = I_D + I_A = I_D = 5{,}000\beta - 100\beta\%D + \beta\%D^2$$

In this case, allocating all D to one neighborhood or the other yields I_T = 5,000β, which is a higher (positive) value than if D were equally allocated in the smallest possible percentage across all neighborhoods (here, 50%), whereupon I_T = 2,500β.

Case 8: Group A and group D generate growing marginal positive externalities, but only for neighbors not like themselves.

This is formally analogous to case 6, wherein both A and D produce positive externalities whose marginal benefits are proportional to the other group in the area.

$$I_D = 200\beta\%D - 2\beta\%D^2 \quad \beta > 0$$
$$I_A = 200\varphi\%D - 2\varphi\%D^2 \quad \varphi > 0$$
$$I_T = I_D + I_A = 200\beta\%D - 2\beta\%D^2 + 200\varphi\%D - 2\varphi\%D^2$$
$$= 200(\beta+\varphi)\%D - 2(\beta + \varphi)\%D^2$$

As in case 7, the maximum of I_T occurs here at a 50-50 split of D between neighborhoods, as can be seen by setting $dI_T/d\%D$ [= $200(\beta + \varphi) - 4(\beta + \varphi)\%D$] to zero.

Case 9: Group A and group D generate growing marginal negative externalities but only for neighbors not like themselves.

This is formally analogous to case 8, wherein both A and D produce negative instead of positive externalities whose marginal benefits are proportional to the other group in the area.

$$I_D = 200\beta D - 2\beta\%D^2 \quad \beta < 0$$
$$I_A = 200\varphi D - 2\varphi\%D^2 \quad \varphi < 0$$
$$I_T = I_D + I_A = 200\beta\%D - 2\beta\%D^2 + 200\varphi\%D - 2\varphi\%D^2$$
$$= 200(\beta+\varphi)\%D - 2(\beta + \varphi)\%D^2$$

The minimum of IT occurs here at a 50-50 split of D between neighborhoods, as can be seen by setting $dIT/d\%D$ [= $200(\beta + \varphi) - 4(\beta + \varphi)\%D$] to zero. Thus, to avoid this low IT situation, group A and D households should be completely segregated.

Case 10: Group D generates constant negative externality β for all neighbors if D exceeds threshold Z .

If $Z < 100 - Z$, then no matter how D is allocated in this simplified situation, at least one neighborhood will exceed Z and the negative externality will result. That is, the externality functions can be specified:

$$I_D = I_T$$
$$= \beta \text{ if } \%D \leq Z;$$
$$= 2\beta \text{ if } Z < \%D \leq 100 - Z$$
$$= \beta \text{ if } \%D > 100 - Z \qquad \beta < 0$$

In this case, the reductions in I_T can be minimized by allocating D such that one neighborhood is below the threshold: that is, $\%D \leq Z$, with the other neighborhood $\%D > 100 - Z$.

If $Z > 100 - Z$, the externality function becomes

$$I_D = I_T$$
$$= \beta \text{ if } \%D \leq 100 - Z;$$
$$= 0 \text{ if } 100 - Z < \%D \leq Z$$
$$= \beta \text{ if } \%D > Z \qquad \beta < 0$$

In this case, the reductions in I_T can be avoided altogether by allocating D such that both neighborhoods are below the threshold—that is, if $100 - Z < \%D \leq Z$.

PART 4

Remaking Neighborhoods
for Our Better Selves

TEN

Toward a Circumscribed, Neighborhood-Supportive Suite of Public Policies

Introduction: The Case for a Three-Pronged Neighborhood Intervention Strategy

The foregoing chapter suggests an unmistakable case of market failure. For a variety of reasons, changes in the flows of households and resources across space will produce socially inefficient outcomes. I have also suggested that these outcomes are inequitable; they likely produce the largest penalties for the most vulnerable households. There is thus a prima facie case on efficiency and equity grounds for some sort of collective intervention, whether it is to come from informal social processes, nonprofit community-based organizations, the governmental sector, or some combination of the above. If we do not like how the market is making neighborhoods that shape us in inefficient and inequitable ways—and indeed we should not —we must intervene to remake neighborhoods in the image of our better selves.[1]

Informal social processes might take the form of sanctions and rewards meted out by neighbors who try to enforce compliance with collective norms regarding civil behavior and building upkeep. Community-based organizations might politically organize, establish bonds of mutual solidarity, or foment a positive public image of the neighborhood.[2] Governments might offer information, financial incentives, regulations, and investments of infrastructure and public services, and target them to neighborhoods at crucial threshold points. In concert, these actions can help alter the perceptions of key neighborhood investors and thus leverage their investments, provide compensatory resource flows, minimize destructive gaming behaviors, internalize externalities, and moderate expectations, thereby defusing self-fulfilling prophecies. Because governments typically represent the primary source of the revenues that will be required to fund adequately the policies that I advocate below, I will direct my recommendations toward them.

In this chapter I will propose a suite of policies in three neighborhood domains: physical quality, economic diversity, and racial diversity. Collectively they comprise what I call a "circumscribed, neighborhood-supportive" set of recommendations. The goals of these recommendations are threefold:

1. to improve conditions in low-quality residential environments while maintaining them in decent-quality ones,
2. to increase the economic and racial diversity in neighborhoods and local political jurisdictions across the metropolitan area, and
3. to reduce "forced" (involuntary) residential mobility associated with inefficient neighborhood race and class transitions.

Clearly, worthy goals do not justify all conceivable means of achieving them, so policy makers must carefully assess the equity and efficacy dimensions of particular programs being considered for enhancing neighborhood investment and population diversity. I would argue that programmatic means are most likely to be efficient and equitable if they employ *voluntary, gradualist, option-enhancing* strategies. I employ these criteria as filters for the particular policy reforms I advocate in the following sections. In particular, my recommendations emphasize voluntary[3] but incentivized choices by households and property owners that ultimately will change neighborhoods in cities and suburbs gradually, so that all of them move toward the aforementioned goals. It took generations of market-driven, state-abetted forces of segregation and disinvestment to get where we are; it will undoubtedly take a while to get where we want to be, even with unstinting efforts.

Which Governments Should Undertake
Neighborhood-Supportive Policies?

What, then, about the public sector delivery systems that should be energized for enhancing neighborhood investment and population diversity? Ideally, the answer would involve mutually supportive actions at the federal, state, and local levels.

At the federal level, a range of programs that would provide better income and housing support for low-income households and financial support for lower-income jurisdictions would be extremely helpful in achieving the aforementioned neighborhood-supportive goals. It is inconceivable that we could ever eliminate low-quality, undermaintained neighborhoods entirely without the federal government guaranteeing both (1) subsidized housing and/or adequate income supports as a right of all citizens, and (2) revenue sharing or community development block grants of such magnitude that they would effectively equalize fiscal capacity across local jurisdictions. The former federal guarantee would affect the rental stream that a property owner can expect, and without which they cannot supply decent middle-quality housing. Making decent, affordable housing a fully funded right in the United States would be tremendously pro-neighborhood, as it would eliminate the financial incentives for landlords to provide low-quality stock because there would be no demand for it.[4] The same consequence would result from a generalized, guaranteed income-support program, such as a more robust earned income tax credit. The latter federal guarantee would affect nondwelling aspects of the residential environment related to the local jurisdiction's ability to finance quality services, infrastructure, facilities, and agencies.[5] Jointly, these two guarantees would eliminate the economic motivations to have a low-quality housing submarket, and permit those receiving person- or place-based housing subsidies to be far less concentrated geographically than they now are.

States also could undertake forms of people-based income and housing assistance and place-based financial assistance analogous to the ones I have just advocated for the federal government. Indeed, many states have their own programs for social welfare assistance, subsidized housing, and intergovernmental revenue sharing, though they vary greatly in their scope and efficacy. States could enable neighborhood-supportive policies even more directly, however, by mandating more regional, metropolitan-area-wide governance structures.[6] Clearly, the most efficacious governance structure for intervening comprehensively and holistically in neighborhoods would be one that corresponds in scale to the metropolitan area over which the market-driven forces of neighborhood change reverberate across the housing submarket array. We have several examples of such "bigger box" governmental structures tackling key forces shaping the flows of financial and human resources across neighborhoods, such as metropolitan growth boundaries in Oregon; regional tax base sharing in the Minneapolis–St. Paul metropolitan area; unified school districts in Charlotte–Mecklenburg County, North Carolina; and inclusionary zoning in Montgomery County, Maryland.[7]

Despite the unambiguous advantages in having more neighborhood-supportive federal, state, and regional policies, I will not discuss them in more detail. Rather, my focus in this chapter will be on policies and programs that local governments can undertake, regardless of the degree to which they receive collaborative, financial, and programmatic supports from other levels of government, foundations, and community-based organizations. Certainly, local governments will be more successful when such support is stronger; indeed, at the end of this chapter I will suggest a great deal of circumspection about what local governments can accomplish if they are forced to go it alone. Nevertheless, even when such supports are massive, there are indispensable roles that local governments must play in delivering neighborhood-supportive policies. As I will amplify below, local governments are in the best position to operationalize the nuanced strategic targeting required for a successful neighborhood policy.

The Foundation of Neighborhood-Supportive Policy: Strategic Targeting

Strategic targeting provides a framework within which policy makers must devise and deliver effective programs comprising a neighborhood-supportive policy. *Strategic targeting* means that policymakers should develop initiatives holistically within the context of metropolitan housing submarket projections, and then direct them at particular neighborhoods with sufficient intensity that the behaviors of private market actors (especially households and residential property owners) will change substantially there. Formulating policies and programs holistically means both recognizing causal interrelationships among neighborhoods within and across jurisdictional boundaries, and trying to achieve the tripartite goals of neighborhood reinvestment, economic diversity, and racial diversity.

Operationalizing strategic targeting means making decisions in three realms: *context, composition,* and *concentration.*[8] *Context* refers to the current and projected opportunities and constraints on the jurisdiction's neighborhood trajectories that a metropolitan area's housing market affords. Before one can logically decide how and where to intervene, one must be aware of the current and the projected future regional context, as well as local conditions. Long-run forecasts of metro-wide population, incomes, employment, and infrastructure investments must form the foundation strategic targeting. This is necessary to anticipate the forces that are likely to impinge most strongly on particular neighborhoods throughout the region, using the predictive logic of the metropolitan housing submarket model developed in chapters 3 and 4. The appropriate region-wide planning entity or council of governments typically would undertake this geographically disaggregated forecasting. Ideally, a strategic targeting plan would be collaboratively drawn

Table 10.1. Representative typology for neighborhood strategic targeting policy

Expected physical conditions, private investment flows	Expected diversity of residents	
	Acceptable	Unacceptable
Abandoned, no investment	N/A	N/A
Badly deteriorated, insufficient investment	A	E
Mildly deteriorating, insufficient investment	B	F
Renovating, sufficient investment	C	G
Stable, sufficient investment	D	H

up for the metropolitan region as a whole, and executed comprehensively at the regional level. Since these powerful, regional bodies are scarce in the United States, however, cities by default will often bear the responsibility for strategic targeting plans. Even when done in a decentralized fashion, these plans must be cognizant of region-wide forecasts and the behaviors of other jurisdictions. Only then will they know where to expect changes of what sort in their own constituent neighborhoods, and rationally target their scarce resources most efficaciously. Strategic targeting also depends on ongoing, up-to-date information about neighborhoods, to monitor and assess progress of past interventions and direct new ones. By implication, this means that cities must have access to a battery of virtually real-time neighborhood indicators.[9]

Composition means that the programmatic particulars of interventions contemplated for any neighborhood must be contingent on the current and projected future characteristics of that place and the particular goals appropriate for that place. Clearly, not all neighborhoods require intervention, and those that might do not all require the same sort of intervention. I amplify my point with the help of the typology of neighborhoods presented in table 10.1.

Strategic targeting requires that each neighborhood in the relevant geography for planning purposes be categorized in terms of a typology analogous to that in table 10.1, so that the broad contours of the treatment, if any, is specified unambiguously. The categories are intuitive:

·   *abandoned, no investment cases*: no intervention until potential for market revival, because no amount of public investment will jump-start market

· *neighborhoods of type C or D*: no intervention required because market is producing desired investment levels and acceptable economic and racial diversity

· *neighborhoods of type A* (an unusual type) *and E that would typically be areas of concentrated poverty or occupied "slums"*: interventions that should be aimed at stimulating private investment and deconcentrating low-income minority households

· *neighborhoods of type B* (diverse areas of incipient physical decline and disinvestment, perhaps because of some previous downward income succession): interventions that should be aimed at stimulating private investment

· *neighborhoods of type F* (homogeneous areas of incipient physical decline and disinvestment): interventions that should be aimed at stimulating private investment and increasing economic and/or racial diversity

· *neighborhoods of type G* (gentrifying areas where wholesale displacement of previous lower-income residents are predicted): interventions that should be aimed at preserving economic and racial diversity

· *neighborhoods of type H* (homogeneous areas of decent quality): interventions that should be aimed at increasing economic and/or racial diversity.

Concentration means that policymakers must apply the tangible public interventions (e.g., financial subsidies, infrastructure investments, community building) at a sufficient spatial density in the targeted area so that the private actors' thresholds for undertaking positive actions vis-à-vis this neighborhood are surmounted. Evidence regarding public intervention thresholds for encouraging neighborhood population diversity is lacking, but the evidence for physical investment thresholds is compelling. Recall that I showed in chapter 6 that theory and evidence strongly support the existence of neighborhood investment thresholds. These must be exceeded before private property owners will spend their own funds improving their properties. Four studies of local government efforts to revitalize neighborhoods provide remarkably consistent evidence on what amount of public investment is needed to surmount these thresholds. Kenneth Bleakly and colleagues examined policies that spatially targeted Community Development Block Grant (CDBG) and other investments in thirty Neighborhood Strategy Areas in twenty cities during the period 1979 to 1981. They reported that substantial improvements in neighborhood physical conditions only occurred when there was a higher than average concentration of CDBG expenditures per block.[10] Peter Tatian, John Accordino, and I investigated the impacts of Richmond's Neighborhoods in Bloom initiative, which consistently targeted CDBG and Local Initiative Support Corporation funds during the 1999–2004 period. We also found that significant improvements in property values only occurred when the investments per block exceeded the sample mean amount.[11] With colleagues Chris Walker, Chris Hayes, Patrick Boxall, and Jennifer Johnson, I measured the relationship between CDBG expenditures and subsequent changes in a variety of neighborhood indicators across seventeen cities during the 1990s. Once again, we found that such expenditures did not have a noticeable relationship with improved census tract trajectories unless they exceeded the sample mean expenditure.[12] Finally, Jennifer Pooley analyzed the impact of Philadelphia's allocation of CDBG funds during the 1990–2009 period and determined that these dollars resulted in significant property value improvements in census tracts only when targeted at greater than median amounts.[13] When we adjust the particular investments analyzed in these four studies for the periods over which they were invested, their spatial scales, and subsequent inflation, consistent dollar thresholds emerge. The first two studies indicate that the public sector needs to invest (measured in 2017 dollars) at least roughly $54,000 annually for five years or $62,000 annually for three years in each target block. The last two studies indicate thresholds of $138,000 annually for ten years or $271,000 annually for five years in each target census tract (measured in 2017 dollars). These sums are not trivial; by implication, local jurisdictions need to focus their neighborhood investments spatially instead of falling prey to the temptation of "doing something for every neighborhood."[14]

Strategic targeting tells neighborhood policy makers that they must carefully consider context, composition, and concentration. It does not ultimately specify, however, which types of neighborhoods displayed in table 10.1 policy makers should select as targets for intervention. The appropriate decision will depend on the particulars of metropolitan housing market forces, the competitive position of the particular jurisdiction's neighborhoods and the resources at its disposal, and, of course, local political considerations. Fundamentally, the choice is whether a jurisdiction intervenes with its limited resources in the worst-off neighborhoods (types A and E), or in those showing early signs of incipient decline (types B and F).

To address this question is to engage in a long-standing controversy over the notion of *triage*. To extend the analogy from battlefield emergency medicine, where it was first coined, neighborhoods can be classified into three groups depending on the severity of their "injuries": "fatally injured" (types A and E), "critically injured" (types B and F), and "mildly injured" (types C, D, G and H). The triage approach advocates for focusing attention solely on the second, "critically injured" group, which can be "saved" only if we intervene quickly and effectively. By contrast, triage argues that we should

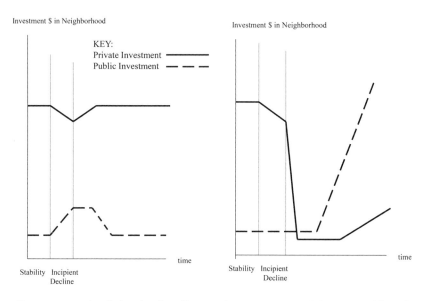

Figure 10.1. A rationale for triage-based intervention: two scenarios of alternative public and private investments flows into a neighborhood

not intervene in the other groups because the first will expire regardless of whatever intervention we attempt, and the last will heal without intervention. The medical metaphor is not fully apt, of course, because sufficiently massive investments could bring even the most moribund neighborhood back to life. Nevertheless, the triage approach does point to a valid consideration about where investments of limited public resources can generate the most efficacious impacts.

Figure 10.1 helps illustrate the point. It portrays flows of public and private investments into a hypothetical neighborhood over time. In the earliest period shown, the neighborhood is perfectly healthy (type D), with substantial flows of investment by private property owners for the upkeep of their residential and nonresidential buildings, and by the public sector in form of services, facilities, and infrastructure maintenance. At some point, however, some unspecified external force, reverberating through the metropolitan housing submarket array, reduces the competitive position of this neighborhood, such that the private sector begins to reduce its investments (type B neighborhood). If this incipient decline is not countered, private investment may eventually fall precipitously, as negative externalities and signaling behaviors associated with undermaintenance and downgrading of residential and nonresidential buildings generate self-reinforcing responses by nearby owners. This downward spiral of disinvestment eventually produces a neighborhood of type A, or an abandoned one, shown in scenario 2.

The triage position argues that it is a wiser use of public resources to intervene in type B neighborhoods as soon as incipient decline is visible. Policymakers would hope that only a relatively modest amount of new public investments here, applied over a relative short period, will be required to exceed owners' reinvestment thresholds in this context and return the neighborhood to full health quickly, as shown in scenario 1. By contrast, a massive investment of public resources will be required to resuscitate the private market in a moribund neighborhood, as shown in scenario 2.

This core argument of the triage position is compelling. Why would policymakers not invest a modest amount in helping a neighborhood recover from a "minor illness," instead of waiting until it requires more expensive critical care when it is near death? Nevertheless, on both efficiency and equity grounds one can make several convincing counterarguments. To do triage effectively, one needs a reliable early warning system of indicators that can identify when incipient neighborhood decline has begun and which ill neighborhoods are closest to the critical threshold of disinvestment. When a jurisdiction confronts neighborhoods that have become type A in the past, should they indeed keep a "benign neglect" stance indefinitely while awaiting external market forces to push the neighborhood into type C? Because those living in such type A neighborhoods are likely to be the jurisdiction's most disadvantaged, some might argue on equity grounds that interventions designed to improve their quality of life might be justified. The opposite side of the same equity coin is the argument that public investments in type B neighborhoods will benefit primarily middle-class households and property owners, instead of the neediest citizens. Nevertheless, one can forward an equity-based rejoinder. Triage-based interventions are the most fiscally prudent way to preserve a jurisdiction's local tax base, which provides the foundation for decent public services and facilities that redound to the benefit of all citizens, not the least of whom may be disadvantaged. Ultimately, the appropriateness of a triage approach will depend upon the particular housing market and the fiscal, social, and political circumstances facing the policymakers in question.

Regardless of the position one takes on the triage issue, it is imperative that policymakers and planners adopt strategic targeting as the guiding principle for developing neighborhood-supportive interventions. Local jurisdictions simply do not have sufficient resources at their command to effect all the neighborhood changes they might view as desirable. They thus must use their precious resources to leverage private resources aimed at the same goals. Accomplishing this effectively requires that they employ an evidence-based system for identifying (1) the current and future flows of private resource into all neighborhoods, (2) what particular programs will enhance these flows most powerfully in the areas chosen, and (3) how intensely these programs must be applied there to trigger the requisite supportive private responses.[15]

Encouraging Neighborhood Investments

There are three general programmatic strategies that the public sector could pursue for encouraging additional private investments in neighborhoods strategically targeted for intervention. The first improves in a variety of ways the physical, social, and psychological aspects of the residential context surrounding property owners, and thereby stimulates their dwelling re-investment efforts. The second incentivizes reinvestment activities directly through both "sticks" (housing code enforcement) and "carrots" (grants or low-interest loans intended to defray costs of dwelling improvements). The third strategy augments neighborhood-wide upkeep levels indirectly, by increasing the number of dwellings that are owner-occupied. As I will demonstrate below, the latter two strategies hold more potential as potent, effective tools of neighborhood reinvestment policy.

Improving Neighborhood Context

A common program that local policy makers often employ as a stimulant for residential reinvestments by the private sector is that of refurbishing and improving public neighborhood infrastructure. This would include sewer, road, and sidewalk improvements; decorative light fixtures; streetscaping; and the like. There is no doubt that such public investments enhance the physical quality and property values of the targeted blocks. There is no evidence that they induce further private investment, however, unless they include a much more comprehensive set of subsidies and related area-based initiatives. My research in Minneapolis and Wooster demonstrated that improved physical conditions in the public sphere of the block face affected the housing upkeep behavior of homeowners only minimally.[16] Furthermore, these improvements did significantly abet their optimism about the future quality of life in the neighborhood. Beyond the blocks where infrastructure investments were made, the consequences may prove deleterious, because homeowners on nontargeted blocks may perceive that the relative quality of their own areas has now fallen, and they are more likely to engage in free-rider gaming behavior. Therefore, the aggregate net result on private reinvestment may not even be positive.

Land-use zoning regulations are another potential policy option for influencing the neighborhood's physical environment and thus stimulating private investment. The results from my aforementioned study, however, give no indication that areas currently with mixed land use have lower home upkeep levels than areas with homogeneous residential uses. Indeed, for certain homeowners the effect was just the opposite.[17]

As for altering the social-psychological milieu of the dwelling owner, the evidence from my work is more mixed. I found that manipulating homeowners' expectations in a way that encourages optimism about the neighborhood as a place to live significantly enhances dwelling upkeep.[18] Unfortunately, in lower-valued neighborhoods, if such optimism also carries over into property-value expectations, the beneficial upkeep results disappear. The prickly policy problem here is how to engender crowd-following behavior through optimistic qualitative neighborhood expectations without simultaneously engendering free-rider behavior due to optimistic property-value expectations. "Building neighborhood confidence" thus is a policy prescription rife with half-truth, and a prescription we have no proven policy instruments to fill successfully.[19]

Public efforts aimed at the maintenance and creation of neighborhood social cohesion also appear to be a double-edged policy sword. On the one hand, neighborhoods with strong solidarity sentiments and collective identification clearly produce far superior levels of homeowner upkeep activity, all else being equal. They improve efficiency by providing a social means for internalizing home upkeep externalities and simultaneously coordinating otherwise destructive strategic gaming behaviors by homeowners in the area. I found that owners in the most cohesive neighborhoods who identified most closely with their neighbors annually spent 28 to 45 percent more on home maintenance and improvements, and evinced a 66 percent lower likelihood of exterior home defects, compared to average homeowners in noncohesive neighborhoods.[20] On the other hand, the dangers of intensified neighborhood parochialism that may attend enhanced cohesion may be nontrivial. Again, it is doubtful whether local planners and policy makers have mastered the manipulation of neighborhood social dynamics sufficiently to attain only benefits from a potential cohesion-building program. Nevertheless, the potential payoffs for stabilizing neighborhood investment levels appear so great as to warrant significant amounts of further study.

A final neighborhood context-alteration strategy is that of working with financial institutions (either as collaborators or as antagonists through Community Reinvestment Act or fair lending challenges) to ensure adequate home purchase and improvement loan flows into targeted neighborhoods. Though we surely can laud such actions, in themselves they are insufficient as cornerstones of neighborhood reinvestment policy. Coordinating lenders' behaviors can profitably reduce their prisoner's-dilemma situation and spur financial resource availability, but the ultimate impact on housing rehabilitation activity depends on the desire by property owners to take advantage of these resources.

Thus, it is apparent that the first overall neighborhood reinvestment strategy of altering the context surrounding individual property owners' upkeep decisions has severe limitations. There is no evidence that changes in the physical infrastructure will induce them to undertake significantly more dwelling investments. Changes in the sociopsychological context have more potential for shaping homeowners' upkeep behavior. Unfortunately, the programmatic means for influencing expectations and social cohesion in controlled, net-beneficial ways have yet to be developed. Moreover, the possibilities of major unintended consequences spawned by public policy blunders in this area are rife. Policies to augment home purchase and improvement loan flows may have positive effects, but have limited applicability for dealing with reinvestment psychology in more challenged neighborhoods.

Incentivizing Incumbent Upgrading

The second general policy approach of directly incentivizing current property owners' reinvestment efforts in strategically targeted neighborhoods is far more effective and less fraught with unintended outcomes. A coordinated incentive policy should involve a package of both positive and negative incentives, delivered with contingencies related to owners' abilities to pay and other quid pro quos to which they must agree as a condition for receiving subsidies.

The primary positive incentives here consist of dwelling rehabilitation grants and/or low-interest (or forgivable) loans to incumbent property owners in the target neighborhoods.[21] Garry Hesser and I conducted a benefit-cost analysis of the rehabilitation grant and low-interest or deferred-loan programs in Minneapolis.[22] All else being equal, the homeowner's receipt of a low-interest loan or grant for home rehabilitation was associated with significantly higher home upkeep expenditures: $35 per $100 in loans and $262 per $100 in grants received. There also was a modest indirect effect of such loan-grant policies on the neighbors of recipients. Homeowners who did not personally receive a subsidy, but who lived in areas where others did, had more optimism about the future quality of their neighborhoods. This, in turn, translated into a 4 percent larger upkeep expenditure stream from them, and a 13 percent lower incidence of exterior home defects manifested on their homes. Whether such increments to property upkeep prove to be "worth" (in a strict budgetary sense) the allocation of local public monies depends on the assumptions one makes about (1) how such housing upkeep increments and positive externalities ultimately become capitalized into the neighborhood's property values, (2) the public sector's discount rate, (3) the terms and conditions of the grants and loans, and (4) the jurisdiction's property tax rate.

Hesser and I found that rehabilitation loans and especially grants had benefit-cost ratios in excess of one under wide ranges of plausible parameter assumptions, regardless of whether one took the viewpoint of a local public official or a geographically broader perspective. However, most loans repaid over terms exceeding about five years were unlikely to be net beneficial from a local public-sector budgetary standpoint. The relative superiority of grants to loans in terms of comparative budgetary benefit-cost ratios depends on the public discount rate (that is, the opportunity cost of funds), and the terms of the loan. Grants will generally be the preferable option (1) the longer the deferment of loan repayment, (2) the higher the discount rate, (3) the lower the loan's interest rate, and (4) the lower the indirect leveraging and externality effects of the subsidies. Even assuming a high loan interest rate of 8 percent, a high discount rate of 9 percent, and generous indirect leveraging and externality effects, loans are superior to grants only if owners can repay within ten years. This, of course, may be financially impossible for many lower-income homeowners whom policy makers would wish to participate in such a program, unless policy makers structure the loan to be repayable only upon sale of the property. Thus, the efficiency of a housing rehabilitation subsidy program will be improved if subsidies are packaged in such a way that, whenever possible, recipients who can afford to do so are only allocated loans that have benefit-cost ratios superior to those of grants (that is, loans that carry a nontrivial interest rate and are repayable within five years). Policy makers then would reserve grants for recipients where affordability concerns suggest that only inefficient low-interest, long-repayment-schedule loans could be offered otherwise.

Of course, to secure maximum neighborhood-wide increases in private residential investments, the public sector may wish to compel participation, instead of relying solely on positive externalities and the endogenous contagion effects among property investors I have documented in prior chapters.[23]

One way to do so is through targeted housing code enforcement. Violators would have a defined period during which they would need to complete necessary repairs and improvements satisfactorily before fines would be exacted. Owners of properties with code violations could then voluntarily apply for the aforementioned need-based grants or loans, should they qualify.

Depending on the generosity of the subsidy proffered, the local public sector could reasonably extract a variety of potential concessions from the beneficiary property owners. For owner occupants of single-family dwellings, this could take the form of a minimum residency requirement post-subsidy or an agreement on sharing some amount of capital gain due to home appreciation between time of subsidy and sale. For absentee owners, the quid pro quo might consist of a period during which rents are frozen at original, presubsidy levels, or constrained to rise at a below-market rate of inflation.

In sum, directly influencing property owners' reinvestment calculus through public incentives commends itself as an important tool of a neighborhood reinvestment strategy. If packaged correctly, a grant and loan program can generate increments of residential benefits far larger than budgetary costs. Because such benefits will largely if not completely manifest themselves as enhanced property values in the jurisdiction, it is conceivable that such a housing rehabilitation program could be self-funding in the long run. That is, even if local governments reassess only part of the property-value gains for tax purposes, their property tax revenues will likely increase enough to offset the original subsidy provided. When coupled with targeted code enforcement to ensure participation, and an appropriate menu of quid pro quos required of subsidy recipients, this strategy has much to recommend it.

Expanding Homeownership in Target Neighborhoods

The third broad category of neighborhood reinvestment policy options does not take as predetermined the number of homeowners in strategically targeted neighborhoods, as do the previous two categories. This third approach tries to produce a net increase in the number of homeowners (with a concomitant reduction in absentee owners) throughout the metropolitan housing market, especially among lower-income households and those living in targeted areas. Crucially, this policy does not aim to move existing homeowners from one neighborhood to a targeted one; rather, it is aimed at assisting those who might not otherwise be able to become homeowners, or at least not very quickly. This strategy offers promise primarily because owneroccupants generate several forms of positive neighborhood externalities. First, they maintain their dwellings at levels far superior to those evidenced by absentee owners, controlling for cross-tenure variations in occupant, dwelling, and neighborhood characteristics.[24] Second, they augment social capital by participating more actively in local social organizations and civic groups.[25] Third, they create superior environments for the development of healthy, higher-performing children, thus reducing the chances that youth incivilities, vandalism, and the like will afflict the neighborhood.[26] Fourth, they arguably create greater collective efficacy that, in conjunction with the previous consequences, may produce a safer neighborhood.[27]

There are several proven ways in which policy can help modest-income households to overcome barriers to owning a home.[28] It is likely, however, that these interventions would raise the overall homeownership rate in a jurisdiction, and not concentrate the new homeowners in the neighborhoods targeted for revitalization. What would be preferable is a program that ties the assistance for attaining homeownership to the targeted neighborhoods. At least two options suggest themselves. First, properties that have been foreclosed by the local taxing authority in the target neighborhoods could be selected for rehabilitation and resale at below-market rates to first-time, low-income households, perhaps in combination with requirements on the new buyer for a sweat equity component, pre- and postpurchase counseling and financial management, a minimum stay in the dwelling, and shared home appreciation capture. Second, spatially nonspecific homeownership assistance (such as down-payment grants, counseling, case management aimed at improving and stabilizing income, and credit repair) might be granted only on the condition that the new home purchased is in a designated target area.

Regardless of programmatic particulars, it is clear that if policy makers can expand and maintain more homeowners in target neighborhoods at moderate cost, the payoffs in the form of enhanced property upkeep, housing values, residential stability, and social cohesion will be dramatic. Bev Wilson and Shakil Bin Kashem found that if a census tract's homeownership rate increased by ten percentage points, the value of homes there would appreciate by 1.6 percent more.[29] Edward Coulson, Seok-Joon Hwang, and Susumu Imai estimated a marginal social benefit of about six thousand dollars for each dwelling that switched from absentee- to occupant-owned in neighborhoods having low homeownership rates initially.[30]

Toward a People-in-Place-Oriented Neighborhood Reinvestment Strategy

Recall the upshot of chapter 9 that motivated the foregoing policy discussion. Our market-dominated system for determining the flows of human and financial resources across neighborhoods has produced a systematic bias toward too little investment in housing. These inefficiencies arise primarily due to the presence of externalities of several sorts, strategic gaming, and self-fulfilling prophecies. I have argued here that policies that focus on improving the neighborhood physical environment or the resident's expectations of it will likely not be as successful in spurring investments by property owners as those that focus on altering their financial incentives and the aggregate tenure characteristics of residents there. A strategy involving dwelling improvement requirements, coupled with subsidies if necessary, attacks a major source of inefficiently low reinvestment levels: strategic gaming among owners. A strategy that expands homeownership directly boosts incentives to invest, and establishes the prerequisite for abetted social identification and cohesion at the neighborhood level, which further intensifies reinvestment indirectly. In sum, I advocate a *"people-in-place"* reinvestment component of strategic targeting that focuses on the selected neighborhoods' owners of residential property, both those who have owned for a considerable period and those who can attain stable homeownership through the policies applied.

Encouraging Economically Diverse Neighborhoods

As table 10.1 emphasizes, policy makers may wish to intervene in neighborhoods receiving appropriate flows of investment but are inappropriately diverse in their populations. In the next two sections, I consider strategies for altering the economic and racial mix of neighborhoods.

Policies for altering the economic diversity of neighborhoods fundamentally depend on some sort of assisted housing, whether one attaches the assistance to a specific dwelling or to a lower-income tenant; I consider both below. To be "neighborhood-supportive," public policymakers, developers, and operators of assisted housing (both site- and tenant-based) must pay close attention to (1) concentration, (2) development type and scale, (3) monitoring of tenants, (4) management of buildings, (5) collaboration with neighborhoods, and (6) public relations. Neighbors and the housing market clearly can distinguish between low concentrations of assisted households residing in small-scale buildings that reflect good design, maintenance, and management and those that are not. The former sort of "good" assisted housing can become cognitively invisible to neighbors as a potential concern contributing to neighborhood disinvestment and decline.[31] Thus, I design my policy recommendations holistically to confound negative public stereotypes about deconcentrated assisted housing by striving for universally well conceived and well operated programs. Most recommendations will apply to federal policies and programs since, unlike in the case of financial investments in neighborhoods, they control how the vast majority of assisted housing plays out on the local level.

Overarching Reforms

Before considering reforms that should be made to particular federal assisted housing programs, there are five neighborhood-supportive yet not budget-busting reforms I would advocate that overarch all such programs.[32]

Regional assisted housing institution building. The federal government or state governments cannot fulfill most of the above criteria for a neighborhood-supportive housing policy; only a more local organization can accomplish these ends. Undoubtedly, some public housing authorities (PHAs) and local governments have proven that they have the requisite human, technological, and financial resources to oversee successful assisted housing programs; others clearly do not. Moreover, even competent organizations rarely have region-wide authority. How, then, can programmatic reforms be delivered in a consistently effective manner across each metropolitan area in the nation with the current institutional structure?

I believe that we need considerable experimentation to find the best method for enhancing institutional capacity to operate metro-wide, neighborhood-sensitive assisted housing programs. An innovative proposal forwarded by Bruce Katz and Margery Turner offers an illustration.[33] They argue that the Department of Housing and Urban Development (HUD) should allow interagency competition for administering a single, seamless public housing / Housing Choice Voucher (HCV) program spanning each metropolitan region. HUD could solicit bids from PHAs, state housing agencies, and other nonprofit organizations. This regional organization would also coordinate with the state authority administering the Low Income Housing Tax Credit (LIHTC) program. Whatever new organizational structures emerge, it is crucial that the various programmatic elements collaborate closely across the entire metropolitan area.[34]

Fair housing law revisions. New legislation should add source of income as a protective class in federal, state, and local fair housing law, similar to how the law treats such classes as race, color, religion, gender, and national origin. This hopefully would change the behavior of landlords who currently can slough off requests to lease by a voucher holder on the perfectly legal basis that "they do not wish to participate in a housing assistance program." An undetermined number of landlords may now be using this excuse as camouflage for illegal discriminatory intent regarding a currently protected class of tenant. More landlords likely decline to participate because of their aversion to the housing inspections associated with the voucher lease-up process, onerous bureaucratic procedures by the local housing authority, or negative reactions by their unsubsidized tenants. Of course, eliminating one vehicle for not renting to a voucher holder does not eliminate them all; so this policy reform, though likely helpful, will not in and of itself be sufficient to increase substantially the scale and geographic scope of dwellings to voucher holders.[35] Other reforms, discussed below, will be required as complements.

Impaction standards. The aforementioned regional housing authority should promulgate regulations for both assisted households and developers that would limit the concentration and scale of assisted housing of various types in all types of neighborhoods.[36] At minimum, these regulations should establish threshold concentrations of poverty and assisted housing past which further site- or tenant-based assistance would be ineligible; racial-ethnic contingencies could also be applied to encourage racial diversity. Many precedents for such restrictions on HCV usage have arisen in the context of settling PHA desegregation cases.[37] Developers of scattered-site assisted housing similarly should be restricted in which neighborhoods they can develop units, and how many they can develop there within certain separations. There also are ample precedents for such supply-side impaction standards.[38]

Encourage the rehabilitation of structures as assisted housing. A key component of a neighborhood-supportive policy involves transforming a neighborhood eyesore into a well-maintained assisted housing site because it will provide substantial positive externalities and public relations gains.[39] To the extent that is feasible, site-based assisted housing programs should attempt to acquire and rehabilitate vacant, poorly maintained properties. HUD might alter its expense reimbursement formulas for PHAs in ways that encourage development through rehabilitation rather than new construction. States might also alter scoring formulas for LIHTC applications to better incentivize rehabilitation. Tenant-based assisted housing programs could seek to recruit owners of deteriorated properties, especially in otherwise strong neighborhoods, and then offer financial incentives for the rehabilitation of said properties in exchange for long-term availability of units for HCV lease-up.

Diversity incentives built into AFFH. HUD's 2016 Final Rule for Affirmatively Furthering Fair Housing requires state and local governments receiving HUD funds to demonstrate how their housing and community development programs promote fair housing; but it lacks sufficient teeth to elicit major changes.[40] These localities should be incentivized financially to move toward more economic and racial diversity in their constituent neighborhoods. I recommend "opportunity housing" bonuses for local governments, funneled through a formula-altered community development block grant program or some other vehicle. Homeowner constituent political support for such a policy could be encouraged through modified Internal Revenue Service rules, which could permit, for example, enhanced deductions of local property taxes and/or mortgage interest payments on residents' federal taxes if their community met its "fair share" of assisted housing sites, or made progress toward neighborhood diversification.[41]

Reforms for Site-Based Assistance Programs

Repeal and replacement of the QCT bonus. Current federal regulations specify that developers of LIHTC projects located in "qualified census tracts" (QCTs) having poverty rates over 25 percent receive bonus credits. Although there is logic in the QTC provision because such areas are more difficult to develop, this provides a perverse incentive, explaining why most LIHTC units have been developed in places that reinforce concentrations of minority poverty.[42] This bonus system should be reversed so that it incentivizes development in high-opportunity neighborhoods with little affordable housing, consistent with my suggested impaction standards.

Diversification/preservation incentives for existing assisted private developments. Some privately owned assisted housing developments will have their affordability contracts expire in the future, whereupon owners may convert the units to market rate, especially in hot-market contexts. Instead of foregoing such opportunities to lock in affordability in revitalizing neighborhoods, we should provide incentives for continuing a share of these units as affordable, consistent with my suggested impaction standards.[43]

Preserving public housing in revitalizing neighborhoods.[44] Sometimes public housing is strategically located in areas that are gentrifying, and maintaining them as good-quality housing in such area would help to lock in affordable options. The new Rental Assistance Demonstration offers more flexibility for PHAs to use HUD funds in combination with other programs to support the renovation and redevelopment of public housing.[45] HUD should better target such initiatives toward preserving affordability in revitalizing neighborhoods.[46]

Reforms for Tenant-Based Assistance Programs

Adopt small area fair market rents (SAFMRs). The standard HCV program establishes a subsidy for each particular size of dwelling based on fair market rent (FMR), defined as the 40th percentile in the metropolitan-wide rent distribution for that dwelling size.[47] This formulation creates a perverse incentive structure that reinforces concentrations of disadvantage. FMRs are often above the rents the market will bear for lower-quality dwellings in high-poverty neighborhoods; thus, landlords in those neighborhoods will be eager to recruit HCV holders actively. Analogously, HCV holders will find that they can reduce their contribution to rent if they settle on lower-quality dwellings in high-poverty neighborhoods renting for less than FMR. Just the opposite disincentives apply for landlords and HCV holders in opportunity neighborhoods. HUD should remove these perverse incentives by adopting a policy whereby FMRs are calculated for each zip code.[48]

Require premove and postmove mobility counseling. Low-income households have limited resources with which to undertake housing searches once local authorities issue them a voucher, and typically they and others in their networks have had little experience with and information about opportunity neighborhoods.[49] Local voucher providers must provide to each HCV holder intensive, hands-on mobility counseling and relocation assistance in locating and inspecting apartments in opportunity neighborhoods. There also should be postmove follow-ups to provide counseling, information, and other assistance aimed at heading off HCV holders from becoming discouraged and wishing to move out.[50]

Provide ancillary family supports after the move. Counseling alone may be insufficient to yield residential stability and satisfaction by HCV holders residing in opportunity neighborhoods. HUD affiliates and other social welfare agencies should provide HCV holders with a wider set of supports — including, where appropriate, subsidized day care and a used automobile.

Reduce barriers to leasing. Administrators of HCV programs should enact several reforms that would help voucher holders lease dwellings in high-opportunity areas more quickly, with less frustration and fear of expiration of the lease-up window.[51] Illustrations include (1) financial assistance for moving costs, furnishings, and apartment and utility security deposits; (2) recruiting and communication with landlords so that they will be more willing to welcome HCV applicants; and (3) extension of the lease-up period beyond the conventional sixty to ninety days.

Change diversification incentives in HUD regulations governing PHAs. The current regulatory structure through which HUD assesses and rewards the performance of each PHA, the Section Eight Management Assessment Program (SEMAP), does not reward placing HCV holders in opportunity neighborhoods or punish them if they place HCV holders in disadvantaged neighborhoods.[52] Moreover, portability of vouchers across jurisdictions is implicitly discouraged. No extra financial assistance is provided to PHAs who receive incoming HCV holders from outside their jurisdictions, or to those PHAs where HCV holders originate, despite the additional administrative burdens.[53] Revising these assessment policy and portability limitations would become less vital, of course, were my proposed strong impaction standards established as substitute criteria as part of SEMAP.

Do Low-Income Households Want to Move to More Economically Diverse Neighborhoods?

I have argued for reforming serious flaws in federal assisted housing policy because thus far it clearly has not accomplished much economic or racial desegregation or improved access of low-income (often minority) households to high-opportunity neighborhoods.[54] At this point I must acknowledge a contrary perspective. Some have argued that the weak past performance of assisted-housing programs in deconcentrating poverty is not due to shortcomings in program design or administration, but rather because low-income households typically do not wish to leave their current neighborhoods, despite aggregate statistical indicators that may suggest that they are "disadvantaged" or even "dysfunctional" places.[55] The residents' purported reasons for wishing to stay include deep place attachments,[56] strong kin and friend networks,[57] preferences for race-class homophily,[58] and ability to negotiate the microspaces within seemingly undesirable neighborhoods to obtain safety, comfort, community, and, ultimately a modicum of residential satisfaction.[59]

I do not doubt that some, perhaps even many, low-income residents of concentrated poverty neighborhoods evince many of the aforementioned attributes. To admit this does not, however, challenge the desirability and likely efficacy of reforms along the lines suggested above, for two reasons.

First, according to the behavioral economics and psychology I reviewed in chapter 5, virtually everyone manifests a status quo bias: a tendency to overvalue present circumstances in comparison to alternatives.[60] It typically takes substantial incentives, which are not present or are perverse in current assisted-housing programs, to induce a substantial change in place of residence. It is neither a matter of "preference" nor of "choice," but rather of inertia. Second, residents' preexisting preferences are not immutable, but instead are contingent on experience. Since so few low-income residents in high-poverty neighborhoods (or their parents) have ever experienced high-quality, safe neighborhoods with functional school systems,[61] their expectations become leveled: they expect all prospective neighborhoods to suffer from the same maladies, so they perceive little prospective gain from moving. Recent evidence from the Baltimore Housing Mobility Program (BHMP), garnered by Stefanie DeLuca, Peter Rosenblatt, and colleagues, powerfully demonstrated this point.[62] They found that poor black families' exposure to economically and racially diverse neighborhoods with better safety and schools changed their preferences regarding future moves, because of the positive experiences their children had living in these places. This seminal research demonstrates how social structure, personal experience, and policy opportunities influence stated and revealed preferences.

Importantly, the BHMP involves many of the components I have advocated previously. Postmove counseling, especially regarding potential second moves, and information about school quality in better neighborhoods were crucial elements of success not present in previous demonstrations like Gautreaux or Moving to Opportunity, let alone the standard voucher program. Regional administration meant that tenants did not need to negotiate with PHAs to "port out" their vouchers for use in a suburban location. Landlord recruitment meant that tenants were rarely discouraged by prospective landlords turning them away.[63] BHMP represents an invaluable prototype for key components of a reformed HCV program that would constitute the centerpiece of a neighborhood-supportive policy.

Encouraging Racially Diverse Neighborhoods

The final domain of a comprehensive neighborhood-supportive policy is a suite of programs for enhancing racial diversity. I advocate these programs because they represent gradualist, option-enhancing, voluntary (but incentive-driven) initiatives. Collectively, they aim at achieving a stable integrative process (SIP) in targeted neighborhoods.

Programs for Encouraging a Stable Integrative Process

SIP is a housing market dynamic in which dwelling seekers representing two or more races actively seek to occupy the same vacant dwellings in a substantial proportion of a jurisdiction's neighborhoods over an extended period. The meaning of "substantial portion" depends on the particulars of the geographic context. Those metropolitan areas having relatively few minorities might expect that SIP would mean that a smaller fraction of their neighborhoods would exhibit active demands by two or more races. SIP is thus consistent with a variety of diversity racial occupancy outcomes across neighborhoods, and of intertemporal changes in these outcomes. "Integration" is thus a flexible, contingent construct from the perspective of SIP.[64]

It would be mistaken to view the goal of SIP in terms of precise percentages of various racial groups living in neighborhoods that constitute a static outcome called "integration." All we can say definitively about the outcome of SIP is that it would tend over time to desegregate racially homogeneous areas and promote more racially diverse ones. Homogeneous neighborhoods could not remain so indefinitely, and diverse neighborhoods would tend to remain so, if a racially diverse set of households with comparable willingness and ability to compete for the dwelling greeted each vacancy.

Perhaps one can more clearly understand SIP by contrasting it with its opposite: a process in which only dwelling seekers of one race actively seek to occupy vacant dwellings in a particular neighborhood. Such a segregative process leads to one of two alternatives. If the race of the in-movers perpetually matches that of the out-movers, stable racial segregation will persist. If the race of the in-movers differs over an extended period from that of the out-movers, temporary racial integration results, followed inevitably by transition and resegregation. SIP seeks to avoid producing these two outcomes through its component programs, which are described next.

Enhanced fair housing enforcement. Policies to deter differential treatment discrimination by housing and mortgage market agents are required if minorities are to be free to exercise their neighborhood choices as their economic circumstances and preferences would dictate. This does not mean merely enhancing existing penalties for violators, increasing outreach to inform victims of their rights and means of redress, improving the speed of case adjudication, or expanding civil rights training of those involved in the various urban market contexts where discrimination occurs, although we can applaud all such efforts. Rather, enhancing deterrence requires an enforcement strategy based on vastly intensified matched-testing investigations conducted by civil rights agencies that create a viable obstacle to discrimination. The fundamental flaw in the federal Fair Housing Act of 1986 (strengthened in 1988) is that it relies on the victim to recognize and formally complain about suspected acts of discrimination.[65] Due to the subtlety of discrimination as it is typically practiced today, such reliance is misplaced. As a result, there is little chance of violators fearing detection or litigation, and consequently there is minimal deterrence. Effective deterrence requires a substantial commitment of resources to empower private and governmental fair housing agencies to conduct ongoing enforcement testing programs, which employ pairs of matched investigators who pose as housing or mortgage seekers. These enforcement testing programs would not merely respond to complaints of alleged victims, but would provide an ongoing presence in areas rendered suspicious by other evidence or, resources permitting, in areas randomly located throughout the market.[66] Only through such a comprehensive enforcement testing policy, backed up by legal suits exacting heavy penalties, can people prone to discriminate be deterred from using race to constrain the opportunities of others.[67] Significant increases in funds and concomitant expansion in the geographic scope of enforcement testing will be required, however, if this strategy is to create a credible deterrent to differential treatment discrimination in housing and mortgage markets.

Affirmative marketing. Affirmative marketing is advertising that through content, medium, and distribution tries to increase the attractiveness of particular properties or neighborhoods in the perceptions of households who are members of racial groups that are currently underrepresented in the area being addressed. The key facet of affirmative marketing is that it explicitly directs its encouragement toward a particular group of households whose increased representation is vital for achieving SIP. Though superficially this might appear to be a version of "steering," the US Supreme Court has upheld the selective provision of housing market information based on the race of the home seeker and the race of the neighborhood if the goal is affirmative marketing and desegregation.

Real estate counseling services. Local jurisdictions or nonprofit organizations could sponsor agencies designed to provide free information to prospective renters and homebuyers about communities in which their racial group is underrepresented. Counseling would include firsthand tours of targeted neighborhoods, preferably with the races of the client and counselor matched. The counselors in such agencies, who have themselves lived in diverse areas and whose children attend integrated schools, are key to making this programmatic component successful. While taking prospective in-movers to schools, shopping areas, recreation facilities, and other community amenities in targeted areas, there is considerable advantage in being able to invite a person of the same race to experience what you have.

Financial incentives. Policymakers should institute a variety of financial incentives to encourage households to move into neighborhoods where their actions would promote SIP there. In chapter 9 I demonstrated that more racially diverse neighborhoods would generate positive social externalities; incentivizing individual actions to move in pro-diversity ways offers a straightforward and voluntary means of achieving this. Several forms of such pro-SIP financial incentives have been used in the past. Many municipalities across the country have offered low-interest second mortgages (sometimes granting deferred payment until time of sale) to buyers of homes in neighborhoods where their racial group has been deemed underrepresented by local policymakers.[68] During the 1980s the state of Ohio earmarked a pool of low-interest mortgage loans for exclusive use by first-time, low-income homebuyers of all races who agreed to purchase in neighborhoods designated by the state for pro-diversity purposes. Oak Park, Illinois, developed a repair grant program for landlords of rental buildings who were able to achieve SIP. Various levels of government could offer grants or tax credits aimed at defraying moving costs when households' moves into neighborhoods increased the racial diversity there, based on the latest American Community Survey data.

Ancillary activities. Community activities related to neighborhoods' and schools' social capital, infrastructure, and quality ideally can reinforce the aforementioned pillars of a pro-diversity strategy.[69] Community organizing should be encouraged, probably at the block or large-building level, so that interracial networks are built and nurtured. If possible, the public sector must maintain and enhance the quality of its infrastructure, to defuse stereotypes about how racial diversity leads to deterioration of the public realm. Public school administrators also should coordinate carefully with housing diversity administrators so that their actions are mutually reinforcing. School administrators might well adjust boundaries of catchment areas to avoid the creation of predominantly white and predominantly minority school buildings. Of course, the quality of public education must be a top priority.

What if People Prefer to Live in Racially Homogeneous Neighborhoods?

In the earlier discussion of policies encouraging economic diversity of neighborhoods, I acknowledged and then challenged a contrary position alleging that low-income households did not support such efforts. In the realm of racial diversity policies, there is an analogous critique: many households, especially disproportionate numbers of whites, prefer neighborhoods overwhelmingly comprised of residents of their own racial group.[70] Because of these supposedly "natural," immutable preferences, the argument goes, policies such as those I have advocated are neither appropriate nor efficacious. There is substantial support from public opinion polls and analyses of residential mobility patterns that indeed many households wish to self-segregate, as I documented in chapter 8. What is fallacious in this argument is that these preferences are somehow "natural" or unalterable. On the contrary, as the aforementioned work by Stefanie DeLuca and colleagues has shown definitively, social structure, personal experience, and policy opportunities influence stated and revealed preferences for neighborhood attributes.[71]

In the case of racial segregation, it is obvious that the legacy of generations of legal, and then illegal but still widespread, housing and mortgage market discrimination created a potent stereotype about what desegregation and racially diverse neighborhoods meant. Discriminatory barriers in white communities (restrictive covenants, exclusionary practices by agents and lenders, etc.) conspired to overcrowd minority households into the oldest, most decrepit parts of central cities, where unscrupulous landlords extracted excessive rent for badly undermaintained dwellings. Historically, the entrance of a few minority people into a formerly all-white neighborhood (often adjacent to the minority one) meant that lenders would start to redline the area, blockbusters would move in to scare away white homeowners, and real estate agents would start steering away prospective white in-movers while steering in prospective minority ones. Thus, neighborhoods rapidly tipped from homogeneous-white to homogeneous-minority status. Heightened social tensions, violence, disrupted social networks, and losses of whites' home equity often accompanied this spasmodic tipping. Then the process of physical decay would progress in this newly annexed neighborhood of minority occupancy for all the aforementioned reasons, and the process would continue. Due to this discriminatory legacy, it is also predictable that many minority households would view white neighbors as being potentially hostile to their presence, and would thus express a "preference" for minority communities. With our racist history, it is no wonder that many households, whites and minorities alike, hold negative attitudes about what it means to live in racially diverse neighborhoods! Indeed, this legacy is the basis of the current power of racial composition as a signal for what the future of the neighborhood holds, as I explained in chapter 5.

Legacy need not be destiny. The way desegregation has transpired in the past is not a guide for how it must work in the future. We cannot stop the momentum of our discriminatory history and its associated stereotypes, however, merely by adopting a race-neutral policy stance and ceasing to discriminate. We must adopt pro-diversity policies to encourage a process of residential selection that confounds the conventional stereotypes and promotes neighborhoods that are racially diverse yet also stable, of high quality, and hospitable to all. The evidence is clear that if people can experience such environments, their attitudes about race and diversity change markedly.

The relevant body of social psychological literature here relates to the notion of equal-status residential contact, which I introduced briefly in chapter 9. This long-standing tenet of intergroup relations is that racial prejudice can be reduced if particular sorts of interracial contacts can be promulgated. To have this impact, such contacts must be (1) sustained; (2) noncompetitive; (3) personal, informal, and one-to-one; (4) approved by the relevant public authorities; and (5) designed to confer equal status on both parties.[72] Racially diverse neighborhoods produced by SIP fulfill all these conditions. Neighbors typically share common community concerns. They are most likely to develop interpersonal relationships because of sustained propinquity. Because public policy promoting SIP is not tantamount to mixing races of radically different socioeconomic class backgrounds, the interracial contact will be officially sanctioned and equal-status in nature. The empirical evidence has consistently shown that equal-status interracial contact causes a substantial reduction in whites' prejudices, especially regarding their desire to have only other whites as neighbors.[73]

Is a Successful Racial Diversity Program Possible?

It is fair to ponder whether multifaceted SIP policy holds much promise for unraveling generations of racist public and private policy that has embedded segregation in our history.[74] I believe that my proposal does hold promise of efficacy, and that the city of Shaker Heights, Ohio, offers an encouraging case study in this regard. Shaker Heights is an independent municipality of about thirty thousand residents abutting Cleveland on its southeastern side. It has considerable diversity in the types and cost of its housing stock, of which about a third is renter-occupied. In the late 1950s, its leaders realized that the rapid growth of the black population in Cleveland's eastern core was generating the classic pattern of neighborhood racial tipping described above, and would soon threaten to continue the same in Shaker Heights, as it has in a few other eastern suburbs. In response, the city enacted a comprehensive strategy for achieving SIP that ultimately included all the components I have described.[75] Fortunately, a wider alliance of eastern Cleveland suburbs joined in some of the Shaker Heights programs.

By multiple indicators, SIP has worked in Shaker Heights.[76] According to the 1960 census, the city's population was only about 1 percent black and 99 percent white. Racial diversity in several dimensions steadily grew over the next half century, until by 2014 its population was 55 percent white, 34 percent black, 7 percent Asian, and 3 percent Hispanic. I showed in a statistical analysis that Shaker Heights neighborhoods initially occupied exclusively by whites had much larger increases in black residents than would have been predicted on the basis of patterns evinced elsewhere across the encompassing county for a similar type of housing stock. Similarly, its neighborhoods already having substantial numbers of black residents at the beginning of the study period exhibited larger numbers of new white home seekers than would have predicted otherwise. In other words, SIP emerged both in erstwhile stably segregated white neighborhoods, and in racially mixed neighborhoods that normally would have been unstable and transitory.[77] Shaker Heights has also exhibited a long-term pattern of home price appreciation that has been far superior to that of the surrounding county as a whole. Brian Cromwell evaluated the city's pro-SIP loan program, and found that it produced a significant stabilizing effect on racial composition and home appreciation in neighborhoods that under normal circumstances might have tipped rapidly to predominantly black occupancy.[78] Importantly, Cromwell interpreted his results as indicating that the Shaker Heights SIP financial incentive program confounded the conventional signaling effect of racial composition on white housing demanders' expectations of the area's future.

Synergisms among Neighborhood-Supportive Policies

Multiple synergisms and complementarities emerge when we consider holistically the menu of neighborhood-supportive policies I have advocated. Consider first the realm of increasing economic diversity. From the perspective of HCV holders, the constraint to limit their search in neighborhoods eligible under impaction standards will be offset by SAFMRs, enhanced mobility counseling, expanded search periods, affirmative landlord recruitment, and the addition of source of income as a fair-housing protected class. Residents in high-opportunity neighborhoods will be less likely to oppose (and fear the potential consequences of) assisted households as new neighbors if they know there are strictly enforced and consistently applied impaction standards across all neighborhoods of the region. Similarly, nonassisted residents in high-opportunity neighborhoods will be less likely to flee or avoid neighborhoods with assisted households if they know those circumstances are widely represented in virtually all neighborhoods. Landlords in high-opportunity neighborhoods will have fewer concerns about renting to HCV holders, since they will not only receive appropriate SAFMRs but will know that impaction standards will automatically restrict the number of such households they can have in their building.

Useful synergisms could also arise if communities creatively integrated their programs for improving the physical condition of target neighborhoods with those aiming to increase their diversity. For example, tax-foreclosed homes often become undermaintained and, in severe cases, abandoned. When such properties are located in otherwise decent-quality neighborhoods, policymakers can target them as vehicles for pro-diversification programs. For example, they can be acquired by local government or private nonprofit agencies to operate as scattered-site affordable rental housing, thus enhancing the area's economic diversity. The Denver Housing Authority's "dispersed housing" program successfully employed such a scheme, which has boosted property values near rehabilitated, formerly foreclosed properties.[79] Concomitantly, policy makers could affirmatively market these properties as appropriate, to enhance the area's racial diversity. Housing code enforcement, coupled with need-based financial assistance, could be concentrated on neighborhoods with increasing shares of minority in-movers produced by SIP policies. This intent of this enforcement would be to confound conventional wisdom about the relationship between neighborhood diversification and declining residential quality.

The Rationale for Circumspect Policy: Caveats, Constraints, and Potential Pitfalls

In the title of this chapter, I have used the adjective "circumspect" to describe my proposed neighborhood-supportive suite of policies. I did not choose this word without considerable intention, because wise policy making in this realm requires a keen appreciation of the limitations as well as the potentials for neighborhood interventions. There are at least seven reasons for circumspection.

Limited Efficacy of Governmental Interventions Compared to Driving Forces

My metropolitan housing submarket model makes it clear that the fundamental drivers of neighborhood change—which are primarily economic, demographic, and technological—are not within the control of local governments. Many drivers, such as change in communication, transportation, and energy technologies and most international economic forces, are largely beyond the control of a nation-state, let alone an individual state, regional planning organization, or municipality. At best, these lower levels of government can make only modest direct adjustments (via regulations or economic incentives) and indirect supplements (via their public service and tax packages) in how the market drives resource flow among the neighborhoods within their purview. These public interventions typically pale in power compared to the larger external forces impinging, and therefore are unlikely to change the overall course of all neighborhoods for which they may be stewards.

The case studies of Detroit and Los Angeles presented in chapter 4 illustrate my point. When a city loses most of its economic base and population declines dramatically, many of its neighborhoods will decay and many will become abandoned. The city and probably even the state governments would not be in a position to target sufficient resources to reverse such declines universally. Conversely, when an older city gets a new injection of its economic base and people clamor to move in, even modest-quality neighborhoods will witness upward succession and physical rehabilitation without the local government needing to do anything. In the face of these overwhelming large-scale external forces, government interventions have relatively limited efficacy. The implication is that policy makers should take care not to intervene in the face of overwhelmingly contrary market forces, and should keep their expectations for success modest.

Potential for Zero-Sum Policy Impact

Even if public interventions are sufficiently powerful to change the trajectory of a neighborhood in a desirable direction, another potential pitfall lurks. The augmented private resources (financial and household flows) invested in the target neighborhood may merely have been siphoned from other neighborhoods with which the target was competing, thus creating a zero-sum effect for the jurisdiction's neighborhoods in aggregate.

Zero-sum policy outcomes are most likely when a program improves the absolute attractiveness of a target area enough to alter migration flows so that somewhat higher-income, better educated households move in. This in turn would change the aggregate household socioeconomic and tenure characteristics of the target area, and thus increase aggregate reinvestment behavior there. From the myopic view of the target neighborhood, this seems like an unvarnished success. However, is this ultimately sensible from the jurisdiction's perspective? Certainly not if the net result is a mere reshuffling of residents across different neighborhoods within the same jurisdiction. In such a case, there is a zero-sum outcome: upward succession and improvements in dwelling upkeep in targeted areas is exactly offset by downward succession and declines in upkeep in nontargeted areas.

Obviously, a single local jurisdiction can attempt to avoid such zero-sum outcomes by aggressively marketing its target neighborhoods to desired residents who live in other jurisdictions. Yet, even if it is successful from its own perspective in doing this, from the broader social perspective the zero-sum result persists: the desired households have been pirated from other jurisdictions whose neighborhoods, by implication, now receive less reinvestment. Of course, if all jurisdictions follow suit and make investments to compete for desired households, the overall result is a waste of public resources, with little net gain to any jurisdiction. Thus, attempting to improve target neighborhoods by attracting new households from elsewhere is a strategy fraught with peril and social inefficiencies.

The neighborhood-supportive programs I have advocated sidestep these zero-sum challenges. In the realm of physical reinvestment, people-in-place strategies that incentivize dwelling rehabilitation efforts by those who otherwise would be not maintain their dwelling in decent repair, and which promote renters becoming homeowners in the same places, produce sizable improvements in the condition of neighborhoods. These are net-gain improvements not counterbalanced by losses in housing investments elsewhere. Of course, the relative rankings of neighborhood quality may change, as might future mobility patterns. Yet, such zero-sum-game-producing dynamics become less relevant at this point, because the fillip to neighborhood reinvestment has already occurred. In the realm of neighborhood diversity programs, drawing certain types of households (categorized by economic status or racial group) to a targeted neighborhood may have the inadvertent effect of taking them away from other neighborhoods that thereby become less diverse. But this is not a necessary outcome. On the contrary, it is often the case that when a household moves from one neighborhood to another, it enhances the diversity of both those neighborhoods.

The Perils of Partial Deconcentration of Poverty

In chapters 6 and 9, I demonstrated how the current poverty concentration situation in many communities is highly inefficient, as well as inequitable, from a societal point of view. This follows because, past a threshold of about 15 to 20 percent neighborhood poverty rates, an upsurge in negative

294 / Chapter Ten

individual behaviors arises that also produces a rapid decline in property values. Certainly this evidence implies that the current pattern of economic segregation is not optimal. It is thus tempting to infer that any pattern of neighborhood poverty that represents less concentration is better than the status quo. This is fallacious, however, due to the peculiar, dual-threshold relationship between concentrated poverty and negative social outcomes, as portrayed in figure 6.2. On the contrary, many scenarios representing less extremely concentrated poverty (over 40 percent) but more moderately concentrated poverty (20 to 40 percent) yield inferior social outcomes. Only if policy can increase the number of poor living in low-poverty (under 20 percent) neighborhoods will we see an enhancement in social efficiency on net.

I illustrate my point with a hypothetical numerical example. The stylized facts shown in table 10.2 attempt to capture in a simplified "step function" the essential elements of the social-scientific evidence I summarized earlier in figure 6.2. Total undesirable social costs, here measured by some unspecified "social problem index," associated with percentages of poverty are (1) very low with concentrations below 20 percent, (2) much higher with concentrations between 20 and 40 percent, and (3) only modestly higher on the margin with concentrations above 40 percent. With this critical evidence as foundation, table 10.2 presents the simple calculation of total social costs in the hypothetical city under four alternative scenarios. For expositional ease, I consider scenario A as baseline. Two neighborhoods have extreme concentrations of poverty, with both contributing 30 to the city's total social costs, as measured by the index. The eight other neighborhoods with no poor people contribute only 5 each in social costs, bringing the city's total across all ten of its neighborhoods to 100. By comparison, scenario C portrays a situation with less extremely concentrated poverty and affluence: there is no homogeneously poor neighborhood, and one fewer homogeneously non-poor neighborhood. Scenario D represents an even more diverse pattern of economic groups across neighborhoods. Yet in scenarios C and D the social well-being of this city is *worse off* (that is, it has higher total social costs) than in scenario A with its greater extent of extreme economic segregation!

This important result seems counterintuitive and perhaps even contradictory to the claims I made in chapters 6 and 9 about how economic segregation was socially inefficient. It is neither. The result of inferior social efficiency follows only when one increases (either in a comparative static thought experiment like this, or with real poverty deconcentration housing policies, discussed earlier in this chapter) the number of poor people living in neighborhoods above the threshold poverty rate of 20 percent. Table 10.2 demonstrates that the situation with greatest feasible number of poor

Table 10.2. Hypothetical example of the perils of partially deconcentrating neighborhood poverty

Scenario A	Social costs	Scenario B	Social costs	Scenario C	Social costs	Scenario D	Social costs
8 w/ no poor	8 × 5 = 40	10 w/ 15% poor	10 × 5 = 50	7 w/ no poor	7 × 5 = 35	4 w/ no poor	4 × 5 = 20
1 w/ 50% poor	1 × 30 = 30			3 w/ 50% poor	3 × 30 = 90	6 w/ 25% poor	6 × 20 = 120
1 w/ 100% poor	1 × 30 = 30						
Total	100		50		125		140

Assume 1,000 households in the city: 150 poor, 850 nonpoor (15 percent overall poverty rate), divided equally among ten neighborhoods. Assume further that social science shows the following incidences of social costs associated with neighborhoods with the following poverty percentages:

If the neighborhood poverty rate is less than 20 percent, the social problem index for the neighborhood is 5.

If the neighborhood poverty rate is between 20 and 40 percent, the social problem index for the neighborhood is 20.

If the neighborhood poverty rate is 40 percent or more, the social problem index for the neighborhood is 30.

Now consider various possible distributions of poor households across the city's neighborhoods, and see total social costs for the city.

households housed in neighborhoods below the threshold—in scenario B—is by far the most desirable for the city as a whole.[80] This is, of course, the identical conclusion reached in case 2 during the theoretical discussion of social efficiency in chapter 9.

Now we can turn from the thought experiment depicted in table 10.2 to the real world. It is appropriate to reiterate other evidence I originally presented in chapter 9, approximating the magnitude of the social inefficiency involved here by using property values as indicators of net social costs. My colleagues and I showed that if one replaced the actual distribution of poverty across metropolitan neighborhoods with one in which no neighborhood had more than a 15 percent poverty rate (equivalent to scenario B in table 10.2), aggregate property values for owner-occupied dwellings would rise 13 percent, and monthly rents would rise by 4 percent.[81] The implied capitalization of decreased social cost to our nation in this neighborhood diversification scenario is nearly a trillion dollars in current prices! Such massive gains in value would occur predominantly in neighborhoods that currently have poverty rates above the 20 percent threshold, and thus would disproportionately benefit moderate-income and minority homeowners. We would thus secure gains in both efficiency and equity.

The cautionary policy implications of this discussion should be obvious. Progress in deconcentrating poverty and decreasing economic segregation must not focus myopically on merely reducing the number of poor people living in neighborhoods with more than 40 percent poverty, as scenario D makes transparent. Rather, progress must be measured by how many poor people live in neighborhoods with less than 20 percent poverty (and, equivalently, how many nonpoor people live in neighborhoods that are completely isolated from the poor) instead of in neighborhoods with more than 20 percent poverty.[82] This evaluative criterion undoubtedly creates a serious challenge for policymakers implementing the sorts of economic diversification strategies I advocated earlier in this chapter.

Inappropriate Geographic Scale of Governance

There is typically a significant mismatch between a local political jurisdiction's small geographic scale and that of the metropolitan area—the scale over which most externally generated neighborhood change forces operate. The relative attractiveness of the public service/tax/policy packages that competing jurisdictions proffer influence the inter-neighborhood flow of financial and human resources. Thus, an individual jurisdiction has only limited ability to direct market-based resource flows into its constituent neighborhoods, because relativistic comparisons of neighborhoods over a much broader geographic area fundamentally guide these flows. By implication, the success of one local jurisdiction's neighborhood strategies will depend not only on its own efforts, but also on the actions or inactions of other competing local jurisdictions in the same realm. This is a problem of *governance* related to the fragmented nature of local political jurisdictions over most US metropolitan areas. As I noted earlier in this chapter, this challenge would shrink in importance if the locality were embedded in a metro-wide system of planning and neighborhood policymaking.

Lack of Supportive Federal and State Policies and Local Partners

To the degree that federal and state social welfare, housing assistance, and revenue sharing policies exacerbate socioeconomic inequalities in metropolitan areas, local efforts to encourage diverse high-quality neighborhoods will be thwarted.[83] Similarly, local governmental efforts will prove less efficacious if they cannot marshal support from a powerful group of local community development organizations and foundations.

Constrained Local Public Financial Resources

Closely related to the foregoing point about inadequate local financial assistance from governmental and charitable sources, the next reason for circumspection is local budgetary reality. Most municipalities and states face staggering financial obligations, especially in the domains of health care, education, public pensions, and infrastructure. Perversely, jurisdictions with the most intense problems of neighborhood underinvestment and concentrations of minority poverty are typically those with the weakest fiscal capacity and the greatest accumulated needs. In this context, it is challenging to press for neighborhood-supportive policies unless policymakers can devise new, equitable means of financing them. It is in this spirit that I forward the following ideas.

First, well-established practices for tax-increment financing (TIF) could be creatively applied to generate resources for a broader set of neighborhood-supportive programs than has traditionally been supported by TIF districts. As illustration, local community redevelopment agencies in California established a long record of using TIFs to finance affordable housing development.[84] Policy makers could spatially target the housing rehabilitation grant/loan program I proposed earlier in a way so that it could be financed by a TIF.

Second, a more experimental financing idea involves partial property equity gain recapture. Because strategic targeting is designed to stabilize and improve the quality of life and property values in neighborhoods, property owners there should be obligated to repay a share of those "unearned" capital gains into a revolving trust fund providing the dedicated source of funding for the targeting program. In particular, the partial equity gain recapture would happen via a property transfer fee assessed at time of closing, as a property in the targeted area sells and the deed transfers. The fee would be a percentage of the capital gain (less any improvements) on the property, with gain defined as current sales price less the baseline capital value established before the initiation of the targeting program. Due to the commonly regressive inequities associated with neighborhood dynamics I documented in chapter 9, I strongly recommend a progressively scaled recapture rate, with the percentage levied increasing with the absolute dollar value of the capital gain, and perhaps with an exemption on properties that transfer below a certain threshold sales price if the owner is also the occupant.

While undoubtedly we will need to secure new sources of revenue before an effective, comprehensive, neighborhood-supportive suite of programs can be instituted by localities, such programs need not detrimentally affect the jurisdictions' long-term fiscal capacity. On the contrary, wise strategic targeting can result in a strengthening of the jurisdiction's tax base over time. If it leverages substantial amounts of private capital, and enhances or maintains the number of households with substantial disposable incomes in the jurisdiction, the net increase in discounted present values of property, income, sales, and other tax and fee revenues emanating from target areas may well exceed the jurisdiction's initial investments. This proved to be the case in Richmond's Neighborhoods In Bloom initiative, discussed earlier.[85] Even if such felicitous possibilities fail to materialize, the use of financial incentives repaid partially or in whole with interest when owners sell their properties offers a vehicle for minimizing financial burdens on both property owners and the local public sector.

Unrealistic Hopes for a Panacea for Poverty and Inequality

The final dimension of circumspection concerns expectations about what neighborhood policy can achieve relative to broader issues of poverty and inequality. Neighborhood policy makers and planners should not naively believe that a neighborhood-supportive policy as described here—even at its most successful—is a panacea for socioeconomic disadvantage or inequality.[86] An improved physical, social, and psychological neighborhood environment alone is likely insufficient to change drastically the economic prospects of adult residents who lack basic human capital, social skills, or means of transportation that would unlock doors of opportunity for them. Similarly, resident youth may gain little in payoffs from an economically and racially diverse neighborhood if their networks stubbornly cement them to their previous social worlds of concentrated disadvantage, or if they continue to enroll in inferior, underachieving school systems.[87] Physically improved neighborhoods will have little purchase in eroding structural and individual barriers of racism (though racially diverse ones will help in this regard). Attacking poverty and inequality successfully will take a comprehensive set of social welfare interventions and supports to provide fair opportunities for all citizens, even in a hypothetical world of diverse, high-quality neighborhoods. Fortunately, creative thinking along these lines is already underway that envisions holistic linkages among housing, transportation, income support, childcare, and health policies.[88]

Having argued that good neighborhoods alone will be *insufficient* to ending poverty and inequality, I hasten to add that they are *necessary*. As I demonstrated in chapters 8 and 9, the way we have made our neighborhoods is a prime culprit in generating and perpetuating poverty and inequality. Moreover, as I argued earlier in this chapter, antipoverty efforts carried out by federal and state governments and by nonprofit organizations—regardless of whether they are "people-based" or "place-based"—will aid local governments' efforts in making good neighborhoods. In sum, efforts by different entities aimed at reducing poverty and inequality work synergistically. Conversely, no individual entity can solve these problems on its own unless it gets substantial support from the other entities involved.

Conclusion

To refashion neighborhoods so that they mold our better selves, we should institute a "circumscribed, neighborhood-supportive" suite of policies in three neighborhood domains: physical quality, economic diversity, and racial diversity. Collectively and synergistically they would improve conditions in low-quality residential environments while maintaining them in decent-quality ones. They would also increase the economic and racial diversity of neighborhoods and local political jurisdictions across the metropolitan area, and reduce involuntary residential mobility associated with inefficient race and class transitions. We should develop programs according to the principle of strategic targeting. We should devise initiatives holistically within the context of metropolitan housing submarket projections, and then direct them at particular neighborhoods with sufficient intensity so that the behaviors of private market actors, especially households and residential property owners, will change substantially in these places. In concert, these actions should alter the perceptions of key neighborhood investors and thereby leverage their investments, minimize destructive gaming behaviors, internalize externalities, and moderate expectations, thus defusing self-fulfilling prophecies.

The neighborhood-supportive policies I have advocated represent a middle-ground position that attempts to straddle both political and intellectual extremes. Politically, my proposal should have bipartisan appeal. It should appeal to progressives because of its attention to issues of social equity and diversity. It aims to blunt neighborhood dynamics and outcomes that are most hurtful to the disadvantaged while simultaneously improving their residential quality of life and expanding their opportunities for socioeconomic advancement. It should appeal to conservatives because of its emphasis on improving the efficiency of how we allocate our scarce private and public resources in society; it aims to do so by gradualist, voluntary, choice-enhancing means. It should appeal to all by framing neighborhood-supportive policy as an effective, humane way to reduce the societal incidence of poverty and the extent of inequality over the long run.

As for intellectual extremes, my proposal sits astride the longstanding "people versus place" debate in housing and community development policy. This debate revolves around whether housing policy should aim to assist low-income families in moving out of disadvantaged neighborhoods, or rather aim to improve the conditions of these neighborhoods so that low-income families can move up in status while staying in place.[89] For decades the discourse on this topic has become increasingly factionalized,[90] though recently there have been laudable efforts to find common ground.[91] I also believe that there is ample ground for syntheses between these positions, and we can identify productive synergisms. Indeed, my proposal of a "people-in-place" strategy synthesizes of elements of both "people-based" and "place-based" approaches in ways that make the ultimate impact most supportive of diverse, stable high-quality neighborhoods.

ELEVEN

Conclusion

We make our neighborhoods. In an obvious way, we as residential developers and property owners invest the resources to build, maintain, and modify dwellings and their supportive infrastructure. In a more subtle way, we make our neighborhoods by our occupancy. Collectively, we and our neighbors tautologically constitute the socioeconomic, demographic, and racial-ethnic profile of residents in our neighborhoods. Finally, we make our neighborhoods through the panoply of local social interactions in which we engage and the organizations we develop with our neighbors, both formally and informally, one-on-one and in groups.

Once we occupy them, neighborhoods start to make us. They influence our physical and mental health by shaping our exposures to pollutants and violence and our accessibility to health care services. They influence our attitudes, especially our satisfaction with the quality of our residential lives. They influence the information we receive about the world and how we interpret, evaluate, and respond to it. Therefore, they influence the expectations that drive the pattern of our investments in neighborhoods, and the mobility behaviors that determine when we move and which neighborhood we will move to next. They influence the major life decisions that shape our future prospects: behaviors related to education, fertility, work, and legal and illegal activities.

This book has aimed to enhance our understanding of these mutually causal roles in which we and our neighborhoods are intertwined. At the most basic level, market-guided flows of financial and human resources into and out of neighborhoods make them. We can best comprehend these flows by a systemic approach focusing on the operation of the metropolitan housing market. Though economic drivers play a prominent role in this formulation, they are not exclusive. Social psychological aspects related to how decision makers gather and process information and form expectations are crucial to understanding neighborhood-altering flows of people and money more fully. Moreover, economic and social forces jointly explain why so many nonlinear and threshold effects characterize many individual behaviors that are related to these flows of resources. Finally, these resource flows tend to produce neighborhoods that are segregated both economically and racially, with numerous interlocking patterns of mutual causation being manifested.

During any particular period, a neighborhood will possess a set of physical, demographic, socioeconomic, social-interactive, geographic, and institutional characteristics. These characteristics can influence the children, youths, and adults who reside there through numerous mechanisms. Variations in geographic context across multiple scales (neighborhood, jurisdiction, metropolitan region)—the "spatial opportunity structure"—affect the socioeconomic outcomes that individuals can achieve by altering the payoffs that will be gained from the attributes that individuals possess during any given period, and by influencing the bundle of attributes that individuals will acquire (both passively and actively) during their lifetimes. The statistical evidence is convincing that these context effects are substantial, leading inexorably to the conclusion that neighborhoods provide a key structural link in generating and perpetuating social inequality in America.

Our market-dominated system for determining the flows of human and financial resources across neighborhoods has produced a systematic bias toward too little investment in housing in certain places and too much segregation by race and economic standing, both of which are socially inefficient and inequitable. Inefficiencies arise primarily due to the presence of externalities, strategic gaming, and self-fulfilling prophecies. Inequities arise because disadvantaged residents disproportionately endure inferior neighborhoods in many domains. The forces that maintain this inefficient and inequitable neighborhood system link together in a mutually reinforcing system of cumulative causation that serves to perpetuate race and class disparities in America.

If there ever were a classic illustration of pernicious market failure, it is here. Our system has produced a pattern of neighborhoods that is both wasteful and unjust. There thus are ample grounds to intervene aggressively with "neighborhood-supportive" policies that will overcome these inefficiencies and inequities through strategically targeted interventions that work toward making a set of neighborhoods that represent higher-quality, more economically and racially diverse places. In particular, we should institute programs within three domains—neighborhood reinvestment, economic diversity, and racial diversity—that have proven their effectiveness while emphasizing voluntary but incentivized changes in behavior in the context of choosing among enhanced options. Though these programs require resources, none represents infeasible expansions of the public sector, and several may be effectively self-funding in practice.

Understanding how we make our neighborhoods and how they make us in turn forces us to ask a critical normative question. Do our human-made neighborhoods make all of us *equally*? Sadly, the answer is a resounding "no." Savage inequalities embedded in our neighborhoods, most critically manifested as low-quality environments segregated by economic and racial status, expose the fiction in our cherished notion of "equal opportunity in America." We must intervene strategically in the market-driven processes that govern the flow of resources across metropolitan space, if we as a society want to affirm our better selves and restore "equal opportunity" to its rightful place as a hallowed premise instead of a hollow promise.

ACKNOWLEDGMENTS

When writing this book I had the distinct advantage of standing on the shoulders of giants within the previous generation of scholars. Professor William Grigsby of the University of Pennsylvania first developed the concept of housing submarkets, which Professor Jerome Rothenberg of MIT subsequently operationalized in a comprehensive, neoclassical economic model. I was fortunate and privileged to have these wonderful people as teachers, collaborators, mentors, and friends. I also am grateful for the long-time association with Dr. Anthony Downs of the Brookings Institution, whose constant encouragement and seminal book about why neighborhoods change were vital talismans.

Several peers also played crucial roles throughout my career in helping me develop the concepts, models, and empirical evidence that inform this book in so many fundamental ways. Foremost among them is Professor Anna Maria Santiago of Michigan State University, my collaborator and friend for a quarter of a century. This book would have been impoverished without our amazing research partnership. Professors Roger Andersson of Uppsala University and Sako Musterd of the University of Amsterdam were extraordinarily generous in providing intellectual stimulation, unique data sets, institutional resources, and energizing friendships over the course of a fourteen-year collaboration. Professor Garry Hesser of Augsburg College provided seminal guidance in conducting field research, and first exposed me to the sociology of neighborhoods more than forty years ago.

I also am deeply grateful to Professors Kenneth Gibb, Ade Kearns, Keith Kintrea, and Mark Livingston of Glasgow University; Gwilym Pryce of Sheffield University; Jurgen Friedrichs of the University of Cologne, Frank Kalter of Mannheim University, Michael Darcy of the University of Western Sydney; Talja Blokland of the Technical University of Delft (who is now at

Humboldt University); Hal Pawson of the University of New South Wales; Up Lim of Yonsei University; Lena Magnusson Turner and Viggo Nordvik of the Oslo and Akershus University College of Applied Sciences; Gabriel Pons Rotger of the Danish National Institute for Social Research; and Lena Hedman of Uppsala University. All have provided institutional and intellectual resources that have greatly assisted me in formulating ideas and gaining empirical understandings of neighborhood effects, household mobility, and concentrated disadvantage. I have been extremely fortunate to have such superb collaborators who proved to be even better friends.

I gratefully acknowledge many other exceptional teammates in the joint production of important neighborhood research over the years. At the Urban Institute I worked with Erin Godfrey, Chris Hayes, Leah Hendey, Jennifer Johnson, Maris Mikelsons, Ron Mincy, Kathryn Pettit, Roberto Quercia, Susan Popkin, Robin Smith, Peter Tatian, Margery Turner, Chris Walker, Doug Wissoker, and Wendy Zimmermann. At MDRC I worked with David Greenberg, Sonya Williams, and Nandita Verma. Indispensable Wayne State University quantitative researchers and project managers included Jason Booza, Alvaro Cortes, Jackie Cutsinger, Jessica Lucero, Ron Malega, Erica Raleigh, Ana Santiago-San Roman, and Lisa Stack.

I could not have undertaken much of my work represented in this book without the financial support from many governmental agencies and foundations whose grants I gratefully acknowledge. In particular, I recognize grants for my research on neighborhoods from the following public sector entities: the US Department of Housing and Urban Development, the National Institute of Mental Health, the National Institute of Child and Human Development / National Institutes of Health, the Social Science Research Council, the Ohio Department of Mental Health, and the city of Wooster. The following private foundations also provided grant support: the Annie E. Casey Foundation, the Fannie Mae Foundation, the Ford Foundation, the Kellogg Foundation, the MacArthur Foundation, and the Rockefeller Foundation. Above all, the generous terms of the Clarence Hilberry Professorship of Urban Affairs at Wayne State University provided me with an unrivaled platform of scholarly support from 1996 through 2017.

In comprehensively tackling a complex topic like urban neighborhoods, one must break out of the narrow disciplinary perspectives that characterize graduate training in many of the social sciences today. Doing so often comes at the cost of being marginalized by one's home discipline. Fortunately, in my case I was able to find substitute sources of personal and professional support and validation from a set of interdisciplinary professional organizations whose rise to prominence coincidentally corresponded with my academic career. In particular, I wish to thank the Urban Affairs Association, the Association of Public Policy and Management, the European Network for Housing Research, and the Association of Collegiate Schools of Planning—executives, staff, and members—for the invaluable role they have played over forty years in directly and indirectly helping me develop the ideas in this book.

I must express my debt to several generations of graduate students in the Master of Urban Planning program at Wayne State University. The students in my classes served as unwitting guinea pigs as I tested my formulations of neighborhood dynamics on them; their creative responses, challenges, and suggestions proved invaluable in polishing them. Three of these students provided even more crucial contributions to this book as research assistants: Natalie Lyons, Katrina Rinehart, and Timarie Szwed. To them I offer special thanks and deep appreciation for their unstinting and extremely professional efforts. I also greatly appreciate the generous assistance of Drs. Sarah Mawhorter and Meagan Elliott, who provided valuable information about Los Angeles and Detroit neighborhoods, respectively.

I thank the University of Chicago Press for its enthusiastic support for this manuscript from the outset. I acknowledge in particular the efforts of Timothy Mennel, Renaldo Migaldi, and Rachel Kelly.

The closing acknowledgment is most crucial: Nancy Galster. She was the one who invested the most valuable emotional resources in this book, though she may not have known it at the time. She was the one who paid with hours of solitude while I was on writing sabbaticals, whether they were in my home office or overseas. Her unflagging support for my scholarship and the social changes I hoped to accomplish with it have been nothing less than essential. Thank you, thank you, my love.

George C. Galster
May 2018

NOTES

PREFACE
1. For comprehensive reviews of the social scientific literature on neighborhood, see Hunter 1979; Downs 1981; Schwirian 1983; Hallman 1985; Grigsby et al. 1987; Temkin and Rohe 1996; Chaskin 1997; Wilson 2011; Kinahan 2016; and Mawhorter 2016.
2. Illustrations include Birch et al. 1979; Clay 1979; Downs 1981; Taub, Taylor, and Dunham 1984; Grigsby et al. 1987; Galster 1987a; Skogan 1990; and Sampson 2012.
3. Illustrations include Brooks-Gunn, Duncan, and Aber 1997; Rubinowitz and Rosenbaum 2002; Goering and Feins 2003; Briggs, Popkin, and Goering 2010; van Ham et al 2012; and Sampson 2012.
4. Illustrations include Molotch 1972; Saltman 1978; Albrandt and Cunningham 1979; Goodwin 1979; Clay and Hollister 1983; Varady 1986; Galster 1987a; Varady and Raffel 1995; Keating and Krumholz 1999; Bright 2000; Zielenbach 2000; Peterman 2000; Massey et al. 2013; Pagano 2015; Chaskin and Joseph 2015; and Brophy 2016.
5. Two seminal works covering multiple domains of neighborhood causes, effects, and policy responses are by Wilson (1987, 1996).
6. Sharkey 2013.
7. Sampson 2012.
8. The private housing market is virtually invisible in Sampson 2012 and Sharkey 2013. The following housing terms, singly or jointly, are absent from their indexes: *abandonment, downgrading, filtering, investment, investor, maintenance, market, price, profit, property, rate of return, reinvestment, rent,* and *upgrading.* Only public housing, proportionately a tiny segment of the housing market in most metropolitan areas, is considered in any depth.
9. In this regard I heed the remonstration of Sampson: "The field of social science will profit from a turn toward deeper engagement with contextual mechanisms of causality from bottom to top and back again, and how they are shaped by the enduring spatial logic of urban life and the interconnected social worlds we inhabit" (2012: 426).

CHAPTER 1
1. Doff 2010 and Hedman 2011 have also provided distinctive but complementary treatises attempting to link conceptually the neighborhood effects and residential mobility literatures.

2. The notion that neighborhood is both a cause and an effect of human behavior is not original with me. See, for example, Sampson 2012: 22.

3. The details of this process are the subject of chapter 5.

4. For an integrated model of these decisions for homeowners, see Galster 1987a: ch. 3.

5. Clark and Onaka (1983) distinguish "voluntary moves" (involving both "adjustment" and "induced" mobility) and "forced" moves. My discussion deals with the former only.

6. For comprehensive reviews of the vast, international urban mobility literature, see Kingsley and Turner 1993; Clark and Dieleman 1996; Dieleman 2001; and Strassman 2001.

7. The seminal formulations are in Rossi 1955 and Clark and Dieleman 1996.

8. Seminal works include Wolpert 1966; Brown and Moore 1970; and Clark and Huff 1978.

9. Seminal works include Speare 1974; Speare, Goldstein, and Frey 1975; Morris, Crull, and Winter 1976; and Newman and Duncan 1979.

10. Seminal works include Goodman 1976; Quigley and Weinberg 1977; and Hanushek and Quigley 1978.

11. Galster 1987a: ch. 8.

12. This is developed fully in chapter 5.

13. This is not to say that it is always the predominant reason households cite as rationale for moving (Clark and Onaka 1983), nor do I imply that neighborhood characteristics as a group explain a relatively large proportion of mobility. Cf. Newman and Duncan 1979; Clark and Onaka 1983; Böheim and Taylor 2002; Kearns and Parkes 2005; and Clark and Ledwith 2006.

14. Boehm and Ihlanfeldt 1986; Clark and Huang 2003; Rabe and Taylor 2010.

15. Bailey and Livingston 2007; van Ham and Clark 2009; Lee 2014.

16. Galster 1990a, 1990c; South and Crowder 1998, 2000; Harris 1999; Sampson and Sharkey 2008; Sampson 2012; Lee 2014.

17. Harris 1999; Quillian 1999; Feijten and van Ham 2009.

18. Musterd et al. 2016; Galster and Turner 2017.

19. Sampson 2012.

20. Birch et al. 1979.

21. Sampson 2012; Hedman 2013; Spring et al. 2017.

22. Ioannides and Zabel 2003; Sampson 2012; Quillian 2014; Musterd et al. 2016.

23. Ellen 2000b; Ioannides and Zabel 2008; Quillian 2014.

24. Boehm 1981; Goodman 1988.

25. For formal models and empirical tests of these simultaneous sets of choices, see Boehm 1981; Goodman 1988; Ioannides and Kan 1996; and Kan 2000.

26. See the seminal theoretical models and supportive empirical studies of Asmus and Iglarsh 1975; Chinloy 1980; Shear 1983; and Boehm and Ihlanfeldt 1986.

27. This point is explored more fully in chapter 5.

28. See, for example, Harris 1999.

29. This point is explored more fully in chapter 5.

30. Hoff and Sen 2005.

31. Such collective influences can be exerted both blatantly and subtly (path N). Individual behavior that imposes negative externalities on neighbors (for example, undermaintaining property) may be blatantly greeted with angry phone calls, public scorn, alienated friends, and ostracism from the group. Conversely, upkeep behavior that generates positive externalities may be accompanied by a host of positive social

reinforcements. In a more subtle sense, individual homeowners may find over time that they inculcate the value of neighbors, internalize their neighbors' norms, and ultimately identify with their neighbors' interests. These solidarity sentiments encourage individual behaviors that are simultaneously self-serving and group-serving. See Galster and Hesser 1982.

32. Galster 1983, 1987a.

33. For a review of models of how households sorting across space endogenously change the characteristics of those spaces, see Kuminoff, Smith, and Timmins 2010.

CHAPTER 2

1. Aber and Nieto 2000:188. Perhaps a critical reason for this lack of scholarly consensus is that the public's conceptualization and representation of the urban neighborhood has undergone significant historical evolution since World War II; Looker 2015. For reviews of conceptual and operational issues related to defining neighborhoods, see Chaskin 1997; Kallus and Law-Tone 2000; Forrest and Kearns 2001; Nicotera 2007; and Park and Rogers 2015.

2. Keller 1968: 89.

3. Morris and Hess 1975: 6.

4. Chaskin 1995: 1.

5. Pagano 2015: 6.

6. Hallman 1984: 13.

7. Warren 1981: 62.

8. Downs 1981: 15.

9. Schoenberg 1979: 69.

10. Lancaster 1966.

11. For more on this dimension, see Hunter 1979 and Temkin and Rohe 1996.

12. For more on this dimension, see Warren 1975; Warren and Warren 1977; Fischer 1982; Sampson 1997, 2012; Sampson, Raudenbush, and Earls 1997; and Sampson, Morenoff, and Earls 1999.

13. Greer 1962; Hunter 1974; and Warren 1975. For more recent examples of neighborhood typologies, see Vicino, Hanlon, and Short 2011; Kinahan 2016; and Mawhorter 2016.

14. Visitors may also consume neighborhoods in which they do not reside by the act of working, shopping, or seeking entertainment there. For simplicity, I omit them as key consumers when analyzing the main determinants of neighborhood change.

15. My view is consonant with that expressed by several other scholars. Garner and Raudenbush state, "Neighborhoods are not uni-dimensional, spatial units. . . . They vary in their definition, depending on the type of problem to be studied and the supposed relationship between their characteristics and the phenomenon under study" (1991: 252). Gephart (1997: 10) notes: "Insofar as neighborhood has a geographic referent, its meaning depends on context and function. The relevant units vary by behavior and domain, and they depend on the outcome or process of interest." Similarly, Peterman (2000: 21) states, "What we consider our 'neighborhood' may be quite different at different times and for different purposes."

16. Suttles 1972. Suttles built upon the seminal insights of Janowitz 1952 and Greer 1962.

17. As valuable as this insight is, shortcomings remain. First, it is unclear how one moves from individual perceptions to collective representations of neighborhood. At whatever spatial level, how do neighborhood boundaries spawned by one individual's

perceptions coincide with those of other, proximate residents? Does the aggregation of individual perceptions result in the establishment of unanimously agreed-upon boundaries that delineate a mutually exclusive and exhaustive set of "neighborhoods" over urban space? If not (as is likely), what leads to variations in this degree of perceptual coincidence? At what point does a lack of perceptual coincidence render the existence of "neighborhood" problematic? Second, there is no compelling a priori reason why one can specify a meaningful ecological neighborhood in terms of social interaction, sentiment, and symbolism. Such dimensions may prove to be sufficient for the unambiguous specification of neighborhood boundaries, but not necessarily so. Third, a spatial neighborhood delineated solely by these social dimensions may be the inappropriate scale when one is attempting to analyze investment or mobility behaviors that lead to changes in the physical condition or demographic composition of a specified area.

18. Keller 1968; Hunter 1974; Birch et al. 1979: ch. 3; Guest and Lee 1984; Burton and Price-Spratlen 1999; Lee and Campbell 1997; Pebley and Vaiana 2002; Campbell et al. 2009; Pebley and Sastry 2009; and Coulton et al. 2013.

19. Changes initiated by others, not the individual in question, are implicit in the notion of externality.

20. For more on the distinction between "realist" and "nominalist" approaches to boundary definition, see Laumann, Marsden, and Prensky 1983: 20–22.

21. This is consistent with a growing multidisciplinary consensus that neighborhood has inherent objective and subjective aspects. Cf. Chaskin 1995; Wachs 1999; Lawton 1999; and Sampson 2000.

22. This view of neighborhood owes an intellectual debt to the seminal suggestions of two scholars. Segal (1979: 6) claimed that neighborhoods might be specified in terms of externalities, and Warren (1972: ch. 1) noted that a vital dimension of a community is the extent to which service areas of local units coincide.

23. Note that this usage is somewhat more general than the way in which economists conventionally use the term "externality." See Schreiber and Clemmer 1982.

24. The approach of specifying neighborhood in the context or individual behavioral responses to external stimuli is consistent with the theory propounded by Franz (1982). He asserts that it is only in the reactions to these disturbances that the boundaries of neighborhoods become empirically visible.

25. It has been suggested that individuals' ability to produce clear "mental maps" of urban space is enhanced by their frequency of travel through the area. See Lynch 1960; Jacobs 1961; and Milgram et al. 1972.

26. One should not infer from the above that externality spaces necessarily have regular shapes. The algorithms presented below make no assumptions in this regard. None of the measures are unique, however; an infinite number of topological configurations could produce the same value for congruence, generality, or accordance.

27. Hunter 1974.

28. These dimensions, though distinct, are not independent; see the appendix to chapter 2.

29. Note that the definition of congruence used here is very different from that employed in Michelson 1976: 26, which refers to "states of variables in one system coexisting better with states of variables in another system than with other alternative states."

30. Note, however, that values of accordance and generality influence the degree of congruence possible; see the appendix to chapter 2.

31. This body of scholarship employs the "hedonic index methodology" to assess the

spatial extent of externalities. There is now a longstanding literature that originally began to apply this technique for estimating the property value impacts of proximate externalities generated by, for example, nonresidential and multifamily land uses (Grether and Mieszowski 1980), racial composition (Galster 1982), and human service facilities (Gabriel and Wolch 1984).

32. See Nicotera 2007 for a thorough review of alternative methods for soliciting information from residents about their views on neighborhood.

33. Pettigrew 1973; Farley et al. 1978.

34. Bruch and Mare 2012.

35. For illustrations of how GIS can be applied to operationalizing the neighborhood concept, see Coulton et al. 2001; Lohmann and McMurran 2009; Coulton, Chan, and Mikelbank 2011; and Coulton 2012.

36. Kramer 2017.

37. For examples, see Hunter 1974; Pebley and Vaiana 2002; Pebley and Sastry 2009; Campbell et al. 2009; and Hwang 2015.

38. Hunter 1974, 1979.

39. See Wellman 1979 and Wellman and Leighton 1979 for seminal treatments of this topic.

40. Hunter 1974.

41. Hwang (2015) finds that race is the primary determinant of perceived neighborhood boundaries, for example.

42. Lynch 1960; Jacobs 1961.

43. Hunter 1974: ch. 2; Noonan 2005 provides a more recent replication of these findings.

44. Grannis 2005.

45. Lynch 1960.

46. Suttles 1972. Birch et al. 1979 replicated this observation. Sampson 2012: 361–62 also advanced this notion of multiple scales of neighborhood, each with potentially distinctive influences.

47. Methods for devising neighborhood typologies have evolved considerably. Cf. Schoenberg and Rosenbaum 1980; Warren 1981; Mawhorter 2016; and Kinahan 2016.

48. Gans 1962.

49. Wellman 1972, 1979; Wellman and Leighton 1979.

50. For a variety of studies indicating that residents' perceptual boundaries differ from those defined administratively, see Ahlbrandt, Charney and Cunningham 1977: 338; Schoenberg and Rosenbaum 1980: ch. 7; Warren 1981: 88; Hallman 1984: 57–59; and Vaskowics and Franz 1984: 152.

51. Social Science Panel 1974: 77.

CHAPTER 3

1. We may consider metropolitan areas the appropriate geography for housing markets inasmuch as this corresponds to local labor market areas and to the scope of most real estate marketing activities.

2. I am intentionally not invoking the standard neoclassical assumptions here about strict optimizing behavior based on full information subjected to careful, rational analysis by individuals. On the contrary, chapter 5 explores in detail why housing-related decisions by households and investors are necessarily founded on expectations that are uncertain, even though they may be based on an active market search

process. I will consider the implications of such imperfect, spatially biased information for neighborhood change in chapter 5.

3. I am not assuming that households have identical preferences for the various components of the housing bundle. On the contrary, we know that households' willingness to pay for a specific dwelling will depend how the idiosyncratic elements of that structure and its neighborhood resonate with the household's individual preferences.

4. For a detailed discussion of housing hedonic value and an application of how it can be estimated and then employed in specifying submarkets, see Rothenberg et al. 1991.

5. For the seminal example of how a hedonic index can be used to array a metropolitan area's housing stock along the metric of "quality" and then subdivide this spectrum into submarkets, see Rothenberg et al. 1991.

6. I use the term "market valuation" to suggest that the principles discussed are independent of whether the dwellings in question are rented or sold to their occupants.

7. For simplicity, I do not distinguish here between continuing an ongoing occupancy with a current tenant or turning over the dwelling to a different tenant. The key point is that whether the current MV is sufficient for the owner to wish to have the dwelling occupied. Similarly, I make no distinction about whether the desired occupant is a tenant who is different from the owner, or whether it is one and the same person—-i.e., a case of owner occupancy. Even owner occupants each market period are implicitly making the choice to "offer their dwelling to the market" when they continue to occupy it themselves.

8. The aforementioned arguments are most clear for landlords of existing rental dwellings and developers of dwellings built speculatively for sale. One can make analogous arguments for owner occupants, however. Determining the reservation prices of owner occupants is complicated by the fact that offering the dwelling to market for another to occupy (and perhaps buy) implies an intended move by the owner. One would expect, however, that owner occupants' reservation prices will be inversely related to the gain in household well-being associated with moving to an alternative dwelling (differentials in satisfaction and occupancy costs net of moving costs) but also by their pessimism about future residential property value trends in their current submarket.

9. Homeowners' actions involving home upkeep and modification represent a more complex amalgam of consumption and investment motivations; Galster 1987a: ch. 3. For example, they may be induced by favorable prospective returns in higher-quality submarkets into more upgrading than their own consumption preferences would dictate, or into downgrading in opposition to these preferences, if prospective downward conversion returns are especially favorable.

10. Economists usually reserve the term "long run" for a context in which all production facilities for the product can be retooled. This seems inappropriate for housing because of its durability and imperfect malleability.

11. For estimates of the determinants of housing supply elasticities for US metropolitan areas, see Saiz 2010.

12. In more technical terms, this can be explained because both own- and cross-price elasticities for all qualities of housing are likely to be less than unity (and the latter also tend to be progressively smaller the more remote the alternative submarket); see Rothenberg et al. 1991 for evidence.

13. More formally, economists call these two parameters the cross-price elasticities of demand and the elasticities of medium-run aggregate supply.

14. For alternative mathematical models of housing markets and neighborhood change, see Herbert and Stevens 1960; Anas 1978; Arnott 1980; Wheaton 1982; Braid 2001; Brueckner and Rosenthal 2009; and Guerrieri, Hartley, and Hurst 2012. For multivariate statistical models of the predictors of neighborhood change, see Brueckner and Rosenthal 2009; Guerrieri, Hartley, and Hurst, 2011; Jun 2013, 2014; and Landis 2016.

CHAPTER 4

1. These are theoretical expositions. For descriptive information about the sorts of changes that actually have been occurring recently in US metropolitan neighborhoods, see Lee and Leigh 2007; Ellen and O'Regan 2008; and Landis 2016.

2. For reviews of these alternative definitions, see Myers 1983; Grigsby et al. 1987; Weicher and Thibodeau 1988; and Baer and Williamson 1988.

3. See Ratcliff 1949: 321–22; Lowry 1960: 363; Grigsby 1963: 97; Ahlbrandt and Brophy 1975: 9; and Leven et al. 1976: 46.

4. There is compelling statistical evidence supporting both of these responses. See Ioannides 2002; Helms 2012; and Bian 2017.

5. For an ethnographic study of the landlord economics of the low-quality housing submarket, see Desmond 2016.

6. The exception here would be that some "hidden" households could emerge as occupiers that previously either had been forced to double up with other households or had been unable to afford any accommodation due to the originally unaffordable market valuations in the low-quality submarket.

7. Note that the Housing Submarket Model's mechanism of filtering is considerably different from others in the literature. See especially Grigsby 1963; Smith 1964; Sweeney 1974b; and Ohls 1975. None of these has done much to model the induced conversion supply response, especially its variability across the submarket quality spectrum. None has modeled endogenous household moves induced by inter-submarket alterations in relative valuations, or their variability across the quality spectrum. Yet, as we have seen, it is precisely such systematic, nonuniform dynamics that provide a means of evaluating the consequences of filtering.

8. We would alter this conclusion to the degree that the posited new construction primarily took the form of infill developments (perhaps involving demolition and reconstruction) in or adjacent to existing neighborhoods.

9. For a more comprehensive analysis of the local retail sector in the inner city, see Chapple and Jacobus 2008.

10. Helms (2003) verified the importance of dwelling- and neighborhood-specific attributes in predicting renovations.

11. Saiz 2010.

12. For the purposes of this scenario, it is irrelevant whether this growth in households occurs due to immigration from outside of the metro area or by the demographic transition of a large age cohort forming new households.

13. The application of the Housing Submarket Model here permits these cross-submarket comparisons that provide a holistic portrait of changes across the entire metropolitan housing market. This contrasts favorably with most prior explanatory models that tend to focus myopically on the low-quality submarket. Cf. Smith 1979; Lees 1994; Bostic and Martin 2003, Lees, Slater, and Wyly 2008; Skaburskis 2010; Hwang and Lin 2016. But for exceptions, see Brueckner and Rosenthal 2009 and Guerrieri, Hartley, and Hurst 2011.

14. Unless otherwise noted, all statistics quoted for the metropolitan areas come from author's calculations of census data aggregated for the following counties in the areas of Detroit (Wayne, Oakland, Macomb) and Los Angeles (Los Angeles, Orange, Riverside, San Bernardino, and Ventura). For insights and data regarding recent housing and neighborhood dynamics in Los Angeles, I relied heavily on Mawhorter (2016) and gratefully acknowledge her assistance in interpreting puzzling trends and providing supplemental information.

15. Galster 2012a.

16. Saiz 2010.

17. For statistical models of these dynamics, see Goodman 2005 and Guerieri, Hartley, and Hurst 2012.

18. Mawhorter 2016.

19. Saiz 2010.

20. Green, Malpezzi, and Mayo 2005; Pendall, Puentes, and Martin 2006.

21. Saiz 2010.

22. These price increases in Los Angeles were, as predicted by the model, exhibited almost uniformly across the array of submarkets; Mawhorter 2016.

23. Chafets 1990.

24. Raleigh and Galster 2015.

25. Data Driven Detroit 2010.

26. Detroit Blight Removal Task Force 2014.

27. Sampson, Schachner and Mare 2017.

28. Mawhorter 2016.

29. In both cities, retail establishments and employment had contracted by the post-recession measurement in 2012. Data come from the US Economic Census for Retail Trades (NAICS 44–45) in Detroit and Los Angeles for 1997 and 2007. The 1992 NAICS values were estimated for both cities by using the ratio between SIC and NAICS reporting for their respective states for 1997, applied to appropriate total employment figures.

30. Perversely, the city's property tax and income tax bases eroded at the same time as its operating costs increased. More firefighters were needed to deal with arson, more health and social services were needed for an ever poorer population, more abandoned buildings had to be demolished, and more clouded titles on abandoned properties had to be cleared so that the land could be transferred to the city for potential sale or redevelopment. The Detroit Blight Removal Task Force (2014) estimated that it would cost $1.5 billion to tear down all 72,000 structures in Detroit that needed demolition.

31. Detroit emerged from the bankruptcy courts in November 2014. Detroit's fiscal stress stands in marked contrast to that of most of its suburbs. The Metropolitan Area Research Corporation estimated that the 2000 property tax base—the assessed value of all residential and nonresidential properties—was only $21,546 per resident in Detroit, less than a third of the regional average of $68,286 per resident. Yet Detroit tries to squeeze much more out of that base. Its property tax rate of sixty-eight dollars per thousand dollars of assessed property value was twenty-eight dollars higher than the metro-wide median, meaning that a Detroit property owner pays $2,800 more in property taxes annually for each $100,000 in assessed value than the regional median. Galster 2012a.

32. The statistics in this paragraph are the author's calculations based on the 1992 Census of Governments (ref: https://www.census.gov//govs/cog/historical_data_1992.html)

and the 2014 Census of Governments (Individual Unit File—Public Use Format available at https://www.census.gov/govs/local/).

33. Tax rates based on data in https://www.smartasset.com/taxes.
34. For a holistic analysis of what decline has meant for the quality of life in Detroit, see Galster 2012a.
35. Temkin and Rohe 1996.
36. Galster 1987a.
37. For more on this, see, for example, Logan and Molotch 1987; and Lees 1994.
38. For a sampling of important works that comprehensively address these aspects of neighborhood change, see Goering and Wienk 1996; Squires 1997, 2004; and Immergluck 2004, 2011.
39. For a more detailed review and critique of these theories, see Schwirian 1983. In fairness, there have been other theories of neighborhood change that do not neatly fall into these three categories; see Leven et al. 1976; Segal 1979; Downs 1981; and Grigsby et al. 1987. For alternative mathematical models of housing markets and neighborhood change, see Herbert and Stevens 1960; Anas 1978; Arnott 1980; Wheaton 1982; Braid 2001; Brueckner and Rosenthal 2009; and Guerrieri, Hartley, and Hurst 2012.
40. Hoyt 1933; Park 1936.
41. Public Affairs Counseling 1975.
42. Rosenthal 2008a; Brueckner and Rosenthal 2009.
43. Though this force may be abetted by the negative externalities associated with lower-income households that end up concentrated in the oldest, lowest-quality dwellings; Rosenthal 2008a, 2008b.
44. Ratcliff 1949; Fisher and Winnick 1951; Lowry 1960; Grigsby 1963.
45. For alternative formulations of this process, see Sweeney 1974a; Weicher and Thibodeau 1988; and Baer and Williamson 1988.

CHAPTER 5

1. An amendment to this claim is that some attributes may have associated with them an absolute minimum threshold value below which no one will ever bid, as in the case of air quality.
2. For a review of theory and evidence on the hedonic index approach for quantifying the valuation of these attributes, see Rothenberg et al. 1991 and Malpezzi 2003.
3. Kurlat and Stroebel (2015) have provided empirical support for this.
4. I acknowledge earlier efforts to model this process: Speare, Goldstein, and Frey 1975; Clark 1982; Maclennan 1982; Tu and Goldfinch 1996; Wong 2002; Marsh and Gibb 2011; Maclennan and O'Sullivan 2012.
5. This view is consistent with the "symbolic interaction" approach in social psychology; Faules and Alexander 1978. The notion of people as "information processors" is more fully developed in Simon 1957 and in Newell and Simon 1972.
6. Kahneman 2011.
7. For a comprehensive review of alternative theories of housing market search, see Dunning 2017.
8. My formulation owes a debt to Fishbein and Ajzen 1975, and represents an extension of the traditional "cognition-affectation-conation" triad used in social psychology for conceptualizing human information processing and resulting behaviors.
9. I borrow these terms from Faules and Alexander 1978: ch.7.
10. Klapp 1978.

11. Fishbein and Ajzen 1975: 11.

12. A long-standing experimental literature has confirmed the direct correlation between the perceived uncertainty of decisions and a resultant increase in active acquisition of information. See Simon 1957; Lanzetta 1963; and Newell and Simon 1972.

13. See Clark 1971; Birch et al. 1979; Clark 1982; Maclennan and O'Sullivan 2012; Hedman 2013; and Bader and Krysan 2015. This spatial bias may be weakening, however, with the wider use of online search engines; Rae 2014.

14. Brown and Moore (1970) refer to this area where secondhand information is gained as "contact space," in contrast to "activity space," the area where firsthand information is gained.

15. DeLuca, Garboden, and Rosenblatt 2013; Darrah and Deluca 2014, and DeLuca and Rosenblatt 2017. Desmond 2016 provides qualitative evidence about limited, network-driven search patterns of low-income households.

16. Marsh and Gibb 2011.

17. This has also been termed "ambiguity aversion" and "preference for the familiar;" DellaVigna 2009.

18. For reviews of the satisfaction literature, see Galster 1987a: ch. 6; and Hipp 2009. For moving intention literature, see Galster 1987a: ch. 8. For urban mobility literature, see Harris 1999, 2001; Dieleman 2001; and Strassman 2001.

19. Wurdock 1981.

20. Galster 1987a: ch. 8. Surprisingly, more pessimism about future quality of life in the neighborhood was associated with plans to remain there longer.

21. Scholars have estimated several variants of these models, each addressing a specific neighborhood outcome, such as housing prices (Li and Rosenblatt 1997), population density (Guest 1972, 1973), income or social class (Guest 1974; Galster and Peacock 1985; Galster and Mincy 1993; Galster, Mincy, and Tobin 1997; Carter, Schill, and Wachter 1998; Wyly and Hammel 1999; 2000), home ownership rates (Baxter and Lauria 2000), female headship rates (Krivo et al. 1998), and racial composition (Schwab and Marsh 1980; Galster 1990a, 1990c; Ottensmann, Good, and Gleeson 1990; Denton and Massey 1991; Lee and Wood 1991; Ottensmann and Gleeson 1992; Lauria and Baxter 1999; Baxter and Lauria 2000; Crowder 2000; Ellen 2000b).

22. Hipp 2010.

23. The exception was Hipp (2010), who indeed identified an endogenous feedback relationship.

24. Galster and Tatian 2009.

25. Hwang and Sampson 2014.

26. Hipp, Tita, and Greenbaum 2009.

27. Ellen, Lacoe, and Sharygin 2012.

28. Katz, Wallace, and Hedberg 2011.

29. Williams, Galster, and Verma 2013. All three studies here used variants of Granger causality tests to conduct their analysis of leading and lagging neighborhood indicators.

30. Because both samples originated in cities containing atypically low black concentrations for larger metropolitan areas, however, these findings may not be generalizable.

31. Galster (1987a: ch. 6) observed this.

32. Taub, Taylor, and Dunham 1984.

33. Quillian and Pager 2001.

34. Skogan 1990.

35. Sampson and Raudenbush 2004.

36. This result held even though in all cases physical and class composition characteristics of neighborhoods were identical in the videos. Krysan, Couper, Farley, and Forman (2009) also observed that black respondents held the most positive opinions about racially mixed scenarios. Emerson, Chai, and Yancey (2001) reached a similar conclusion regarding whites' neighborhood stereotyping in the vignette-based national survey of whites' preferences for where they would buy a house; they also found that Asian and Hispanic neighborhood composition did not matter to whites. Analyses of surveys in Houston by Lewis, Emerson, and Klineberg (2011) also found that whites found neighborhoods less attractive as the proportion of black or Hispanic residents increased, independent of crime, school quality, and property values; the proportion of Asian residents had no impact. By contrast, racial composition had little impact on Hispanics' and blacks' neighborhood preferences. Similarly, Bader and Krysan (2015) found in Chicago that neighborhood desirability in the eyes of white (and to a lesser degree, Hispanic) households was crucially shaped by the percentage of black residents. The aforementioned surveys are problematic to interpret, however, insofar as they may be revealing that whites eschew predominantly black-occupied neighborhoods because whites are using race as a proxy for expectations or for other unmeasured features of the neighborhood, or because of an aversion to black neighbors per se.

37. Hipp (2012) provides indirect support for this conclusion as well, though his study does not explicitly consider how residents use race as a predictor of future neighborhood conditions. He found that the racial composition of the census tract, the smaller-scale neighborhood surrounding a home, and the race of the prior occupant all possessed strong signaling power for the race of the next occupant.

38. Harris 1999.

39. Harris 2001.

40. Ellen 2000b: chs. 5–7.

41. She does not find these relationships for black homeowners or renters of either race, however.

CHAPTER 6

1. For classic formulations of collective socialization, see Simmel 1971; and Weber, 1978.

2. Wilson 1987.

3. Galster 1987a: ch. 3.

4. Economists have also developed several mathematical models involving collective socialization effects in which thresholds often emerge as solutions to complex decision problems under certain assumptions. See Akerlof 1980; and Brock and Durlauf 1999.

5. Sampson and Groves 1989.

6. Lim and Galster 2009.

7. Schelling 1978.

8. Granovetter 1978.

9. Subsequent work by Granovetter and Soong (1986) builds on and generalizes this work for various dimensions of neighborhood change.

10. Galster 1987a: ch. 3.

11. Schelling (1971, 1978); Schnare and MacRae (1975); and Taub, Taylor, and Dunham (1984) conducted seminal work in this vein.

12. Crane 1991.

13. Crane (1991) drew out implications of this process for the aggregate situation in neighborhoods. He hypothesized that social problems should increase nonlinearly as neighborhood quality declined, assuming that the aforementioned two resident susceptibility conditions were inversely related to neighborhood quality. Thus, somewhere near the bottom of the distribution of neighborhood quality there should be a threshold relationship: an extremely large, sharp increase in the incidence of social problems.

14. Murphy, Shleifer, and Vishny (1993) developed a theoretical model demonstrating how a small criminal group can create synergism among different neighborhood forces that ultimately encourages a dominant criminal culture. As the number of criminals in an area grows, three things may happen simultaneously. First, returns from noncriminal activities will be reduced progressively as crime siphons a portion away. Second, the number of individuals who monitor, report, and/or directly sanction criminal behavior (that is, collective efficacy) will fall, relatively and perhaps absolutely. Finally, the stigma associated with criminal activity (that is, collective norms) will be eroded as crime becomes normative. In concert, these three factors likely interact to alter in a nonlinear fashion the relative economic and social payoffs from crime relative to noncriminal activities.

15. Hipp and Yates 2011.

16. For a full exposition of this point, see Sharkey and Faber 2014.

17. Pinkster 2008.

18. Kleinhans 2004; Kleit 2008.

19. Turley 2003; Burdick-Will et al. 2010; Galster, Andersson, and Musterd 2010; Clampet-Lundquist et al. 2011; Sanbonmatsu et al. 2011; Ludwig 2012; Musterd et al. 2012; Andersson and Malmberg 2013; Chetty, Hendren, and Katz 2015; Galster, Santiago, and Lucero 2015; Galster, Santiago, Stack, and Cutsinger 2016.

20. The only US exception is Crane 1991, whose study I discuss below.

21. Galster and Santiago 2006.

22. Wolf 1963. See the review of early work in this field in Goering 1978.

23. Crowder 2000.

24. Ellen 2000b.

25. Ioannides and Zabel (2008) did not observe any nonlinearity in the positive relationship between the percentage of white residents in the potential destination neighborhood and the probability that a white household would move there.

26. Quillian 2014.

27. Taub, Taylor and Dunham 1984: ch. 6.

28. Galster 1987a: ch. 9.

29. This critical value was estimated as the mean for each variable.

30. Vartanian 1999a, 1999b; Weinberg, Reagan, and Yankow 2004.

31. The Western European evidence on nonlinear relationships between neighborhood conditions and individual outcomes is understandably less consistent because of the various national contexts, different indicators used, and research methods employed, and much less consistent in conclusions; see the review in Galster 2014.

32. Crane 1991; Duncan et al. 1997; Chase-Lansdale et al. 1997.

33. Crane (1991: 1234, 1241) interpreted these findings as consistent with intraneighborhood social interactions, but was unable to distinguish whether the high-status neighbors created an endogenous effect (such as serving as positive role models) or a correlated effect (such as bringing resources that made local institutions and services better).

34. Duncan et al. (1997) did not explicitly test for a critical point at or below-average percentage of affluent residents, however, so their results are not directly comparable to those in Crane 1991.
35. Turley 2003. Unfortunately, with this neighborhood indicator one cannot be certain whether the relationship is being generated by the share of affluent or by the share of poor residents.
36. Galster, Santiago, Stack, and Cutsinger 2016. Social vulnerability was measured as the sum of the neighborhood percentages of poverty, renters, female-headed households, and unemployed.
37. Unfortunately, the data on census tracts impose limitations on interpreting the results of these studies. First, the aggregate nature of the data does not permit us to distinguish the contributions to the observed aggregate change in the tract made by in-movers, outmovers, and stayers. Third, we cannot identify the precise behavioral mechanisms through which any observed nonlinear effects occur.
38. Giles et al. 1975; Galster 1990c; Lee and Wood 1991; Card, Mas, and Rothstein 2008; Lee, Seo, and Shin 2011, 2017. See the reviews in Crowder 2000; and Ellen 2000b.
39. Galster 1990c. Note that both Galster 1990c and Crowder 2000 estimate cubic models with comparable estimated shapes.
40. Hwang and Sampson 2014.
41. Ding 2014.
42. Schuetz, Been, and Ellen 2008.
43. Han 2017a.
44. Galster, Quercia, and Cortes 2000.
45. Galster, Cutsinger, and Lim (2007) also found this same self-stabilizing relationship when modeling annual changes in neighborhood poverty rates across a sample of cities.
46. Galster, Quercia, and Cortes (2000) also observed thresholdlike changes in the neighborhood female headship and unemployment rates when the percentage of nonprofessional employment rose from 77 to 83 percent. These findings are complementary to those of Crane (1991) and Chase-Lansdale et al. (1997).
47. Krivo and Peterson 1996.
48. Hannon 2005.
49. Lauritsen and White (2001) also observed this increasingly positive marginal relationship for victimization and neighborhood disadvantage, though they investigated this only in a bivariate test. McNulty (2001) claimed to have found a positive but diminishing marginal relationship between violent crime and neighborhood disadvantage, but Hannon and Knapp (2003) demonstrated that this was an artifact of their logarithmic transformation of crime. After making the appropriate transformation, Hannon and Knapp claimed that McNulty's findings actually replicated those of Hannon (2005) and Lauritsen and White (2001).
50. Their investigation is noteworthy because it (1) employs a large number of census tracts across twenty-five cities, (2) tests a variety of nonlinear function forms, and (3) employs spatial lags of crime to control for spatial autocorrelation.
51. Krivo and Peterson 1996.
52. Hipp and Yates 2011.
53. Hannon 2002.
54. Galster, Cutsinger, and Malega 2008.
55. Meen 2005.
56. Flippen (2004) also observed this 20 percent poverty rate threshold, though her

model did not permit a precisely comparable estimation of nonlinear functional relationships.

57. For more comprehensive reviews of the literature examining the impacts of affordable housing on neighborhoods, see Galster 2004; and Dillman, Horn, and Verrilli (2016).

58. Schwartz, Ellen, and Voicu (2002).

59. Johnson and Bednarz (2002) also observed that diminishing positive marginal impact from increasing the concentration of Low Income Housing Tax Credit developments could become a negative impact once concentrations exceeded a threshold amount.

60. Galster et al. 1999; Santiago, Galster, and Tatian 2001.

61. Galster et al. 1999; Galster, Tatian, and Smith 1999.

62. For a more detailed review of the impact of housing choice voucher holders on neighborhoods, see Owens 2017.

63. Popkin et al. 2012.

64. Hendey et al. 2016.

65. Schuetz, Been, and Ellen 2008, also identified a threshold effect whereby neighborhood property values only declined once a critical concentration of foreclosed homes was exceeded.

CHAPTER 7

1. Watson 2009; Fry and Taylor 2012; Bischoff and Reardon 2014; Jargowsky 1996, 2003, 2015; Reardon and Bischoff 2011, 2016.

2. See the review in Rosenthal and Ross 2015.

3. Reardon and Bischoff 2016.

4. Economic segregation within racial and ethnic groups has been rising over time, particularly for black and Hispanic families since 2000. Bischoff and Reardon 2014.

5. Rosenthal and Ross 2015.

6. Galster, Booza, and Cutsinger 2008.

7. Galster and Booza 2007.

8. Booza, Cutsinger, and Galster (2006); Ioannides (2004); and Talen (2006) used multivariate techniques to probe the correlates of neighborhood income diversity, and found a greater likelihood of mixing in neighborhoods with more owner occupants and nonwhite households, higher densities, lower vacancy rates and housing values, and greater diversity of housing by tenure and values. Galster et al. (2005) developed an econometric model of the metropolitan forces influencing the degree to which very low-income households reside in neighborhoods with great income diversity. This also demonstrates the importance of owner occupancy rates and slack rental markets in expanding these opportunities.

9. Reardon and Bischoff 2011; Bischoff and Reardon 2014; Pendall and Hedman 2015; Reardon and Bischoff 2016.

10. Jargowsky 2003, 2015.

11. Jargowsky 2015.

12. As illustrations of alternative measurements and temporal analysis frames, Rosenthal (2008a) categorizes neighborhoods by quartiles based on the average income of a neighborhood *relative* to the average income of all census tracts in his balanced panel of thirty-five metropolitan areas for the year in which one observes the neighborhood, measured from 1950 to 2000. Rosenthal (2008b) defines both five categories of absolute neighborhood poverty rates and those based on the quartiles associated

with *relative* poverty rates within a metropolitan area and year, for all metropolitan areas over the period from 1970 to 2000. Galster, Booza and Cutsinger (2008) define a neighborhood's category based on which of six ranges of neighborhood median income relative to metro-wide median income it falls into, for all metropolitan areas during the 1990s. Sampson, Mare, and Perkins (2015) and Sampson, Schachner, and Mare (2017) use median neighborhood income compared to the national median and index of concentration at the extremes of income, for both the 1990s and 2000s, separately for Chicago and for Los Angeles.

13. Rosenthal 2008b.
14. Rosenthal (2008b) also finds that persistence of neighborhood status is greater in larger metropolitan areas.
15. Galster, Quercia, Cortes, and Malaga (2003).
16. Rosenthal 2008a.
17. This notion that neighborhood dynamics are subject to mean reversion for a large number of neighborhood indicators was first suggested by Galster, Cutsinger, and Lim (2007). Rosenthal (2008a) buttressed this claim with his finding that neighborhood poverty rates varied around a stable long run mean.
18. For a multidisciplinary variety of models and empirical studies of gentrification, see Smith 1979; Lees 1994; Bostic and Martin 2003; Lees, Slater, and Wyly 2008; Brueckner and Rosenthal 2009; Skaburskis 2010; Guerrieri, Hartley, and Hurst 2011; Hwang and Sampson 2014; and Hwang and Lin 2016.
19. Ellen and Ding 2016.
20. Rosenthal 2008a, 2008b.
21. Vandell 1981; Rosenthal 2008b; Ellen and O'Regan 2008; Hwang and Sampson 2014; Jun 2016.
22. Baxter and Lauria 2000; Rosenthal 2008b.
23. Quillian 2012.
24. Scholars most commonly measure residential segregation with three indices: (1) the dissimilarity index, which captures the comparative evenness of the overall distribution of two racial or ethnic groups across the neighborhoods of a metropolitan area; (2) the isolation index, which captures the degree to which members of a particular racial or ethnic group live in neighborhoods occupied by members of the same group; and (3) the exposure index, which captures the degree to which members of a particular racial or ethnic group live in neighborhoods occupied by members of another group.
25. Logan, Stults, and Farley 2004; Logan and Stults 2011; Glaeser and Vigdor 2012; De la Roca, Ellen, and O'Regan 2014.
26. All the foregoing statistics are from Logan 2011. Another interesting aspect of segregation is the degree to which minorities of high socioeconomic status are moving into predominantly white middle- or upper-class suburban neighborhoods that are not declining ("spatial assimilation"). Smith, Pride, and Schmitt-Sands (2017) found that this process stalled during the 2000s, after decades of progress.
27. Owens 2017.
28. Ellen, Horn, and O'Regan 2012.
29. Notably, there was no evidence that integrated neighborhoods that lost white population shares began the decade with higher shares of minorities, on average, thus casting some doubt on the conventional wisdom about racial tipping points. One must interpret this result with extreme caution, however, since the measurement of change was crude and no multivariate modeling was employed.

30. Ellen and Ding 2016.
31. For an alternative model of how neighborhoods jointly change their race and class composition, see Bond and Coulson 1998.
32. Note this is fundamentally different than some classic treatments of this topic. Schelling (1971) focused on endogenous processes that would make whites leave the neighborhood, and simply assumed that all vacancies would be occupied by blacks.
33. Schnare and MacRae (1978) first developed this model; Colwell (1991) and Card, Mas, and Rothstein (2008) subsequently modified it. Taub, Taylor and Dunham (1984) devised a related version of this approach.
34. For simplicity, it does not matter whether the one does the allocation via dwelling rental or purchase.
35. At this point, the rate of racially motivated out-migration by white residents may also accelerate, as per the model of Schelling 1971, though this endogenous process is not formally a dynamic associated with the Willingness to Pay Model.
36. The earliest work in this realm was by Bailey (1959, 1966), who focused on preferences for distance from another household group. Schelling (1971, 1972, 1978) developed conceptual models wherein residential choice behaviors among socially interacting individuals produced macro-outcomes of segregation that were often unintended and undesired. Rose-Akerman (1975); Yinger (1976); and Courant and Yinger (1977) undertook early efforts to include segregationist preferences in the classic monocentric city model of residential locations. They concluded that prejudice alone was insufficient to explain much segregation due to within-race variations in income producing variations in willingness to pay both within and between races.
37. See, for example, Zhang 2004; Pancs and Vriend 2007; and Fossett 2011.
38. Bruch and Mare 2006.
39. For a contrary view alleging that preferences can largely explain racial segregation, see Clark 2009.
40. Myrdal (1944) undertook the seminal formulation of how racial prejudices, residential segregation, and interracial economic disparities were linked in a mutually reinforcing pattern of cumulative causation. I have elaborated and expanded on this sort of conceptual model of racial segregation in Galster 1988a, 1992a, and 2012b. I operationalized and estimated parameters of statistical versions of this model in Galster 1987b and 1991; and in Galster and Keeney 1988. To my knowledge, no one has tried to understand the causes of both class and racial segregation within a unified model of cumulative causation. Bayer and McMillan (2012) and Bayer, Fang, and McMillan (2014) developed static theoretical models that included both class and racial segregation as outcomes. Smith, Pride, and Schmitt-Sands (2017) provide a rich, descriptive portrait of how metropolitan neighborhoods have jointly changed their economic and racial composition since 1970.
41. In my presentation, I skirt a longstanding debate over which of the various causes of segregation holds the most explanatory power. See, for example, Clark 1986, 1989 versus Galster 1988b, 1989. Because causes and effects are ultimately blurred in a cumulative causation model, this debate seems sterile. Moreover, I acknowledge that my model likely holds somewhat different explanatory power. That is, the strength of different linkages varies, depending on which racial group is being considered. It is well established, for example, that the correlates of segregation for blacks and Hispanic are somewhat different; see Santiago and Galster 1995; Bayer, McMillan, and Rueben 2004; Iceland and Nelson 2008; and Rugh and Massey 2014.
42. Sampson and Sharkey (2008) and Sampson (2012) have documented the powerful

intersections of race and class in structuring the flows of population movement across Chicago neighborhoods.

43. For reviews of the causes of class segregation, see Grigsby et al. 1987; and Rosenthal and Ross 2015.

44. There has been a considerable evolution in assumptions and evidence about how income groups weigh these alternatives. In the earliest formulations of the classic urban model, Alonso (1964); Mills (1967); and Muth (1969) assumed that the marginal value of time does not grow as rapidly with income as the marginal value of housing consumption. Thus, higher-income households will outbid other groups for locations farther from employment, typically near the fringe of the built-up metropolitan area. Wheaton (1977) found that these relative valuations did not differ substantially by income, however. More recently, Glaeser, Kahn, and Rappaport (2008) claimed that the relative weighting of the classical model has now been reversed.

45. Rosenthal 2008a, 2008b; Brueckner and Rosenthal 2009.

46. Brueckner, Thisse, and Zenou 1999; Bayer, McMillan, and Rueben 2005; Epple, Gordon, and Sieg 2010.

47. Banzhof and Walsh 2008.

48. Glaeser, Kahn, and Rappaport 2008; Brueckner and Rosenthal 2009.

49. Guerrieri, Hartley, and Hurst 2011.

50. Musterd et al. 2016; Galster and Turner 2017.

51. Benabou 1993, 1996; Bayer, Ferreira, and McMillan 2007.

52. O'Sullivan 2005; Guerrieri, Hartley, and Hurst 2013.

53. Tiebout 1956. For newer theoretical formulations and empirical tests, see Epple and Romer 1991; Alesina, Baquir, and Easteerly 1999; Ross and Yinger 1999; DeBartoleme and Ross 2003, 2008; and Nechyba and Walsh 2004.

54. Calabrese, Epple, Romer, and Sieg (2006) provide a model of this sorting. Evidence using several different measures of segregation studies show that households with children are distributed less evenly across neighborhoods of different economic status (and racial or ethnic composition) than are households without children. Logan et al. 2001; Jargowsky 2015; Owens 2017. For a summary of trends in class and racial segregation in schools, see Galster and Sharkey 2017.

55. Eberts and Gronberg 1981.

56. Vandell 1995.

57. Massey and Kanaiaupuni 1993; Rosenthal 2008b.

58. For reviews of the causes of racial segregation, see Galster 1988a, 1988b; Massey and Denton 1993; Ellen 2000b; Charles 2003; Dawkins 2004; Massey 2008.

59. Taeuber and Taeuber 1965; and Darden and Kamel 2000. Crowder, South, and Chavez 2006, Iceland and Wilkes 2006; and Kucheva and Sander 2017, have estimated how much interracial income and wealth differences contribute to racial segregation.

60. Pascal 1965.

61. Farley, Danziger, and Holzer 2000; Emerson, Chai, and Yancey 2001; Krysan, Couper, Farley, and Forman 2009; Clark 2009; Lewis, Emerson, and Klineberg 2011; Bader and Krysan 2015; Havekes et al. 2016.

62. Galster 1977, 1982; Cutler, Glaeser, and Vigdor 1999.

63. Bayer, McMillan, and Rueben 2004; Bayer, Fang, and McMillan 2014.

64. See Turner et al. 2002, 2013 for the latest two national studies of housing market discrimination, which used paired-testing methods. They reveal that while the incidence of discrimination against blacks has decreased in rental markets, levels remain

stubbornly high in home sales markets and when directed against Hispanics. Adelman (2005) and Havekes et al. (2016) provide survey data suggesting that minorities may be prevented from moving into neighborhoods that have the racial composition they desire, and in which they have searched for housing. See Goering 2007 and Quillian 2006, for a broader discussion of these discrimination issues.

65. Ross 2011.
66. Galster and Godfrey 2005; Besbirs and Faber 2017.
67. Gotham 2002.
68. Roychoudhury and Goodman 1992; Ondrich, Ross, and Yinger 2003; Fisher and Massey 2004; Galster and Godfrey 2005.
69. For evidence on racial discrimination in mortgage markets, see Yinger 1995; Ladd 1998; Turner and Skidmore 1999; Ross and Yinger 2002; Engel and McCoy 2008; Immergluck 2011; and Rugh, Albright, and Massey 2015.
70. Hirsch 1983; Sugrue 1996; Freund 2007; Massey 2008.
71. Galster 2012c.
72. Farley, Danziger, and Holzer 2002.
73. Bader and Krysan 2015.
74. See Pendall 2000a and Rothwell and Massey 2009 for empirical estimates of how much these local land use regulations contribute to segregation.
75. Galster 1990b.
76. Yinger 1995.
77. Several recent federal legal suits against major lenders have alleged that many minority applicants were discriminatorily charged higher subprime mortgage interest rates when in fact they qualified for lower prime rates and otherwise were targeted for predatory lending practices. Engel and McCoy 2008; Immergluck 2011.
78. Yinger 1995; Ondrich, Ross, and Yinger 2003.
79. For reviews of the voluminous literature that this hypothesis has spawned since its formulation in the 1960s, see Kain 1968, 1992, 2004; and Turner 2008.
80. Sturdivant 1969.
81. Fusfeld and Bates 1984.
82. Bates 1997.
83. Massey and Denton 1993; Massey 2008.
84. Clark 1989.
85. Allport 1979; Jackman and Crane 1986; Pettigrew and Tropp 2011.
86. Fischel 2001.
87. Acs et al. 2017.

CHAPTER 8

1. Galster and Killen (1995) introduced similar notions of "opportunity structure" and "geography of opportunity." For an analysis of the normative implications of this framework, see Dawkins 2017.
2. Of course, *within* any of these three fundamental spatial scales there can be contextual variations in all the domains noted.
3. We recognize that there is a voluminous literature on human decision making and considerable debate over the most appropriate model (see the review in Galster and Killen 1995). We think it irrelevant for our model which particular view is taken, so long as one rejects the notion that these life choices are purely instinctual or random, having no relationship with the social construction of a current and prospective reality. We think these choices may generally be described as based on "bounded

rationality": imperfect (perhaps even incorrect) information, subjective assessments, and varying degrees of dispassionate, analytical thought in comparison to impulse and snap judgments contingent on many personal and contextual aspects of the situation. Though my model has many features in common with the "rational actor" model of Eriskon and Jonsson (1996) and Becker (2003), we stress that sociospatial context is a prime source of information and values related to an individual's assessments of expected benefits and costs.

4. McConnell et al. 2010; Lovasi et al. 2011.
5. Rau, Reyes, and Urzúa 2013.
6. Sharkey and Sampson 2010; Sharkey et al. 2012, 2014.
7. O'Regan 1993.
8. Wilson 1987.
9. Haveman and Wolfe 1994.
10. Galster and Santiago 2006.
11. Sharkey 2013.
12. Jencks and Mayer 1990; Duncan, Brooks-Gunn, and Aber 1997; Gephart 1997; Ellen and Turner 1997; Wandersman and Nation 1998; Friedrichs 1998; Green and Ottoson 1999; Atkinson et al. 2001; Booth and Crouter 2001; Sampson 2001; Ellen, Mijanovich, and Dillman 2001; Haurin, Dietz, and Weinberg 2002; Sampson, Morenoff, and Gannon-Rowley 2002; Ellen and Turner 2003; Ioannides and Loury 2004; Pinkster 2008; and Phibbs 2009.
13. By contrast, Manski (1995) groups them into "endogenous," "exogenous," and "correlated" categories. Ellen and Turner (1997) group them into five categories: concentration, location, socialization, physical, and services. Leventhal and Brooks-Gunn (2000) use the rubrics "institutional resources," "relationships," and "norms/collective efficacy."
14. Sampson, Morenoff, and Earls 1999.
15. Note that this discussion relates to but is distinct from the question of how to measure accurately the magnitude of this dosage-response relationship, about which I wrote in Galster 2008.
16. I combine the competition and relative deprivation mechanisms because, to my knowledge, there is little extant statistical evidence that can distinguish between them.
17. Though in this review of mechanisms I only cite US-based scholarship, this generalization applies to scholarly literatures emanating from the United States, Europe, and Australia. For a broader review that encompasses this literature, see Galster 2012b.
18. Here I focus on studies of neighborhood social interrelationships; for a review of such effects within schools, see Ross 2012 and Sharkey and Faber 2014.
19. Darling and Steinberg 1997; Simons et al. 1996; Dubow, Edwards, and Ippolito 1997; Gonzales 1996.
20. Case and Katz 1991.
21. Billings, Deming, and Ross 2016. For more supportive evidence on the importance of role models and peer effects in disadvantaged neighborhoods, see Sinclair et al. 1994; Briggs 1997a; South and Baumer 2000; Ginther, Haveman, and Wolfe 2000; and South 2001.
22. However, it is not definitive about the extent to which such negative socialization is general across races. Turley (2003) probes beyond her discovery of overall positive correlations between median family income of neighborhood and youths' behavioral and psychological test scores to see whether there were interaction effects with

proxies for number of peer interactions and time spent in neighborhood. She found such strong interaction effects for white but not black youths in her sample, and concluded, "Differences in neighborhood socializing may explain why neighborhood income affects black and white children differently" (2003: 70).

23. Rosenbaum, 1991, 1995; and Rosenbaum et al. 2002.
24. Rosenbaum 1991.
25. Patillo-McCoy 1999; Freeman 2006; Boyd 2008; Hyra 2008.
26. Chaskin and Joseph 2015.
27. Fernandez and Harris 1992; O'Regan 1993; Tiggs, Brown, and Greene 1998.
28. Bertrand, Luttmer, and Mullainathan 2000.
29. Bayer, Ross, and Topa 2004.
30. Bayer, Ross, and Topa 2004.
31. Briggs, 1998.
32. Popkin, Harris, and Cunningham 2002; Rosenbaum, Harris, and Denton 2003.
33. Schill 1997; Clampet-Lundquist 2004; Kleit 2001a, 2001b, 2002, 2005, 2008; Kleit and Carnegie 2009; Chaskin and Joseph 2015.
34. Sampson 1992; Sampson and Groves 1989; Sampson, Raudenbush, and Earls 1997; Morenoff, Sampson and Raudenbush 2001; Sampson 2012.
35. See the review in Sampson, Morenoff, and Gannon-Rowley 2002.
36. Aneshensel and Sucoff (1996) find that neighborhood social cohesion explains a large portion of the relationship between neighborhood socioeconomic status and adolescent depression. Kohen et al. (2002) find that neighborhood disorder is negatively related and neighborhood cohesion is positively related to children's verbal ability, and that neighborhood cohesion (though not disorder) is negatively associated with child behavioral problems.
37. Galster and Santiago 2006.
38. Ginther, Haveman, and Wolfe 2000; Galster, Santiago, and Stack 2016; Galster, Santiago, Stack, and Cutsinger 2016; Galster, Santiago, Lucero, and Cutsinger 2016.
39. Compare Freeman 2006; Hyra 2008; and Boyd 2008.
40. Klebanov et al. 1997; Spencer 2001.
41. Elder et al. 1995; Linares et al. 2001.
42. Klebanov et al., 1994; Earls, McGuire, and Shay 1994; Simons et al. 1996; Briggs 1997a.
43. Simons et al. 1996.
44. Greenberg et al. 1999.
45. Briggs 1997a, 1997b; Goering and Feins 2003.
46. Katz, Kling, and Liebman 2000; Goering and Feins 2003; Sanbonmatsu et al. 2011.
47. Aneshensel and Sucoff 1996; Martinez and Richter 1993; Ceballo et al. 2001; Hagan et al. 2001.
48. Ganz 2000.
49. Geronimus 1992.
50. Linares et al. 2001; Guerra, Huesmann, and Spindler 2003.
51. Ross et al. 2001.
52. Stansfeld, Haynes, and Brown 2000; Schell and Denham 2003; Van Os 2004.
53. Lopez, Russell, and Hynes 2006.
54. Goering and Feins 2003; Sanbonmatsu et al. 2011.
55. Holguin (2008) and Mills et al. (2009) elucidated potential physiological mechanisms by which pollution can create health risks. For critical reviews, discussions, and evaluations of this vast research literature on pollution and health, see Bernstein et al.

2004; Stillerman et al. 2008; Ren and Tong 2008; Chen, Goldberg, and Villeneuve 2008; and Clougherty et al. 2009.

56. McConnochie et al. 1998; Brunekreef and Holgate 2002; Ritz, et al. 2002; Clancy et al. 2002; McConnell et al. 2002; Kawachi and Berkman 2003; Chay and Greenstone 2003a, 2003b; Neidell 2004; Currie and Neidell 2005; Brook, 2008; and Hassing et al. 2009.

57. Ebenstein, Lavy, and Roth 2016.

58. Litt, Tran, and Burke 2009.

59. Needleman and Gastsonis 1991; Pocock et al. 1994; Reyes 2005. For a recent review of the lead poisoning evidence, see Muller, Sampson and Winter 2018.

60. For reviews, see Kain 1992 and Ihlanfeldt and Sjoquist 1998.

61. Sullivan 1989; Newman 1999; Wilson 1997.

62. Cutler and Glaeser 1997; Weinberg, Reagan, and Yankow 2004; Dawkins, Shen, and Sanchez 2005.

63. Kozol 1991; Lankford, Loeb, and Wyckoff 2002; Condron and Roscigno 2003.

64. Jargowsky and Komi 2010.

65. Loeb et al. 2004.

66. Andersen et al. 2002.

67. Rasmussen 1994; Bauder 2001.

68. Galster and Santiago 2006; Phibbs 2009.

69. Jarrett 1997.

70. Morland et al. 2002; Block, Scribner, and DeSalvo 2004; Zenk et al. 2005.

71. Briggs 1997b.

72. Gallagher 2006, 2007; and Morland, Wing, and Diez-Roux 2002.

73. Wilson 1996; Wacquant 2008.

74. After their review, Leventhal and Brooks-Gunn (2000) similarly concluded that the strongest support seems to be for the combined role of norms, collective efficacy (informal social controls), and peers as major neighborhood influences on adolescent behaviors.

75. There is growing empirical consensus around the contingency of neighborhood effects by age, gender and ethnicity. Cf. Galster, Andersson, and Musterd 2010; Sharkey and Faber 2014; Galster, Santiago and Stack 2016; Galster, Santiago, Stack, and Cutsinger 2016; Galster, Santiago, Lucero, and Cutsinger 2016; and Galster and Santiago 2017a.

76. For an extensive discussion, see Galster 2008.

77. Manski 1995, 2000; Duncan et al. 1997; Ginther, Haveman, and Wolfe 2000; Dietz 2002.

78. The direction of the bias has been the subject of debate, with Jencks and Mayer (1990) and Tienda (1991) arguing that measured contextual impacts are biased upwards, and Brooks-Gunn, Duncan, and Aber (1997) arguing the opposite. Gennetian, Ludwig, and Sanbonmatsu (2011) show that these biases can be substantial enough to seriously distort conclusions about the magnitude and direction of context effects.

79. For a conceptual and empirical comparison of these approaches, see Galster and Hedman 2013.

80. Illustrations include Bolster et al. 2007; Galster et al. 2008; Musterd et al. 2008; Van Ham and Manley 2009; and Galster, Andersson, and Musterd 2010.

81. Illustrations include Weinberg, Reagan, and Yankow 2004; Musterd, Galster, and Andersson 2012.

82. Illustrations include Duncan et al. 1997; Crowder and South 2003; Crowder and

Teachman 2004; Galster et al. 2007; Kling, Liebman, and Katz 2007; Ludwig et al. 2008; Cutler, Glaeser, and Vigdor 2008; Sari 2012; Hedman and Galster 2013; and Damm 2014.

83. Bayer, Ross, and Topa 2008.

84. Weinhardt 2014.

85. Sharkey 2010; Sharkey et al. 2012, 2014.

86. Harding 2003.

87. This method is used by Sharkey and Elwert (2011) in combination with a formal sensitivity analysis to estimate the cumulative effect of multigenerational exposure to neighborhood poverty on cognitive development.

88. Illustrations include Sharkey 2012; Galster and Hedman 2013; and Gibbons, Silva, and Weinhardt 2013, 2014.

89. Aaronson 1998.

90. Rosenbaum 1991; Briggs 1997; Fauth, Leventhal, and Brooks-Gunn,2007.

91. Schwartz 2010; Casciano and Massey 2012.

92. Santiago et al. 2014.

93. Oreopoulos 2003; Damm 2009, 2014; Rotger and Galster 2017.

94. Edin, Fredricksson, and Åslund 2003; Åslund and Fredricksson 2009.

95. Smolensky 2007; Sanbonmatsu et al. 2011; Ludwig 2012.

96. Cf. Clampet-Lundquist and Massey 2008; Sampson 2008; Burdick-Will et al. 2010; Briggs, Popkin, and Goering 2010; Briggs et al. 2008, 2011; Sanbonmatsu et al. 2011; Ludwig 2012.

97. This section was cowritten with Patrick Sharkey, whose contributions are gratefully acknowledged.

98. Employing propensity score matching, Ahern et al. (2008) found that an individual's propensity to drink and the neighborhood's culture of alcohol use were related, but Novak et al. (2006) found only a small, barely discernable effect of the density of retail tobacco outlets on youth cigarette smoking. Jokela (2014) used the fixed-effect modeling approach and found no impact of neighborhood disadvantage on the probability of smoking. Gibbons, Silva and Weinhardt (2013) also used fixed effects but found that the share of neighbors from lower-status backgrounds increased the chances of teen boys engaging in antisocial behaviors like graffiti, vandalism, shoplifting, fighting, or public disturbance. Two approaches employing inverse probability weighting (marginal structural model) methods found a strong relationship between neighborhood poverty and the odds of binge drinking (Cerda et al. 2010) and the odds of drug injecting (Nandi et al. 2010).

99. Sanbonmatsu et al. 2011.

100. Santiago, et al. 2017.

101. Niewenhuis and Hooimeijer 2014; Sharkey and Faber 2014.

102. For reviews, see Sastry 2012 and Sharkey and Faber 2014.

103. Sampson, Sharkey, and Raudenbush 2008.

104. Sharkey and Elwert 2011.

105. Sharkey 2010.

106. Sharkey et al. 2012.

107. Sanbonmatsu et al. 2006, 2011.

108. Sanbonmatsu et al. 2006.

109. Turner et al. 2012.

110. Ludwig, Ladd, and Duncan 2001; Burdick-Will et al. 2011; Sanbonmatsu et al. 2011.

111. The methods have included propensity score matching (Harding 2003), sibling com-

parisons (Aaronson 1998; Plotnick and Hoffman 1999), fixed-effects (Plotnick and Hoffman 1999; Vartanian and Gleason 1999; Jargowsky and El Komi 2011), instrumental variables (Duncan, Connell, and Klebanov 1997; Crowder and South 2003; Galster, et al. 2007a), nonmovers (Gibbons, Silva, and Weinhardt 2014) and timing of exogenous events (Sharkey et al. 2014; Weinhardt 2014; Carlson and Cowan 2015).

112. Plotnick and Hoffman (1999), using US data; and Gibbons, Silva, and Weinhardt (2013) and Weinhardt (2014), using UK data.

113. Rosenbaum 1995; Fauth, Leventhal, and Brooks-Gunn 2007; DeLuca et al. 2010.

114. Jacob 2004; Clampet-Lundquist 2007.

115. Schwartz 2010; Casciano and Massey 2012.

116. Tach et al. 2016.

117. Santiago et al. 2014; Galster et al. 2015, Galster, Santiago, and Stack 2016; Galster, Santiago, Stack, and Cutsinger 2016; Galster, Santiago, Lucero, and Cutsinger 2016; Galster and Santiago 2017a.

118. There was little context effect observed in Jacob 2004, because the experimental households did not use their housing vouchers to change their neighborhood characteristics significantly.

119. Chetty, Hendren, and Katz 2015. These findings were replicated in the natural experiment analyzed by Galster and Santiago (2017b).

120. Plotnick and Hoffman (1999) found that neighborhood effects on teen childbearing disappeared when using a model of fixed effects with only observations of sisters, whereas Harding (2003) found that neighborhood effects remained significant despite propensity score matching, and argued that selection bias would need to be unreasonably large to rule out causal effects of neighborhood socioeconomic conditions on teen childbearing.

121. Santiago et al. 2014.

122. Popkin, Leventhal, and Weismann 2010; Sanbonmatsu et al. 2011.

123. Chetty, Hendren, and Katz 2015.

124. Oakes et al. (2015) recently completed a comprehensive review of the empirical literature related to neighborhood effects on health. After reviewing 1,369 articles, he concluded that only about one percent produced plausibly causal estimates, using criteria similar to those I employ.

125. Schootman et al. 2007; Johnson et al. 2008; Hearst et al. 2008.

126. Do, Wang, and Elliott 2013.

127. Glymour et al. 2010.

128. Jokela 2014.

129. Ludwig et al. 2011; Sanbonmatsu et al. 2011.

130. Leventhal and Brooks-Gunn 2003; Kessler et al. 2014.

131. Moulton, Peck, and Dillman 2014.

132. Cohen et al. 2006.

133. Vortuba and King 2009.

134. Santiago et al. 2014.

135. Santiago et al. 2014.

136. Several studies using US data (Weinberg, Reagan, and Yankow 2004; Dawkins, Shen, and Sanchez 2005; Cutler, Glaeser, and Vigdor 2008; Bayer, Ross, and Topa 2008; Sharkey 2012), several using Swedish data (Galster et al. 2008; Galster, Andersson, and Musterd 2010, 2015, 2017; Musterd, Galster, and Andersson 2012; Hedman and Galster 2013), one Danish study (Damm 2014) and one French study (Sari 2012) find nontrivial neighborhood effects on various adult labor market outcomes such as

income and employment rates. One US-based study (Plotnick and Hoffman 1999) and three UK-based analyses (Bolster et al. 2007; Propper et al. 2007; van Ham and Manley 2010) find minor, if any, neighborhood effects, and instead suggest that geographic selection dominates.

137. Rosenbaum (1991, 1995); Rubinowitz and Rosenbaum (2000); DeLuca et al. (2010); Galster, Santiago, and Lucero (2015a, 2015b); Galster et al. (2015); Galster and Santiago (2017b); and Chyn (2016) conducted analyses in the United States. Edin, Fredricksson, and Åslund (2003) and Åslund and Fredricksson (2009) employ a natural experiment in Sweden. Damm (2009, 2014) does so in Denmark. Oreopoulos (2003) does so in Canada.

138. Oreopoulos 2003.

139. Ludwig, Duncan, and Pinkston 2005; Katz, Kling, and Liebman 2001; Ludwig, Ladd, and Duncan 2001; Ludwig, Duncan, and Hirschfield 2001; Orr et al. 2003; Kling, Leibman, and Katz 2007; Ludwig et al. 2008; Sanbonmatsu et al. 2011; Ludwig 2012.

140. Clampet-Lundquist and Massey 2008; Turner et al. 2012.

141. Chetty, Hendren, and Katz 2015.

142. Livingston et al., 2014.

143. Santiago et al., 2014.

144. Damm and Dustmann 2014.

145. Rotger and Galster 2017.

146. Billings, Deming, and Ross 2016.

147. Katz, Kling, and Liebman 2001; Ludwig, Duncan, and Hirshfeld 2001.

148. Kling, Ludwig, and Katz 2005; Sanbonmatsu et al. 2011.

149. This corresponds to the conclusion reached in Sharkey 2016.

CHAPTER 9

1. Economists refer to the latter aspect as the lack of a clear "social welfare function."

2. This sufficient condition for assessing changes in social efficiency is termed by economists "Pareto improvement."

3. Another less important source of inefficiency is information asymmetries. Those who reside in or own properties in a particular neighborhood have more information about that place than do prospective in-movers and property buyers because of their firsthand experiences and more dense social networks there. This can produce inefficient choices by prospective in-movers and property buyers since the market cannot accurately capitalize "inside information" about quality of life and appreciation prospects in a neighborhood into market valuations.

4. Scafidi et al. 1998.

5. Galster 1987a: ch.7.

6. Seo and Von Rabenau (2011) included such an explicit measure in their hedonic home price model and found that a deteriorated house adjacent to the one sold would reduce its value by about 10 percent, though the estimate was not statistically significant by conventional standards.

7. Simons, Quercia, and Maric 1998; Whitaker and Fitzpatrick 2013.

8. Immergluck and Smith 2006; Schuetz, Been, and Ellen 2008; Mikelbank 2008; Harding, Rosenblatt, and Yao 2009; Han 2013.

9. Lin, Rosenblatt, and Yao 2007; Schuetz, Been, and Ellen 2008; Zhang, Leonard, and Murdoch 2016.

10. Cf. Han 2013; Griswold and Norris 2007; and Shlay and Whitman 2006; though Han (2017a) demonstrates that impact is larger in neighborhoods with higher crime rates.

11. Seo and von Rabenau 2011.
12. Han 2013; but see Mikelbank 2008.
13. Ding and Knaap 2003.
14. Ellen et al. 2001.
15. Galster, Tatian, and Accordino 2006; Rossi-Hansberg, Sarte, and Owens 2010.
16. Wilson and Bin Kashem 2017.
17. Coulson and Li 2013.
18. Coulson, Hwang, and Imai 2003.
19. Wilson and Bin Kashem 2017.
20. Lang and Nakamura 1993.
21. Ding 2014.
22. Taub, Taylor, and Dunham 1984: ch. 6.
23. Taub, Taylor, and Dunham 1984: 134.
24. Galster, 1987a: ch.10.
25. This relationship controlled for expectations about property appreciation; Galster 1987a: ch. 10.
26. Ioannides 2002; Helms 2012.
27. Vigdor 2010.
28. This claim of neighborhood diversity eroding social capital has been made, for example, by Putnam (2007).
29. Over time, income certainly could change. Indeed, several of the potential intraneighborhood externalities would be expected to affect the incomes of A or D residents; it is the nature of the externality itself.
30. I explicate this remarkable and important conclusion more fully in Galster 2002.
31. Note that I express this threshold here in proportionate terms; it is theoretically equivalent to an absolute number under the simplifying assumption of a fixed neighborhood population. In empirical work, however, identifying whether the threshold is based on an absolute or proportionate number of a group is critical.
32. There is no necessary reason why past the threshold the relationship is linear; I assume this for simplicity here.
33. Figure 9.2 portrays $Y > X$, but this is not necessary and the textual discussion does not depend on this.
34. DeBartolomé (1990) and Benabou (1993) formally model this case. They assume that positive role model and/or peer effects imparted by higher-skilled residents (or their offspring) reduce the costs of skill acquisition and, ultimately, labor force participation. Their models reach the same conclusion as here: the residential segregation of high-skilled residents is inefficient for the economy as a whole.
35. Pettigrew and Tropp 2011.
36. An alternative form of this mechanism can be envisioned: one that has the externality negatively related to %D in a continuous fashion. This is equivalent to case 2, so I do not replicate it here.
37. My review in chapter 6 of the statistical evidence of nonlinear behavioral responses and property value dynamics associated with changing neighborhood poverty rates supports the threshold notion embedded implicitly in this mechanism.
38. There is a substantial and consistent literature rejecting the notion that neighborhood economic diversity generates the intimate intergroup social interactions, social networks, and collective socialization that would enhance employment information and other resources for the poor. See Rosenbaum, 1991; Briggs 1997a, 1997b, 1998; Schill 1997; Kleit 2001a, 2001b, 2002; Rosenbaum, Harris, and Denton 2003;

334 / Notes to Chapter Nine

Chaskin and Joseph 2015. It is also noteworthy that these same studies of social interactions among different income groups in mixed neighborhoods do not reveal compelling evidence of relative deprivation or intergroup competition that would harm disadvantaged neighbors.

39. Briggs, Popkin and Goering 2010; Sanbonmatsu et al. 2011; Chaskin and Joseph 2015; Galster and Santiago 2017a. An Australian study also offers indirect evidence in support of this claim, assuming that the results are general. Baum, Arthurson, and Rickson (2010) find that low-income individuals are much more likely to be satisfied with their neighborhood if they live in places with more income diversity and a smaller ratio of low-to-high-income households.

40. Galster, Cutsinger, and Malega 2008. This is a lower-bound estimate because it assumes that all the negative externalities associated with concentrated poverty capitalize into property values and rents within the neighborhood, ignoring likely spillover effects on proximate neighborhoods. Moreover, residential property markets may not capitalize many other externalities to society, such as lost productivity from premature school-leaving, teen pregnancies, or costs of incarceration.

41. Galster 1991; Cutler and Glaeser 1997.

42. Galster and Santiago 2017b.

43. Ellen, Steil, and De la Roca 2016.

44. Acs et. al. 2017.

45. The differences in conclusions between the studies may be due to differences in the units of observation, measures of racial segregation employed, and/or controls applied. Neither study employs a method designed to provide plausible causal estimates.

46. Hipp 2007. This result has been replicated by Boessen and Chamberlain 2017.

47. Putnam 2007.

48. There is evidence that households can dramatically change their preconceptions about certain types of neighborhoods after they actually experience them; see Darrah and DeLuca 2014.

49. Allport 1954. Note, however, that several preconditions are required for these benefits to transpire (Gans 1961:176).

50. See, for example, Ihlanfeldt and Scafidi 2002; Emerson, Kimbro, and Yancey 2002; and the review by Pettigrew and Tropp (2006, 2011).

51. Sampson and Raudenbush 2004.

52. Taub, Taylor, and Dunham 1984.

53. This was first argued by Downs, (1981: 16–19) and later confirmed empirically by Galster (1987a) and Helms (2012).

54. For a thorough discussion of the harms of racial and economic segregation, see Dreier, Mollenkopf and Swanstrom 2014. For more on racial inequities in neighborhood contexts, see Firebaugh et al. 2015; Ellen, Steil, and De la Roca 2016; Firebaugh and Farrell 2016; and Intrator, Tannen, and Massey 2016. For more on class-based inequities in neighborhood contexts, see Pendall and Hedman 2015.

55. For an overview of this history, see Galster and Santiago 2017a.

56. These sophisticated statistical investigations either employ instrumental variables techniques (Galster 1987b; 1991; Galster and Keeney 1988; Santiago and Galster 1995; Cutler and Glaeser 1997) or multilevel modeling of individual outcomes nested in metropolitan areas (Price and Mills 1985; Ellen 2000a; Chang 2006; Lee and Ferraro 2007; Nelson 2013; Steil, De la Roca. and Ellen 2015; Ellen, Steil, and De la Roca 2016).

57. Steil, De la Roca, and Ellen 2015. Note that their models were not estimated in a fashion that permits definitive causal inferences. Also see Ellen, Steil, and De la Roca 2016.

58. Supporting evidence on the harms of racial segregation for blacks' chances for economic success has recently been provided by Acs et al. (2017), who found that higher levels of metropolitan racial segregation were associated with lower median incomes, per capita incomes, and college graduations rates for blacks in the metropolitan area. Hispanics also manifested these relationships, but they were not statistically significant. Note that their models were not estimated in a fashion that permits definitive causal inferences.

59. For a review of this literature, see Sharkey 2016.

60. Chetty et al., 2014.

61. Graham and Sharkey 2013.

62. Acs, et al. 2017.

63. Acs et al. (2017) find that higher levels of metropolitan segregation in both racial and economic dimensions were consistently associated with lower median incomes, per capita incomes, and college graduations rates for blacks in the metropolitan area. Logan (2011) finds that metropolitan racial segregation, not interracial differences in income, is the main predictor of interracial differences in exposure to disadvantaged places. Woldoff and Ovadia (2009) find that segregation creates a context where blacks have a much more difficult time converting their income, wealth, and education into residential quality.

64. Logan 2011; the average Asian person's exposure to neighborhood poverty is only 5 percent higher.

65. Poor Asians are exposed to 41 percent higher neighborhood poverty rates than poor whites; the interracial gaps are somewhat lower for affluent minorities; Logan 2011.

66. Jargowsky 2015.

67. Sharkey 2014.

68. Reardon, Fox, and Townsend 2015.

69. The evidence is clear that blacks and Hispanics suffer absolute losses in well-being from living in racially segregated areas. The evidence is mixed about the degree to which whites gain in absolute terms (instead of just relatively) from racial segregation. Cf. Ellen, Steil, and De la Roca 2016; Acs et. al., 2017.

70. Only recently have researchers made statistical efforts to disentangle which of these mechanisms are most powerful in mediating the impacts of racial segregation on socioeconomic disparities. Cutler and Glaeser (1997), added to their cross-metropolitan area models of aggregate rates of black high school graduation, employment, earnings, and single parenting three variables measuring the degree to which blacks were relatively concentrated in the central city municipality, were exposed to college-educated neighbors, and resided far from their places of employment, on average across the metro area. The addition of these variables reduced the coefficient of their dissimilarity index of segregation by 40 percent, suggesting that only a minor part of segregation's harmful effects were operating by constraining blacks to inferior places. Using the metropolitan area as unit of observation weakens this inference, however. It does not permit the measurement of a wide range of conditions that blacks may be experiencing in their neighborhoods. Steil, De La Roca, and Ellen (2015) attempted to overcome this weakness by measuring neighborhood-level variations in density of private establishments, school quality, violent crime, and college-educated members of one's own racial group across a large sample of metropolitan areas. They

concluded that the three latter factors play important roles in establishing the strong relationship observed between metro-level residential segregation of blacks and Hispanics and a variety of their socioeconomic outcomes. Galster and Santiago (2017a) found that a similar set of outcomes for low-income black and Hispanic youth and young adults in Denver varied according to their childhood exposure to different racial groups. Consistent with Steil, De La Roca, and Ellen, they demonstrated that exposure to property crime and neighbors of higher occupational status mediated virtually all of the negative effects of greater neighborhood-level concentrations of black and Hispanic households associated with segregation.

71. Bleachman, 1991.
72. Clark 1965; Anderson 1994; Massey 1996.
73. Kirschenman and Neckerman, 1991; Wilson 1996.
74. MacDonald and Nelson 1991; Shaffer 2002.
75. Moore and Roux 2006.
76. Caskey 1994; Steil, De La Roca, and Ellen 2015.
77. Fellowes 2008.
78. Fellowes and Mabanta 2008.
79. Wyly et al. 2006; Been, Ellen, and Madar 2009; Richter and Craig 2010; Faber 2013; Hyra et al. 2013; Hwang, Hankinson, and Brown 2015.
80. Rugh, Albright, and Massey 2015.
81. Galster, Wissoker, and Zimmermann 2001; Galster 2006; Galster and Booza 2008.
82. Dreier, Mollenkopf, Swanstrom 2014.
83. Kozol 1991; Wilson 1991; Wolman et al. 1991; Card and Krueger 1992, Lankford, Loeb, and Wyckoff 2002; Condron and Roscigno 2003; Steil, De La Roca, and Ellen 2015.
84. Ennett et al. 1997; Teitler and Weiss 1996.
85. Hedges, Laine, and Greenwald 1994; Jargowsky and Komi 2010.
86. Logan 2011. The comparable figure for Asian students is 42 percent.
87. Fuller et al. 1997; Steil, De La Roca, and Ellen 2015.
88. McKnight 1995; Minkler 1997.
89. Galster and Santiago 2006; Phibbs 2009.
90. Jarrett 1997.
91. Kawachi and Berkman 2003; Acevedo-Garcia and Osypuk 2008; Currie 2011.
92. Farr and Dolbeare, 1996; Acevedo-Garcia and Osypuk, 2008.
93. Ross 2001.
94. US Environmental Protection Agency 1992; Litt, Tran, and Burke 2009; Saha 2009.
95. Downey and Hawkins 2008.
96. McConnochie et al. 1998; Brunekreef and Holgate 2002; Ritz, et al. 2002; Clancy et al. 2002; McConnell et al. 2002; Kawachi and Berkman 2003; Chay and Greenstone 2003a, 2003b; Neidell 2004; Currie and Neidell 2005; Brook 2008; Hassing et al. 2009.
97. Litt, Tran, and Burke 2009.
98. Lanphear 1998.
99. Reyes 2005.
100. Needleman and Gastsonis 1991; Pocock et al. 1994.
101. Walker, Kane, and Burke 2010.
102. Sanbonmatsu et al. 2011.
103. Acevedo-Garcia and Osypuk 2008; Budrys 2010; Currie 2011.
104. Geronimus 1992.

105. Kawachi, Kennedy, and Wilkinson 1999.
106. Fick and Thomas 1995; Ganz 2000.
107. Sampson (2012), Papachristos (2013), and Hegerty (2017) find a positive relationship between crime and neighborhood poverty, controlling for racial composition, though Hipp (2007) does not. Hipp (2007), Peterson and Krivo (2010), Hegerty, (2017), and Boessen and Chamberlain (2017) find a positive relationship between crime rates and racial composition of the neighborhood, after controlling for poverty rates, though Morenoff, Sampson, and Raudenbush (2001) do not.
108. Aneshensel and Sucoff 1996; Martinez and Richter 1993; Ceballo et al. 2001; Hagan et al. 2001.
109. Zapata et al. 1992; Duncan and Laren 1990.
110. Hagan et al. 2001; Lord and Mahoney 2007; Harding 2009; Sampson and Sharkey 2014; Sharkey et al. 2014.
111. Linares et al. 2001; Guerra, Huesmann, and Spindler 2003.
112. Galster and Santiago 2006.
113. Fick and Thomas 1996; Linares et al. 2001.
114. Johnson 2011.
115. Sullivan 1989; Newman 1999.
116. Newman 1999; Wilson 1996; Li, Campbell, and Fernandez 2013; Kneebone and Holmes 2015.
117. Rosenbaum 1995.
118. For reviews, see Kain 1992; Ihlanfeldt 1999. For recent evidence, see Li, Campbell, and Fernandez 2013.
119. Waldinger 1996; Hellerstein, Neumark, and McInerney 2008; Hellerstein, Kutzbach, and Neumark, 2014.
120. Lipman 2006.
121. Oliver and Shapiro 1995; Kochhar, Fry, and Taylor 2011; Shapiro, Meschede, and Osoro 2013.
122. Conley 1999.
123. Kochhar, Fry, and Taylor (2011); Kuebler and Rugh (2013); and Shapiro, Meschede, and Osoro (2013) estimate that 27 percent of the rise in the interracial wealth gap over the last twenty-five years—the single biggest component—is related to years of homeownership, though they do not separate ownership of a home from the appreciation of that home.
124. Galster 1992b; Cloud and Galster 1993; Yinger 1995; Ross and Yinger 2002; Freund 2007.
125. Wyly et al. 2006; Been, Ellen, and Madar 2009; Richter and Craig 2010; Faber 2013; Hyra et al. 2013; Hwang, Hankinson, and Brown 2015.
126. Rugh, Albright, and Massey 2015.
127. Also see Gruenstein, Bocian, Smith, and Li 2012 for an estimate of total negative externality costs on minority communities due to foreclosures.
128. Pandey and Coulton 1994; Kim 2000, 2003; Flippen 2004; Galster, Cutsinger, and Malega 2008.
129. Flippen 2004.
130. Kim (2000, 2003); Flippen (2004); and Anaker (2010, 2012) all find that the static level of share of black households reduces values, though their findings were not replicated by Macpherson and Sirmans (2001). Phares (1971); Devaney and Rayburn (1993); Macpherson and Sirmans (2001); Flippen (2004); and Coate and Schwester (2011) all find that growth in share of black households reduces values.

131. Flippen 2004.
132. Flippen 2004; Anaker 2010, 2012. However, Macpherson and Sirmans (2001) were unable to replicate their findings.
133. Macpherson and Sirmans 2001; Flippen 2004.
134. Flippen 2004. Note that this result is entangled with increases in shares of foreign-born residents.
135. Vandell 1981; Jun 2016.
136. For example, Rugh, Albright, and Massey (2015) found that from 2000 to the neighborhood-specific peak in 2006–7, local home prices in Baltimore rose by 139 percent for a sample of black borrowers from a major lender, as compared with 168 percent for white borrowers. From 2008 to 2012 they dropped by 40 percent among the former but only 35 percent among the latter. Also see Oliver and Shapiro 1995; Loving, Finke, and Salter 2012; and Faber and Ellen 2016.
137. Flippen 2004.
138. Gyourko and Linneman (1993) found that homes starting in the lowest decile of value in 1960 appreciated overall from 1960 to 1989 at about a 1 percent annual rate, whereas those beginning in the 90th percentile appreciated at a 3.67 percent annual rate (though the rates varied depending on the specific era). By contrast, using different time scales, price delineations, and data sets, Oliver and Shapiro (1995) and Loving, Finke, and Salter (2012) found that lower-valued properties appreciated more rapidly.
139. For reviews and overviews of this literature, see Freeman 2006; Lees, Slater, and Wyly 2008, 2010; Brown-Saracino 2010; and Hyra, 2008, 2017.
140. Hwang and Lin 2016.
141. Newman and Wyly 2006.
142. Vigdor, Massey, and Rivlin 2002; Freeman and Braconi 2004; Freeman 2005; Ellen and O'Regan 2011; McKinnish, Walsh, and White 2010; Ellen and O'Regan 2011; Landis 2016.
143. Ding, Hwang, and Divringi 2016.
144. Dastrup and Ellen 2016.
145. Knotts and Haspel 2006; Martin 2007; Zukin 2010; Hyra 2014; Michener and Wong 2015; Elliott 2017. Note, however, that the displacement of local retailers may be exaggerated; Meltzer 2016.
146. Hyra 2017.
147. Hartley 2013; Ellen and O'Regan 2011; Ding and Hwang 2016; Dastrup and Ellen 2016.
148. Cf. Lester and Hartley 2014; and Meltzer and Ghorbani 2015.
149. Freeman 2006, Ellen and O'Regan 2011.
150. Flippen (2004) shows that owners who experienced a decrease in their neighborhood's poverty rate since they purchased their home saw a 3 percent higher (albeit only modestly statistically significant) appreciation of home value than those who experienced no change in their neighborhood's poverty rate, controlling for changes in the racial composition of the neighborhood and a variety of other characteristics.
151. Sampson and Sharkey (2008) provide powerful evidence of how racially and economically distinct flows of households across Chicago neighborhoods produce self-perpetuating patterns of segregation and inequality.
152. Farley 1998.
153. Yinger (1995) wrote the seminal treatise on motives for discrimination. For recent

reviews of the evidence on such motives, see Oh and Yinger 2015; and Galster, Mac-Donald, and Nelson 2018.

154. Freund 2007.

CHAPTER 10

1. For a review of how neighborhood planning has evolved, see Rohe 2009. There is a long-standing multidisciplinary literature that evaluates and advances public policies aimed at improving various aspects of US neighborhoods. Illustrations include Molotch 1972; Saltman 1978; Albrandt and Cunningham 1979; Goodwin 1979; Clay and Hollister 1983; Varady 1986; Galster 1987a; Varady and Raffel 1995; Keating and Krumholz 1999; Bright 2000; Zielenbach 2000; Peterman 2000; Massey et al. 2013; Pagano 2015; Chaskin and Joseph 2015; Brophy 2016.

2. For encouraging examples of efficacious community interventions, see Deng et al. 2018.

3. Many past neighborhood renewal strategies, particularly those that have demolished large tracts of private rental housing or public housing estates, have imposed heavy costs on disadvantaged households by involuntarily displacing them. See, for example, Goetz 2003, 2018.

4. Bratt, Stone, and Hartman 2006.

5. Unfortunately, the primary federal program for doing so, the Community Development Block Grant Program, has steadily declined in inflation-adjusted, per capita value by five-sixths since its peak in 1978. Rohe and Galster 2014.

6. For more on the rationale for doing so and the political challenges that such reforms entail, see Rusk, 1993, 1999; Orfield 1997.

7. For details of these various strategies, see Rusk, 1993, 1999; Orfield 1997; and Dreier, Mollenkopf, and Swanstrom 2014.

8. For a practical guide on how communities can develop an operational system of strategic targeting, see Accordino and Fasulo 2013.

9. Galster, Hayes, and Johnson (2005) provide a parsimonious yet powerfully predictive set of neighborhood indicators. For comprehensive discussions about how analysts can develop and employ neighborhood indicators using new Geographic Information System technologies, see Kingsley, Coulton, and Pettit 2014; Chapple and Zuk 2016.

10. Bleakly et al. 1982.

11. Galster, Tatian, and Accordino 2006.

12. Galster et al. 2004.

13. Pooley 2014.

14. My recommendation echoes that advanced earlier by the US Government Accounting (now Accountability) Office (2005) and numerous scholars: Thomson 2008, 2011; Accordino and Fasulo 2013; Wilson and Bin Kashem 2017.

15. For further discussion of and justification for strategic targeting, see Thomson 2008, 2011; Accordino and Fasulo 2013.

16. Galster 1987a.

17. Galster 1987a.

18. Galster 1987a.

19. Goetze (1976) was a noted advocate of the building neighborhood confidence strategy.

20. This impact was larger in magnitude than that associated with a twenty-thousand-dollar difference in homeowners' incomes. Galster 1987a.

21. Reduced-tax zones are another strategy that fit within this policy category. I do not advocate them, however, because of their large horizontal and vertical inequities and the large share of zero-sum behavioral responses they induce.
22. Galster and Hesser 1988.
23. Ioannides 2002; Rossi-Hansberg, Sarte, and Owens 2010; Helms 2012; Wilson and Kashem 2017.
24. Galster 1983.
25. See the reviews in Haurin, Dietz, and Weinberg 2002; Rohe, van Zandt, and McCarthy 2013.
26. Green and White 1997; Haurin, Parcel, and Haurin 2002; Harkness and Newman 2003; Dietz and Haurin 2003; Galster et al. 2007b; Green, Painter, and White 2012.
27. Both Hipp (2007) and Hegerty (2017) find that higher homeownership rates are associated with lower neighborhood crime rates, controlling for residents' economic and racial composition.
28. For a review of alternative programmatic means for enhancing rates of homeownership among lower-income households, see Galster and Santiago 2008 and Lubbell 2016. Santiago, Galster, and Smith (2017) favorably evaluated an especially innovative and effective program in this regard developed by the Denver Housing Authority.
29. Wilson and Bin Kashem 2017.
30. Coulson, Hwang, and Imai 2003.
31. Galster et al. 2003.
32. I draw here from discussions for a quarter century of wide-ranging policy reform proposals aimed at (among other things) improving the geographic distribution of federal housing assistance. See Goering 1986; Turner 1998; Katz and Turner 2001, 2008; Pendall 2000b; Galster et al. 2003; Grigsby and Bourassa 2004; Popkin et al. 2004; Khadduri 2005; McClure 2008; Khadduri and Wilkins 2008; de Souza Briggs, Popkin, and Goering 2010; Landis and McClure 2010; Kleit 2013; Sard and Rice 2014; Pendall and Hendey 2016; Turner 2017; Boggs 2017.
33. Katz and Turner 2001.
34. Significant organizational capacity and procedural precedent of the type envisioned exists in many metropolitan areas. The court-ordered settlements in more than a dozen PHA racial desegregation suits mandated similar sorts of interorganizational competitions for administering deconcentration HCV programs. Popkin et al., 2003.
35. Freeman 2012; Freeman and Yunjing 2014; Metzger 2014; Tighe, Hatch, and Mead 2017.
36. De Souza Briggs, 1997; Hartung and Henig, 1997.
37. The Gautreaux remedy, for example, required that recipients used their vouchers in neighborhoods where black residents made up less than 30 percent of the population; both Memphis and Cincinnati consent decrees placed the limit at 40 percent, and a Dallas settlement restricted HCV use to areas with less than 10 vouchers per census tract (Goering, Stebbins, and Siewert 1995). More recently, the Baltimore Housing Mobility Program limited participants' vouchers to use in tracts with no more than 10 percent poverty, 30 percent black population, and 5 percent assisted households (DeLuca and Rosenblatt 2017).
38. The FY2001 HUD appropriations bill set a maximum of 25 percent of units with project-based assistance in any apartment complexes newly developed by PHAs. The 1996 consent decree settling the public housing desegregation suit in Baltimore required that authorities build scattered-site public housing in areas with less than 26 percent minorities, less than 10 percent poverty, and less than 5 percent assisted

households. The 1984 consent decree resolving the Cincinnati public housing suit required that more than half the new scattered-site public housing units be constructed in areas with less than 20 percent minorities and less than 15 percent subsidized housing (Varady and Preiser 1998). Since the early 1990s, Denver has limited the concentration of scattered site public housing and supportive housing (Galster et al. 2003).

39. Galster et al. 2003.
40. O'Regan 2016. At this writing, the Trump administration, acting through HUD Secretary Ben Carson, has put a moratorium on requiring local recipients of federal grants to file AFFH documents, though this is being challenged in court.
41. Boger 1996.
42. Galster 2013.
43. Levy, Comey, and Padilla 2006a, 2006b; Lubbell 2016.
44. For a broader discussion of past and proposed federal, state, and local initiatives to preserve and promote diversity in gentrifying neighborhoods, see Levy, Comey, and Padilla, 2006a, 2006b; Lees and Ley, 2008; and Lubbell, 2016.
45. O'Regan 2016.
46. Lubbell 2016.
47. For broader discussions of not only federal but also state and local policies and programs that could help the HCV program become a more effective vehicle for deconcentrating poverty, see Turner, 1998; Katz and Turner, 2001, 2008; Pendall, 2000; Grigsby and Bourassa, 2004; Khadduri, 2005; McClure, 2008; Khadduri and Wilkins, 2008; Mallach, 2008; de Souza Briggs, Popkin, and Goering, 2010; Landis and McClure, 2010; Sard and Rice, 2014; Pendall and Hendey, 2016; and Freeman and Schuetz, 2017.
48. HUD has already begun experimenting with this scheme in several metropolitan areas. Early evaluations give cause for optimism about the power of SAFMRs in deconcentrating poverty (Collinson and Ganong 2016). Unfortunately, at this writing the Trump administration, acting through HUD Secretary Ben Carson, has halted the implementation of SAFMRs.
49. DeLuca, Garboden, and Rosenblatt 2013; Darrah and DeLuca 2014.
50. Deluca and Rosenblatt 2017.
51. Sard and Rice 2014.
52. DeLuca, Garboden, and Rosenblatt 2013.
53. Greenlee 2011.
54. For recent reviews, see Galster 2013; DeLuca, Garboden, and Rosenblatt 2013; Schwartz, McClure, and Taghavi, 2016.
55. Imbroscio 2012; Diamond 2012; Shelby, 2017.
56. Manzo 2014.
57. Stack 1975.
58. Clark 2008.
59. Hunter et al. 2016; Shelby 2017; Basolo and Yerena 2017.
60. Marsh and Gibb 2011.
61. Sharkey 2013.
62. DeLuca, Garboden, and Rosenblatt 2013; Darrah and DeLuca 2014; Deluca and Rosenblatt 2017.
63. DeLuca, Garboden, and Rosenblatt 2013.
64. For more on SIP and the concept of integration, see Galster 1998.
65. Galster 1990d.

66. The Clinton and Obama administrations' Departments of Justice pursued such policies, as did local private fair housing groups supported through the auspices of the federal Fair Housing Initiatives Program (Squires 2017).
67. There is strong evidence that well-publicized court findings of discrimination, coupled with large penalties, do deter discrimination by market agents (Ross and Galster 2006).
68. Saltman 1990.
69. For amplification of these points, see Carmon, 1976, 1997.
70. The central advocate of this position is William Clark. See, for example, Clark, 2008.
71. Recent statistical evidence related to changing mobility behaviors over time suggests that preferences for neighborhood racial composition are subject to modification over time. During the 2000s, white households seemed to be less prone to avoid moving into minority-occupied areas than in prior decades (Lee 2017).
72. Pettigrew, 1973 2011; Jackman and Crane 1986.
73. For comprehensive reviews, see Pettigrew and Tropp 2006; Pettigrew 2011.
74. Smith 1993.
75. For a deeper discussion and details of the SIP program in Shaker Heights, see De-Marco and Galster 1993; for histories of comparable programs in other communities, see Saltman, 1978, 1990.
76. DeMarco and Galster, 1993.
77. Galster 1990a.
78. Cromwell 1990.
79. Galster et al. 2003.
80. I demonstrate these propositions more formally in Galster 2003.
81. Galster, Cutsinger, and Malega 2008.
82. I previously exposed this fallacious reasoning in the case of how commentators viewed the altered distribution of neighborhood poverty rates during the 1990s; Galster 2005.
83. Sadly, this is what is happening at the federal level. At this writing, HUD's proposed FY 2018 budget cuts HCVs by one-third.
84. Blount et al. 2014; Freeman and Schuetz 2017.
85. Galster, Tatian and Accordino 2006.
86. Joseph 2006.
87. Briggs et al. 2010.
88. Briggs et al. 2010; Fraser et al. 2013; Hyra 2013; Joseph 2013; Khare 2013; Chaskin and Joseph 2015.
89. Goetz 2003; Galster 2017.
90. See the reviews in Shelby 2017; and Squires 2017.
91. Turner 2017; O'Regan 2017; Boggs 2017; Squires 2017; Goetz 2018; Dawkins 2018.

REFERENCES

Aaronson, Daniel. 1998. "Using Sibling Data to Estimate the Impact of Neighborhoods on Children's Educational Outcomes." *Journal of Human Resources* 33(4): 915–946.

Aber, Mark S., and Martin Nieto. 2000. "Suggestions for the Investigation of Psychological Wellness in the Neighborhood Context: Toward a Pluralistic Neighborhood Theory." In *The Promotion of Wellness in Children and Adolescents*, edited by Dante Cicchetti, Julian Rappaport, Irwin Sandler, and Roger P. Weissberg, 185–219. Washington: CWLA Press.

Accordino, John, and Fabrizio Fasulo. 2013. "Fusing Technical and Political Rationality in Community Development: A Prescriptive Model of Efficiency-Based Strategic Geographic Targeting." *Housing Policy Debate* 23(4): 615–642.

Acevedo-Garcia, Dolores, and Theresa L. Osypuk. 2008. "Impacts of Housing and Neighborhoods on Health: Pathways, Racial/Ethnic Disparities and Policy Directions." In *Segregation: The Rising Costs for America*, edited by James H. Carr and Nandine K. Kutty, 197–235. New York: Routledge.

Acs, Gregory, Rolf Pendall, Mark Treskon, and Amy Khare. 2017. *The Cost of Segregation: National Trends and the Case of Chicago, 1990–2010.* Washington: Urban Institute. Available at http://www.urban.org/policy-centers/metropolitan-housing-and-communities -policy-center/projects/cost-segregation.

Adelman, Robert M. 2005. "The Roles of Race, Class, and Residential Preferences in the Neighborhood Racial Composition of Middle-Class Blacks and Whites." *Social Science Quarterly* 86(1): 209–228.

Ahern, Jennifer, Sandro Galea, Alan Hubbard, Lorraine Midanik, and S. Leonard Syme. 2008. "'Culture of Drinking' and Individual Problems with Alcohol Use." *American Journal of Epidemiology* 167(9): 1041–1049.

Ahlbrandt, Roger S., and Paul C. Brophy. 1975. *Neighborhood Revitalization: Theory and Practice.* Lexington, MA: Lexington Books / D. C. Heath and Co.

Ahlbrandt, Roger S., Margaret Charney, and James V. Cunningham. 2000. "Citizen Perceptions of Their Neighborhoods." *Journal of Housing* 7:338–341.

Akerlof, George. 1980. "A Theory of Social Custom, of Which Unemployment May Be One Consequence." *Quarterly Journal of Economics* 94(4): 749–775.

Albrandt, Roger S., and James V. Cunningham. 1979. *A New Public Policy for Neighborhood Preservation.* New York: Praeger Publishers.

Alesina, Alberto, Reza Baqir, and William Easterly. 1999. "Public Goods and Ethnic Divisions." *Quarterly Journal of Economics* 114(4): 1243–1284.

Allport, Gordon W. 1954. *The Nature of Prejudice*. Cambridge, MA: Perseus.

———. 1979. *The Nature of Prejudice: 25th Anniversary Edition*. New York: Basic Books.

Alonso, William. 1964. *Location and Land Use*. Cambridge, MA: Harvard University Press.

Anacker, Katrin B. 2010. "Still Paying the Race Tax? Analyzing Property Values in Homogeneous and Mixed-Race Suburbs." *Journal of Urban Affairs* 32(1): 55–77.

Anacker, Katrin B. 2012. "Shaky Palaces? Analyzing Property Values and Their Appreciation in Minority First Suburbs." *International Journal of Urban and Regional Research* 36(4): 791–816.

Anas, Alex. 1978. "Dynamics of Urban Residential Growth." *Journal of Urban Economics* 5(1): 66–87.

Andersson, Eva. 2004. "From Valley of Sadness to Hill of Happiness: The Significance of Surroundings for Socioeconomic Career." *Urban Studies* 41(3): 641–659.

Andersson, Eva, and Bo Malmberg. 2013. "Contextual Effects on Educational Attainment in Individualized Neighborhoods: Differences across Gender and Social Class." Paper presented at ENHR Conference; Tarragona, Spain, June.

Anderson, Ronald M., Hongjian Yu, Roberta Wyn, Pamela L. Davidson, and E. Richard Brown. 2002. "Access to Medical Care for Low-Income Persons: How Do Communities Make a Difference?" *Medical Care Research and Review* 59(4): 384–411.

Aneshensel, Carol S., and Clea A. Sucoff. 1996. "The Neighborhood Context and Adolescent Mental Health." *Journal of Health and Social Behavior* 37(4): 293–310.

Arnott, Richard J. 1980. "A Simple Urban Growth Model with Durable Housing." *Regional Science and Urban Economics* 10(1): 53–76.

Åslund, Olaf, and Peter Fredriksson. 2009. "Peer Effects in Welfare Dependence: Quasi-Experimental Evidence." *Journal of Human Resources* 44(3): 798–825.

Asmus, Karl H., and Harvey J. Iglarsh. 1975. "Dynamic Model of Private Incentives to Housing Maintenance: Comment." *Southern Economic Journal* 42(2): 326–329.

Atkinson, Rowland, and Keith Kintrea. 2001. "Area Effects: What Do They Mean for British Housing and Regeneration Policy?" *European Journal of Housing policy* 2(2): 147–166.

Bader, Michael D. M., and Maria Krysan. 2015. "Community Attraction and Avoidance in Chicago: What's Race Got to Do with it?" *The ANNALS of the American Academy of Political and Social Science* 660(1): 261–281.

Baer, William C., and Christopher B. Williamson. 1988. "The Filtering of Households and Housing Units." *Journal of Planning Literature* 3(2): 127–152.

Bailey, Martin J. 1959. "A Note on the Economics of Residential Zoning and Urban Renewal." *Land Economics* 35(3): 288–292.

———. 1966. "Effects of Race and Other Demographic Factors on Values of Single-Family Homes." *Land Economics* 42(2): 215–220.

Bailey, Nick, and Mark Livingston. 2007. *Population Turnover and Area Deprivation*. Bristol, UK: Policy Press.

Banzhaf, H. Spencer, and Randall P. Walsh. 2008. "Do People Vote with Their Feet? An Empirical Test of Tiebout's Mechanism." *American Economic Review* 98(3): 843–863.

Basolo, Victoria, and Anaid Yerena. 2017. "Residential Mobility of Low-Income, Subsidized Households: A Synthesis of Explanatory Frameworks." *Housing Studies* 32(6): 841–862.

Bates, Timothy. 1997. *Race, Self-Employment and Upward Mobility*. Washington and Baltimore: Woodrow Wilson Center Press and Johns Hopkins University Press.

Bauder, Harald. 2001. "Culture in the Labor Market: Segmentation Theory and Perspectives of Place." *Progress in Human Geography* 25(1): 37–52.

Baum, Scott, Kathryn Arthurson, and Kara Rickson. 2010. "Happy People in Mixed-Up Places: The Association Between the Degree and Type of Local Socioeconomic Mix and Expressions of Neighborhood Satisfaction." *Urban Studies* 47(3): 467–485.

Baxter, Vern, and Mickey Lauria. 2000. "Residential Mortgage Foreclosures and Neighborhood Change." *Housing Policy Debate* 11(3): 675–699.

Bayer, Patrick, Hangming Fang, and Robert McMillan. 2014. "Separate When Equal? Racial Inequality and Residential Segregation." *Journal of Urban Economics* 82:32–48.

Bayer, Patrick, and Robert McMillan. 2012. "Tiebout Sorting and Neighborhood Stratification." *Journal of Public Economics* 96(11): 1129–1143.

Bayer, Patrick, Robert McMillan, and Kim Rueben. 2004. "What Drives Racial Segregation? New Evidence Using Census Microdata." *Journal of Urban Economics* 56(3): 514–535.

———. 2005. "Residential Segregation in General Equilibrium." National Bureau of Economic Research, NBER Working Paper no. 11095, January.

Bayer, Patrick, Fernando Ferreira, and Robert McMillan. 2007. "A Unified Framework for Measuring Preferences for Schools and Neighborhoods." *Journal of Political Economy* 115(4): 588–638.

Bayer, Patrick, Stephen Ross, and Giorgio Topa. 2004. "Place of Work and Place of Residence: Informal Hiring Networks and Labor Market Outcomes." Working paper, Economics Department, Yale University.

———. 2008. "Place of Work and Place of Residence: Informal Hiring Networks and Labor Market Outcomes." *Journal of Political Economy* 116(6): 1150–1196.

Becker, Rolf. 2003. "Educational Expansion and Persistent Inequalities of Education." *European Sociological Review* 19(1): 1–24.

Been, Vicki, Ingrid Gould Ellen, and Josiah Madar. 2009. "The High Cost of Segregation: Exploring Racial Disparities in High-Cost Lending." *Fordham Urban Law Journal* 36: 361–393.

Benabou, Roland. 1993. "Workings of a City: Location, Education, and Production." *Quarterly Journal of Economics* 108(3): 619–652.

———. 1996. "Heterogeneity, Stratification, and Growth: Macroeconomic Implications of Community Structure and School Finance." *American Economic Review* 86(3): 584–609.

Bender, Annah, Molly Metzger, Vithya Murugan, and Divya Ravindranath. 2016. "Housing Choices as School Choices: Subsidized Renters' Agency in an Uncertain Policy Context." *City & Community* 15 (4): 444–467.

Bernstein, Jonathan A., Neil Alexis, Charles Barnes, I. Leonard Bernstein, Andre Nel, David Peden, David Diaz-Sanchez, Susan M. Tarlo, and P. Brock Williams. 2004. "Health Effects of Air Pollution." *Journal of Allergy and Clinical Immunology* 114(5): 1116–1123.

Bertrand, Marianne, Ezro F. P. Luttmer, and Sendhil Mullainathan. 2000. "Network Effects and Welfare Cultures." *Quarterly Journal of Economics* 115(3): 1019–1055.

Besbirs, Max, and Jacob W. Faber. 2017. "Investigating the Relationship between Real Estate Agents, Segregation, and House Prices: Steering and Upselling in New York State." *Sociological Forum* 32(4): 850-873..

Bian, Xun. 2017. "Housing Equity Dynamics and Home Improvements." *Journal of Housing Economics* 37:29–41.

Billings, Stephen, David Deming, and Stephen Ross. 2016. "Partners in Crime: Schools, Neighborhoods and the Formation of Criminal Networks." Cambridge, MA: NBER Working Paper w21962.

Birch, David L., Eric S. Brown, Richard P. Coleman, Dolores W. da Lomda, William L. Parsons, Linda C. Sharpe, and Sheryll A. Weber. 1979. *The Behavioral Foundations of Neighborhood Change*. Washington: Office of Policy Development and Research, US Department of Housing and Urban Development.

Bischoff, Kendra, and Sean Reardon. 2014. "Residential Segregation by Income: 1970–2009." In *Diversity and Disparities: America Enters a New Century*, edited by John R. Logan, 208–234. New York: Russell Sage Foundation.

Bleachman, Eileen. 1991. "Mentors for High-Risk Minority Youth: From Effective Communication to Bicultural Competence." *Journal of Clinical Child Psychology* 21(2): 160–169.

Bleakly, Kenneth, Mary Joel Holin, Laura Fitzpatrick, and Constance Newman. 1982. *A Case Study of Local Control over Housing Development: The Neighborhood Strategy Area Demonstration*. Washington: Office of Policy Development and Research, US Department of Housing and Urban Development.

Block, Jason P., Richard A. Scribner, and Karen B. DeSalvo. 2004. "Fast Food, Race/Ethnicity, and Income: A Geographic Analysis." *American Journal of Preventive Medicine* 27(3): 211–217.

Blount, Casey, Wendy Ip, Ikuo Nakano, and Elaine Ng. 2014. "Redevelopment Agencies in California: History, Benefits, Excesses and Closure." Washington: US Department of Housing and Urban Development, Economic Market Analysis Working Paper Series no. EMAD-2014–01.

Boehm, Thomas. 1981. "Tenure Choice and Expected Mobility: A Synthesis." *Journal of Urban Economics* 10(3): 375–389.

Boehm, Thomas, and Keith Ihlanfeldt. 1986. "The Improvement Expenditures of Urban Homeowners." *American Real Estate and Urban Economics Association Journal* 14(1): 48–60.

Boessen, Adam, and Alyssa Chamberlain. 2107. "Neighborhood Crime, the Housing Crisis, and Geographic Space: Disentangling the Consequences of Foreclosure and Vacancy." *Journal of Urban Affairs* 39(8): 1122–1137.

Boger, John C. 1996. "Toward Ending Racial Segregation: A Fair Share Proposal for the Next Reconstruction." *North Carolina Law Review* 71(5): 1573–1618.

Boggs, Erin. 2017. "People and Place in Low-Income Housing Policy: Unwinding Segregation in Connecticut." *Housing Policy Debate* 27(2): 320–326.

Böheim, René, and Mark P. Taylor. 2002. "Tied Down or Room to Move? Investigating the Relationships between Housing Tenure, Employment Status and Residential Mobility in Britain." *Scottish Journal of Political Economy* 49(4): 369–392.

Bolster, Anne, Simon Burgess, Ron Johnston, Kelvyn Jones, Carol Propper, and Rebecca Sarker. 2007. "Neighbourhoods, Households and Income Dynamics: A Semi-Parametric Investigation of Neighbourhood Effects." *Journal of Economic Geography* 7(1): 1–38.

Bond, Eric W., and N. Edward Coulson. 1989. "Externalities, Filtering, and Neighborhood Change." *Journal of Urban Economics* 26(2): 231–249.

Booth, Alan, and Ann C. Crouter, eds. 2001. *Does It Take a Village? Community Effects on Children, Adolescents and Families*. London and Mawah, NJ: Lawrence Erlbaum Publishers.

Booza, Jason A., Jackie M. Cutsinger, and George C. Galster. 2006. *Where Did They Go? The Decline of Middle-Income Neighborhoods in Metropolitan America*. Washington: Brookings Institution.

Bostic, Raphael, and Richard Martin. 2003. "Black Home-owners as a Gentrifying Force?

Neighbourhood Dynamics in the Context of Minority Home-ownership." *Urban Studies* 40: 2427–2449.

Boyd, Michelle R. 2008. *Jim Crow Nostalgia: Reconstructing Race in Bronzeville*. Minneapolis: University of Minnesota Press.

Braid, Ralph M. 2001. "Spatial Growth and Redevelopment with Perfect Foresight and Durable Housing." *Journal of Urban Economics* 49(3): 425–452.

Bratt, Rachel G., Michael E. Stone, and Chester Hartman, eds. 2006. *A Right to Housing: Foundation for a New Social Agenda*. Philadelphia: Temple University Press.

Briggs, Xavier de Souza. 1997a. "Moving Up versus Moving Out: Neighborhood Effects in Housing Mobility Programs." *Housing Policy Debate* 8(1): 195–234.

———. 1997b. *Yonkers Revisited: The Early Impacts of Scattered-Site Public Housing on Families and Neighborhoods*. New York: Teachers College, Columbia University.

———. 1998. "Brown Kids in White Suburbs: Housing Mobility and the Many Faces of Social Capital." *Housing Policy Debate* 9(1), 177–221.

Briggs, Xavier de Souza, ed. 1995. *The Geography of Opportunity*. Washington: Brookings Institution Press.

Briggs, Xavier de Souza, Elizabeth Cove, Cynthia Duarte, and Margery Austin Turner. 2011. "How Does Leaving High-Poverty Neighborhoods Affect the Employment Prospects of Low-Income Mothers and Youth?" In *Neighborhood and Life Chances: How Place Matters in Modern America*, edited by Harriet Newburger, Eugenie Birch, and Susan Wachter, 179–203. Philadelphia: University of Pennsylvania Press.

Briggs, Xavier de Souza, Kadija Ferryman, Susan Popkin, and Maria Rendon. 2008. "Why Did the Moving to Opportunity Experiment Not Get Young People into Better Schools?" *Housing Policy Debate* 19(1): 53–91.

Briggs, Xavier de Souza, Susan J. Popkin, and John Goering. 2010. *Moving to Opportunity: The Story of an American Experiment to Fight Ghetto Poverty*. New York: Oxford University Press.

Bright, Elsie M. 2000. *Reviving America's Forgotten Neighborhoods: An Investigation of Inner City Revitalization Efforts*. New York and London: Garland Press.

Brock, William, and Steven Durlauf. 1999. "Interactions-Based Models." Paper presented at the Neighborhood Effects Conference, Joint Center for Poverty Research, Chicago.

Brook, Robert D. 2008. "Cardiovascular Effects of Air Pollution." *Clinical Science* 115(6):175–187.

Brooks-Gunn, Jeanne, Greg J. Duncan, and J. Lawrence Aber, eds. 1997. *Neighborhood Poverty: Volume 1. Context and Consequences for Children*. New York: Russell Sage Foundation.

Brophy, Paul, ed. 2016. *On the Edge: America's Middle Neighborhoods*. New York: American Assembly, Columbia University.

Brown, Lawrence A., and Eric G. Moore. 1970. "The Intra-Urban Migration Process: A Perspective." *Geografiska Annaler B, Human Geography* 52(1): 1–13.

Brown-Saracino, Japonica. 2010. *The Neighborhood That Never Changes: Gentrification, Social Preservation, and the Search for Authenticity*. Chicago: University of Chicago Press.

Bruch, Elizabeth E., and Robert D. Mare. 2006. "Neighborhood Choice and Neighborhood Change." *American Journal of Sociology* 112(3): 667–709.

———. 2012. "Methodological Issues in the Analysis of Residential Preferences, Residential Mobility, and Neighborhood Change." *Sociological Methodology* 42:103–154.

Brueckner, Jan, and Stuart Rosenthal. 2009. "Gentrification and Neighborhood Cycles: Will America's Future Downtowns Be Rich?" *Review of Economics and Statistics* 91(4): 725–743.

Brueckner, Jan, Jacques-François Thisse, and Yves Zenou. 1999. "Why Is Central Paris Rich and Downtown Detroit Poor? An Amenity-Based Theory." *European Economic Review* 43(1): 91–107.

Brunekreef, Bert, and Stephen T. Holgate. 2002. "Air Pollution and Health." *The Lancet* 360(9341): 1233–1242.

Budrys, Grace. 2010. *Unequal Health; How Inequality Contributes to Health and Illness.* 2nd ed. Lanham, MD: Rowman and Littlefield.

Burdick-Will, Julia, Jens Ludwig, Stephen W. Raudenbush, Robert J. Sampson, Lisa Sanbonmatsu, and Patrick W. Sharkey. 2010. *Converging Evidence for Neighborhood Effects on Children's Test Scores: An Experimental, Quasi-Experimental, and Observational Comparison.* Washington: Brookings Institution.

Burton, Linda M., and Townsand Price-Spratlen. 1999. "Through the Eyes of Children: An Ethnographic Perspective on Neighborhoods and Child Development." In *Cultural Processes in Child Development*, edited by Ann S. Masten, 77–96. Mahwah, NJ: Lawrence Erlbaum Associates.

Calabrese, Stephen, Dennis Epple, Thomas Romer, and Holger Sieg. 2006. "Local Public Good Provision: Voting, Peer Effects, and Mobility." *Journal of Public Economics* 90(6): 959–981.

Campbell, Elizabeth, Julia R. Henly, Delbert S. Elliott, and Katherine Irwin. 2009. "Subjective Constructions of Neighborhood Boundaries: Lessons from a Qualitative Study of Four Neighborhoods." *Journal of Urban Affairs* 31(4): 461–490.

Card, David, and Alan B. Krueger. 1992. "Does School Quality Matter? Returns to Education and the Characteristics of Public Schools in the United States." *Journal of Political Economy* 100(1): 1–40.

Card, David, Alexandre Mas, and Jesse Rothstein. 2008. "Tipping and the Dynamics of Segregation." *Quarterly Journal of Economics* 123(1): 177–218.

Carlson, Deven, and Joshua Cowen. 2015. "Student Neighborhoods, Schools, and Test Score Growth: Evidence from Milwaukee, Wisconsin." *Sociology of Education* 88(1): 38–55.

Carmon, Naomi. 1976. "Social Planning of Housing." *Journal of Social Policy* 5(1): 49–59.

———. 1997. "Neighborhood Regeneration: The State of the Art." *Journal of Planning Education and Research* 17(2): 131–144.

Carter, William H., Michael H. Schill, and Susan M. Wachter. 1998. "Polarisation, Public Housing, and Racial Minorities in US Cities." *Urban Studies* 35(10): 1889–1911.

Casciano, Rebecca, and Douglas Massey. 2012. "School Context and Educational Outcomes: Results from a Quasi-Experimental Study." *Urban Affairs Review* 48(2): 180–204.

Case, Anne C., and Lawrence F. Katz. 1991. *The Company You Keep: The Effects of Family and Neighborhood on Disadvantaged Youth.* NBER Working Paper 3705. Cambridge, MA: National Bureau of Economic Research, May.

Caskey, John P. 1994. *Fringe Banking: Check-Cashing Outlets, Pawnshops, and the Poor.* NY: Russell Sage Foundation.

Ceballo, Rosario, Trayci A. Dahl, Maria T. Aretakis, and Cynthia Ramirez. 2001. "Inner-City Children's Exposure to Community Violence: How Much Do Parents Know?" *Journal of Marriage and Family* 63(4): 927–940.

Cerdá, Magdalena, Ana Diez-Roux, Eric Tchetgen Tchetgen, Penny Gordon-Larsen, and Catarina Kiefe. 2010. "The Relationship between Neighborhood Poverty and Alcohol Use: Estimation by Marginal Structural Models." *Epidemiology* 21(4): 482–489.

Chafets, Ze'ev. 1990. *Devil's Night and Other True Tales of Detroit.* New York: Random House.

Chang, Virginia W. 2006. "Racial Residential Segregation and Weight Status Among US Adults." *Social Science & Medicine* 63(5): 1289–1303.

Chapple, Karen, and Rick Jacobus. 2008. "Retail Trade as a Route to Neighborhood Revitalization." In *Urban and Regional Policy and Its Effects: Building Resilient Regions*, edited by Margery Austin Turner, Howard Wial, and Harold Wolman, 19–68. Washington: Brookings Institution Press.

Chapple, Karen, and Miriam Zuk. 2016. "Forewarned: The Use of Neighborhood Early Warning Systems for Gentrification and Displacement." *Cityscape* 18(3): 109–130.

Charles, Camille Zubrinsky. 2003. "The Dynamics of Racial Residential Segregation." *Annual Review of Sociology* 29:167–207.

Chase-Lansdale, P. Lindsay, Rachel A. Gordon, Jeanne Brooks-Gunn, and Pamela K. Klebanov. 1997. "Neighborhood and Family Influences on the Intellectual and Behavioral Competence of Preschool and Early School-Age Children." In *Neighborhood Poverty: Volume 1. Context and Consequences for Children*, edited by Jeanne Brooks-Gunn, Greg J. Duncan, and J. Lawrence Aber, 79–118. New York: Russell Sage Foundation.

Chaskin, Robert J. 1995. *Defining Neighborhoods: History, Theory, and Practice*. Chicago: Chapin Hall Center for Children, University of Chicago.

———. 1997. "Perspectives on Neighborhood and Community: A Review of the Literature." *Social Service Review* 71(4): 521–547.

Chaskin, Robert J., and Mark Joseph. 2015. *Integrating the Inner City: The Promise and Perils of Mixed-Income Public Housing Transformation*. Chicago: University of Chicago Press.

Chay, Kenneth Y., and Michael Greenstone. 2003. "The Impact of Air Pollution on Infant Mortality: Evidence from Geographic Variation in Pollution Shocks Induced by a Recession." *Quarterly Journal of Economics* 118(3): 1121–1167.

Chen, Hong, Mark S. Goldberg, and Paul J. Villeneuve. 2008. "A Systematic Review of the Relation between Long-Term Exposure to Ambient Air Pollution and Chronic Diseases." *Reviews on Environmental Health* 23(4): 243–297.

Chetty, Raj, Nathaniel Hendren, Patrick Kline, and Emmanuel Saez. 2014. "Where Is the Land of Opportunity? The Geography of Intergenerational Mobility in the United States." *Quarterly Journal of Economics* 129(4): 1553–1623.

Chetty, Raj, Nathanial Hendren, and Lawrence Katz. 2015. "The Effects of Exposure to Better Neighborhoods on Children: New Evidence from the Moving to Opportunity Experiment." NBER Working Paper no. 21156. Cambridge, MA: National Bureau of Economic Research.

Chinloy, Peter. 1980. "The Effect of Maintenance Expenditures on the Measurement of Depreciation in Housing." *Journal of Urban Economics* 8(1): 86–107.

Chyn, Eric. 2016. "Moved to Opportunity: The Long-Run Effect of Public Housing Demolition on Labor Market Outcomes of Children." Unpublished working paper, Department of Economics, University of Michigan.

Clampet-Lundquist, Susan. 2004. "HOPE VI Relocation: Moving to New Neighborhoods and Building New Ties." *Housing Policy Debate* 15(3): 415–447.

———. 2007. "No More 'Bois Ball: The Impact of Relocation from Public Housing on Adolescents." *Journal of Adolescent Research* 22(3): 298–323.

Clampet-Lundquist, Susan, Kathryn Edin, Jeffery R. Kling, and Greg J. Duncan. 2011. "Moving At-Risk Youth Out of High-Risk Neighborhoods: Why Girls Fare Better Than Boys." *American Journal of Sociology* 116(4): 1154–1189.

Clampet-Lundquist, Susan, and Douglas Massey. 2008. "Neighborhood Effects on Economic Self-Sufficiency: A Reconsideration of the Moving to Opportunity Experiment." *American Journal of Sociology* 114(1): 107–143.

Clancy, Luke, Pat Goodman, Hamish Sinclair, and Douglas W. Dockery. 2002. "Effect of Air Pollution Control on Death Rates in Dublin, Ireland." *The Lancet* 360(9341): 1210–1214.

Clark, Kenneth B. 1989. *Dark Ghetto: Dilemmas of Social Power*. 2nd ed. Middletown, CT: Wesleyan University Press.

Clark, William A.V. 1971. "A Test of Directional Bias in Residential Mobility." In *Perspectives in Geography 1: Models of Spatial Variations*, edited by H. McConnell and D. Yaseen, 1–27. DeKalb: Northern Illinois University Press.

———. 1982. *Modeling Housing Market Search*. London: Palgrave Macmillian.

———. 1986. "Residential Segregation in American Cities: A Review and Interpretation." *Population Research and Policy Review* 5(2): 95–127.

———. 2008. "Reexamining the Moving to Opportunity Study and Its Contribution to Changing the Distribution of Poverty and Ethnic Concentration." *Demography* 45(3): 515–535.

———. 2009. "Changing Residential Preferences across Income, Education, and Age: Findings from the Multi-City Study of Urban Inequality." *Urban Affairs Review* 44(3): 334–355.

Clark, William A.V., and Frans M. Dieleman. 1996. *Households and Housing: Choices and Outcomes in the Housing Market*. New Brunswick, NJ: Rutgers University Center for Urban Policy Research.

Clark, William A.V., and Youquin Huang. 2003. "The Life Course and Residential Mobility in British Housing Markets." *Environment and Planning A* 35(2): 323–339.

Clark, William A. V., and James O. Huff. 1978. "Cumulative Stress and Cumulative Inertia: A Behavioral Model of Decision to Move." *Environment and Planning A* 10(10): 1357–1376.

Clark, William A.V., and Valerie Ledwith. 2006. "Mobility, Housing Stress, and Neighborhood Contexts: Evidence from Los Angeles." *Environment and Planning A* 38(6): 1077–1093.

Clark, William A.V., and Jun L. Onaka. 1983. "Life Cycle and Housing Adjustment as Explanations of Residential Mobility." *Urban Studies* 20(1): 47–57.

Clay, Phillip L. 1979. *Neighborhood Renewal: Middle-Class Resettlement and Incumbent Upgrading in American Neighborhoods*. Lexington, MA: Lexington Books.

Clay, Phillip L., and Robert M. Hollister. 1983. *Neighborhood Policy and Planning*. Lexington, MA: Lexington Books.

Cloud, Cathy, and George C. Galster. 1993. "What Do We Know about Racial Discrimination in Mortgage Markets?" *Review of Black Political Economy* 22:101–120.

Clougherty, Jane E., and Laura D. Kubzansky. 2009. "A Framework for Examining Social Stress and Susceptibility to Air Pollution in Respiratory Health." *Environmental Health Perspectives* 117(9): 1351–1358.

Coate, Douglas, and Richard W. Schwester. 2011. "Black-White Appreciation of Owner-Occupied Homes in Upper Income Suburban Integrated Communities: The Cases of Maplewood and Montclair, New Jersey." *Journal of Housing Research* 20(2): 127–139.

Cohen, Deborah, Bonnie Ghosh-Dastidar, Richard Scribner, Angela Miu, Molly Scott, Paul Robinson, Thomas Farley, Ricky Bluthenthal, and Didra Brown-Taylor. 2006. "Alcohol Outlets, Gonorrhea, and the Los Angeles Civil Unrest: A Longitudinal Analysis." *Social Science and Medicine* 62(12): 3062–3071.

Collinson, Robert A., and Peter Ganong. 2016. "The Incidence of Housing Voucher Generosity." Available at http://dx.doi.org/10.2139/ssrn.2255799.

Colwell, Peter F. 1991. "Economic Views of Segregation and Integration," *ORER Letter* (summer) 8–11. Champaign-Urbana: Office of Real Estate Research, University of Illinois.

Condron, Dennis J., and Vincent J. Roscigno. 2003. "Disparities Within: Unequal Spending and Achievement in an Urban School District." *Sociology of Education* 76(1): 18–36.

Conley, Dalton. 1999. *Being Black, Living in the Red: Race, Wealth, and Social Policy in America.* Berkeley and Los Angeles: University of California Press.

Coulson, N. Edward, Seok-Joon Hwang, and Susumu Imai. 2003. "The Benefits of Owner-Occupation in Neighborhoods." *Journal of Housing Research* 14(1): 21–48.

Coulson, N. Edward, and Herman Li. 2013. "Measuring the External Benefits of Homeownership." *Journal of Urban Economics* 77:57–67.

Coulton, Claudia J. 2012. "Defining Neighborhoods for Research and Policy." *Cityscape* 14(2): 231–236.

Coulton, Claudia J., Tsui Chan, and Kristen Mikelbank. 2011. "Finding Place in Community Change Initiatives: Using GIS to Uncover Resident Perceptions of Their Neighborhoods." *Journal of Community Practice* 19(1): 10–28.

Coulton, Claudia J., M. Zane Jennings, and Tsui Chan. 2012. "How Big Is My Neighborhood? Individual and Contextual Effects on Perceptions of Neighborhood Scale." *American Journal of Community Psychology* 51(1-2): 140–150.

Coulton, Claudia J., Jill Korbin, Tsui Chan, and Marilyn Su. 2001. "Mapping Residents' Perceptions of Neighborhood Boundaries: A Methodological Note." *American Journal of Community Psychology* 29(2): 371–383.

Courant, Paul N., and John M. Yinger. 1977. "On Models of Racial Prejudice and Urban Residential Structure." *Journal of Urban Economics* 4(3): 272–291.

Crane, Jonathan. 1991. "The Epidemic Theory of Ghettos and Neighborhood Effects on Dropping Out and Teenage Childbearing." *American Journal of Sociology* 96:1226–1259.

Cromwell, Brian. 1990. "Prointegrative Subsidies and Their Effect on the Housing Market: Do Race-Based Loans Work?" Working paper #9018, Federal Reserve Bank of Cleveland.

Crowder, Kyle. 2000. "The Racial Context of White Mobility: An Individual-Level Assessment of the White Flight Hypothesis." *Social Science Research* 29(2): 223–257.

Crowder, Kyle, and Scott J. South. 2003. "Neighborhood Distress and School Dropout: The Variable Significance of Community Context." *Social Science Research* 32(4): 659–698.

Crowder, Kyle, Scott J. South, and Erick Chavez. 2006. "Wealth, Race, and Inter-Neighborhood Migration." *American Sociological Review* 71(1): 72–94.

Crowder, Kyle, and Jay Teachman. 2004. "Do Residential Conditions Explain the Relationship between Living Arrangements and Adolescent Behavior?" *Journal of Marriage and the Family* 66(3): 721–738.

Currie, Janet. 2011. "Health and Residential Location." In *Neighborhood and Life Chances: How Place Matters in Modern America,* edited by Harriett B. Newburger, Eugenie L. Birch, and Susan M. Wachter, 3–17. Philadelphia: University of Pennsylvania Press.

Currie, Janet, and Matthew Neidell. 2005. "Air Pollution and Infant Health: What Can We Learn from California's Recent Experience?" *Quarterly Journal of Economics* 120(3): 1003–1030.

Cutler, David M., and Edward Glaeser. 1997. "Are Ghettos Good or Bad?" *Quarterly Journal of Economics* 112(3): 827–872.

Cutler, David M., Edward L. Glaeser, and Jacob L. Vigdor. 1999. "The Rise and Decline of the American Ghetto." *Journal of Political Economy* 107(3): 455–506.

———. 2008. "When Are Ghettos Bad? Lessons from Immigrant Segregation in the United States." *Journal of Urban Economics* 63(3): 759–774.

Damm, Anna Piil. 2009. "Ethnic Enclaves and Immigrant Labor Market Outcomes: Quasi-Experimental Evidence." *Journal of Labor Economics* 27(2): 281–314.

———. 2014. "Neighborhood Quality and Labor Market Outcomes: Evidence from a Quasi-Random Neighborhood Assignment of Immigrants." *Journal of Urban Economics* 79: 139–166.

Damm, Anna Piil, and Christian Dustmann. 2014. "Does Growing Up in a High Crime Neighborhood Affect Youth Criminal Behavior?" *American Economic Review* 104(6): 1806–1832.

Darden, Joe T., and Sameh M. Kamel. 2000. "Black Residential Segregation in the City and Suburbs of Detroit: Does Socioeconomic Status Matter?" *Journal of Urban Affairs* 22(1): 1–13.

Darling. Nancy, and Lawrence Steinberg. 1997. "Assessing Neighborhood Effects Using Individual-Level Data." In *Neighborhood Poverty: Vol. 2. Policy Implications in Studying Neighborhoods*, edited by Jeanne Brooks-Gunn, Greg J. Duncan, and J. Lawrence Aber, 120–131. New York: Russell Sage Foundation.

Darrah, Jennifer, and Stefanie DeLuca. 2014. "'Living Here Has Changed My Whole Perspective': How Escaping Inner-City Poverty Shapes Neighborhood and Housing Choice." *Journal of Policy Analysis and Management* 33(2): 350–84.

Dastrup, Samuel, and Ingrid Gould Ellen. 2016. "Linking Residents to Opportunity: Gentrification and Public Housing." *Cityscape* 18(3): 87–107.

Data Driven Detroit. 2010. Detroit Residential Parcel Survey. Accessed at http://datadrivendetroit.org.

Dawkins, Casey. 2004. "Recent Evidence on the Continuing Causes of Black-White Residential Segregation." *Journal of Urban Affairs* 26(3): 379–400.

———. 2017. "Putting Equality in Place: The Normative Foundations of Geographic Equality of Opportunity." *Housing Policy Debate* 27(6): 897–912.

———. 2018. "Toward Common Ground in the US Fair Housing Debate." *Journal of Urban Affairs* 40(4): 475–493.

Dawkins, Casey, Qing Shen, and Thomas Sanchez. 2005. "Race, Space and Unemployment Duration." *Journal of Urban Economics* 58(1): 91–113.

DeBartolomé, Charles A.M. 1990. "Equilibrium and Inefficiency in a Community Model with Peer Group Effects." *Journal of Political Economy* 98(1): 110–133.

DeBartolomé, Charles A.M., and Stephen L. Ross. 2003. "Equilibria with Local Governments and Commuting: Income Sorting vs. Income Mixing." *Journal of Urban Economics* 54(1): 1–20.

———. 2007. "The Race to the Suburb: The Location of the Poor in a Metropolitan Area." Economics Department, University of Colorado at Boulder. Accessed at https://ssrn.com/abstract=1011203.

De la Roca, Jorge, Ingrid Gould Ellen, and Katherine M. O'Regan. 2014. "Race and Neighborhoods in the 21st Century: What Does Segregation Mean Today?" *Regional Science and Urban Economics* 47:138–151.

Della Vigna, Stefano. 2009. "Psychology and Economics: Evidence from the Field." *Journal of Economic Literature* 47(2): 315–372.

DeLuca, Stefanie, and Peter Rosenblatt. 2017. "Walking Away from the Wire: Housing Mobility and Neighborhood Opportunity in Baltimore." *Housing Policy Debate* 27(4): 519–546.

DeLuca, Stefanie, Greg J. Duncan, Michere Keels, and Ruby M. Mendenhall. 2010. "Gautreaux Mothers and Their Children: An Update." *Housing Policy Debate* 20(1): 7–25.

DeLuca, Stefanie, Philip M. E. Garboden, and Peter Rosenblatt. 2013. "Segregating Shelter: How Housing Policies Shape the Residential Locations of Low-Income Minority Families." *Annals of the American Academy of Political and Social Science* 647(1): 268–299.

DeMarco, Donald, and George Galster. 1993. "Prointegrative Policy: Theory and Practice." *Journal of Urban Affairs* 15(2): 141–60.

Deng, Lan, Eric Seymour, Margaret Dewar, and June Manning Thomas. 2018. "Saving Strong Neighborhoods from the Destruction of Mortgage Foreclosures: The Impact of Community-Based Efforts in Detroit, Michigan." *Housing Policy Debate* 28(2): 153–179.

Denton, Nancy A., and Douglas S. Massey. 1991. "Patterns of Neighborhood Transition in a Multiethnic World: US Metropolitan Areas, 1970–1980." *Demography* 28(1): 41–63.

Desmond, Matthew. 2016. *Evicted: Poverty and Profit in the American City*. New York: Broadway Books.

Detroit Blight Removal Task Force. 2014. Detroit Blight Removal Task Force Plan. Accessed at http://report.timetoendblight.org/.

Devaney, Michael, and William B. Rayburn. 1993. "Neighborhood Racial Transition and Housing Returns: A Portfolio Approach." *Journal of Real Estate Research* 8(2): 239–252.

Diamond, Michael. 2012. "Deconcentrating Poverty: Deconstructing a Theory and the Failure of Hope." In *Community, Home, And Identity*, 47–76. Farnham, UK: Ashgate.

Dieleman, Frans M. 2001. "Modelling Residential Mobility: A Review of Recent Trends in Research." *Journal of Housing and the Built Environment* 16(3): 249–265.

Dietz, Robert D. 2002. "The Estimation of Neighborhood Effects in the Social Sciences." *Social Science Research* 31(4): 539–575.

Dietz, Robert D., and Donald Haurin. 2003. "The Social and Private Micro-Level Consequences of Homeownership." *Journal of Urban Economics* 54: 401–450.

Dillman, Keri-Nicole, Keren Mertens Horn, and Ann Verrilli. 2017. "The What, Where, and When of Place-Based Housing Policy's Neighborhood Effects." *Housing Policy Debate* 27(2): 282–305.

Ding, Chengri, and Gerrit Knaap. 2003. "Property Values in Inner-City Neighborhoods: The Effects of Homeownership, Housing Investment and Economic Development." *Housing Policy Debate* 13(4): 701–727.

Ding, Lei. 2014. "Information Externalities and Residential Mortgage Lending in the Hardest Hit Housing Market: The Case of Detroit." *Cityscape* 16(1): 233–252.

Ding, Lei, Jackelyn Hwang, and Eileen Divringi. 2016. "Gentrification and Residential Mobility in Philadelphia," *Regional Science and Urban Economics* 61(1): 38–51.

Do, Phuong, Lu Wang, and Michael Elliott. 2013. "Investigating the Relationship between Neighborhood Poverty and Mortality Risk: A Marginal Structural Modeling Approach." *Social Science & Medicine* 91:58–66.

Doff, Wenda. 2010. *Puzzling Neighbourhood Effects*. Amsterdam: IOS Press.

Downey, Liam, and Brian Hawkins. 2008. "Race, Income, and Environmental Inequality in the United States." *Sociological Perspectives* 51(4): 759–781.

Downs, Anthony. 1981. *Neighborhoods and Urban Development*. Washington: Brookings Institution.

Dreier, Peter, John Mollenkopf, and Todd Swanstrom. 2014. *Place Matters: Metropolitics for the Twenty-First Century*. 3rd ed. Lawrence: University Press of Kansas.

Dubow, Eric F., Stanley Edwards, and Maria F. Ippolito. 1997. "Life Stressors, Neighborhood

Disadvantages, and Resources: A Focus on Inner City Children's Adjustment." *Journal of Clinical Child Psychology* 26(2): 130–144.

Duncan, Greg J., and J. Lawrence Aber. 1997. "Neighborhood Models and Measures." In *Neighborhood Poverty, Volume 1: Context and Consequences for Children*, edited by Jeanne Brooks-Gunn, Greg J. Duncan, and J. Lawrence Aber, 219–250. New York: Russell Sage Foundation.

Duncan, Greg J., Jeanne Brooks-Gunn, and J. Lawrence Aber, eds. 1997. *Neighborhood Poverty: Context and Consequences for Children*, vol. 1. New York: Russell Sage Foundation.

Duncan, Greg J., James Patrick Connell, and Pamela Klebanov. 1997. "Conceptual and Methodological Issues in Estimating the Causal Effects of Neighborhood and Family Conditions on Individual Development." In *Neighborhood Poverty: Context and Consequences for Children*, edited by Jeanne Brooks-Gunn, Greg J. Duncan, and J. Lawrence Aber, 219–250. New York: Russell Sage Foundation.

Duncan, Greg J., and Deborah Laren. 1990. *Neighborhood and Family Correlates of Low Birthweight: Preliminary Results on Births to Black Women from the PSID Geocode File*. Ann Arbor, MI: Survey Research Center.

Dunning, Richard J. 2017. "Competing Notions of Search for Home: Behavioural Economics and Housing Markets." *Housing, Theory, and Society* 34(1): 21–37.

Earls, Felton, Jacqueline McGuire, and Sharon Shay. 1994. "Evaluating a Community Intervention to Reduce the Risk of Child Abuse: Methodological Strategies in Conducting Neighborhood Surveys." *Child Abuse and Neglect* 18(5): 473–485.

Ebenstein, Avraham, Victor Lavy, and Sefi Roth. 2016. "The Long-Run Economic Consequences of High- Stakes Examinations: Evidence from Transitory Variation in Pollution." *American Economic Journal: Applied Economics* 8(4): 36–65.

Eberts, Randall W., and Timothy J. Gronberg. 1981. "Jurisdictional Homogeneity and the Tiebout Hypothesis." *Journal of Urban Economics* 10(2): 227–239.

Edin, Per-Anders, Peter Fredriksson and Olof Åslund. 2003. "Ethnic Enclaves and the Economic Success of Immigrants: Evidence from a Natural Experiment." *Quarterly Journal of Economics* 118(1): 329–357.

Elder, Glen H., Jacquelynne S. Eccles, Monika Ardelt, and Sarah Lord. 1995. "Inner-City Parents under Economic Pressure: Perspectives on the Strategies of Parenting." *Journal of Marriage and the Family* 57(3): 771–784.

Ellen, Ingrid Gould. 2000a. "Is Segregation Bad for Your Health? The Case of Low Birth Weight." *Brookings-Wharton Papers on Urban Affairs*, 203–238.

Ellen, Ingrid Gould. 2000b. *Sharing America's Neighborhoods: The Prospects for Stable Racial Integration*. Cambridge, MA: Harvard University Press.

Ellen, Ingrid Gould, and Lei Ding. 2016. "Guest Editors' Introduction: Advancing Our Understanding of Gentrification." *Cityscape* 18(3): 3–8.

Ellen, Ingrid Gould, Keren Horn, and Katherine O'Regan. 2012. "Pathways to Integration: Examining Changes in the Prevalence of Racially Integrated Neighborhoods." *Cityscape* 14(3): 33–53.

Ellen, Ingrid Gould, Johanna Lacoe, and Claudia Ayanna Sharygin. 2012. "Do Foreclosures Cause Crime?" *Journal of Urban Economics* 74: 59–70.

Ellen, Ingrid Gould, Tod Mijanovich, and Keri-Nicole Dillman. 2001. "Neighborhood Effects on Health: Exploring the Links and Assessing the Evidence." *Journal of Urban Affairs* 23(3-4): 391–408.

Ellen, Ingrid Gould, and Brenan O'Flaherty. 2013. "How New York Housing Policies Are Different—and Maybe Why." In *New York City-Los Angeles: The Uncertain Future*, edited by Andrew Beveridge and David Halle, 286–309. New York: Oxford University Press.

Ellen, Ingrid Gould, and Katherine O'Regan. 2008. "Reversal of Fortunes? Lower-Income Urban Neighbourhoods in the US in the 1990s." *Urban Studies* 45(4): 845–869.

———. 2011. "How Low-Income Neighborhoods Change: Entry, Exit, and Enhancement." *Regional Science and Urban Economics* 41(2): 89–97.

Ellen, Ingrid Gould, Michael H. Schill, Scott Susin, and Amy Ellen Schwartz. 2001. "Building Homes, Reviving Neighborhoods: Spillovers from Subsidized Construction of Owner-Occupied Housing in New York City." *Journal of Housing Research* 12(2): 185–216.

Ellen, Ingrid Gould, Justin P. Steil, and Jorge De la Roca. 2016. "The Significance of Segregation in the 21st Century." *City & Community* 15(1): 8–13.

Ellen, Ingrid Gould, and Margery Austin Turner. 1997. "Does Neighborhood Matter? Assessing Recent Evidence." *Housing Policy Debate* 8(4): 833–866.

———. 2003. "Do Neighborhoods Matter and Why?" In *Choosing a Better Life? Evaluating the Moving to Opportunity Experiment*, edited by John M. Goering and Judith D. Feins, 313–338. Washington: Urban Institute Press.

Elliott, Meagan. 2017. "Cultural Displacement: Making Sense of Population Growth alongside Decline in Contemporary Detroit." Unpublished PhD dissertation, Department of Sociology, University of Michigan.

Emerson, Michael O., Karen J. Chai, and George Yancey. 2001. "Does Race Matter in Residential Segregation? Exploring the Preferences of White Americans." *American Sociological Review* 66(6): 922–935.

Emerson, Michael O., Rachel Tolbert Kimbro, and George Yancey. 2002. "Contact Theory Extended: The Effects of Prior Racial Contact on Current Social Ties." *Social Science Quarterly* 83(3): 745–761.

Engle, Kathleen C., and Patricia A. McCoy. 2008. "From Credit Denial to Predatory Lending: The Challenge of Sustaining Minority Homeownership." In *Segregation: The Rising Costs for America*, edited by James H. Carr and Nandinee K. Kutty, 81–124. New York: Routledge.

Ennett, Susan T., Robert L. Flewelling, Richard C. Lindrooth, and Edward C. Norton. 1997. "School and Neighborhood Characteristics Associated with School Rates of Alcohol, Cigarette, and Marijuana Use." *Journal of Health and Social Behavior* 38(1): 55–71.

Epple, Dennis, Brett Gordon, and Holger Sieg. 2010. "A New Approach to Estimating the Production Function for Housing." *American Economic Review* 100(3): 905–924.

Epple, Dennis, and Thomas Romer. 1991. "Mobility and Redistribution." *Journal of Political Economy*, 99(4): 828–858.

Erikson, Robert, and Jan Jonsson. 1996. "Explaining Class Inequality in Education: The Swedish Test Case." In *Can Education Be Equalized? The Swedish Case in Comparative Perspective*, edited by Robert Erikson and Jan Jonsson, 1–63. Boulder, CO: Westview Press.

Faber, Jacob. 2013. "Racial Dynamics of Subprime Mortgage Lending at the Peak." *Housing Policy Debate* 23(2): 328–349.

Faber, Jacob, and Ingrid Gould Ellen. 2016. "Race and the Housing Cycle: Differences in Home Equity Trends among Long-Term Homeowners." *Housing Policy Debate* 26(3): 456–473.

Farley, Reynolds, Sheldon Danziger, and Harry J. Holzer. 2000. *Detroit Divided*. A volume in the Multi-City Study of Urban Inequality. New York: Russell Sage Foundation.

Farley, Reynolds, Howard Schuman, Suzanne Bianchi, Diane Colastano, and Shirley

Hatchett. 1978. "Chocolate City, Vanilla Suburbs: Will the Trend toward Racially Separate Communities Continue?" *Social Science Research* 7(4): 319–344.

Farr, Nick, and Cushing Dolbeare. 1996. "Childhood Lead Poisoning: Solving a Health and Housing Problem." *Cityscape* 2(3): 176–182.

Faules, Don, and Dennis Alexander. 1978. *Communication and Social Behavior: A Symbolic Interaction Perspective.* Reading, MA: Addison-Wesley.

Fauth, Rebecca, Tama Leventhal, and Jeanne Brooks-Gunn. 2007. "Welcome to the Neighborhood? Long-Term Impacts of Moving to Low-Poverty Neighborhoods on Poor Children's and Adolescents' Outcomes." *Journal of Research on Adolescence* 17(2): 249–284.

Feijten, Peteke, and Maarten van Ham. 2009. "Neighbourhood Change . . . Reason to Leave?" *Urban Studies* 46(10): 2103–2122.

Fellowes, Matt. 2008. "Reducing the High Cost of Being Poor." Testimony before the House Committee on Financial Services, Subcommittee on Housing and Community Opportunity, March 8.

Fellowes, Matt and Mia Mabanta. 2008. *Banking on Wealth: America's New Retail Banking Infrastructure and Its Wealth-Building Potential.* Washington: Brookings Institution Metropolitan Policy Program.

Fernandez, Roberto, and David Harris. 1992. "Social Isolation and the Underclass." In *Drugs, Crime, and Social Isolation: Barriers to Urban Opportunity,* edited by Adele V. Harrell and George E. Peterson, 257–293. Washington: Urban Institute.

Fick, Ana Correa, and Sarah Moody Thomas. 1996. "Growing Up in a Violent Environment: Relationship to Health-Related Beliefs and Behavior." *Youth and Society* 27(2): 136–147.

Firebaugh, Glenn, and Chad R. Farrell. 2016. "Still Large, but Narrowing: The Sizable Decline in Racial Neighborhood Inequality in Metropolitan America, 1980–2010." *Demography* 53(1): 139–64.

Firebaugh, Glenn, John Iceland, Stephen A. Matthews, and Barrett A. Lee. 2015. "Residential Inequality: Significant Findings and Policy Implications." *Annals of the American Academy of Political and Social Science* 660:360–366.

Fischel, William A. 2001. *The Homevoter Hypothesis: How Home Values Influence Local Government Taxation, School Finance, and Land Use Policies.* Cambridge, MA: Harvard University Press.

Fischer, Claude. 1982. *To Dwell among Friends.* Chicago: University of Chicago Press.

Fischer, Mary, and Douglas Massey. 2004. "The Ecology of Racial Discrimination." *City & Community* 3(3): 221–241.

Fishbein, Martin, and Icek Ajzen. 1975. *Belief, Attitude, Intention and Behavior.* Reading, MA: Addison-Wesley.

Fisher, Ernest M, and Louis Winnick. 1951. "A Reformulation of the Filtering Concept." *Journal of Social Issues* 7(1-2): 47–58.

Flippen, Chenoa A. 2004. "Unequal Returns to Housing Investments? A Study of Real Housing Appreciation among Black, White, and Hispanic Households." *Social Forces* 82(4): 1527–1555.

Forrest, Ray and Ade Kearns. 2001. "Social Cohesion, Social Capital and the Neighbourhood." *Urban Studies* 38(12): 2125–2143.

Fossett, Mark. 2011. "Generative Models of Segregation: Investigating Model-Generated Patterns of Residential Segregation by Ethnicity and Socioeconomic Status." *Journal of Mathematical Sociology* 35(1–3): 114–145.

Franz, P. 1982. "Zur Analyse der Bezlehung von sozialokologischen Prozessen und socialen Problemen." In *Zur Raumbezogenheit socialer Probleme*, edited by L. Vaskovics, 96–119. Opladen, Germany: Springer.

Fraser, James C., Robert J. Chaskin, and Joshua Theodore Bazuin. 2013. "Making Mixed-Income Neighborhoods Work for Low-Income Households. *Cityscape* 15(2): 83–100.

Freeman, Lance. 2005. "Displacement or Succession? Residential Mobility in Gentrifying Neighborhoods." *Urban Affairs Review* 40(4): 463–491.

———. 2006. *There Goes the 'Hood: Views of Gentrification from the Ground Up*. Philadelphia: Temple University Press.

———. 2012. "The Impact of Source of Income Laws on Voucher Utilization." *Housing Policy Debate* 22(2): 297–318.

Freeman, Lance, and Hillary Botein. 2002. "Subsidized Housing and Neighborhood Impacts: A Theoretical Discussion and Review of the Evidence." *Journal of Planning Literature* 16(3): 359–378.

Freeman, Lance, and Frank Braconi. 2004. "Gentrification and Displacement: New York City in the 1990s." *Journal of the American Planning Association* 70(1): 39–52.

Freeman, Lance, and Yunjing Li. 2014. "Do Source of Income Anti-Discrimination Laws Facilitate Access to Less Disadvantaged Neighborhoods?" *Housing Studies* 29(1): 88–107.

Freeman, Lance, and Jenny Schuetz. 2017. "Producing Affordable Housing in Rising Markets: What Works?" *Cityscape* 19(1): 217–236.

Freund, David M. P. 2007. *Colored Property: State Policy and White Racial Politics in Suburban America*. Chicago: University of Chicago Press.

Friedrichs, Jürgen. 1998. "Do Poor Neighborhoods Make their Residents Poorer? Context Effects of Poverty Neighborhoods on their Residents." In *Empirical Poverty Research in a Comparative Perspective*, edited by Hans-Jürgen Andreß, 77–99. Aldershot, UK: Ashgate.

Fry, Richard, and Paul Taylor. 2012. *The Rise of Residential Segregation by Income*. Washington: Pew Research Center.

Fuller, Bruce, Casey Coonerty, Fran Kipnis, and Yvonne Choong. 1997. "An Unfair Head Start: California Families Face Gaps in Preschool and Child Care Availability: Second Edition." Education Resources Information Center. Accessed at https://eric.ed.gov/?id =ED417799.

Fusfeld, Daniel R. and Timothy Bates. 1984. *The Political Economy of the Black Ghetto*. Carbondale and Edwardsville: Southern Illinois University Press.

Gabriel, Stuart, and Jennifer Wolch. 1984. "Spillover Effects of Human Service Facilities in a Racially Segmented Housing Market." *Journal of Urban Economics* 16(3): 339–350.

Gallagher, Mari. 2006. *Examining the Impact of Food Deserts on Public Health in Chicago*. Chicago: Mari Gallagher Research and Consulting Group.

Galster, George C. 1977. "A Bid-Rent Analysis of Housing Market Discrimination," *American Economic Review* 67 (2): 144–155.

———. 1982. "Black and White Preferences for Neighborhood Racial Composition." *American Real Estate and Urban Economics Association Journal* 10(1): 39–66.

———. 1983. "Empirical Evidence on Cross-Tenure Differences in Home Maintenance and Conditions." *Land Economics* 59(1): 107–113.

———. 1987a. *Homeowners & Neighborhood Reinvestment*. Durham, NC: Duke University Press.

———. 1987b. "Residential Segregation and Interracial Economic Disparities: A Simultaneous-Equations Approach." *Journal of Urban Economics* 21(1): 22–44.

———. 1988a. "Assessing the Causes of Residential Segregation: A Methodological Critique." *Journal of Urban Affairs* 10(4): 395–407.

———. 1988b. "Residential Segregation in American Cities: A Contrary Review." *Population Research and Policy Review* 7(2): 93–112.

———. 1990a. "Neighborhood Racial Change, Segregationist Sentiments, and Affirmative Marketing Policies." *Journal of Urban Economics* 27(3): 344–361.

———. 1990b. "Racial Steering by Real Estate Agents: Mechanisms and Motives." *Review of Black Political Economy* 19(39): 39–63.

———. 1990c. "White Flight from Racially Integrated Neighbourhoods in the 1970s: The Cleveland Experience." *Urban Studies* 27(3): 385–399.

———. 1990d. "Federal Fair Housing Policy: The Great Misapprehension," In *Building Foundations: Housing and Federal Policy*, edited by Denise DiPasquale and Langley C. Keyes, 137–157. Philadelphia: University of Pennsylvania Press.

———. 1991. "Housing Discrimination and Urban Poverty of African-Americans." *Journal of Housing Research* 2(2): 87–122.

———. 1992a. "A Cumulative Causation Model of the Underclass: Implications for Urban Economic Development Policy." In *The Metropolis in Black and White: Place, Power, and Polarization*, edited by George C. Galster and Edward W. Hill, 190–215. New Bruswick, NJ: Rutgers University Press / Transaction Publishers.

———. 1992b. "Research on Discrimination in Housing and Mortgage Markets: Assessment and Future Directions." *Housing Policy Debate* 3(2): 639–684.

———. 1998. "A Stock/Flow Model of Defining Racially Integrated Neighborhoods." *Journal of Urban Affairs* 20(1): 43–51.

———. 2002. "An Economic Efficiency Analysis of Deconcentrating Poverty Populations." *Journal of Housing Economics* 11(4): 303–329.

———. 2003. "MTO's Impact on Sending and Receiving Neighborhoods." In *Choosing a Better Life? Evaluating the Moving to Opportunity Social Experiment*, edited by John Goering and Judith Feins, 365–382. Washington: Urban Institute Press.

———. 2004. "The Effects of Affordable and Multifamily Housing on Market Values of Nearby Homes." In *Growth Management and Affordable Housing: Do They Conflict*, edited by Anthony Downs, 176–201. Washington: Brookings Institution Press.

———. 2005. "Consequences from the Redistribution of Urban Poverty during the 1990s: A Cautionary Tale." *Economic Development Quarterly* 19(2): 119–125.

———. 2006. "Do Home Insurance Base Premium-Setting Policies Create Disparate Racial Impacts? The Case of Large Insurance Companies in Ohio." *Journal of Insurance Regulation* 24 (4): 7–20.

———. 2008. "Quantifying the Effect of Neighbourhood on Individuals: Challenges, Alternative Approaches and Promising Directions." *Journal of Applied Social Science Studies [Schmollers Jahrbuch / Zeitscrift fur Wirtschafts- und Sozialwissenschaften]* 128(1): 7–48.

———. 2012a. *Driving Detroit: The Quest for Respect in the Motor City*. Philadelphia, PA: University of Pennsylvania Press.

———. 2012b. "The Mechanism(s) of Neighbourhood Effects: Theory, Evidence, and Policy Implications." In *Neighbourhood Effects Research: New Perspectives*, edited by Maarten van Ham, David Manley, Nick Bailey, Ludi Simpson, and Duncan Maclennan, 23–56. Dordrecht, Netherlands: Springer.

———. 2012c. "Urban Opportunity Structure and Racial/Ethnic Polarization." In *Research on Schools, Neighborhoods, and Communities: Toward Civic Responsibility*, edited by William F. Tate IV, 47–66. Lanham, MD: Rowman and Littlefield.

———. 2013. US Assisted Housing Programs and Poverty Deconcentration: A Critical Geographic Review. In *Neighbourhood Effects or Neighbourhood Based Problems?: A Policy*

Context, edited by David Manley, Maarten van Ham, Nick Bailey, Ludi Simpson, and Duncan Maclennan, 215–249. Dordrecht, Netherlands: Springer.

———. 2014. "Nonlinear and Threshold Aspects of Neighborhood Effects." In *Soziale Kontexte und soziale Mechanismen [Social Contexts and Social Mechanisms]*, edited by Jurgen Friedrichs and Alexandra Nonnenmacher, 117–133. Wiesbaden, Germany: Springer.

———. 2017. "People versus Place, People and Place, or More? New Directions for Housing Policy." *Housing Policy Debate* 27(2): 261–265.

Galster, George C., Roger Andersson, and Sako Musterd. 2010. "Who Is Affected by Neighbourhood Income Mix? Gender, Age, Family, Employment and Income Differences." *Urban Studies* 47(14): 2915–2944.

———. 2015. "Are Males' Incomes Influenced by the Income Mix of Their Male Neighbors? Explorations into Nonlinear and Threshold Effects in Stockholm." *Housing Studies* 30(2): 315–343.

———. 2017. "Neighborhood Social Mix and Adults' Income Trajectories: Longitudinal Evidence from Stockholm," *Geografisker Annaler B Human Geography* 98(2): 145–170.

Galster, George C., Roger Andersson, Sako Musterd, and Timo Kauppinen. 2008. "Does Neighborhood Income Mix Affect Earnings of Adults?" *Journal of Urban Economics* 63(3): 858–870.

Galster, George C., and Jason A. Booza. 2007. "The Rise of the Bipolar Neighborhood." *Journal of the American Planning Association* 73(4): 421–435.

———. 2008. "Are Home and Auto Insurance Policies Excessively Priced in Cities? Recent Evidence from Michigan." *Journal of Urban Affairs* 30(5): 507–527.

Galster, George C., Jason A. Booza, and Jackie M. Cutsinger. "Income Diversity within Neighborhoods and Very Low-Income Families." *Cityscape* 10(2): 257–300.

Galster, George C., Jason A. Booza, Jackie M. Cutsinger, Kurt Metzger, and Up Lim. 2005. *Low-Income Households in Mixed-Income Neighborhoods: Extent, Trends, and Determinants.* Washington: Office of Policy Development and Research, US Department of Housing and Urban Development.

Galster, George C., Jackie M. Cutsinger, and Up Lim. 2007. "Are Neighborhoods Self-Stabilizing? Exploring Endogenous Dynamics." *Urban Studies* 44(1): 1–19.

Galster, George C., Jackie M. Cutsinger, and Ron Malega. 2008. "The Costs of Concentrated Poverty: Neighborhood Property Markets and the Dynamics of Decline." In *Revisiting Rental Housing: Policies, Programs, and Priorities*, edited by Nicolas P. Retsinas and Eric S. Belsky, 93–113. Washington: Brookings Institution Press.

Galster, George C., and Erin Godfrey. 2005. "By Words and Deeds: Racial Steering by Real Estate Agents in the US in 2000." *Journal of the American Planning Association* 71(3): 1–19.

Galster, George C., Chris Hayes, and Jennifer Johnson. 2005. "Identifying Robust, Parsimonious Neighborhood Indicators." *Journal of Planning Education and Research* 24(3): 265–280.

Galster, George C., and Lina Hedman. 2013. "Measuring Neighborhood Effects Non-Experimentally: How Much Do Alternative Methods Matter?" *Housing Studies* 28(3): 473–498.

Galster, George C., and Gary W. Hesser. 1981. "Residential Satisfaction: Compositional and Contextual Correlates." *Environment and Behavior* 13(6): 735–758.

———. 1982. "The Social Neighborhood: An Unspecified Factor in Homeowner Maintenance?" *Urban Affairs Quarterly* 18(2): 235–254.

———. 1988. "Evaluating and Redesigning Subsidy Policies for Home Rehabilitation." *Policy Sciences* 21(1): 67–95.

Galster, George C., and W. Mark Keeney. 1988. "Race, Residence, Discrimination, and Economic Opportunity: Modeling the Nexus of Urban Racial Phenomena." *Urban Affairs Quarterly* 24(1): 87–117.

Galster, George C. and Sean Killen. 1995. "The Geography of Metropolitan Opportunity: A Reconnaissance and Conceptual Framework." *Housing Policy Debate* 6(1): 7–44.

Galster, George C., Heather MacDonald, and Jacqueline Nelson. 2018. "What Explains the Differential Treatment of Renters Based on Ethnicity? New Evidence from Sydney." *Urban Affairs Review* 54(1): 107-136.

Galster, George C., David Marcotte, Marvin Mandell, Hal Wolman, and Nancy Augustine. 2007a. "The Impact of Childhood Neighborhood Poverty on Young Adult Outcomes." *Housing Studies* 22(5): 723–752.

———. 2007b. "The Impacts of Parental Homeownership on Children's Outcomes during Early Adulthood." *Housing Policy Debate* 18:785–827.

Galster, George C., and Ronald B. Mincy. 1993. "Understanding the Changing Fortunes of Metropolitan Neighborhoods." *Housing Policy Debate* 4(3): 303–352.

Galster, George C., Ronald B. Mincy, and Mitchell Tobin. 1997. "The Disparate Racial Neighborhood Impacts of Metropolitan Economic Restructuring." *Urban Affairs Review* 32(6): 797–824.

Galster, George C., and Stephen Peacock. 1985. "Urban Gentrification: Evaluating Alternative Indicators." *Social Indicators Research* 18(3): 321–337.

Galster, George C., Roberto G. Quercia, and Alvaro Cortes. 2000. "Identifying Neighborhood Thresholds: An Empirical Exploration," *Housing Policy Debate* 11(3): 701–732.

Galster, George C., Roberto G. Quercia, Alvaro Cortes, and Ron Malega. 2003. "The Fortunes of Poor Neighborhoods." *Urban Affairs Review* 39(2): 205–227.

Galster, George C., and Jerome Rothenberg. 1991. "Filtering in Urban Housing: A Graphical Analysis of a Quality-Segmented Market." *Journal of Planning Education and Research* 11(1): 37–50.

Galster, George C., Anna M. Santiago. 2006. "What's the Hood Got to Do with It? Parental Perceptions about How Neighborhood Mechanisms Affect Their Children." *Journal of Urban Affairs* 28(3): 201–226.

———. 2008 "Low-Income Homeownership as an Asset-Building Tool: What Can We Tell Policymakers?" In *Urban and Regional Policy and Its Effects*, edited by Margery A. Turner, Harold Wial, and Howard Wolman, 60–108. Washington: Brookings Institution Press.

———. 2017a. "Do Neighborhood Effects on Low-Income Minority Children Depend on Their Age? Evidence from a Public Housing Natural Experiment." *Housing Policy Debate* 27(4): 584–610.

———. 2017b. "Neighborhood Ethnic Composition and Outcomes for Low-Income Latino and African American Children." *Urban Studies* 54(2): 482–500.

Galster, George C., Anna M. Santiago, and Jessica Lucero. 2015. "Adrift at the Margins of Urban Society: What Role Does Neighborhood Play?" *Urban Affairs Review* 51(1): 10–45.

Galster, George C., Anna M. Santiago, Jessica Lucero, and Jackie Cutsinger. 2016. "Adolescent Neighborhood Context and Young Adult Economic Outcomes for Low-Income African Americans and Latinos." *Journal of Economic Geography* 16(2): 471–503.

Galster, George C., Anna M. Santiago, Robin Smith, and Peter Tatian. 1999. *Assessing Property Value Impacts of Dispersed Housing Subsidy Programs*. Washington: Office of Policy Development and Research, US Department of Housing and Urban Development.

Galster, George C., Anna M. Santiago and Lisa Stack. 2016. "Elementary School Difficulties of Low-Income Latino and African American Youth: The Role of Geographic Context." *Journal of Urban Affairs* 38(4): 477–502.

Galster, George C., Anna M. Santiago, Lisa Stack, and Jackie Cutsinger. 2016. "Neighborhood Effects on Secondary School Performance of Latino and African American Youth: Evidence from a Natural Experiment in Denver." *Journal of Urban Economics* 93:30–48.

Galster, George C., and Patrick Sharkey. 2017. "Spatial Foundations of Inequality: An Empirical Overview and Conceptual Model." *RSF: The Russell Sage Journal of the Social Sciences* 3(2): 1–34.

Galster, George C., and Peter Tatian. 2009. "Modeling Housing Appreciation Dynamics in Disadvantaged Neighborhoods." *Journal of Planning Education and Research* 29(1): 7–23.

Galster, George C., Peter Tatian, and John Accordino. 2006. "Targeting Investments for Neighborhood Revitalization." *Journal of the American Planning Association* 72(4): 457–474.

Galster, George C., Peter Tatian, Anna M. Santiago, Kathryn A. Pettit, and Robin Smith. 2003. *Why NOT in My Backyard? The Neighborhood Impacts of Assisted Housing.* New Brunswick, NJ: Rutgers University / Center for Urban Policy Research / Transaction Press.

Galster, George C., Peter Tatian, and Robin Smith. 1999. "The Impact of Neighbors Who Use Section 8 Certificates on Property Values." *Housing Policy Debate* 10(4): 879–917.

Galster, George C., and Lena Magnusson Turner. 2017. "Status Discrepancy as a Driver of Residential Mobility: Evidence from Oslo." *Environment and Planning A* 49(9): 2155–2175.

Galster, George C., Christopher Walker, Chris Hayes, Patrick Boxall, and Jennifer Johnson. 2004. "Measuring the Impact of Community Development Block Grant Spending on Urban Neighborhoods." *Housing Policy Debate* 15(4): 903–934.

Galster, George C., Doug Wissoker, and Wendy Zimmermann. 2001. "Testing for Discrimination in Home Insurance: Results from New York City and Phoenix." *Urban Studies* 38(1): 141–156.

Gans, Herbert. 1961. "The Balanced Community: Homogeneity or Heterogeneity in Residential Areas?" *Journal of the American Institute of Planners* 27(3): 176–184.

———. 1962. *The Urban Villagers.* New York: Free Press.

Ganz, M. L. 2000. "The Relationship between External Threats and Smoking in Central Harlem." *American Journal of Public Health* 90(3), 367–371.

Garner, Catherine L., and Stephen W. Raudenbush. 1991. "Neighborhood Effects on Educational Attainment: A Multilevel Analysis." *Sociology of Education* 64(4): 251–262.

Gennetian, Lisa A., Lisa Sanbonmatsu, and Jens Ludwig. 2011. "An Overview of Moving to Opportunity: A Random Assignment Housing Mobility Study in Five US Cities." In *Neighborhood and Life Chances: How Place Matters in Modern America*, edited by Harriet B. Newburger, Eugenie L. Birch, and Susan M. Wachter, 163–178. Philadelphia: University of Pennsylvania Press.

Gephart, Martha A. 1997. "Neighborhoods and Communities as Contexts for Development." In *Neighborhood Poverty, Volume 1: Context and Consequences for Children*, edited by Jeanne Brooks-Gunn, Greg J. Duncan, and J. Lawrence Aber, 1–43. New York: Russell Sage Foundation.

Geronimus, Arline T. 1992. "The Weathering Hypothesis and the Health of African-American Women and Infants: Evidence and Speculations." *Ethnicity & Disease* 2(3): 207–221.

Gibbons, Stephen, Olmo Silva, and Felix Weinhardt. 2013. "Everybody Needs Good Neighbours? Evidence from Students' Outcomes in England." *Economic Journal* 123(571): 831–874.

Gibbons, Stephen, Olmo Silva, and Felix Weinhardt. 2014. "Neighbourhood Turnover and Teenage Achievement." Discussion paper 8381, Institute for the Study of Labour (IZA), Bonn, Germany.

Giles, Michael W., Everett F. Cataldo, and Douglas S. Gatlin. 1975. "White Flight and Percent Black: The Tipping Point Re-examined." *Social Science Quarterly* 56(1): 85–92.

Ginther, Donna, Robert Haveman, and Barbara Wolfe. 2000. "Neighborhood Attributes as Determinants of Children's Outcomes." *Journal of Human Resources* 35(4): 603–642.

Glaeser, Edward L., Matthew E. Kahn, and Jordan Rappaport. 2008. "Why Do the Poor Live in Cities? The Role of Public Transportation." *Journal of Urban Economics* 63(1): 1–24.

Glaeser, Edward, and Jacob Vigdor. 2012. *The End of the Segregated Century: Racial Separation in America's Neighborhoods, 1890–2010*. New York: Manhattan Institute for Policy Research.

Glymour, M. Maria, Mahasin Mujahid, Qiong Wu, Kellee White, and Eric J. Tchetgen. 2010. "Neighborhood Disadvantage and Self-Assessed Health, Disability, and Depressive Symptoms: Longitudinal Results from the Health and Retirement Study." *American Journal of Epidemiology* 20(11): 856–61.

Goering, John M. 1978. "Neighborhood Tipping and Racial Transition: A Review of Social Science Evidence." *Journal of the American Institute of Planners* 44(1): 68–78.

Goering, John. M., ed. 1986. *Housing Desegregation and Federal Policy*. Chapel Hill: University of North Carolina Press.

Goering, John M., ed. 2007. *Fragile Rights within Cities: Government, Housing, and Fairness.* Lanham, MD: Rowman and Littlefield.

Goering, John M., and Judith Feins, eds. 2003. *Choosing a Better Life? Evaluating the Moving to Opportunity Experiment*. Washington: Urban Institute Press.

Goering, John M., Helene Stebbins, and Michael Siewert. 1995. "Promoting Housing Choice in HUD's Rental Assistance Programs: A Report to Congress." Office of Policy Development and Research, US Department of Housing and Urban Development.

Goering, John M., and Ron Wienk, eds. 1996. *Mortgage Lending, Racial Discrimination, and Federal Policy*. Washington: Urban Institute Press.

Goetz, Edward. 2003. *Clearing the Way: Deconcentrating the Poor in Urban America*. Washington: Urban Institute Press.

———. 2018. *The One-Way Street of Integration: Fair Housing and the Pursuit of Racial Justice in American Cities*. Ithaca, NY: Cornell University Press.

Goetze, Rolf. 1976. *Building Neighborhood Confidence*. Cambridge, MA: Ballinger.

———. 1983. *Rescuing the American Dream*. New York and London: Holmes and Meier Publishers.

Goetze, Rolf, and Kent W. Colton. 1980. "The Dynamics of Neighborhood: A Fresh Approach to Understanding Housing and Neighborhood Change." *Journal of the American Planning Association* 46(2): 184–194.

Golab, Caroline. 1982. "The Geography of Neighborhood." In *Neighborhoods in Urban America*, edited by R. Bayor, 70–85. Port Washington, NY: Kennikat.

Goodman, Allen. 1988. "An Econometric Model of Housing Price, Permanent Income, Tenure Choice, and Housing Demand." *Journal of Urban Economics* 23(3): 27–353.

———. 2005. "Central Cities and Housing Supply: Growth and Decline in US Cities." *Journal of Housing Economics* 14(4): 315–335.

Goodman, John, Jr. 1976. "Housing Consumption Disequilibrium and Local Residential Mobility." *Environment and Planning A* 8(8): 855–874.

Goodwin, Carol. 1979. *The Oak Park Strategy*. Chicago: University of Chicago Press.

Gotham, Kevin Fox. 2002. "Beyond Invasion and Succession: School Segregation, Real Estate Blockbusting, and the Political Economy of Neighborhood Racial Transition." *City & Community* 1(1): 83–111.

Graham, Bryan, and Patrick Sharkey. 2013. "Mobility and the Metropolis: The Relationship Between Inequality in Urban Communities and Economic Mobility." Washington: Pew Charitable Trusts.

Grannis, Richard. 2005. "T-Communities: Pedestrian Street Networks and Residential Segregation in Chicago, Los Angeles, and New York." *City & Community* 4(3): 295–321.

Granovetter, Mark. 1978. "Threshold Models of Collective Behavior." *American Journal of Sociology* 83(6): 1420–1443.

Granovetter, Mark, and Ronald Soong. 1986. "Threshold Models of Diversity: Chinese Restaurants, Residential Segregation, and the Spiral of Silence." *Journal: Sociological Methodology* 18:69–104.

Gray, Robert, and Steven Tursky. 1986. "Location and Racial/Ethnic Occupancy Patterns for HUD-Subsidized Family Housing in Ten Metropolitan Areas." In *Housing Desegregation and Federal Policy*, edited by John M. Goering, 232–252. Chapel Hill: University of North Carolina Press.

Green, Lawrence W., and Judith M. Ottoson. 1999. *Community and Population Health*, 8th ed. Boston: WCB/McGraw-Hill.

Green, Richard. K., and Stephen Malpezzi. 2003. *A Primer on US Housing Markets and Housing Policy*. Washington: Urban Institute Press.

Green, Richard K., Stephen Malpezzi, and Stephen K. Mayo. 2005. "Metropolitan-Specific Estimates of the Price Elasticity of Supply of Housing, and Their Sources." *American Economic Review* 95(2): 334–339.

Green, Richard, and Michelle White. 1997. "Measuring the Benefits of Homeowning: Effects on Children." *Journal of Urban Economics* 41:441–461.

Green, Richard, Garry Painter, and Michelle White. 2012. *Measuring the Benefits of Homeowning: Effects on Children Redux*. Washington: Research Institute for Housing America.

Greenlee, Andrew J. 2011. "A Different Lens: Administrative Perspectives on Portability in Illinois' Housing Choice Voucher Program." *Housing Policy Debate* 21(3): 377–403.

Greenberg, Mark T., Liliana J. Lenqua, John D. Coie, Ellen E. Pinderhughes. 1999. "Predicting Developmental Outcomes at School Entry Using Multiple-Risk Model: Four American Communities." *Developmental Psychology* 35(2): 403–417.

Greer, Scott. 1962. *The Emerging City*. New York: Free Press.

Grether, David, and Peter Mieszkowlki. 1980. "The Effects of Nonresidential Land Use on the Prices of Adjacent Housing: Some Estimates of Proximity Effects." *Journal of Urban Economics* 8(1): 1–15.

Grigsby, William G. 1963. *Housing Markets and Public Policy*. Philadelphia: University of Pennsylvania Press.

Grigsby, William G., Morton Baratz, George C. Galster, and Duncan Maclennan. 1987. *The Dynamics of Neighborhood Change and Decline*. Progress in Planning Series #28. London: Pergamon.

Grigsby, William G., and Steven C. Bourassa. 2004. "Section 8: The Time for Fundamental Program Change?" *Housing Policy Debate* 15(4): 805- 834.

Griswold, Nigel G., and Patricia E. Norris. 2007. *Economic Impacts of Residential Property*

Abandonment and the Genesee County Land Bank in Flint, Michigan. Flint: Michigan State University Land Policy Institute.

Gruenstein Bocian, Debbie, Peter Smith, and Wei Li. 2012. *Collateral Damage: The Spillover Costs of Foreclosures*. Washington: Center for Responsible Lending.

Guerra, Nancy, L. Rowell Huesmann, and Anja Spindler. 2003. "Community Violence Exposure, Social Cognition, and Aggression among Urban Elementary School Children." *Child Development* 74(5): 1561–1576.

Guerrieri, Veronica, Daniel Hartley, and Erik Hurst. 2012. "Within-City Variation in Urban Decline: The Case of Detroit." *American Economic Review: Papers and Proceedings* 102(3).

———. 2013. "Endogenous Gentrification and Housing Price Dynamics." *Journal of Public Economics* 100:45–60.

Guest, Avery M. 1972. "Urban History, Population Densities, and Higher-Status Residential Location." *Economic Geography* 48(4): 375–387.

———. 1973. "Urban Growth and Population Densities." *Demography* 10(1): 53–69.

———. 1974. "Neighborhood Life Cycles and Social Status." *Economic Geography* 50(3): 228–243.

Guest, Avery M., and Barret A. Lee. 1984. "How Urbanites Define Their Neighborhoods." *Population and Environment* 7(1): 32–56.

Gyourko, Joseph, and Peter Linneman. 1993. "The Affordability of the American Dream: An Examination of the Last 30 Years." *Journal of Housing Research* 4(1): 39–72.

Hagan, John, and Holly Foster. 2001. "Youth Violence and the End of Adolescence." *American Sociological Review* 66(6): 874–899.

Hallman, Howard W. 1984. *Neighborhoods: Their Place in Urban Life*. Sage Library of Social Research, vol. 154. Beverly Hills: Sage Publications.

Han, Hye-Sung. 2013. "The Impact of Abandoned Properties on Nearby Property Values." *Housing Policy Debate* 24(2): 311–334.

———. 2017a. "Exploring Threshold Effects in the Impact of Housing Abandonment on Nearby Property Values." *Urban Affairs Review*, accessed at https://doi.org/10.1177/1078087417720303.

———. 2017b. "Neighborhood Characteristics and Resistance to the Impacts of Housing Abandonment." *Journal of Urban Affairs* 39(6): 833–856.

Hannon, Lance E. 2002. "Criminal Opportunity Theory and the Relationship between Poverty and Property Crime." *Sociological Spectrum* 22(3): 363–381.

———. 2005. "Extremely Poor Neighborhoods and Homicide." *Social Science Quarterly* 86(1): 1418–1434.

Hannon, Lance, and Peter Knapp. 2003. "Reassessing Nonlinearity in the Urban Disadvantage / Violent Crime Relationship: An Example of Methodological Bias from Log Transformation." *Criminology* 41(4): 1427–1448.

Hanushek, Eric, and John Quigley. 1978. "An Explicit Model of Intra-Metropolitan Mobility." *Land Economics* 54:411–429.

Harding, David. 2003. "Counterfactual Models of Neighborhood Effects: The Effect of Neighborhood Poverty on Dropping Out and Teenage Pregnancy." *American Journal of Sociology* 109(3): 676–719.

Harding, John P., Eric Rosenblatt, and Vincent W. Yao. 2009. "The Contagion Effect of Foreclosed Properties." *Journal of Urban Economics* 66(3): 164–178.

Harkness, Joseph, and Sandra Newman. 2003. "Differential Effects of Homeownership on Children from Higher- and Lower-Income Families." *Journal of Housing Research* 14:1–19.

Harris, David R. 1999. "Property Values Drop When Blacks Move In, Because . . . : Racial and Socioeconomic Determinants of Neighborhood Desirability." *American Sociological Review* 64(3): 461–479.

———. 2001. "Why Are Whites and Blacks Averse to Black Neighbors?" *Social Science Research* 30: 100–116.

Hartley, Daniel. 2013. "Gentrification and Financial Health." *Federal Reserve Bank of Cleveland Economic Trends.* Accessed at https://www.clevelandfed.org/newsroom-and-events/publications/economic-trends/2013-economic-trends/et-20131106-gentrification-and-financial-health.aspx.

Hartung, John M., and Jeffrey R. Henig. 1997. "Housing Vouchers and Certificates as a Vehicle for Deconcentrating the Poor: Evidence from the Washington, DC, Metropolitan Area." *Urban Affairs Review* 32(3): 403–419.

Hassing, Carlijne, Marcel Twickler, Bert Brunekreef, Flemming Cassee, Pieter Doevendans, John Kastelein, and Maarten Jan Cramer. 2009. "Particulate Air Pollution, Coronary Heart Disease and Individual Risk Assessment: A General Overview." *European Journal of Preventitive Cardiology* 16(1): 10–15.

Haurin, Donald R., Robert D. Dietz, and Bruce A. Weinberg. 2002. "The Impact of Neighborhood Homeownership Rates: A Review of the Theoretical and Empirical Literature." Department of Economics Working Paper, Ohio State University.

Haurin, Donald R., Toby Parcel, and Ruth J. Haurin. 2002. "Does Home Ownership Affect Child Outcomes?" *Real Estate Economics* 30:635–666.

Havekes, Esther, Michael Bader, and Maria Krysan. 2016. "Realizing Racial and Ethnic Neighborhood Preferences? Exploring the Mismatches between What People Want, Where They Search, and Where They Live." *Population Research and Policy Review* 35(1): 101–126.

Haveman, Robert, and Barbara Wolfe. 1994. *Succeeding Generations: On the Effects of Investments in Children.* New York: Russell Sage Foundation.

Hearst, Mary, Michael Oakes, Pamela Johnson. 2008. "The Effect of Racial Residential Segregation on Black Infant Mortality." *American Journal of Epidemiology* 168(11): 1247–1254.

Hedges, Larry V., Richard D. Laine, and Rob Greenwald. 1994. "An Exchange: Part 1: Does Money Matter? A Meta-Analysis of Studies of the Effects of Differential School Inputs on Student Outcomes." *Educational Researcher* 23(3): 5–14.

Hedman, Lina. 2011. "The Impact of Residential Mobility on Measurements of Neighbourhood Effects." *Housing Studies* 26(4): 501–519.

———. 2013. "Moving Near Family? The Influence of Extended Family on Neighbourhood Choice in an Intra-Urban Context." *Population, Space and Place* 19:32–45.

Hedman, Lina, and George Galster. 2013. "Neighborhood Income Sorting and the Effects of Neighborhood Income Mix on Income: A Holistic Empirical Exploration." *Urban Studies* 50(1): 107–127.

Hedman, Lina, Maarten van Ham, and David Manley. 2011. "Neighbourhood Choice and Neighbourhood Reproduction." *Environment and Planning A* 43(6): 1381–1399.

Hegerty, Scott. 2017. "Crime, Housing Tenure, and Economic Deprivation: Evidence from Milwaukee, Wisconsin." *Journal of Urban Affairs* 39(8): 1103–1121.

Hellerstein, Judith, Mark. Kutzbach, and David Neumark. 2014. "Do Labor Market Networks Have an Important Spatial Dimension?" *Journal of Urban Economics* 79:39–58.

Hellerstein, Judith, David Neumark, and Melissa McInerney. 2008. "Spatial Mismatch or Racial Mismatch?" *Journal of Urban Economics* 64(2): 464–479.

Helms, Andrew C. 2003. "Understanding Gentrification: An Empirical Analysis of the Determinants of Urban Housing Renovation." *Journal of Urban Economics* 54(3).

———. 2012. "Keeping Up with the Joneses: Neighborhood Effects in Housing Renovation." *Regional Science and Urban Economics* 42(1-2): 303–313.

Hendey, Leah, George C. Galster, Susan J. Popkin, and Chris Hayes. 2016. "Housing Choice Voucher Holders and Neighborhood Crime: A Dynamic Panel Analysis from Chicago." *Urban Affairs Review* 52(4): 471–500.

Herbert, John D., and Benjamin H. Stevens. 1960. "A Model for the Distribution of Residential Activity in Urban Areas." *Journal of Regional Science* 2(2): 21–36.

Hipp, John R. 2007. "Income Inequality, Race and Place: Does the Distribution of Race and Class Within Neighborhoods Affect Crime Rates?" *Criminology* 45(3): 665–697.

———. 2009. "Specifying the Determinants of Neighborhood Satisfaction: A Robust Assessment in 24 Metropolitan Areas over Four Time Points." *Social Forces* 88:395–424.

———. 2010. "A Dynamic View of Neighborhoods: The Reciprocal Relationship between Crime and Neighborhood Structural Characteristics." *Social Problems* 57(2): 205–230.

———. 2012. "Segregation Through the Lens of Housing Unit Transition: What Roles Do the Prior Residents, the Local Micro-Neighborhood, and the Broader Neighborhood Play?" *Demography* 49(4):1285–1306.

Hipp, John R., George E. Tita, and Robert T. Greenbaum. 2009. "Drive-Bys and Trade-Ups: Examining the Directionality of the Crime and Residential Instability Relationship." *Social Forces* 87(4): 1777–1812.

Hipp, John R., and Daniel K. Yates. 2011. "Ghettos, Thresholds, and Crime: Does Concentrated Poverty Really Have an Accelerating Increasing Effect on Crime?" *Criminology* 49(4): 955–990.

Hirsch, Arnold R. 1983. *Making the Second Ghetto: Race and Housing in Chicago, 1940–1960*. Cambridge: Cambridge University Press.

Hoff, Karla, and Arijit Sen. 2005. "Homeownership, Community Interactions, and Segregation." *American Economic Review* 95(4): 1167–1189.

Holguin, Fernando. 2008. "Traffic, Outdoor Air Pollution, and Asthma." *Immunology and Allergy Clinics in North America* 28(3): 577–588.

Hoyt, Homer. 1933. *A Hundred Years of Land Values in Chicago*. Chicago: University of Chicago Press.

Hunter, Albert. 1974. *Symbolic Communities*. Chicago: University of Chicago Press.

———. 1979. "The Urban Neighborhood: Its Analytical and Social Contexts." *Urban Affairs Quarterly* 14(3): 267–288.

Hunter, Marcus Anthony, Mary Pattillo, Zandria F. Robinson, and Keeanga-Yamahtta Taylor. 2016. "Black Placemaking: Celebration, Play and Poetry." *Theory, Culture and Society* 33(7-8): 31–56.

Hwang, Jackelyn. 2015. "The Social Construction of a Gentrifying Neighborhood: Reifying and Redefining Identity and Boundaries in Inequality." *Urban Affairs Review* 52 (1): 98–128.

Hwang, Jackelyn, Michael Hankinson, and Kreg Steven Brown. 2015. "Racial and Spatial Targeting: Segregation and Subprime Lending within and across Metropolitan Areas." *Social Forces* 93(3): 1081–1108.

Hwang, Jackelyn, and Jeffrey Lin. 2016. "What Have We Learned about the Causes of Recent Gentrification?" *Cityscape* 18(3): 9–26.

Hwang, Jackelyn, and Robert J. Sampson. 2014. "Divergent Pathways of Gentrification: Racial Inequality and the Social Order of Renewal in Chicago Neighborhoods." *American Sociological Review* 79 (4): 726–751.

Hyra, Derek S. 2008. *The New Urban Renewal: The Economic Transformation of Harlem and Bronzeville*. Chicago: University of Chicago Press.

———. 2013. "Mixed-Income Housing: Where Have We Been and Where Do We Go from Here?" *Cityscape* 15(2): 123–134.

———. 2014. "The Back-to-the-City Movement: Neighborhood Redevelopment and Processes of Political and Cultural Displacement." *Urban Studies* 52(10): 1753–1773.

———. 2017. *Race, Class and Politics in Cappuccino City*. Chicago: University of Chicago Press.

Hyra, Derek S., Gregory D. Squires, Robert N. Renner, and David S. Kirk. 2013. "Metropolitan Segregation and the Subprime Lending Crisis." *Housing Policy Debate* 23(1): 177–198.

Iceland, John, and Kyle A. Nelson. 2008. "Hispanic Segregation in Metropolitan America: Exploring the Multiple Forms of Spatial Assimilation. *American Sociological Review* 73(5): 741–765.

Iceland, John, and Rima Wilkes. 2006. "Does Socioeconomic Status Matter? Race, Class, and Residential Segregation." *Social Problems* 53(2): 248–273.

Ihlanfeldt, Keith R. 1999. "The Geography of Economic and Social Opportunity in Metropolitan Areas." In *Governance and Opportunity in Metropolitan America*, edited by Alan Altshuler, William Morrill, Harold Wolman, and Faith Mitchell, 213–250. Washington: National Academy Press.

Ihlanfeldt, Keith, and Benjamin Scafidi. 2002. "The Neighborhood Contact Hypothesis." *Urban Studies* 39:619–641.

Ihlanfeldt, Keith R., and David L. Sjoquist. 1998. "The Spatial Mismatch Hypothesis: A Review of Recent Studies and their Implications for Welfare Reform." *Housing Policy Debate* 9(4): 849–892.

Imbroscio, David. 2012. "Beyond Mobility: The Limits of Liberal Urban Policy." *Journal of Urban Affairs* 34(1): 1–20.

Immergluck, Dan. 2011. *Foreclosed: High-Risk Lending, Deregulation, and the Undermining of America's Mortgage Market*. Ithaca, NY: Cornell University Press.

———. 2004. *Credit to the Community: Community Reinvestment and Fair Lending Policy in the United States*. New York: M. E. Sharpe.

Immergluck, Dan, and Geoff Smith. 2006. "The External Costs of Foreclosure: The Impact of Single-Family Mortgage Foreclosures on Property Values." *Housing Policy Debate* 17(1): 57–79.

Intrator, Jake, Jonathan Tannen, and Douglas S. Massey. 2016. "Segregation by Race and Income in the United States 1970–2010." *Social Science Research* 60:45–60.

Ioannides, Yannis. 2002. "Residential Neighborhood Effects." *Regional Science and Urban Economics* 32:145–165.

Ioannides, Yannis, and Kamhon Kan. 1996. "Structural Estimation of Residential Mobility and Housing Tenure Choice." *Journal of Regional Science* 36(3): 335–363.

Ioannides, Yannis, and Linda Datcher Loury. 2004. "Job Information Networks, Neighborhood Effects, and Inequality." *Journal of Economic Literature* 42(4): 1056–1093.

Ioannides, Yannis, and Jeffrey Zabel. 2003. "Neighborhood Effects and Housing Demand." *Journal of Applied Econometrics* 18: 563–584.

———. 2008. "Interactions, Neighborhood Selection, and Housing Demand." *Journal of Urban Economics* 63(1): 229–252.

Jackman, Mary R., and Marie Crane. 1986. "Some of My Best Friends are Black: Interracial Friendship and Whites' Racial Attitudes." *Public Opinion Quarterly* 50(4): 459–486.

Jacob, Brian. 2004. "Public Housing, Housing Vouchers, and Student Achievement: Evidence from Public Housing Demolitions in Chicago." *American Economic Review* 94(1): 233–58.

Jacobs, Jane. 1961. *The Death and Life of Great American Cities.* New York: Random House.

Janowitz, Morris. 1952. *Community Press in an Urban Setting.* New York: Free Press.

Jargowsky, Paul A. 2015. *The Architecture of Segregation: Civil Unrest, the Concentration of Poverty, and Public Policy.* New York: Century Foundation.

Jargowsky, Paul A., and Mohamed El Komi. 2011. "Before or After the Bell? School Context and Neighborhood Effects on Student Achievement." In *Neighborhood and Life Chances: How Place Matters in Modern America,* edited by Harriet B. Newburger, Eugenie L. Birch, and Susan M. Wachter, 50–72. Philadelphia: University of Pennsylvania Press.

Jarret, Robin L. 1997. "Bringing Families Back In: Neighborhoods' Effects on Child Development." In *Neighborhood Poverty: Volume 2. Policy Implications in Studying Neighborhoods,* edited by Jeanne Brooks-Gunn, Greg J. Duncan, and J. Lawrence Aber, 48–64. New York: Russell Sage Foundation.

Jencks, Cristopher, and Susan Mayer. 1990. "The Social Consequences of Growing Up in a Poor Neighborhood." In *Inner-City Poverty in the United States,* edited by Lawrence Lynn and Michael MacGeary, 111–186. Washington: National Academy Press.

Johnson, Jennifer, and Beata Bednarz. 2002. *Neighborhood Effects of the Low-Income Housing Tax Credit Program: Final Report.* Washington: Office of Policy Development and Research, US Department of Housing and Urban Development.

Johnson, Pamela Jo, J. Michael Oakes, and Douglas L. Anderton. 2008. "Neighborhood Poverty and American Indian Infant Death: Are the Effects Identifiable?" *American Journal of Epidemiology* 18(7): 552–559.

Johnson, Rucker C. 2011. "The Place of Race in Health Disparities: How Family Background and Neighborhood Conditions in Childhood Impact Later-Life Health." In *Neighborhood and Life Chances: How Place Matters in Modern America,* edited by Harriett B. Newburger, Eugenie L. Birch, and Susan M. Wachter, 18–36. Philadelphia: University of Pennsylvania Press.

Jokela, Markus. 2014. "Are Neighborhood Health Associations Causal? A 10-Year Prospective Cohort Study with Repeated Measurements." *American Journal of Epidemiology* 180(8): 776–784.

Joseph, Mark L. 2006. "Is Mixed-Income Development an Antidote to Urban Poverty?" *Housing Policy Debate* 17(2): 209–234.

———. 2013. "Cityscape Mixed-Income Symposium Summary and Response: Implications for Antipoverty Policy." *Cityscape* 15(2): 215–222.

Jun, Hee-Jung. 2013. "Determinants of Neighborhood Change: A Multilevel Analysis." *Urban Affairs Review* 49(3): 319–352.

———. 2014. "The Role of Municipal-level Factors in Neighborhood Economic Change." *Journal of Urban Affairs* 36(3): 447–464.

———. 2016. "The Effect of Racial and Ethnic Composition on Neighborhood Economic Change: A Multilevel and Longitudinal Look." *Housing Studies* 31(1): 102–125.

Kahneman, Daniel. 2011. *Thinking, Fast and Slow.* New York: Farrar, Strauss and Giroux.

Kain, John F. 1992. "The Spatial Mismatch Hypothesis: Three Decades Later." *Housing Policy Debate* 3(2): 371–460.

Kallus, Rachel, and Hubert Law-Yone. 2000. "What Is a Neighbourhood? The Structure and Function of an Idea." *Environment and Planning B: Planning and Design* 27(6): 815–826.

Kan, Kamhon. 2000. "Dynamic Modeling of Housing Tenure Choice." *Journal of Urban Economics* 48(1): 46–69.

Katz, Bruce, and Margery Turner. 2001. "Who Should Run the Housing Voucher Program? A Reform Proposal." *Housing Policy Debate* 12(2): 239–262.

———. 2008. "Rethinking US Rental Housing Policy: A New Blueprint for Federal, State and Local Action." In *Rethinking Rental Housing: Policies, Programs and Priorities*, edited by Nichola Retsinas and Eric Belsky, 319–358. Washington: Brookings Institution.

Katz, Charles M., Danielle Wallace, and E. C. Hedberg. 2013. "A Longitudinal Assessment of the Impact of Foreclosure on Neighborhood Crime." *Journal of Research in Crime and Delinquency* 50(3): 359–389.

Katz, Lawrence, Jeffrey Kling, and Jeffrey Leibman, 2001. "Moving to Opportunity in Boston: Early Results of a Randomized Mobility Experiment." *Quarterly Journal of Economics* 116(2): 607–654.

Kawachi, Ichirō, and Lisa F. Berkman. 2003. *Neighborhoods and Health*. New York: Oxford University Press.

Kawachi, Ichirō, Bruce P. Kennedy, and Richard G. Wilkinson. 1999. *The Society and Population Health Reader: Volume I: Income Inequality and Health*. New York: The New Press.

Kearns, Ade, and Alison Parkes. 2005. "Living in and Leaving Poor Neighbourhood Conditions." In *Life in Poverty Neighbourhoods: European and American Perspectives*, edited by Jürgen Friedrichs, George C. Galster, and Sako Musterd Sako, 31–56. London: Routledge.

Keating, W. Dennis, and Norman Krumholz, eds. 1999. *Rebuilding Urban Neighborhoods: Achievements, Opportunities and Limits*. Thousand Oaks, CA; London; and New Delhi: Sage Publications.

Keller, Suzanne. 1968. *The Urban Neighborhood: A Sociological Perspective*. New York: Random House.

Kessler, Ronald, Greg Duncan, Lisa Gennetian, Lawrence Katz, Jeffrey Kling, Nancy Sampson, Lisa Sanbonmatsu, Alan Zaslavsky, and Jens Ludwig. 2014. "Associations of Housing Mobility Interventions for Children in High-Poverty Neighborhoods with Subsequent Mental Disorders during Adolescence." *Journal of the American Planning Association* 311(9): 937–948.

Khadduri, Jill. 2005. "Comment on Basolo and Nguyen. 'Does Mobility Matter?'" *Housing Policy Debate* 16(3-4): 325–334.

Khadduri, Jill, and Charles Wilkins. 2008. "Designing Subsidized Rental Housing Programs: What Have We Learned?" In *Rethinking Rental Housing: Policies, Programs, and Priorities*, edited by Nicholas P. Retsinas, and Eric S. Belsky, 161–190. Washington: Brookings Institution.

Khare, Amy T. 2013. "Market-Driven Public Housing Reforms: Inadequacy for Poverty Alleviation." *Cityscape* 15(2): 193–204.

Kim, Sunwoong. 2000. "Race and Home Price Appreciation in Urban Neighborhoods: Evidence from Milwaukee, Wisconsin." *Review of Black Political Economy* 28(2): 9–28.

———. 2003. "Long-Term Appreciation of Owner-Occupied Single-Family House Prices in Milwaukee Neighborhoods." *Urban Geography* 24(3): 212–231.

Kinahan, Kelly L. 2016. "Neighborhood Revitalization and Historic Preservation in US Legacy Cities." Unpublished PhD dissertation, Maxine Goodman Levin College of Urban Affairs, Cleveland State University.

Kingsley, G. Thomas, and Margery Austin Turner, eds. 1993. *Housing Markets and Residential Mobility*. Washington: Urban Institute Press.

Kingsley, G. Thomas, Claudia Coulton, and Kathryn Pettit, eds. 2014. *Strengthening Communities with Neighborhood Data*. Washington: Urban Institute Press.

Kirschenman, Joleen, and Kathryn M. Neckerman. 1991. "We'd Love to Hire Them, but. . . . : The Meaning of Race for Employers." In *The Urban Underclass*, edited by

Christopher Jencks and Paul E. Peterson, 203–232. Washington: Brookings Institution.

Klapp, Orrin. 1978. *Opening and Closing: Strategies of Information Adaptation in Society.* Cambridge: Cambridge University Press.

Kleinhans, Reinout. 2004. "Social Implications of Housing Diversification in Urban Renewal: A Review of Recent Literature." *Journal of Housing and the Built Environment* 19(4): 367–390.

Kleit, Rachel Garshick. 2001a. "Neighborhood Relations in Scattered-Site and Clustered Public Housing." *Journal of Urban Affairs* 23(3–4): 409–430.

———. 2001b. "The Role of Neighborhood Social Networks in Scattered-Site Public Housing Residents' Search for Jobs." *Housing Policy Debate* 12(3): 541–573.

———. 2002. "Job Search Networks and Strategies in Scattered-Site Public Housing." *Housing Studies* 17(1): 83–100.

———. 2005. "HOPE VI New Communities: Neighborhood Relationships in Mixed-Income Housing." *Environment and Planning A* 37(8), 1413–1441.

———. 2008. "Neighborhood Segregation, Personal Networks, and Access to Social Resources." In *Segregation: The Rising Costs for America*, edited by James H. Carr and Nandinee K. Kutty, 237–260. New York: Routledge.

———. 2013. "False Assumptions About Poverty Dispersal Policies." *Cityscape* 15(2): 205–209.

Kleit, Rachel Garshick, and Nicole Bohme Carnegie. 2011. "Integrated or Isolated? The Impact of Public Housing Redevelopment on Social Network Homophily." *Social Networks* 33(2): 152–165.

Klenbanov, Pamela Kato, Jeanne Brooks-Gunn, and Greg J. Duncan. 1994. "Does Neighborhood and Family Poverty Affect Mothers' Parenting, Mental Health, and Social Support?" *Journal of Marriage and the Family* 56(2): 441–455.

Klenbanov, Pamela Kato, Jeanne Brooks-Gunn, P. Lindsay Chase-Lansdale, and Rachel A. Gordon. 1997. "Are Neighborhood Effects on Young Children Mediated by Features of the Home Environment?" In *Neighborhood Poverty: Vol. 1. Context and Consequences for Children*, edited by Jeanne Brooks-Gunn, Greg J. Duncan, and J. Lawrence Aber, 119–145. New York: Russell Sage Foundation.

Kling, Jeffrey, Jens Ludwig, and Lawrence Katz. 2005. "Neighborhood Effects on Crime for Female and Male Youth: Evidence from a Randomized Housing Voucher Experiment." *Quarterly Journal of Economics* 120(1): 87–131.

Kling, Jeffrey., Jeffrey Liebman, and Lawrence Katz. 2007. "Experimental Analysis of Neighborhood Effects." *Econometrica* 75(1): 83–119.

Knapp, Elijah. 2017. "The Cartography of Opportunity: Spatial Data Science for Equitable Urban Policy." *Housing Policy Debate* 27(6): 913–940.

Kneebone, Elizabeth, and Natalie Holmes. 2015. *The Growing Distance between People and Jobs in Metropolitan America.* Washington: Brookings Institution.

Knotts, H. Gibbs, and Moshe Haspel. 2006. "The Impact of Gentrification on Voter Turnout." *Social Science Quarterly* 87(1): 110–121.

Kochhar, Rakesh, Richard Fry, and Paul Taylor. 2011. *Twenty-to-One: Wealth Gaps Rise to Record Highs between Whites, Blacks, and Hispanics.* Washington: Pew Research Center.

Kohen, Dafna E., Jeanne Brooks-Gunn, Tama Leventhal, and Clyde Hertzman. 2002. "Neighborhood Income and Physical and Social Disorder in Canada: Associations with Young Children's Competencies." *Child Development* 73(6): 1844–1860.

Kozol, Jonathan. 1991. *Savage Inequalities: Children in America's Schools.* New York: Crown.

Kramer, Rory. 2017. "Defensible Spaces in Philadelphia: Exploring Neighborhood Boundaries through Spatial Analysis." *RSF: The Russell Sage Foundation Journal of the Social Sciences* 3(2): 81–101.

Krivo, Lauren J., and Ruth D. Peterson. 1996. "Extremely Disadvantaged Neighborhoods and Urban Crime." *Social Forces* 75(2): 619–648.

Krivo, Lauren J., Ruth D. Peterson, Helen Rizzo, and John R. Reynolds. 1998. "Race, Segregation, and the Concentration of Disadvantage: 1980–1990." *Social Problems* 45(1): 61–80.

Krysan, Maria, Mick P. Couper, Reynolds Farley, and Tyrone A. Forman. 2009. "Does Race Matter in Neighborhood Preferences? Results from a Video Experiment." *American Journal of Sociology* 115(2): 527–559.

Kucheva, Yana, and Richard Sander. 2017. "Structural versus Ethnic Dimensions of Housing Segregation." *Journal of Urban Affairs* 40(3): 329–348.

Kuebler, Meghan, and Jacob Rugh. 2013. "New Evidence on Racial and Ethnic Disparities in Homeownership." *Social Science Research* 42(5): 1357–1374.

Kuminoff, Nicolai V., Kerry Smith, and Christopher Timmins. 2010. *The New Economics of Equilibrium Sorting and Its Transformational Role for Policy Evaluation*. Working paper 16349, National Bureau of Economic Research, Cambridge, MA.

Kurlat, Pablo, and Johannes Stroebel. 2015. "Testing for Information Asymmetries in Real Estate Markets." *Review of Financial Studies* 28(8): 2429–2461.

Ladd, Helen F. 1998. "Evidence on Discrimination in Mortgage Lending." *Journal of Economic Perspectives* 12(2): 41–62.

Lancaster, Kelvin J. 1966. "A New Approach to Consumer Theory." *Journal of Political Economy* 74(2): 132–157.

Landis, John D. 2015. "Tracking and Explaining Neighborhood Socioeconomic Change in US Metropolitan Areas between 1990 and 2010." *Housing Policy Debate* 26(1): 2–52.

Landis, John D., and Kirk McClure. 2010. "Rethinking Federal Housing Policy." *Journal of the American Planning Association* 76(3): 319–348.

Lang, William M., and Leonard I. Nakamura. 1993. "A Model of Redlining." *Journal of Urban Economics* 33(2): 223–234.

Lankford, Hamilton, Susanna Loeb, and James Wyckoff. 2002. "Teacher Sorting and the Plight of Urban Schools: A Descriptive Analysis." *Educational Evaluation and Policy Analysis* 24(1): 37–62.

Lanphear, Bruce P. 1998. "The Paradox of Lead Poisoning Prevention." *Science* 281(5383): 1617–1618.

Lanzetta, John T. 1963. "Information Acquisition in Decision Making." In *Motivation and Social Interaction*, edited by O. J. Harvey, 239–265. New York: Ronald Press.

Laumann, Edward O., Peter V. Marsden, and David Prensky. 1983. "The Boundary Definition Problem in Network Analysis." In *Applied Network Analysis*, edited by Ronald Burt and M. Michael Minor. Beverly Hills, CA: Sage Publications.

Lauria, Mickey, and Vern Baxter. 1999. "Residential Mortgage and Racial Transition in New Orleans." *Urban Affairs Review* 34(6): 757–786.

Lauritsen, Janet L., and Norman A. White. 2001. "Putting Violence in Its Place: The Influence of Race, Gender, Ethnicity and Place on the Risk for Violence," *Criminology and Public Policy* 1(1): 37–59.

Lawton, M. Powell. 1999. "Environmental Taxonomy: Generalizations from Research with Older Adults." In *Measuring Environment across the Life Span: Emerging Methods and Concepts*, edited by Sarah L. Freidman and Theodore D. Wachs, 91–126. Washington: American Psychological Association.

Lee, Barrett A., and Karen E. Campbell. 1997. "Common Ground? Urban Neighborhoods as Survey Respondents See Them." *Social Science Quarterly* 78(4): 922–936.

Lee, Barrett A., R. S. Oropesa, and James W. Kanan. 1994. "Neighborhood Context and Residential Mobility." *Demography* 31(2): 249–270.

Lee, Barrett A., and Peter B. Wood. 1991. "Is Neighborhood Racial Succession Place-Specific?" *Demography* 28(1): 21–40.

Lee, Chang-Moo, Dennis P. Culhane, and Susan M. Wachter. 1999. "The Differential Impacts of Federally Assisted Housing Programs on Nearby Property Values: A Philadelphia Case Study." *Housing Policy Debate* 10(1): 75–93.

Lee, Kwan O. 2014. "Why Do Renters Stay in or Leave Certain Neighborhoods?" *Journal of Regional Science* 54(5): 755–787.

———. 2017. "Temporal Dynamics of Racial Segregation in the United States: An Analysis of Household Residential Mobility." *Journal of Urban Affairs* 39(1): 40–67.

Lee, Min-Ah, and Kenneth F. Ferraro. 2007. "Neighborhood Residential Segregation and Physical Health among Hispanic Americans: Good, Bad, or Benign?" *Journal of Health and Social Behavior* 48(2): 131–148.

Lee, Sokbae, Myung Hwan Seo, and Youngki Shin. 2011. "Testing for Threshold Effects in Regression Models." *Journal of the American Statistical Association* 106(493): 220–231.

———. 2017. "Testing for Threshold Effects in Regression Models: Correction." *Journal of the American Statistical Association* 112(518): 883.

Lee, Sugie, and Nancy Green Leigh. 2007. "Intrametropolitan Spatial Differentiation and Decline of Inner-Ring Suburbs: A Comparison of Four US Metropolitan Areas." *Journal of Planning Education and Research* 27(2): 146–164.

Lees, Loretta. 1994. "Rethinking Gentrification: Beyond the Positions of Economics or Culture." *Progress in Human Geography* 18(2): 137–150.

Lees, Loretta, and David Ley. 2008. "Introduction to Special Issue on Gentrification and Public Policy." *Urban Studies* 45(12): 2379–2384.

Lees, Loretta, Thomas Slater, and Elvin K. Wyly. 2008. *Gentrification.* New York: Routledge.

———. 2010. *The Gentrification Reader.* New York: Routledge.

Lester, William T., and Daniel A. Hartley. 2014. "The Long-Term Employment Impacts of Gentrification in the 1990s." *Regional Science and Urban Economics* 45:80–89.

Leven, Charles, James Little, Hugh Nourse, and R. Read. 1976. *Neighborhood Change: Lessons in the Dynamics of Urban Decay.* Cambridge, MA: Ballinger.

Leventhal, Tama, and Jeanne Brooks-Gunn. 2000. "The Neighborhoods They Live In: The Effects of Neighborhood Residence on Child and Adolescent Outcomes." *Psychological Bulletin* 126(2): 309–337.

———. 2003. "Moving to Opportunity: An Experimental Study of Neighborhood Effects on Mental Health." *American Journal of Public Health* 93(9): 1576–1582.

Levy, Diane K., Jennifer Comey, and Sandra Padilla. 2006a. *In the Face of Gentrification: Case Studies of Local Efforts to Mitigate Displacement.* Washington: Urban Institute.

———. 2006b. *Keeping the Neighborhood Affordable: A Handbook of Housing Strategies for Gentrifying Areas.* Washington: Urban Institute.

Lewis, Valerie A., Michael O. Emerson, and Stephen L. Klineberg. 2011. "Who We'll Live with: Neighborhood Racial Composition Preferences of Whites, Blacks and Latinos." *Social Forces* 89(4): 1385–1407.

Li, Huiping, Harrison Campbell, and Steven Fernandez. 2013. "Residential Segregation, Spatial Mismatch, and Economic Growth across US Metropolitan Areas." *Urban Studies* 50(13): 2642–2660.

Li, Ying, and Eric Rosenblatt. 1997. "Can Urban Indicators Predict Home Price Apprecia-tion? Implications for Redlining Research." *Real Estate Economics* 25(1): 81–104.

Lim, Up, and George C. Galster. 2009. "The Dynamics of Neighborhood Property Crime Rates." *Annals of Regional Science* 43(4): 925–945.

Lin, Zhenguo, Eric Rosenblatt, and Vincent W. Yao. 2007. "Spillover Effects of Foreclosures on Neighborhood Property Values." *Journal of Real Estate Finance and Economics* 38(4): 387–407.

Linares, L. Oriana, Timothy Heeren, Elisa Bronfman, Barry Zuckerman, Marilyn Augustyn, and Edward Tronick. 2001. "A Mediational Model for the Impact of Exposure to Com-munity Violence on Early Child Behavior Problems." *Child Development* 72(2): 639–652.

Lipman, Barbara. 2006. A Heavy Load: The Combined Housing and Transportation Bur-den of Working Families. Washington: Center for Housing Policy, available at: http://www.cnt.org.

Litt, Jill S., Nga L. Tran, and Thomas A. Burke. 2009. "Examining Urban Brownfields through the Public Health 'Macroscope.'" In *Urban Health: Readings in the Social, Built, and Physical Environments of U.S. Cities*, edited by H. Patricia Hynes and Russ Lopez, 217–236. Sudbury, MA: Jones and Bartlett Publishers.

Livingston, Mark, George Galster, Ade Kearns, and Jon Bannister. 2014. "Criminal Neigh-borhoods: Does the Density of Prior Offenders in an Area Encourage Others to Com-mit Crime?" *Environment and Planning A* 46(10): 2469–2488.

Loeb, Susanna, Bruce Fuller, Sharon Lynn Kagan, Bidemi Carrol. 2004. "Child Care in Poor Communities: Early Learning Effects of Type, Quality, and Stability." *Child Development* 75(1): 47–65.

Logan, John R. 2011. *Separate and Unequal: The Neighborhood Gap for Blacks, Hispanics, and Asians in Metropolitan America*. Providence, RI: Brown University.

Logan, John R., and Harvey L. Molotch. 1987. *Urban Fortunes: The Political Economy of Place*. Berkeley and Los Angeles: University of California Press.

Lohmann, Andrew, and Grant Mcmurran. 2009. "Resident-Defined Neighborhood Map-ping: Using GIS to Analyze Phenomenological Neighborhoods." *Journal of Prevention and Intervention in the Community* 37(1): 66–81.

Looker, Benjamin. 2015. *A Nation of Neighborhoods: Imagining Cities, Communities, and Democracy in Postwar America*. Chicago: University of Chicago Press.

Lopez, Russell, and Patricia Hynes. 2006. "Obesity, Physical Activity, and the Urban En-vironment: Public Health Research Needs." *Environmental Health* 5(1): 25–35.

Lord, Heather, and Joseph L. Mahoney. 2007. "Neighborhood Crime and Self-Care: Risks for Aggression and Lower Academic Performance." *Developmental Psychology* 43(6): 1321–1333.

Lovasi, Gina, James Quinn, Virginia Rauh, Frederica Perera, Howard Andrews, Robin Gar-finkel, Lori Hoepner, Robin Whyatt, and Andrew Rundle. 2011. "Chlorpyrifos Exposure and Urban Residential Environment Characteristics as Determinants of Early Child-hood Neurodevelopment." *American Journal of Public Health* 101(1): 63–70.

Loving, Ajamu C., Michael S. Finke, and John R. Salter. 2012. "Does Home Equity Explain the Black Wealth Gap?" *Journal of Housing and the Built Environment* 27(4): 427–451.

Lowry, Ira. 1960. "Filtering and Housing Standards: A Conceptual Analysis." *Land Econom-ics* 36(4): 362–370.

Lubbell, Jeffrey. 2016. "Preserving and Expanding Affordability in Neighborhoods Experi-encing Rising Rents and Property Values." *Cityscape* 18(3): 131–150.

Ludwig, Jens. 2012. "Moving to Opportunity: Guest Editor's Introduction." *Cityscape* 14(2): 1–28.

Ludwig, Jens, Greg J. Duncan, and Paul Hirschfield. 2001. "Urban Poverty and Juvenile Crime: Evidence from a Randomized Experiment." *Quarterly Journal of Economics* 116(2): 655–679.

Ludwig, Jens, Greg J. Duncan, and Joshua Pinkston. 2005. "Neighborhood Effects on Economic Self-Sufficiency: Evidence from a Randomized Housing-Mobility Experiment." *Journal of Public Economics* 89(1): 131–156.

Ludwig, Jens, Helen Ladd, and Greg J. Duncan. 2001. "The Effects of Urban Poverty on Educational Outcomes: Evidence from a Randomized Experiment." In *Brookings-Wharton Papers on Urban Affairs*, edited by William Gale and Jennifer Pack, 147–201. Washington: Brookings Institution.

Ludwig, Jens, Jeffrey Liebman, Jeffrey Kling, Greg Duncan, Lawrence Katz, Ronald Kessler, and Lisa Sanbonmatsu. 2008. "What Can We Learn about Neighborhood Effects from the Moving to Opportunity Experiment?" *American Journal of Sociology* 114(1): 144–188.

Ludwig Jens, Lisa Sanbonmatsu, Lisa Gennetian, Adam Emma, Greg Duncan, and Lawrence Katz. 2011. "Neighborhoods, Obesity, and Diabetes: A Randomized Social Experiment." *New England Journal of Medicine* 365(16): 1509–1519.

Lynch, Kevin. 1960. *The Image of the City*. Cambridge, MA: MIT Press.

MacDonald, James M., and Paul E. Nelson. 1991. "Do the Poor Still Pay More? Food Price Variations in Large Metropolitan Areas." *Journal of Urban Economics* 30(3): 344–359.

Maclennan, Duncan. 1982. *Housing Economics: An Applied Approach*. Singapore: Longman Group.

Maclennan, Duncan, and Tony O'Sullivan. 2012. "Housing Markets, Signals and Search." *Journal of Property Research* 29(4): 324–340.

Macpherson, David A., and G. Stacy Sirmans. 2001. "Neighborhood Diversity and House-Price Appreciation." *Journal of Real Estate Finance and Economics* 22(1): 81–97.

Mallach, Alan. 2008. *Managing Neighborhood Change: A Framework for Sustainable and Equitable Revitalization*. Montclair, NJ: National Housing Institute.

Malpezzi, Stephen. 2003. "Hedonic Pricing Models." In *Housing Economics and Public Policy*, edited by Tony O'Sullivan and Kenneth Gibb, 67–89. Oxford, UK: Blackwell Publishing.

Manski, Charles. 1995. *Identification Problems in the Social Sciences*. Cambridge, MA: Harvard University Press.

———. 2000. "Economic Analysis of Social Interactions." *Journal of Economic Perspectives* 14(3): 115–136.

Manzo, Lynne C. 2014. "On Uncertain Ground: Being at Home in the Context of Public Housing Redevelopment." *International Journal of Housing Policy* 14(2): 389–410.

Marsh, Alex, and Kenneth Gibb. 2011. "Uncertainty, Expectations, and Behavioural Aspects of Housing Market Choices." *Housing Theory and Society* 28(3): 215–235.

Martin, Leslie. 2007. "Fighting for Control: Political Displacement in Atlanta's Gentrifying Neighborhoods." *Urban Affairs Review* 42(5): 603–628.

Martinez, Pedro, and John E. Richters. 1993. "The NIMH Community Violence Project: II. Children's Distress Symptoms Associated with Violence Exposure." *Psychiatry* 56(1): 22–35.

Massey, Douglas S. 1996. "The Age of Extremes: Concentrated Affluence and Poverty in the Twenty-First Century." *Demography* 33(4): 395–412.

Massey, Douglas S., Len Albright, Rebecca Casciano, Elizabeth Derickson and David N.

Kinsey. 2013. *Climbing Mount Laurel: The Struggle for Affordable Housing and Social Mobility in an American Suburb*. Princeton, NJ: Princeton University Press.

Massey, Douglas S., and Nancy A. Denton. 1993. *American Apartheid: Segregation and the Making of the Underclass*. Cambridge, MA: Harvard University Press.

Massey, Douglas S., and Shawn M. Kanaiaupuni. 1993. "Public Housing and the Concentration of Poverty." *Social Science Research* 74(1): 109–122.

Mawhorter, Sarah L. 2016. "Reshaping Los Angeles: Housing Affordability and Neighborhood Change." Unpublished PhD dissertation, Sol Price School of Public Affairs, University of Southern California.

McClure, Kirk. 2008. "Deconcentrating Poverty with Housing Programs." *Journal of the American Planning Association* 74(1): 90–99.

McConnell, Rob, Kiros Berhane, Frank Gilliland, Stephanie J. London, Talat Islam, W. James Gauderman, Edward Avol, Helene G. Margolis, and John M. Peters. 2002. "Asthma in Exercising Children Exposed to Ozone: A Cohort Study." *The Lancet* 359(9304): 386–391.

McConnell, Rob, Talat Islam, Ketan Shankardass, Michael Jerrett, Fred Lurmann, Frank Gilliland, Jim Gauderman, Ed Avol, Nino Künzli, Ling Yao, John Peters, and Kiros Berhane. 2010. "Childhood Incident Asthma and Traffic-Related Air Pollution at Home and School." *Environmental Health Perspectives* 118(7): 1021–1026.

McConnochie, Kenneth, Mark Russo, John McBride, Peter Szilagyi, Ann-Marie Brooks, and Klaus Roghmann. 1999. "Socioeconomic Variation in Asthma Hospitalization: Excess Utilization or Greater Need?" *Pediatrics* 103(6): 75–82.

McKinnish, Terra, Randall Walsh, and T. Kirk White. 2010. "Who Gentrifies Low-Income Neighborhoods?" *Journal of Urban Economics* 67(2): 180–193.

McKnight, John. 1995. *The Carless Society: Community and Its Counterfeits*. New York: Basic Books.

McNulty, Thomas L. 2001. "Assessing the Race-Violence Relationship at the Macro Level: The Assumption of Racial Invariance and the Problem of Restricted Distributions." *Criminology* 39(2): 467–488.

Meen, Geoffrey. 2005. "Local Housing Markets and Segregation in England." *Economic Outlook* 29(1): 11–17.

Meltzer, Rachel. 2016. "Gentrification and Small Business: Threat or Opportunity?" *Cityscape* 18(3): 57–85.

Meltzer, Rachel, and Pooya Ghorbani. 2015. "Does Gentrification Increase Employment Opportunities in Low-Income Neighborhoods?" Paper presented at the 37th annual fall conference of the Association for Public Policy and Management, Miami, November 13.

Metzger, Molly. 2014. "The Reconcentration of Poverty: Patterns of Housing Voucher Use, 2000–2008." *Housing Policy Debate* 24(3): 544–567.

Michelson, William. 1976. *Man and His Urban Environment: A Sociological Approach*. Reading, MA: Addison-Wesley.

Michener, Jamila, and Diane Wong. 2015. "Gentrification and Political Destabilization: What, Where & How." Paper presented at the 45th Urban Affairs Association Annual, Miami, April 10.

Mikelbank, Brian A. 2008. "Spatial Analysis of the Impact of Vacant, Abandoned and Foreclosed Properties." Cleveland: Office of Community Affairs, Federal Reserve Bank of Cleveland. Accessed online at https://www.clevelandfed.org/newsroom-and-events/publications/special-reports/sr-200811-spatial-analysis-of-impact-ofvacant-abandoned-foreclosed-properties.aspx.

Milgram, Stanley, Judith Greenwald, Suzanne Kessler, Wendy McKenna, and Judith Waters. 1972. "A Psychological Map of New York City." *American Scientist* 60(2): 194–200.

Mills, Nicholas L., Ken Donaldson, Paddy W. Hadoke, Nicholas A. Boon, William Mac-Nee, Flemming R. Cassee, Thomas Sandström, Anders Blomberg, and David E. Newby. 2009. "Adverse Cardiovascular Effects of Air Pollution." *Nature Clinical Practice Cardiovascular Medicine* 6(1): 36–44.

Minkler, Meredith. 1997. "Community Organizing among the Elderly Poor in San Francisco's Tenderloin District." In *Community Organizing & Community Building for Health*, edited by Meredith Minkler, 244–260. New Brunswick, NJ, and London: Rutgers University Press.

Molotch, Harvey. 1972. *Managed Integration*. Berkeley: University of California Press.

Morenoff, Jeffrey D., Robert J. Sampson, and Stephen W. Raudensbush. 2001. "Neighborhood Inequality, Collective Efficacy, and the Spatial Dynamics of Homicide." *Criminology* 39(3): 517–560.

Moore, Latetia V., and Ana Diez Roux. 2006. "Associations of Neighborhood Characteristics with the Location and Type of Food Stores." *American Journal of Public Health* 96(2): 325–331.

Morland, Kimberly, Steve Wing, Ana Diez-Roux, and Charles Poole. 2002 "Neighborhood Characteristics Associated with the Location of Food Stores and Food Service Places." *American Journal of Preventive Medicine* 22(1): 23–29.

Morris, David J., and Karl Hess. 1975. *Neighborhood Power: The New Localism*. Boston: Beacon Press.

Morris, Earl W., Sue R. Crull, and Mary Winter. 1976. "Housing Norms, Housing Satisfaction, and the Propensity to Move." *Journal of Marriage and the Family* 38(2): 309–320.

Moulton, Stephanie, Laura Peck, and Keri-Nicole Dillman. 2014. "Moving to Opportunity's Impact on Health and Well-Being among High-Dosage Participants." *Housing Policy Debate* 24(2): 415–445.

Muller, Christopher, Robert Sampson, and Alix Winter. 2018. "Environmental Inequality: The Social Causes and Consequences of Lead Exposure." *Annual Review of Sociology* (forthcoming).

Murphy, Kevin M., Andrei Shleifer, Robert W. Vishny. 1993. "Why Is Rent Seeking So Costly to Growth?" *American Economic Review* 83:409–414.

Musterd, Sako, Roger Andersson, George Galster, and Timo Kauppinen. 2008. "Are Immigrants' Earnings Influenced by the Characteristics of their Neighbours?" *Environment and Planning A* 40(4): 785–805.

Musterd, Sako, George Galster, and Roger Andersson. 2012. "Temporal Dimensions and the Measurement of Neighbourhood Effects." *Environment and Planning A* 44(3): 605–627.

Musterd, Sako, Wouter P. C. van Gent, Marjolijn Das, and Jan Latten. 2016. "Adaptive Behaviour in Urban Space: Residential Mobility in Response to Social Distance." *Urban Studies* 53(2): 227–246.

Myers, Dowell. 1983. "Upward Mobility and the Filtering Process." *Journal of Planning Education and Research* 2(2): 101–112.

Nandi, Arijit, Thomas Glass, Stephen Cole, Haitao Chu, Sandro Galea, David Celentano, Gregory Kirk, David Vlahov, William Latimer, and Shruti Mehta. 2010. "Neighborhood Poverty and Injection Cessation in a Sample of Injection Drug Users." *American Journal of Epidemiology* 171(4): 391–398.

Needleman, H., and B. Gatsonis. 1991. "Meta-Analysis of 24 Studies of Learning Disabilities Due to Lead Poisoning." *Journal of the American Medical Association* 265:673–678.

Neidell, Matthew. 2004. "Air Pollution, Health, and Socio-Economic Status: The Effect of Outdoor Air Quality on Childhood Asthma." *Journal of Health Economics* 23(6): 1209–1236.

Nelson, Kyle Anne. 2013. "Does Residential Segregation Help or Hurt? Exploring Differences in the Relationship Between Segregation and Health Among US Hispanics by Nativity and Ethnic Subgroup." *Social Science Journal* 50(4): 646–657.

Newell, Allen, and Herbert Simon. 1972. *Human Problem Solving*. Englewood Cliffs, NJ: Prentice-Hall.

Newman, Kathe, and Elvin K. Wyly. 2006. "The Right to Stay Put, Revisited: Gentrification and Resistance to Displacement in New York City." *Urban Studies* 43(1): 23–57.

Newman, Katherine S. 1999. *No Shame in My Game: The Working Poor in the Inner City*. New York: Knopf Doubleday and Russell Sage Foundation.

Newman, Sandra J., and Greg J. Duncan. 1979. "Residential Problems, Dissatisfaction, and Mobility." *Journal of the American Planning Association* 45(2): 154–166.

Nicotera, Nicole. 2007. "Measuring Neighborhood: A Conundrum for Human Services Researchers and Practitioners." *American Journal of Community Psychology* 40(1): 26–51.

Nieuwenhuis, Jaap, and Pieter Hooimeijer. 2016. "The Association between Neighbourhoods and Educational Achievement: A Systematic Review and Meta-Analysis." *Journal of Housing and the Built Environment* 31(2): 321–347.

Noonan, Douglas S. 2005. "Neighbours, Barriers and Urban Environments: Are Things 'Different on the Other Side of the Tracks?'" *Urban Studies* 42 (10): 1817–1835.

Novak, Scott, Sean Reardon, Stephen Raudenbush, and Stephen Buka. 2006. "Retail Tobacco Outlet Density and Youth Cigarette Smoking: A Propensity-Modeling Approach." *American Journal of Public Health* 96(4): 670–676.

Oakes, Michael, Kate Andrade, Ifrah Biyoow, and Logan Cowan. 2015. "Twenty Years of Neighborhood Effect Research: An Assessment." *Current Epidemiology Reports* 2(1): 1–8.

Oh, Sun Jung, and John Yinger. 2015. "What Have We Learned from Paired Testing in Housing Markets?" *Cityscape* 17(3): 15–59.

Ohls, James C. 1975. "Public Policy toward Low-Income Housing and Filtering in Housing Markets." *Journal of Urban Economics* 2(2): 144–171.

Oliver, Melvin L., and Thomas M. Shapiro. 1995. *Black Wealth/White Wealth: A New Perspective on Racial Inequality*. New York: Routledge.

O'Regan, Katherine M. 1993, "The Effect of Social Networks and Concentrated Poverty on Black and Hispanic Youth Unemployment," *Annals of Regional Science* 27(4): 327–342.

———. 2016. "Commentary: A Federal Perspective on Gentrification." *Cityscape* 18(3): 151–162.

———. 2017. "People and Place in Low-Income Housing Policy." *Housing Policy Debate* 27(2): 316–319.

Oreopoulos, Philip. 2003. "The Long-Run Consequences of Living in a Poor Neighborhood." *Quarterly Journal of Economics* 118(4): 1533–1575.

Orfield, Myron. 1997. *Metropolitics*. Washington: Brookings Institution.

Orr, Larry, Judith Feins, Robin Jacob, Eric Beecroft, Lisa Sanbonmatsu, Lawrence Katz, Jeffrey Liebman, and Jeffrey Kling. 2003. *Moving to Opportunity: Interim Impacts Evaluation*. Washington: Office of Policy Development and Research, US Department of Housing and Urban Development.

Ottensmann, John R., David H. Good, and Michael E. Gleeson. 1990. "The Impact of Net Migration on Neighborhood Racial Composition." *Urban Studies* 27(5): 705–717.

Ottensmann, John R., and Michael E. Gleeson. 1992. "The Movement of Whites and

Blacks into Racially Mixed Neighborhoods: Chicago, 1960–1980." *Social Science Quarterly* 73(3): 645–662.

Owens, Ann. 2017. "How Do People-Based Housing Policies Affect People (and Place)?" *Housing Policy Debate* 27(2): 266–281.

Pagano, Michael A., ed. 2015. *The Return of the Neighborhood as an Urban Strategy.* Urbana, Chicago, and Springfield: University of Illinois Press.

Pandey, Shanta, and Claudia Coulton. 1994. "Unraveling Neighborhood Change Using Two-Wave Panel Analysis: A Case Study of Cleveland in the 1980s." *Social Work Research* 18(2): 83–96.

Papachristos, Andrew. 2013. "48 Years of Crime in Chicago: A Descriptive Analysis of Serious Crime Trends from 1965 to 2013." Working paper ISPS 13-023, ISPS, Institution for Social and Policy Studies, Yale University.

Park, Robert E. 1936. "Succession, an Ecological Concept." *American Sociological Review* 1 (2): 171–179.

Park, Yunmi, and George O. Rogers. 2015. "Neighborhood Planning Theory, Guidelines, and Research: Can Area, Population, and Boundary Guide Conceptual Framing?" *Journal of Planning Literature* 30(1): 18–36.

Pascal, Anthony H. 1965. *The Economics of Housing Segregation.* Santa Monica, CA: Rand Corporation.

Patillo-McCoy, Mary. 1999. *Black Picket Fences: Privilege and Peril in the Black Middle Class.* Chicago: University of Chicago Press.

Pebley, Anne R., and Narayan Sastry. 2009. "Our Place: Perceived Neighborhood Size and Names in Los Angeles." Working paper #2009–026. Los Angeles: California Center for Population Research. Accessed at http://papers.ccpr.ucla.edu/papers/PWP-CCPR -2009–026/ PWP-CCPR-2009–026.pdf.

Pebley, Anne, and Mary Vaiana. 2002. *In Our Backyard.* Santa Monica, CA: Rand Corporation.

Pendall, Rolf. 2000a. "Local Land Use Regulation and the Chain of Exclusion." *Journal of the American Planning Association* 66(2): 125–142.

———. 2000b. "Why Voucher Holder and Certificate Users Live in Distressed Neighbourhoods." *Housing Policy Debate* 11(4): 881–910.

Pendall, Rolf, and Carl Hedman. 2015. *Worlds Apart: Inequality between American's Most and Least Affluent Neighborhoods.* Washington: Urban Institute.

Pendall, Rolf, Robert Puentes, and Jonathan Martin. 2006. "From Traditional to Reformed: A Review of the Land Use Regulations in the Nation's 50 Largest Metropolitan Areas." Research brief. Brookings Institution, Washington.

Peterman, William. 2000. *Neighborhood Planning and Community-Based Development: The Potential and Limits of Grassroots Action.* Thousand Oaks, CA; London; and New Delhi: Sage Publications.

Peterson, Ruth D., and Lauren J. Krivo. 2010. *Divergent Social Worlds: Neighborhood Crime and the Racial-Spatial Divide.* New York: Russell Sage Foundation.

Pettigrew, Thomas W. 1973. "Attitudes on Race and Housing: A Social-Psychological View." In *Segregation in Residential Areas: Papers on Racial and Socioeconomic Factors in Choice of Housing,* edited by Amos H. Hawley and Vincent P. Rock, 21–84. Washington: National Academy of Sciences.

Pettigrew, Thomas, and Linda R. Tropp. 2006. "A Meta-Analytic Test of Intergroup Contact Theory." *Journal of Personality and Social Psychology* 90(5): 751–783.

———. 2011. *When Groups Meet: The Dynamics of Intergroup Contact.* New York: Psychology Press.

Phares, Donald. 1971. "Racial Change and Housing Values: Transition in an Inner Suburb." *Social Science Quarterly* 52(3): 560–573.

Phibbs, Peter. 2009. *The Relationship between Housing and Improved Health, Education and Employment Outcomes: The View from Australia.* Paper delivered at the 50th annual Association of Collegiate Schools of Planning conference, Crystal City, VA.

Pinkster, Fenne M. 2009. "Living in Concentrated Poverty." Unpublished PhD dissertation, Department of Geography, Planning, and International Development Studies, University of Amsterdam.

Plotnick, Robert, and Saul Hoffman. 1999. "The Effect of Neighborhood Characteristics on Young Adult Outcomes: Alternative Estimates." *Social Science Quarterly* 80(1): 1–18.

Pocock, Stuart J., Marjorie Smith, and Peter Baghurst. 1994. "Environmental Lead and Children's Intelligence: A Systematic Review of the Epidemiological Evidence." *British Medical Journal* 309(6963): 1189–1197.

Pooley, Jennifer. 2014. "Using Community Development Block Grant Dollars to Revitalize Neighborhoods: The Impact of Program Spending in Philadelphia." *Housing Policy Debate* 24(1): 172–191.

Popkin, Susan J., George C. Galster, Kenneth Temkin, Carla Herbig, Diane K. Levy, and Elise K. Richer. 2003. "Obstacles to Desegregating Public Housing: Lessons Learned from Implementing Eight Consent Decrees." *Journal of Policy Analysis and Management* 22(2): 179–200.

Popkin, Susan J., Laura E. Harris, and Mary K. Cunningham. 2002. *Families in Transition: A Qualitative Analysis of the MTO Experience.* Washington: US Department of Housing and Urban Development.

Popkin, Susan J., Bruce Katz, Mary K. Cunningham, Karen D. Brown, Jeremy Gustafson, and Margery A. Turner. 2004. *A Decade of HOPE VI: Research Findings and Policy Challenges.* Washington: Urban Institute and Brookings Institution.

Popkin, Susan J., Tama Leventhal, and Gretchen Weismann. 2010. "Girls in the 'Hood: How Safety Affects the Life Chances of Low-Income Girls." *Urban Affairs Review* 45(6): 715–744.

Popkin, Susan J., Michael J. Rich, Leah Hendey, Christopher R. Hayes, Joe Parilla, and George C. Galster. 2012. "Public Housing Transformation and Crime: Making the Case for Responsible Relocation." *Cityscape* 14(3): 137–160.

Price, Richard, and Edwin Mills. 1985. "Race and Residence in Earnings Determination." *Journal of Urban Economics* 17(1): 1–18.

Propper, Carol, Simon Burgess, Anne Bolster, George Leckie, Kelvyn Jones, and Ron Johnston. 2007. "The Impact of Neighbourhood on the Income and Mental Health of British Social Renters." *Urban Studies* 44(2): 393–415.

Public Affairs Counseling. 1975. *The Dynamics of Neighborhood Change.* Policy Development and Research Report 108. Washington: Office of Policy Development and Research, US Department of Housing and Urban Development.

Putnam, Robert. 2007. "E Pluribus Unum: Diversity and Community in the Twenty-First Century: The 2006 Johan Skytte Prize Lecture." *Scandinavian Political Studies* 30(2): 137–174.

Quigley, John M., and Daniel H. Weinberg. 1977. "Intra-Urban Residential Mobility: A Review and Synthesis." *International Regional Science Review* 2(1): 41–66.

Quillian, Lincoln. 1999. "Migration Patterns and the Growth of High-Poverty Neighborhoods, 1970–1999." *American Journal of Sociology* 105(1): 1–37.

———. 2006. "New Approaches to Understanding Racial Prejudice and Discrimination." *Annual Review of Sociology* 32(1): 299–328.

———. 2012. "Segregation and Poverty Concentration: The Role of Three Segregations." *American Sociological Review* 77(3): 354–379.

———. 2014. "Race, Class, and Location in Neighborhood Migration: A Multidimensional Analysis of Locational Attainment." Unpublished working paper, Department of Sociology, Northwestern University.

Qillian, Lincoln, and Devah Pager. 2001. "Black Neighbors, Higher Crime? The Role of Racial Stereotypes in Evaluations of Neighborhood Crime." *American Sociological Review* 107 (3): 717–767.

Rabe, Birgitta, and Mark Taylor. 2010. "Residential Mobility, Quality of Neighbourhood and Life Course Events." *Journal of the Royal Statistical Society A: Statistics in Society* 173(3): 531–555.

Rae, Alistair. 2014. "Online Housing Search and the Geography of Submarkets." *Housing Studies* 30(3): 453–472.

Raleigh, Erica, and George C. Galster. 2015. "Neighborhood Disinvestment, Abandonment and Crime Dynamics." *Journal of Urban Affairs* 37(4): 367–396.

Ratcliff, Richard U. 1949. *Urban Land Economics.* New York: McGraw Hill.

Rau, Tomás, Loreto Reyes, and Sergio Urzúa. 2013. "The Long-Term Effects of Early Lead Exposure: Evidence from a Case of Environmental Negligence." NBER working paper no. 18915. Cambridge, MA: National Bureau of Economic Research. Accessed at http://www.nber.org/papers/w18915.

Reardon, Sean, and Kendra Bischoff. 2011. "Income Inequality and Income Segregation." *American Journal of Sociology* 116(4): 1092–1153.

———. 2016. "The Continuing Increase in Income Segregation, 2007–2012." Retrieved from Stanford Center for Education Policy Analysis. Accessed at http://cepa.stanford.edu/content/continuing-increase-income-segregation-2007-2012.

Reardon, Sean, Lindsay Fox, and Joseph Townsend. 2015. "Neighborhood Income Composition by Race and Income, 1990–2009." *Annals of the American Academy of Political and Social Science* 660(1): 78–97.

Ren, Cizao, and Shilu Tong. 2008. Health Effects of Ambient Air Pollution: Recent Research Development and Contemporary Methodological Challenges. *Environmental Health* 7(1): 56–66.

Reyes, Jessica. 2005. "The Impact of Prenatal Lead Exposure on Health." Working paper, Department of Economics, Amherst College.

Richter, Francisca, and Ben Craig. 2010. "Lending Patterns in Poor Neighborhoods." Working paper 10-06, Federal Reserve Bank of Cleveland.

Ritz, Beate, Fei Yu, Scott Fruin, Guadalupe Chapa, Gary M. Shaw, and John A. Harris. 2002. "Ambient Air Pollution and Risk of Birth Defects in Southern California." *American Journal of Epidemiology* 155(1): 17–25.

Rohe, William M. 2009. "From Local to Global: One Hundred Years of Neighborhood Planning." *Journal of the American Planning Association* 75(2): 209–230.

Rohe, William M., and George C. Galster. 2014. "The Community Development Block Grant Program Turns 40: Proposals for Program Expansion and Reform." *Housing Policy Debate* 24(1): 3–13.

Rohe, William M., Shannon van Zandt, and George McCarthy. 2013. "The Social Benefits and Costs of Homeownership: A Critical Review of the Research." In *The Affordable Housing Reader*, edited by J. Rosie Tighe and Elizabeth J. Mueller, 196–213. New York: Routledge.

Rose-Ackerman, Susan. 1975. "Racism and Urban Structure." *Journal of Urban Economics* 2(1): 85–103.

Rosenbaum, Emily, Laura Harris, and Nancy A. Denton. 2003. "New Places, New Faces: An Analysis of Neighborhoods and Social Ties Among MTO Movers in Chicago." In *Choosing a Better Life? Evaluating the Moving to Opportunity Experiment*, edited by John Goering and Judith D. Feins, 275–310. Washington: Urban Institute Press.

Rosenbaum, James E. 1991. "Black Pioneers: Do Moves to the Suburbs Increase Economic Opportunity for Mothers and Children?" *Housing Policy Debate* 2(4): 1179–1213.

———. 1995. "Changing the Geography of Opportunity by Expanding Residential Choice: Lessons from the Gautreaux Program." *Housing Policy Debate* 6(1): 231–269.

Rosenbaum, James E., Lisa Reynolds, and Stefanie DeLuca. 2002. "How Do Places Matter? The Geography of Opportunity, Self-Efficacy, and a Look Inside the Black Box of Residential Mobility." *Housing Studies* 17(1): 71–82.

Rosenthal, Stuart. 2008a. "Old Homes, Externalities, and Poor Neighborhoods: A Model of Urban Decline and Renewal." *Journal of Urban Economics* 63(3): 816–840.

Rosenthal, Stuart. 2008b. "Where Poor Renters Live in Our Cities: Dynamics and Determinants." In *Revisiting Rental Housing: Policies, Programs, and Priorities*, edited by Nicolas P. Retsinas, and Eric S. Belsky, 59–92. Washington: Brookings Institution.

Rosenthal, Stuart, and Stephen L. Ross. 2015. "Change and Persistence in the Economic Status of Neighborhoods and Cities." In *Handbook of Regional and Urban Economics*, Vol. 5, edited by Gilles Duranton, J. Vernon Henderson, and William C. Strange, 1047–1120. Amsterdam: Elsevier B.V.

Ross, Catherine E., John Mirowksy, and Shana Pribesh. 2001. "Powerlessness and the Amplification of Threat: Neighborhood Disadvantage, Disorder, and Mistrust." *American Sociological Review* 66(4): 443–478.

Ross, Stephen L. 2001. "Employment Access, Neighborhood Quality, and Residential Location Choice." Conference paper, Lincoln Institute of Land Policy.

———. 2011. "Understanding Racial Segregation: What Is Known about the Effect of Housing Discrimination?" In *Neighborhood and Life Chances*, edited by Harriet Newburger, Eugenie Birch, and Susan Wachter, 288–301. Philadelphia: University of Pennsylvania Press.

———. 2012. "Social Interactions Within Cities: Neighborhood Environments and Peer Relationships." In *The Oxford Handbook of Urban Economics and Planning*, edited by Nancy Brooks, Kieran Donaghy, and Gerrit-Jan Knaap, 203–229. Oxford and New York: Oxford University Press.

Ross, Stephen L., and George C. Galster. 2006. "Fair Housing Enforcement and Changes in Discrimination between 1989 and 2000: An Exploratory Study." In *Fragile Rights within Cities*, edited by John Goering, 177–202. Plymouth, UK: Rowman and Littlefield.

Ross, Stephen L., and John Yinger. 1999. "Sorting and Voting: A Review of the Literature on Urban Public Finance." In *Handbook of Regional and Urban Economics*, Vol. 3, edited by Edwin S. Mills and Paul Cheshire, 2001–2060. Amsterdam: Elsevier B.V.

———. 2002. *The Color of Credit: Mortgage Discrimination, Research Methodology and Fair-Lending Enforcement*. Cambridge, MA: MIT Press.

Rossi, Peter H. 1955. *Why Families Move*. Beverly Hills, CA, and London: Sage Publications.

Rossi-Hansberg, Esteban, Pierre-Daniel Sarte, and Raymond Owens III. 2010. "Housing Externalities." *Journal of Political Economy* 118(3): 485–535.

Rotger, Gabriel Pons, and George Galster. 2017. "Neighborhood Context and Criminal Behaviors of the Disadvantaged: Evidence from a Copenhagen Natural Experiment." Paper presented at the Allied Social Sciences Association meetings, Chicago.

Rothenberg, Jerome, George C. Galster, Richard V. Butler, and John R. Pitkin. 1991. *The*

Maze of Urban Housing Markets: Theory, Evidence, and Policy. Chicago: University of Chicago Press.

Rothwell, Jonathan, and Douglas S. Massey. 2009. "The Effect of Density Zoning on Racial Segregation in US Urban Areas." *Urban Affairs Review* 44(6): 779–806.

Roychoudhury, Canopy, and Allen C. Goodman. 1992. "An Ordered Probit Model for Estimating Racial Discrimination Through Fair Housing Audits." *Journal of Housing Economics* 2(4): 358–373.

Rubinowitz, Leonard S., and James A. Rosenbaum. 2002. *Crossing the Class and Color Lines: From Public Housing to White Suburbia*. Chicago: University of Chicago Press.

Rugh, Jacob S., and Douglas S. Massey. 2013. "Segregation in Post-Civil Rights America: Stalled Integration or End of the Segregated Century?" *Du Bois Review: Social Science Research on Race* 11(2): 205–32.

Rugh, Jacob. S., Len Albright, and Douglas S. Massey. 2015. "Race, Space, and Cumulative Disadvantage: A Case Study of the Subprime Lending Collapse." *Social Problems* 62(2): 186–218.

Rusk, David. 1993. *Cities without Suburbs*. Washington: Woodrow Wilson Center Press.

———. 1999. *Inside Game Outside Game: Winning Strategies for Saving Urban America*. Washington: Brookings Institution.

Saha, Robin. 2009. "A Current Appraisal of Toxic Wastes and Race in the United States—2007." In *Urban Health: Readings in the Social, Built, and Physical Environments of U.S. Cities*, edited by Patricia Hynes and Russ Lopez, 237–260. Sudbury, MA: Jones and Bartlett Publishers.

Saiz, Albert. 2010. "The Geographic Determinants of Housing Supply." *Quarterly Journal of Economics* 125(3): 1253–1296.

Saltman, Juliet. 1978. *Open Housing: Dynamics of a Social Movement*. New York: Praeger.

———. 1990. *A Fragile Movement: The Struggle for Neighborhood Stabilization*. New York: Greenwood Press.

Sampson, Robert J. 1992. "Family Management and Child Development: Insights from Social Disorganization Theory." In *Facts, Frameworks, and Forecasts: Advances in Criminological Theory*, Vol. 3, edited by Joan McCord, 63–93. New Brunswick, NJ: Transaction Books.

———. 1997. "Collective Regulation of Adolescent Misbehavior: Validation Results for Eighty Chicago Neighborhoods." *Journal of Adolescent Research* 12(2): 227–244.

———. 2000. "Whither the Sociological Study of Crime?" *Annual Review of Sociology* 26(1): 711–714.

———. 2001. "How Do Communities Undergird or Undermine Human Development? Relevant Contexts and Social Mechanisms." In *Does It Take a Village? Community Effects on Children, Adolescents and Families*, edited by Alan Booth and Ann C. Crouter, 3–30. London and Mawah, NJ: Lawrence Erlbaum Publishers.

———. 2008. "Moving to Inequality: Neighborhood Effects and Experiments Meet Social Structure." *American Journal of Sociology* 114(11): 189–231.

———. 2012. *Great American City: Chicago and the Enduring Neighborhood Effect*. Chicago: University of Chicago Press.

Sampson, Robert J., and W. Byron Groves. 1989. "Community Structure and Crime: Testing Social Disorganization Theory." *American Journal of Sociology* 94(4): 774–802.

Sampson, Robert J., Robert D. Mare, and Kristin L. Perkins. 2015. "Achieving the Middle Ground in an Age of Concentrated Extremes: Mixed Middle-Income Neighborhoods and Emerging Adulthood." *Annals of the American Academy of Political and Social Science* 660(1): 156–174.

Sampson, Robert J., Jeffrey Morenoff, and Felton Earls. 1999. "Beyond Social Capital: Spatial Dynamics of Collective Efficacy for Children." *American Sociological Review* 64(5): 633–660.

Sampson, Robert J., Jeffrey D. Morenoff, and Thomas Gannon-Rowley. 2002. "Assessing 'Neighborhood Effects': Social Processes and New Directions in Research." *Annual Review of Sociology* 28: 443–478.

Sampson, Robert J., and Stephen W. Raudenbush. 2004. "Seeing Disorder: Neighborhood Stigma and the Social Construction of 'Broken Windows.'" *Social Psychology Quarterly* 67(4): 319–342.

Sampson, Robert J., Stephen W. Raudenbush, and Felton Earls. 1997. "Neighborhoods and Violent Crime: A Multilevel Study of Collective Efficacy." *Science* 277(5328): 918–924.

Sampson, Robert J., Jared N. Schachner, and Robert D. Mare. 2017. "Urban Income Inequality and the Great Recession in Sunbelt Form: Disentangling Individual and Neighborhood-Level Change in Los Angeles." *RSF: The Russell Sage Foundation Journal of the Social Sciences* 3(2): 102–128.

Sampson, Robert J., and Patrick Sharkey. 2008. "Neighborhood Selection and the Social Reproduction of Concentrated Racial Inequality." *Demography* 45(1): 1–29.

Sampson, Robert J., Patrick Sharkey, and Stephen W. Raudenbush. 2008. "Durable Effects of Concentrated Disadvantage on Verbal Ability among African-American Children." *Proceedings of the National Academy of Sciences* 105(3): 845–852.

Sanbonmatsu, Lisa, Jeffrey Kling, Greg J. Duncan, and Jeanne Brooks-Gunn. 2006. "Neighborhoods and Academic Achievement: Evidence from the Moving To Opportunity Experiment." *Journal of Human Resources* 41(4): 649–691.

Sanbonmatsu, Lisa, Jens Ludwig, Lawrence F. Katz, Lisa A. Gennetian, Greg J. Duncan, Ronald C. Kessler, Emma Adam, Thomas W. McDade, and Stacy Tessler Lindau. 2011. *Impacts of the Moving to Opportunity for Fair Housing Demonstration Program after 10 to 15 Years.* Washington: Office of Policy Development and Research, US Department of Housing and Urban Development.

Santiago, Anna, and George C. Galster. 1995. "Puerto Rican Segregation: Cause or Consequence of Economic Status?" *Social Problems* 42(3): 361–389.

Santiago, Anna, George C. Galster, Jessica Lucero, Karen Ishler, Eun Lye Lee, Georgios Kypriotakis, and Lisa Stack. 2014. *Opportunity Neighborhoods for Latino and African American Children.* Washington: Office of Policy Development and Research, US Department of Housing and Urban Development.

Santiago, Anna M., George C. Galster, and Richard J. Smith. 2017. "Evaluating the Impacts of an Enhanced Family Self-Sufficiency Program." *Housing Policy Debate* 27(5): 772–788.

Santiago, Anna, George C. Galster, and Peter Tatian. 2001. "Assessing the Property Value Impacts of the Dispersed Housing Subsidy Program in Denver." *Journal of Policy Analysis and Management* 20(1): 65–88.

Santiago, Anna, Eun Lye Lee, Jessica Lucero, and Rebecca Wiersma. 2017. "How Living in the 'Hood Affects Risky Behaviors Among Latino and African American Youth." *RSF: The Russell Sage Foundation Journal of the Social Sciences* 3(2): 170–209.

Sard, Barbara, and Douglas Rice. 2014. *Creating Opportunity for Children: How Location Can Make a Difference.* Washington: Center on Budget and Policy Priorities.

Sari, Florent. 2012. "Analysis of Neighbourhood Effects and Work Behaviour: Evidence from Paris." *Housing Studies* 27(1): 45–76.

Sastry, Narayan. 2012. "Neighborhood Effects on Children's Achievement: A Review of

Recent Research." In *Oxford Handbook on Child Development and Poverty*, edited by Rosalind King and Valerie Maholmes, 423–447. New York: Oxford University Press.

Scafidi, Benjamin. P., Michael H. Schill, Susan M. Wachter, and Dennis P. Culhane. 1998. "An Economic Analysis of Housing Abandonment." *Journal of Housing Economics* 7(4): 287–303.

Schell, Lawrence M., and Melinda Denham. 2003. "Environmental Pollution in Urban Environments and Human Biology." *Annual Review of Anthropology* 32: 111–134.

Schelling, Thomas C. 1971. "Dynamic Models of Segregation." *Journal of Mathematical Sociology* 1(2): 143–186.

———. 1972. "A Process of Residential Segregation: Neighbourhood Tipping." In *Racial Discrimination in Economic Life*, edited by Anthony H. Pascal, 157–184. Lexington, MA: Lexington Books, D. C. Heath.

———. 1978. *Micro-Motives and Macro-Behavior*. New York: Norton.

Schill, M. 1997. "Chicago's New Mixed-Income Communities Strategy: The Future Face of Public Housing?" In *Affordable Housing and Urban Redevelopment in the United States*, edited by Willem van Vliet, 135–157. Thousand Oaks, CA: Sage Publications.

Schnare, Ann B., and C. Duncan MacRae. 1978. "A Model of Neighbourhood Change." *Urban Studies* 15(3): 327–331.

Schoenberg, Sandra Pearlman. 1979. "Criteria for the Evaluation of Neighborhood Viability in Working Class and Low Income Areas in Core Cities." *Social Problems* 27(1): 69–78.

Schoenberg, Sandra Pearlman, and Patricia L. Rosenbaum. 1980. *Neighborhoods That Work: Sources for Viability in the Inner City*. New Brunswick, NJ: Rutgers University Press.

Schootman, Mario, Elena Andresen, Fredric Wolinsky, Theodore Malmstrom, Philip Miller, and Douglas Miller. 2007. "Neighbourhood Environment and the Incidence of Depressive Symptoms among Middle-Aged African Americans." *Journal of Epidemiology and Community Health* 61(6): 527–32.

Schreiber, Arthur, and Richard Clemmer. 1982. *Economics of Urban Problems*. 3rd ed. Boston: Houghton-Mifflin.

Schuetz, Jenny, Vicki Been, and Ingrid Gould Ellen. 2008. "Neighborhood Effects of Concentrated Mortgage Foreclosures." *Journal of Housing Economics* 17(4): 306–319.

Schwab, William A., and E. Marsh. 1980. "The Tipping-Point Model: Prediction of Change in the Racial Composition of Cleveland, Ohio, Neighborhoods, 1940–1970." *Environment and Planning A* 12(4): 385–398.

Schwartz, Alex F. 2015. *Housing Policy in the United States*. 3rd Edition. New York and London: Routledge.

Schwartz, Alex F., Kirk McClure, and Lydia B. Taghavi. 2016. "Vouchers and Neighborhood Distress: The Unrealized Potential for Families with Housing Choice Vouchers to Reside in Neighborhoods with Low Levels of Distress." *Cityscape* 18(3): 207–227.

Schwartz, Amy Ellen, Ellen Ingrid Gould, and Ioan Voicu. 2002. "Estimating the External Effects of Subsidized Housing Investment on Property Values." Report presented at National Bureau of Economic Research Universities Research Conference, Cambridge, MA.

Schwartz, Heather. 2010. *Housing Policy Is School Policy: Economically Integrative Housing Promotes Academic Achievement in Montgomery County, MD*. New York: Century Foundation.

Schwartz, Heather, Kata Mihaly, and Breann Gala. 2017. "Encouraging Residential Moves to Opportunity Neighborhoods: An Experiment Testing Incentives Offered to Housing Voucher Recipients." *Housing Policy Debate* 27(2): 230–260.

Schwirian, Kent. 1983. "Models of Neighborhood Change." *Annual Review of Sociology* 9:83–102.

Segal, David. 1979. *The Economics of Neighborhood*. New York: Academic Press.

Seo, Wonseok, and Burkhard von Rabenau. 2011. "Spatial Impacts of Microneighborhood Physical Disorder on Property Resale Values in Columbus, Ohio." *Journal of Urban Planning and Development* 137(3): 337–345.

Shaffer, Amanda. 2002. *The Persistence of L.A.'s Grocery Gap*. Los Angeles: Occidental College Center for Food and Justice.

Shapiro, Thomas, Tatjana Meschede, and Sam Osoro. 2013. *Widening Roots of the Racial Wealth Gap: Explaining the Black-White Economic Divide*. Waltham, MA: Institute on Assets and Social Policy, Brandeis University.

Sharkey, Patrick. 2010. "The Acute Effect of Local Homicides on Children's Cognitive Performance." *Proceedings of the National Academy of Sciences* 107(26): 11733–11738.

———. 2012. "An Alternative Approach to Addressing Selection into and out of Social Settings: Neighborhood Change and African American Children's Economic Outcomes." *Sociological Methods and Research* 41(2): 251–293.

———. 2013. *Stuck in Place*. Chicago: University of Chicago Press.

———. 2014. "Spatial Segmentation and the Black Middle Class." *American Journal of Sociology* 119(4): 903–954.

———. 2016. "Neighborhoods, Cities, and Economic Mobility." *RSF: The Russell Sage Foundation Journal of the Social Sciences* 2(2): 159–177.

Sharkey, Patrick, and Felix Elwert. 2011. "The Legacy of Disadvantage: Multigenerational Neighborhood Effects on Cognitive Ability." *American Journal of Sociology* 116(6): 1934–1981.

Sharkey, Patrick, and Jacob W. Faber. 2014. "Where, When, Why, and For Whom Do Residential Contexts Matter? Moving Away from the Dichotomous Understanding of Neighborhood Effects." *Annual Review of Sociology* 40(1): 559–579.

Sharkey, Patrick, and Robert J. Sampson. 2010. "The Acute Effect of Local Homicides on Children's Cognitive Performance." *Proceedings of the National Academy of Sciences of the United States of America* 107(26): 11733–11738.

Sharkey, Patrick, Amy Ellen Schwartz, Ingrid Gould Ellen, and Johanna Lacoe. 2014. "High Stakes in the Classroom, High Stakes on the Street: The Effects of Community Violence on Students' Standardized Test Performance." *Sociological Science* 1:199–220.

Sharkey, Patrick, Nicole Tirado-Strayer, Andrew Papachristos, and C. Cybele Raver. 2012. "The Effect of Local Violence on Children's Attention and Impulse Control." *American Journal of Public Health* 102(12): 2287.

Shear, William B. 1983. "Urban Housing Rehabilitation and Move Decisions." *Southern Economic Journal* 49(4): 1030–1052.

Shelby, Hayden. 2017. "Why Place Really Matters: A Qualitative Approach to Housing Preferences and Neighborhood Effects." *Housing Policy Debate* 27(4): 547–569.

Shlay, Anne B., and Gordon Whitman. 2006. "Research for Democracy: Linking Community Organizing and Research to Leverage Blight Policy." *City & Community* 5(2): 153–171.

Simmel, George. 1971. *George Simmel on Individuality and Social Forms*. Chicago: University of Chicago Press.

Simon, Herbert A. 1957. *Models of Man: Social and Rational*. New York: John Wiley and Sons.

Simons, Robert A., Roberto G. Quercia, and Ivan Maric. 1998. "The Value Impact of New Residential Construction and Neighborhood Disinvestment on Residential Sales Price." *Journal of Real Estate Research* 15(1/2): 147–161.

Simons, Ronald L., Christine Johnson, Jay Beaman, Rand D. Conger, and Les B. Whitbeck. 1996. "Parents and Peer Group as Mediators of the Effect of Community Structure on Adolescent Behavior." *American Journal of Community Psychology* 24(1): 145–171.

Sinclair, Jamie J., Gregory S. Petit, Amanda W. Harrist, Kenneth A. Dodge, and John E. Bates. 1994. "Encounters with Aggressive Peers in Early Childhood: Frequency, Age Differences, and Correlates of Risk Behaviour Problems." *International Journal of Behavioral Development* 17(4): 675–696.

Skaburskis, Andrejs. 2010. "Gentrification in the Context of 'Risk Society.'" *Environment and Planning A* 42(4): 895–912.

Skobba, Kimberly, and Edward G. Goetz. 2013. "Mobility Decisions of Very Low-Income Households." *Cityscape* 15(2): 155–171.

Skogan, Wesley G. 1990. *Disorder and Decline: Crime and the Spiral of Decay in American Neighborhoods.* Berkeley: University of California Press.

Smith, Neil. 1979. "Toward a Theory of Gentrification: A Back to the City Movement by Capital, Not People." *Journal of the American Planning Association* 45:538–548.

Smith, Richard A. 1993. "Creating Stable, Racially Integrated Communities: A Review." *Journal of Urban Affairs* 15(2): 115–140.

Smith, Richard J., Theodore T. Pride, and Catherine E. Schmitt-Sands. 2017. "Does Spatial Assimilation Lead to Reproduction of Gentrification in the Global City?" *Journal of Urban Affairs* 39(6): 745–763.

Smith, Wallace F. 1964. *Filtering and Neighborhood Change.* Center for Real Estate and Urban Economics Research Report, Institute of Urban and Regional Development: University of California, Berkeley.

Smolensky, Eugene. 2007. "Children in the Vanguard of the US Welfare State." *Journal of Economic Literature* 45(4): 1011–1023.

Social Science Panel. 1974. *Toward an Understanding of Metropolitan America.* San Francisco: Canfield Press / National Academy of Sciences.

South, Scott J. 2001. "Issues in the Analysis of Neighborhoods, Families, and Children." In *Does It Take a Village? Community Effects on Children, Adolescents and Families,* edited by Alan Booth and Ann C. Crouter, 87–94. London and Mawah, NJ: Lawrence Erlbaum Publishers.

South, Scott J., and Eric P. Baumer. 2000. "Deciphering Community and Race Effects on Adolescent Pre-Marital Childbearing." *Social Forces* 78(4): 1379–1407.

South, Scott J., and Kyle D. Crowder. 1998. "Leaving the 'Hood': Residential Mobility between Black, White, and Integrated Neighborhoods." *American Sociological Review* 63(1): 17–26.

———. 2000. "The Declining Significance of Neighborhoods? Marital Transitions in Community Context." *Social Forces* 78(3): 1067–1099.

Speare, Alden Jr. 1974. "Residential Satisfaction as an Intervening Variable in Residential Mobility." *Demography* 11(2): 173–188.

Speare, Alden Jr., Sidney Goldstein, and William H. Frey. 1975. *Residential Mobility, Migration and Metropolitan Change.* Cambridge, MA: Ballinger.

Spencer, Margaret Beale. 2001. "Resiliency and Fragility Factors Associated with the Contextual Experiences of Low-Resource Urban African-American Male Youth and Families." In *Does It Take a Village? Community Effects on Children, Adolescents and Families,* edited by Alan Booth and Ann C. Crouter, 51–78. London and Mawah, NJ: Lawrence Erlbaum Publishers.

Squires, Gregory D. 2017. *The Fight for Fair Housing: Causes, Consequences, and Future Implications of the 1968 Federal Fair Housing Act.* New York and London: Routledge.

Squires, Gregory D., ed. 1997. *Insurance Redlining: Disinvestment, Reinvestment, and the Evolving Role of Financial Institutions*. Washington: Urban Institute Press.

———. 2004. *Why the Poor Pay More: How to Stop Predatory Lending*. Westport, CT: Praeger.

Stack, Carol B. 1975. *All Our Kin: Strategies for Survival in a Black Community*. New York: Harper and Row.

Stansfeld, Stephen, Mary Haynes, and Bernadette Brown. 2000. "Noise and Health in the Urban Environment." *Reviews on Environmental Health* 15(1-2): 43–82.

Steil, Justin, Jorge de la Roca, and Ingrid Gould Ellen. 2015. "Desvinculado y Desigual: Is Segregation Harmful to Latinos?" *Annals of the American Academy of Political and Social Science* 660(1): 92–110.

Stillerman, Karen Perry, Donald R. Mattison, Linca C. Giudice, and Tracey J. Woodruff. 2008. "Environmental Exposures and Adverse Pregnancy Outcomes: A Review of the Science." *Reproductive Sciences* 15(7): 631–650.

Strassmann, W. Paul. 2001. "Residential Mobility: Contrasting Approaches in Europe and the United States." *Housing Studies* 16(1): 7–20.

Sturdivant, Frederick D., ed. 1969. *The Ghetto Marketplace*. New York: The Free Press.

Sugrue, Thomas J. 1996. *The Origins of the Urban Crisis*. Princeton, NJ: Princeton University Press.

Sullivan, Mercer L. 1989. *Getting Paid: Youth Crime and Work in the Inner City*. Ithaca, NY: Cornell University Press.

Suttles, Gerald. 1972. *The Social Construction of Communities*. Chicago: University of Chicago Press.

Sweeney, James L. 1974a. "A Commodity Hierarchy Model of the Rental Housing Market." *Journal of Urban Economics* 1(3): 288–323.

Sweeney, James L. 1974b. "Quality, Commodity Hierarchies, and Housing Markets." *Econometrica: Journal of the Econometric Society* 42(1): 147–168.

Tach, Laura, Sara Jacoby, Douglas Wiebe, Terry Guerra, and Therese Richmond. 2016. "The Effect of Microneighborhood Conditions on Adult Educational Attainment in a Subsidized Housing Intervention." *Housing Policy Debate* 26(2): 380–397.

Talen, Emily. 2006. "Neighborhood-Level Social Diversity: Insights from Chicago." *Journal of the American Planning Association* 72(4): 431–446.

Taub, Richard P., D. Garth Taylor, and Jan Dunham. 1984. *Paths of Neighborhood Change: Race and Crime in Urban America*. Chicago: University of Chicago Press.

Taeuber, Karl E., and Alma F. Taeuber. 1965. *Negroes in Cities: Residential Segregation & Neighborhood Change*. Chicago: Aldine.

Teitler, Julian O., and Christopher C. Weiss. 1996. "Contextual Sex: The Effect of School and Neighborhood Environments on the Timing of the First Intercourse." Paper presented at the annual meeting of the Population Association of America, New Orleans.

Temkin, Kenneth, and William Rohe. 1996. "Neighborhood Change and Urban Policy." *Journal of Planning Education and Research* 15(3): 159–170.

Thomson, Dale. 2008. "Strategic, Geographic Targeting of Housing and Community Development Resources: A Conceptual Framework and Critical Review." *Urban Affairs Review* 43(5): 629–662.

———. 2011. "Strategic Geographic Targeting in Community Development: Examining the Congruence of Political, Institutional, and Technical Factors." *Urban Affairs Review* 47(4): 564–594.

Tiebout, Charles M. 1956. "A Pure Theory of Local Expenditures." *Journal of Political Economy* 64(5): 416–424.

Tienda, Marta. 1991. "Poor People and Poor Places: Deciphering Neighborhood Effects on Poverty Outcomes." In *Macro-Micro Linkages in Sociology*, edited by Joan Huber. Newbury Park, CA: Sage.

Tigges, Leann M., Irene Browne, and Gary P. Green. 1998. "Social Isolation of the Urban Poor." *Sociological Quarterly* 39(1): 53–77.

Tighe, J. Rosie, Megan E. Hatch, and Joseph Mead. 2017. "Source of Income Discrimination and Fair Housing Policy." *Journal of Planning Literature* 32(1): 3–15.

Tu, Yong, and Judy Goldfinch. 1996. "A Two-Stage Housing Choice Forecasting Model." *Urban Studies* 33(3): 517–538.

Turley, Ruth N. Lopez. 2003. "When Do Neighborhoods Matter? The Role of Race and Neighborhood Peers." *Social Science Research* 32(1):61–79.

Turner, Margery A. 1998. "Moving Out of Poverty: Expanding Mobility and Choice Through Tenant-Based Housing Assistance." *Housing Policy Debate* 9(2): 373- 394.

———. 2008. "Residential Segregation and Employment Inequality." In *Segregation: The Rising Costs for America*, edited by James H. Carr and Nandinee K. Kutty, 151–196. New York: Routledge.

———. 2017. "Beyond People versus Place: A Place-Conscious Framework for Investing in Housing and Neighborhoods." *Housing Policy Debate* 27(2): 306–314.

Turner, Margery Austin, Jennifer Comey, Daniel Kuehn, and Austin Nichols. 2012. *Residential Mobility, High-Opportunity Neighborhoods, and Outcomes for Low-Income Families: Insights from the Moving to Opportunity Demonstration*. Washington: Office of Policy Development and Research, US Department of Housing and Urban Development.

Turner, Margery Austin, Stephen L. Ross, George C. Galster, and John Yinger. 2002. *Discrimination in Metropolitan Housing Markets*. Washington: Office of Policy Development and Research, US Department of Housing and Urban Development.

Turner, Margery Austin, Rob Santos, Diane Levy, Doug Wissoker, Claudia Aranda, and Rob Pitingolo. 2013. *Housing Discrimination against Racial and Ethnic Minorities*. Washington: Office of Policy Development and Research, US Department of Housing and Urban Development.

Turner, Margery Austin, and Felicity Skidmore. 1999. *What We Know about Mortgage Lending Discrimination in America*, Washington: Urban Institute Press.

US Government Accounting Office. 2005. *Community Development Block Grant Formula: Targeting Assistance to High-Need Communities Could Be Enhanced*. Washington: GAO-05-622T.

US Environmental Protection Agency. 1992. *Environmental Equity: Reducing Risks for All Communities*. Vols. 1–2. Washington: Policy, Planning, and Evaluation, Environmental Protection Agency.

Van Ham, Maarten, and William A. V. Clark. 2009. "Neighbourhood Mobility in Context: Household Moves and Changing Neighbourhoods in the Netherlands." *Environment and Planning A* 41(6): 1442–1459.

Van Ham, Maarten, and David Manley. 2009. "The Effect of Neighbourhood Housing Tenure Mix on Labor Market Outcomes: A Longitudinal Perspective." Discussion paper IZA DP no. 4094, Institute for the Study of Labor, Bonn, Germany.

———. 2010. "The Effect of Neighbourhood Housing Tenure Mix on Labour Market Outcomes: A Longitudinal Investigation of Neighbourhood Effects." *Journal of Economic Geography* 10(2): 257–282.

Van Ham, Maarten, David Manley, Nick Bailey, Ludi Simpson, and Duncan Maclennan, eds. 2012. *Neighbourhood Effects Research: New Perspectives*. Dordrecht, Netherlands: Springer.

Van Os, Jim. 2004. "Does the Urban Environment Cause Psychosis?" *British Journal of Psychiatry* 184(4): 287–288.

Vandell, Kerry D. 1981. The Effects of Racial Composition on Neighbourhood Succession. *Urban Studies* 18(3): 315–333.

———. 1995. "Market Factors Affecting Spatial Heterogeneity among Urban Neighborhoods." *Housing Policy Debate* 6(1): 103–139.

Varady, David P. 1986. *Neighborhood Upgrading: A Realistic Assessment.* Albany: State University of New York Press.

Varady, David P., and Wolfgang F. E. Preiser. 1998. "Scattered-Site Public Housing and Satisfaction: Implications for the New Public Housing Program." *Journal of the American Planning Association* 64(2): 189–207.

Varady, David P., and Jeffrey A. Raffel. 1995. *Selling Cities: Attracting Homebuyers through Schools and Housing Programs.* Albany: State University of New York Press.

Vartanian, Thomas P. 1999a. "Adolescent Neighborhood Effects on Labor Market and Economic Outcomes." *Social Service Review* 73(2): 142–167.

———. 1999b. "Childhood Conditions and Adult Welfare Use: Examining Neighborhood and Family Factors." *Journal of Marriage and Family* 67(1): 225–237.

Vartanian, Thomas, and Philip Gleason. 1999. "Do Neighborhood Conditions Affect High School Dropout and College Graduation Rates?" *Journal of Socio-Economics* 28(1): 21–24.

Vaskowics, Laszlo, and Peter Franz. 1984. "Residential Areal Bonds in the Cities of West Germany." In *The Residential Areal Bond: Local Attachments in Delocalized Societies,* edited by Paul Peachey, Erich Bodzenta, and Wlodzimierz Mirowski. New York: Irvington.

Vicino, Thomas J., Bernadette Hanlon, and John Rennie Short. 2011. "A Typology of Urban Immigrant Neighborhoods." *Urban Geography* 32(3): 383–405.

Vigdor, Jacob L. 2010. "Is Urban Decay Bad? Is Urban Revitalization Bad Too?" *Journal of Urban Economics* 68(3): 277–289.

Vigdor, Jacob L., Douglas, S. Massey, and Alice M. Rivlin. 2002. "Does Gentrification Harm the Poor?" *Brookings-Wharton Papers on Urban Affairs,* 133–182.

Votruba, Mark Edward, and Jeffrey Kling. 2009. "Effects of Neighborhood Characteristics on the Mortality of Black Male Youth: Evidence from Gautreaux, Chicago." *Social Science and Medicine* 68(5): 814–823.

Wachs, Theodore D. 1999. "Celebrating Complexity: Conceptualization and Assessment of the Environment. In *Measuring Environment across the Life Span: Emerging Methods and Concepts,* edited by Sarah L. Freidman and Theodore D. Wachs, 357–392. Washington: American Psychological Association.

Wacquant, Loic. 2008. *Urban Outcasts: A Comparative Sociology of Advanced Marginality.* Malden, MA: Polity Press.

Waldinger, Roger. 1996. *Still the Promised City? African Americans and New Immigrants in Postindustrial New York.* Cambridge, MA: Harvard University Press.

Walker, Renee E., Christopher R. Kaine, and Jessica J. Burke. 2010. "Disparities and Access to Healthy Food in the United States: A Review of the Food Deserts Literature." *Health and Place* 16(5): 876–884.

Wandersman, Abraham, and Maury Nation. 1998. "Urban Neighborhoods and Mental Health: Psychological Contributions to Understanding Toxicity, Resilience, and Interventions." *American Psychologist* 53(6): 647–656.

Warren, Donald I. 1975. *Black Neighborhoods: An Assessment of Community Power.* Ann Arbor: University of Michigan Press.

———. 1981. *Helping Networks: How People Cope with Problems in Urban Community.* Notre Dame, IN: University of Notre Dame Press.

Warren, Rachelle B., and Donald I. Warren. 1977. *The Neighborhood Organizer's Handbook.* Notre Dame, IN: University of Notre Dame Press.

Warren, Ronald L. 1972. *The Community in America.* 2nd ed. Chicago: Rand McNally.

Watson, Tara. 2009. "Inequality and the Measurement of Residential Segregation by Income." *Review of Income and Wealth* 55(3): 820–844.

Weber, Max. 1978. *Economy and Society.* Vols. 1–2. Berkeley: University of California Press.

Weicher, John C., and Thomas G. Thibodeau. 1988. "Filtering and Housing Markets: An Empirical Analysis." *Journal of Urban Economics* 23(1): 21–40.

Weinberg, Bruce A., Patricia B. Reagan, and Jeffrey J. Yankow. 2004. "Do Neighborhoods Affect Work Behavior? Evidence from the NLSY79." *Journal of Labor Economics* 22(4): 891–924.

Weinhardt, Felix. 2014. "Social Housing, Neighborhood Quality and Student Performance." *Journal of Urban Economics* 82:12–31.

Wellman, Barry. 1972. "Who Needs Neighborhoods?" In *The City: Attacking Modern Myths,* edited by Alan T. Powell. Toronto: McClelland and Stewart.

———. 1979. "The Community Question: The Intimate Networks of East Yorkers." *American Journal of Sociology* 84(5): 1201–1231.

Wellman, Barry, and Barry Leighton. 1979. "Networks, Neighborhoods and Communities." *Urban Affairs Quarterly* 14(3): 363–390.

Wheaton, William C. 1977. "Income and Urban Residence: An Analysis of Consumer Demand for Location." *American Economic Review* 67(4): 620–631.

———. 1982. "Urban Spatial Development with Durable but Replaceable Capital." *Journal of Urban Economics* 12: 53–67.

Whitaker, Stephan, and Thomas J. Fitzpatrick IV. 2013. "Deconstructing Distressed-Property Spillovers: The Effects of Vacant, Tax-delinquent, and Foreclosed Properties in Housing Submarkets." *Journal of Housing Economics* 22(2): 79–91.

Williams, Sonya, George C. Galster, and Nandita Verma. 2013. "Home Foreclosures as Early Warning Indicator of Neighborhood Decline." *Journal of the American Planning Association* 79(3): 201–210.

Wilson, Bev, and Shakil Bin Kashem. 2017. "Spatially Concentrated Renovation Activity and Housing Appreciation in the City of Milwaukee, Wisconsin." *Journal of Urban Affairs* 39(8): 1085–1102.

Wilson, Florence L. 2011. "Subsidized Housing and Neighborhood Change." Unpublished PhD dissertation, Graduate Program in Social Welfare, University of California, Berkeley.

Wilson, William Julius. 1987. *The Truly Disadvantaged.* Chicago: University of Chicago Press.

———. 1991. "Another Look at 'The Truly Disadvantaged.'" *Political Science Quarterly* 106(4): 639–56.

———. 1996. *When Work Disappears: The World of the New Urban Poor.* New York: Vintage.

Woldoff, Rachael, and Seth Ovadia. 2009. "Not Getting Their Money's Worth: African-American Disadvantages in Converting Income, Wealth, and Education into Residential Quality." *Urban Affairs Review* 45:66–91.

Wolf, Eleanor. 1963. "The Tipping-Point in Racially Changing Neighborhoods." *Journal of the American Institute of Planners* 29(3): 217–222.

Wolman, Hal, Cary Lichtman, and Suzie Barnes. 1991. "The Impact of Credentials, Skill Levels, Worker Training, and Motivation on Employment Outcomes: Sorting Out the

Implications for Economic Development Policy." *Economic Development Quarterly* 5(2): 140–151.

Wolpert, J. 1966. "Migration as an Adjustment to Environmental Stress." *Journal of Social Issues* 22(4): 92–102.

Wong, G. 2002. "A Conceptual Model of the Household's Housing Decision-Making Process: The Economic Perspective." *Review of Urban and Regional Development Studies* 14(3): 217–234.

Wurdock, Clarence J. 1981. "Neighborhood Racial Transition: A Study of the Role of White Flight." *Urban Affairs Review* 17(1): 75–89.

Wyly, Elvin K., Mona Atia, Holly Foxcroft, Daniel J. Hammel, and Kelly Phillips-Watts. 2006. "American Home: Predatory Mortgage Capital and Neighbourhood Spaces of Race and Class Exploitation in the United States." *Geografiska Annaler* 88(1): 105–132.

Wyly, Elvin K., and Daniel J. Hammel. 1999. "Islands of Decay in Seas of Renewal: Housing Policy and the Resurgence of Gentrification." *Housing Policy Debate* 10(4): 711–771.

———. 2000. "Capital's Metropolis: Chicago and the Transformation of American Housing Policy." *Geografiska Annaler: Series B, Human Geography* 82(4): 181–206.

Yinger, John M. 1976. "Racial Prejudice and Racial Residential Segregation in an Urban Model." *Journal of Urban Economics* 3(4): 383–406.

———. 1995. *Closed Doors, Opportunities Lost.* New York: Russell Sage Foundation.

Zapata, B. Cecilia, Annabella Rebolledo, Eduardo Atalah, Beth Newman, and Mary-Claire King. 1992. "The Influence of Social and Political Violence on the Risk of Pregnancy Complications." *American Journal of Public Health* 82(5): 685–690.

Zenk, Shannon N., Amy J. Schulz, Barbara A. Israel, Sherman A. James, Shuming Bao, and Mark L. Wilson. 2005. "Neighborhood Racial Composition, Neighborhood Poverty, and Spatial Accessibility of Supermarkets in Metropolitan Detroit." *American Journal of Public Health* 95(4): 660–667.

Zhang, Junfu. 2004. "Residential Segregation in an All-Integrationist World." *Journal of Economic Behavior and Organization* 54(4): 533–550.

Zhang, Lei, Tammy Leonard, and James C. Murdoch. 2016. "Time and Distance Heterogeneity in the Neighborhood Spillover Effects of Foreclosed Properties." *Housing Studies* 31(2): 133–148.

Zielenbach, Sean. 2000. *The Art of Revitalization: Improving Conditions in Distressed Inner-City Neighborhoods.* New York: Garland Publishing.

Zukin, Sharon. 2010. *Naked City: The Death and Life of Authentic Urban Places.* New York: Oxford University Press.

INDEX